Paul Gosselin

Flight From the Absolute

Cynical Observations on the
Postmodern West

volume I

SAMIZDAT

Library and Archives Canada Cataloguing in Publication

Gosselin, Paul, 1957-
Flight from the absolute: cynical observations on the postmodern West /
Paul Gosselin.
Translation of: Fuite de l'Absolu. volume 1

Includes bibliographical references and index.
ISBN 978-2-9807774-3-1 (v. 1)

1. Postmodernism. 2. Cosmology. 3. Civilization, Western. 4. Religion
and civilization. I. Title.

B831.2.G6713 2012   149'.97   C2012-901723-X

Translated from the French: *Fuite de l'Absolu: Observations cyniques sur
l'Occident postmoderne. volume I (2006)*
Cover: Detail drawn from *Le triangle invisible*
by Constance Cimon, 2002 - Acrylic on canvas.
Cf: www.samizdat.qc.ca/arts/av/cimon

Samizdat 2012©
Succursale Jean-Gauvin
CP 25019
Quebec, QC
G1X 5A3
www.samizdat.qc.ca/publications/

Layout and cover by PogoDesign

"O weariness of men who turn from GOD
To the grandeur of your mind and the glory of your action,
To arts and inventions and daring enterprises,
To schemes of human greatness thoroughly discredited,
Binding the earth and the water to your service,
Exploiting the seas and developing the mountains,
Dividing the stars into common and preferred,
Engaged in devising the perfect refrigerator,
Engaged in working out a rational morality,
Engaged in printing as many books as possible,
Plotting of happiness and flinging empty bottles,
Turning from your vacancy to fevered enthusiasm
For nation or race or what you call humanity;
Thought you forget the way to the Temple,
There is one who remembers the way to your door:
Life you may evade, but Death you shall not.
You shall not deny the Stranger."

T. S. Eliot (Choruses from 'the Rock' 1982: 117)

"O world of spring and autumn, birth and dying!
The endless cycle of idea and action,
Endless invention, endless experiment,
Brings knowledge of motion, but not of stillness;
Knowledge of speech, but not of silence;
Knowledge of words, and ignorance of the Word.
All our knowledge brings us nearer to our ignorance
All our ignorance brings us nearer to death,
But nearness to death no nearer to God.
Where is the Life we have lost in living?
Where is the wisdom we have lost in knowledge?
Where is the knowledge we have lost in information?
The cycles of heaven in twenty centuries
Bring us farther from God and nearer to the Dust."

T. S. Eliot (Choruses from 'the Rock' 1982: 107)

Art of the mosaic

A picture or pattern produced by the arrangement of small coloured pieces of hard material (*tesserae*), such as stone, tile, or glass in a limited space.

figurative: a combination of unrelated elements, giving form to a new concept.

Table of contents

Foreword

A scant century or two ago in the Western world, religion had great influence over several strategic social institutions such as education, justice, science, health care, the arts and culture. But since then things have changed. During the course of the twentieth-century, secularization has marginalized the Judeo-Christian tradition in the West. In most cases, a secular perspective now dominates major social institutions, though the United States may in some respects be considered an exception to the rule that applies elsewhere in the West. It would appear that in general terms the major influences in the West are secular and religion has been relegated to the private sphere. But if one looks past the surface, it is obvious that the yearning for meaning still haunts Western man. Even though the cultural context has changed, ultimate questions remain just as relevant in the twenty-first century as they were in Antiquity or during the Middle Ages. Is it possible that materialism (and its numerous ideological derivatives) has not eliminated religion, but, in the current context, supplanted its functions and has joined, wittingly or not, in the process of providing answers to the question of meaning?

Though the modern or materialist worldview was initially just an idea in the minds of a small group of influential thinkers of the Enlightenment, as time passed it came to shape the attitudes and behaviour of the educated classes and, eventually, of entire societies. This worldview has penetrated the Western psyche so deeply that it has become an invisible, self-explanatory presupposition. Many take it for granted.

In a discussion with an intellectual, I sometimes ask: "How do you define postmodernism? How do you distinguish between modern and postmodern outlooks?" The answers to these questions

typically vary according to the fields of interest or educational background of the person. A relevant definition, in the field of literature
or architecture, may be of little interest in anthropology or history.
In the present work we will be primarily concerned with postmodernism as a system of beliefs.

What then is a worldview, an ideology, or a religion?[1] It is
primarily a system of belief developed to give meaning to human
existence both on an intellectual and emotional level. Initially, a
worldview involves a **cosmology**, i.e. a set of presuppositions concerning the order of the world. A cosmology provides the conceptual framework in which human existence is given meaning. One
could say that a cosmology is the stage where the theatre of life is
played out. It often, but not always, takes the form of an origins
myth. A materialist cosmology[2], for example, offers a rather narrow
framework (or a smaller box) while the various theistic cosmologies
propose boxes comprising additional dimensions, that is categories
of beings unknown (or discounted) in a materialist cosmology.
Cosmology thus has, as a main function, to establish the limits of
the conceivable world. It provides the basis on which one can begin
to answer the big questions of human existence, such as the reasons for human alienation and suffering. Cosmology then supports
and prefigures moral codes, and even eschatology,[3] which are typically part of the development of a mature religion or worldview.

A mature worldview or **ideologico-religious system** is based
on a cosmology and involves an explanation of human alienation
as well as strategies which attempt to mitigate or resolve this problem in some fashion. These strategies may be conceived as leading
to a final resolution, a Utopia. Final resolution can take many forms,
for example Progress, the return of the Messiah, Nirvana, the New
Jerusalem, the unification of the Islamic nations under one Caliph,
the five Hindu heavens,[4] a classless society or cyberspace.[5] The strategies referred to by various worldviews when attempting to rem-
edy human alienation obviously do not make any sense if taken out
of the context of their own cosmologies. For example, the Marxist
utopia of classless society would basically be seen as heresy in the
context of Hindu cosmology. We thus postulate that a religion is an
attempt to impose order, to give meaning to the world. Whether
this system refers to the supernatural or not is of no real consequence. A materialist cosmology can just as easily establish an
ideologico-religious system as a cosmology referring to the supernatural. In its development, a religion is integrative, that is, it con-

stitutes an attempt at a total response to the questions of existence. This attempt may be more or less successful depending on the historical context and the subjective perceptions of its coherence or contradictions in the eyes of the individual. We postulate here that it is impossible to understand the ethical system, the morality of an ideologico-religious system without first understanding its cosmology, since the presuppositions inherent in a cosmology prefigure and provide the basis for further development of taboos, ethical precepts, concepts of alienation, various themes of artistic expression as well as the eschatology of a religion.

The **modern** ideologico-religious system, an outgrowth of the Enlightenment, dominated the twentieth-century in the West and in its early stages set aside Christianity. It asserted that science was now the true source of knowledge and salvation. In the past, clerical hierarchies or the Bible had been considered the guarantors of Truth, but in the modern world Science took over this function. Reason and the empirical world were expected to provide the foundation of all knowledge worthy of interest. To ensure the logical coherence of this system of beliefs, it was necessary, in fact inevitable, to call upon an origins myth[6] legitimized by the prestige of science. Although a materialist worldview has dominated the West since the beginning of the twentieth-century; in the background concepts drawn from the Judeo-Christian cultural heritage have remained in use.[7] For example, the Christian concept of Time as meaningful (History[8]) was maintained and, in the modern context, repackaged under the term "Progress". Initially a theological concept, this concept was reformulated in materialistic terms. When the modern view arrived at the apex of its influence, many assumed that in a generation or two scientists and technologists would lead us to an era of prosperity and peace where technology would perform miracles to eliminate illness as well as push back the conventional limits of human existence. Today, after Auschwitz,[9] the H-bomb, the reappearance of "eradicated" diseases such tuberculosis, the development of genetically modified organisms and the emergence of various environmental problems linked to technological progress, observers are more cautious. On the practical level, politics has become central and modern salvation has frequently taken a political or social form, attempting to enact collective utopias of some sort.

One should view the development of the modern religion as a two-stage affair. The first stage occurred with thinkers such as

Descartes, Hobbes and Voltaire whose most significant contribution was to set up, alongside the authority of the Bible and/or the Church, the authority of Reason and/or Science. These first-stage moderns were for the most part theologically literate deists[10] who accepted the existence of God (as Creator and providing a basis for human reason). Second-stage moderns rose up when there was a critical mass allowing for a mature materialist cosmology. Once the epistemological authority of Science had been established and it was seen as a source of Truth, then thinkers such as Buffon, Lamarck and later on, Darwin became instrumental in breaking down the last vestiges of the old traditional Judeo-Christian cosmology. This opened the door to thinkers such as Nietzsche who proclaimed "God is Dead!" and, later on, Dawkins who commented that Darwin made it possible to be an intellectually fulfilled atheist.

In the **postmodern** era, elements from the Judeo-Christian heritage have been shed in a gradual underground process, slowly questioning and discarding concepts notably in the areas of morality, universal history (unilinear),[11] law, sexual conduct, universal rights and man's status in the natural world.[12] Furthermore, in reaction to modernism, the postmodern worldview has disavowed the collective, universal political projects that characterized the twentieth-century. Political utopias are now *passé*. Cultural relativism has eliminated all moral or political absolutes, except perhaps that of science, at least for the present. The concept of progress has also been deconstructed. The universality of this Enlightenment concept has been denied and it is treated as little more than a Western meta-narrative. Postmodernism is in part a reaction against the rational monotony of modernism, against modernism's faith in technology, in progress and in the postulate of a universal knowledge, which is perceived by academic elites as intellectual "colonialism". Feminism has also contributed to the postmodern current by its rejection of male-influenced Reason, which had been erected on the altar of the Enlightenment. Even science has become a target for deconstruction. Postmoderns propose instead a heterogeneous, fragmented ideology. Postmoderns are wary of universals. If postmoderns reject Revolution and grand political utopias, all that remains for them is salvation found in various forms of sexual or environmental liberation/jihad. While Reason, Truth and Man were at the heart of modernism, there is reason to believe that desire (expressed as self-fulfilment) has become the core value of postmodernism. For this reason, one can view

Existentialism as a precursor of postmodernism in its relativization of modern collective ideologies and in the central place it accords to the individual and his subjectivity, but all the while remaining captive to modern (materialist) cosmology. Existentialism is caught between these two worlds.

One should keep in mind that postmodernism does not reject traditional religion in absolute terms, as did the modern ideology[13] (in its mature, materialistic forms). In the postmodern context, traditional religion's admission to the public arena is conditional. Religious discourse expressed in this context will be expected to yield to the demands of postmodern syncretism, that is religion must give up any claims of an Absolute, of a universal Truth or else face postmodern "tolerance"… Hard core materialism is thus no longer mandatory. Today, even interest in the occult is no longer taboo and can be legitimately pursued. Nor is there any shame in attempting to get shamanism to coexist with Catholic doctrine and Feng Shui. Postmodern religion is custom-made and the customer is always right… Individuals can, of course, belong to a faith community if they like, but this is considered optional, of secondary importance. Rigid collective ideologies or religions are now a thing of the past[14]. In our generation, the *spiritual journey* masks an ideological pick-and-choose approach. Finding Truth is of little concern to postmoderns. The journey itself is what really counts, which boils down to the emotional or aesthetic satisfaction the individual can derive from it. At least this process provides wallpaper and a pleasant colour scheme, masking the inner void…

In the West, postmodern influence is, for the most part, subliminal, non-explicit. Very few people identify themselves as postmoderns and yet one observes that the behaviour and attitudes of the masses are to a great extent moulded by postmodern presuppositions. This should come as no surprise. In medical terms, for example, it is known that individuals can carry an infection without being aware of it. On the ideological level then as well, it is quite possible to be influenced by postmodern thought, its mythology and its presuppositions, without knowingly identifying with this movement. To sort things out, one must then apply some sort of diagnostic test to verify or exclude the presence of postmodern influence. It is important to note here that the subject of this work, postmodernism, is not a movement defined solely by the works of a handful of French intellectuals. Authors such as Derrida, Foucault, Lyotard, Deleuze and others have of course taken part in and contributed to this movement, but it precedes them and goes beyond them. It is not a phenomenon defined by the activities of a few scholars. Other actors such as pop culture, media, advertising, the film industry, media elites and others participate, in various ways, in the development and propagation of this ideologico-religious system.

Deconstruction and meta-narrative analysis are the preferred tools of our academic postmodern elites, but if these tools are turned around to target postmodern discourse itself, then such an initiative may turn up a few issues worthy of interest. Years ago American sociologist Thomas Luckmann observed (1970: 70) that a priori all societies have an ideologico-religious system, a system of meaning, a worldview or, to use postmodern jargon, a meta-narrative. In Luckmann's view, the development of personal and social identity always has a religious dimension. If an ideologico-religious system constitutes the infrastructure of any civilization, what then is the religion of the postmodern West? What are its sacred institutions, its rites, its origins myths, its apostles, its believers and its initiations? In the following pages, we will attempt to examine all these unpleasant and neglected questions and look into the heart of our generation.

What will we find there?

1 / Worldviews

I know not who put me into the world, nor what the world is, nor what I myself am. I am in terrible ignorance of everything. I know not what my body is, nor my senses, nor my soul, not even that part of me which thinks what I say, which reflects on all and on itself, and knows itself no more than the rest. I see those frightful spaces of the universe which surround me, and I find myself tied to one corner of this vast expanse, without knowing why I am put in this place rather than in another, nor why the short time which is given me to live is assigned to me at this point rather than at another of the whole eternity which was before me or which shall come after me. I see nothing but infinities on all sides, which surround me as an atom and as a shadow which endures only for an instant and returns no more. All I know is that I must soon die, but what I know least is this very death which I cannot escape.
(Pascal 1670/1908 sect. 194)

In the collision between the West and the Islamic world, a misperception may occur in the minds of Moslems, rejecting and criticizing what they perceive as the "Christian West". There is a false impression here. It is in fact an illusion, a mirage. The "Christian West" no longer exists[15]. In historical terms, though it is a fact that the Christian cultural heritage established deep roots in the West, it should be understood that the Judeo-Christian worldview has been largely abandoned by Western elites for a long time now. Notwithstanding this fact, politicians[16] at election time may refer to symbols drawn from the Christian cultural heritage in order to garner a few extra votes. But beyond the rhetoric, reality is very different; Westerners live in a post-Christian culture. Dominant intellectual and cultural influences are rarely Christian and past Christian contributions to culture and science are generally ignored or misrepresented. In the course of history, we see signs marking the progress of this drift: genetic racism (eugenics), rejection of traditional morality, materialism, the Gulag, the relativism of the elites, abolition of sexual constraints, worship of consumerism by the masses, abortion, gay ideology, euthanasia, etc.

Obviously, few of our elites would admit a link between the post-Christian worldview and such phenomena. Some things are better not discussed... On the other hand, if Christians have had to come to grips with their responsibility in the Inquisition, perhaps one day our ideologists will come to acknowledge the logical consequences of their own worldview.[17]

In the eyes of modern or postmodern elites, man is no more than an object. He has no particular status and must be content to grope about in time and space, in a world where nothing, in itself, has meaning or particular significance. It is important to understand that modern man's creativity and endeavours are exerted within a particular framework, i.e. that provided, in large measure, by the materialist worldview conceived by Enlightenment philosophers and finding ultimate support, since the nineteenth-century, in the cosmology provided by the theory of evolution. If evolution is true, as Jacques Monod, Richard Dawkins, Stephen Jay Gould or Carl Sagan have proclaimed, humans are indeed little else, but a trivial natural phenomenon. They have no intrinsic meaning or particular status. Man is, at most, a garbage bag-full of pompous molecules interacting in a universe totally indifferent to his existence. Coherent modern men live in a disenchanted world, emptied of meaning, where the human organism labours. No divinity intervenes or cares. It is a closed system.

For the masses, this reality is suppressed as nihilism wears a discreet mask. But artists are generally more sensitive to the lack of meaning resulting from the materialist worldview than are good-thinking scientific gurus.[18] Since the artist's professional status is generally not linked to science as an institution, he enjoys a position tolerating some critical distance. For example, let us examine what Ray Bradbury, sci-fi author, has Spender, one of the main characters in **The Martian Chronicles**, say (1946/1982: 66):

> That's the mistake we made when Darwin showed up. We embraced him and Huxley and Freud, all smiles. And then we discovered that Darwin and our religions didn't mix. Or at least we didn't think they did. We were fools. We tried to budge Darwin and Huxley and Freud. They wouldn't move very well. So, like idiots, we tried knocking down religion. We succeeded pretty well. We lost our faith and went around wondering what life was for. If art was no more than a frustrated outfling of desire, if religion was nor more than self-delusion, what good was life? Faith had always given us answers to all things. But it all went down the drain with Freud and Darwin. **We were and still are a lost people**.

For their part, the rock band U2 echoes the angst of a bloated and dissatisfied generation[19] when they observe: "I still haven't found what I'm looking for..." Thus, when he breaks away from the distractions and pauses to reflect, postmodern man confronts the Void. Jean-Paul Sartre described with stark clarity the loss of meaning in modern man's existence (1938/2007: 129):

> The word absurdity is coming to life under my pen; a little while ago, in the garden, I couldn't find it, but neither was I looking for it, I didn't need it: I thought without words, on things, with things. Absurdity was not an idea in my head, or the sound of a voice, only this long serpent dead at my feet, this wooden serpent. Serpent or claw or root or vulture's talon, what difference does it make. And without formulating anything clearly, I understood that I had found the key to Existence, the key to my Nauseas, to my own life.

In **The Rebel**, Albert Camus considers the life-work of the poet Rimbaud and exposes the ironic paradox at the heart of modern man (1951/1978: 88):

> Rimbaud's greatness does not lie in the first poems from Charleville nor in his trading at Harrar. It shines forth at the moment when, in giving

the most peculiarly appropriate expression to rebellion that it has ever received, he simultaneously proclaims his triumph and his agony, his conception of a life beyond the confines of this world and the inescapability of the world, the yearning for the unattainable and reality brutally determined on restraint, the rejection of morality and the irresistible compulsion to duty.

Yes, the skeletons in the closet come out to play. Dark novels such as Kurt Vonnegut's **Slaughterhouse Five**, juxtapose, in the same scene, destiny crushing both insects and human lives, all the while mumbling his laconic mantra: "So it goes". Vonnegut appears rather cynical about the answers offered by our modern religious elites. In the same novel, he writes (1969/1975: 101): "Another time Billy heard Rosewater say to a psychiatrist, 'I think you guys are going to have to come up with a lot of wonderful *new* lies, or people just aren't going to want to go on living.'" One notices with Vonnegut, as with other postmodern materialist authors, a peculiar schizophrenia. On the one hand, one observes a need to impose, with no room for compromise, the materialism resulting from evolutionary theory and, on the other hand, one notices a more or less subliminal attempt to distance themselves from this same theory because of its brutal consequences on ethical/moral/social levels.

Katherine Hayles, an author belonging to the posthuman movement,[20] explains that traditional belief systems, formerly dominant in the West, provided places of refuge for meaning through their myths. Postmodern ideologies, however, refer to myths whose architecture offers little shelter (1999: 285):

> The work of Eric Havelock, among others, demonstrates how in Plato's Republic this view of originary presence authorized a stable, coherent self that could witness and testify to a stable, coherent reality. Through these and other means, the metaphysics of presence front-loaded meaning into the system. Meaning was guaranteed because a stable origin existed. It is now a familiar story how deconstruction exposed the inability of systems to posit their own origins, thus ungrounding signification and rendering meaning indeterminate.

Hayles emphasizes that postmodernism erodes the meaning of modern and traditional belief systems, but neglects to add that postmodern ideology deconstructs all meaning and, on the interactive level, any concept of a transcendent moral nature. It is ironic to note that deconstruction is the perverted legacy of Judeo-Christian culture. This argument was initially used by Greek philosophers and later on by apologists such as Tertullian (155-225

AD), as they deconstructed traditional Greek and Roman myths. Jean-François Lyotard also defines postmodernism as the rejection of all metanarrative (1979/1984: 7-8). It is about the downfall of heroes and noble causes[21], the end of grand patriotic speeches, legitimizing consensus. As one can see, postmoderns call in question even the most prestigious dogmas of the modern view. Terry Eagleton bluntly notes (1987: 194):

> We are now in the process of wakening from the nightmare of modernity, with its manipulative reason and fetish of the totality, into the laid-back pluralism of the postmodern, that heterogeneous range of lifestyles and language games which has renounced the nostalgic urge to totalize and legitimate itself. (….) science and philosophy must jettison their grandiose metaphysical claims and view themselves more modestly as just another set of narratives.

British anthropologist Ernest Gellner mentions (1992/1999: 23) that postmodernism implies the concept that all is text and that the raw material of texts, speech and societies, is meaning and meaning must be decoded or deconstructed. Consequently even the concept that there is such a thing as "objective reality" is suspect. In anthropology, this leads to absolute relativism, locking up cultures in closed-system incommensurability.[22] One cannot really understand or appreciate the Other, that is humans who do not share our culture, our worldview. Our perception of the Other is then always defective and biased.

Postmodern man nonetheless enjoys Beauty and a good show. Faced with the universe's lack of meaning, postmodern man reacts in various ways. Some go off on a pilgrimage to Tibet, seeking interior illumination. Others avoid the expense of the plane ticket (and the wear and tear on their shoes) and settle for a neighbourhood guru or shrink. It is a banal, but tragic observation that many attempt to find meaning in diverse self-fulfilment schemes. As a result, *salvation* is found in consumption and *communion* amounts to going shopping. Postmodern man denies involvement in any explicit religion or belief in any rigid creed. In attempting to avoid total nihilism, aesthetics is sometimes his only refuge (excluding perhaps sex and drugs). To fill the vacuum, he can seek Beauty in everyday life. He will attend plays, eat in the best restaurants, visit art galleries, buy albums by recognized artists and hang reproductions and posters on the walls of his house. In a large measure, popular culture has replaced religion. It is thus both logical and ironic, in this context, to observe in this day and age unused churches converted into art galleries, theatres, arts centres or circus arts academies.

Since the beginning of time, humans have demonstrated a capacity to enjoy Beauty, but with postmoderns the consumption of Beauty often serves as a pathetic façade, masking the inner void. So many stratagems to flee the Void, always to flee… A number of artistic works produced in the twentieth-century echo this void. A striking example is the French song **Le monde est stone**,[23] drawn from the musical **Starmania** created by Québécois songwriter and producer Luc Plamondon. The same could be said of the song **Lucky Man** by progressive rock band Emerson, Lake & Palmer offering biting irony about the vanity of material and social success when confronted with the reality of death. Famous Anglo-American poet, T. S. Eliot, also echoed modern alienation in his poem **The Hollow Men** (1954/82: 77):

> We are the hollow men
> We are the stuffed men
> Leaning together
> Headpiece filled with straw. Alas!
> Our dried voices, when
> We whisper together
> Are quiet and meaningless
> As wind in dry grass
> Or rats' feet over broken glass
> In our dry cellar.
> Shape without form, shade without colour,
> Paralysed force, gesture without motion;
>
> Those who crossed
> With direct eyes, to death's other kingdom
> Remember us - if at all - not as lost
> Violent souls, but only
> As the hollow men
> The stuffed men.

The well-known existentialist philosopher and French novelist, Jean-Paul Sartre, had to deal with a particular aspect of the loss of meaning in the materialist world and arrived at a paradoxical conclusion. In an interview, he remarked (in de Beauvoir 1984: 39):

> Sartre: Even if one does not believe in God, there are elements of the idea of God that remain in us and that cause to see the world with some

divine aspects.
De Beauvoir: What for example?
Sartre: That varies according to the person.
De Beauvoir: But for you?
Sartre: As for me, I don't see myself as so much dust that has appeared in the world, but as a being that was expected, prefigured, called forth. In short, as a being that could, it seems, come only from a creator; and this idea of a creating hand that created me refers me back to God. Naturally this is not a clear, exact idea that I set in motion every time I think of myself. It contradicts many of my other ideas; but it is there, floating vaguely. And when I think of myself I often think rather in this way, for want of being able to think otherwise.

Is it a coincidence that the darkest utopias, such as **Brave New World**, (1932: A. Huxley), **1984** (1949: George Orwell), graphic novels by Enki Bilal or movies such as **Fahrenheit 451** (1966: Fr. Truffaut), **Clockwork Orange** (1972: S. Kubrick), **Solyent Green** (1973: R. Fleischer), **Blade Runner** (1982: R. Scott) or **Gattacca** (1997: A. Niccol) were written/produced in the twentieth-century? Is it possible that artists perceive realities that our postmodern elites prefer, if possible, to ignore? In the post-Darwinian context, where it is difficult to establish a coherent meaning of life, is it a coincidence that a twentieth-century philosopher such as Camus puts before us such a brutal question (1942/1991: 3)?

There is but one truly serious philosophical problem, and that is suicide. Judging whether life is or is not worth living amounts to answering the fundamental question of philosophy. All the rest — whether or not the world has three dimensions, whether the mind has nine or twelve categories — comes afterwards. These are games; one must first answer [the question of suicide].

Jean-Paul Sartre also examined the void at the heart of modern man. In his novel **Nausea** (1938), he explores this concept. Antoine Roquentin, the novel's main character, experiences a form of uneasiness, a generalized and nameless angst. This anxiety arises in the most commonplace circumstances and cannot be avoided; it is Nausea. The phenomenon is so relentless that Roquentin, sitting at the Mably café, cannot stand to look at his beer mug. It seems disturbing for some reason. Roquentin is not okay. The lack of meaning affects everything and is inexpressible. It eats up everything and, afterwards, nothing is left. Roquentin remarks (Sartre 1938/2007: 8):

Still, somehow I am not at peace: I have been avoiding looking at this glass of beer for half an hour. I look above, below, right and left; but I don't want to see it. And I know very well that all these bachelors around me can be of no help: it is too late, I can no longer take refuge among them. They could come and tap me on the shoulder and say, "Well, what's the matter with that glass of beer?" It's just like all the others. It's bevelled on the edges, has a handle, a little coat of arms with a spade on it and on the coat of arms is written "Sparlenbrau," I know all that, but I know there is something else. Almost nothing. But I can't explain what I see. To anyone. There; I am quietly slipping into the water's depths, towards fear.

Another author, George Orwell, in his novel **1984**, has also encountered this angst and seems to have a glimpse of an answer... that is, if one goes beyond the particular context of the novel. Orwell has his main character say (1949/1984: 52):

Always in your stomach and in your skin there was a sort of protest, a feeling that you had been cheated of something that you had a right to. It was true that he had no memories of anything greatly different. In any time that he would accurately remember, there had never been quite enough to eat, one had never had socks or underclothes that were not full of holes, furniture had always been battered and rickety, rooms underheated, tube trains crowded, houses falling to pieces, bread dark colored, tea a rarity, coffee filthy-tasting, cigarettes insufficient — nothing cheap and plentiful except synthetic gin. And though, of course, it grew worse as one's body aged, was it not a sign that this was not the natural order of things, if one's heart sickened at the discomfort and dirt and scarcity, the interminable winters, the stickiness of one's socks, the lifts that never worked, the cold water, the gritty soap, the cigarettes that came to pieces, the food with its strange evil tastes? Why should one feel it to be intolerable unless one had some kind of ancestral memory that things had once been different?

If one compares the current situation (where modern elites and media institutions are dominant) with that prevailing in the West a few hundred years ago (when Christianity was predominant in ideological and cultural terms), the contrast is striking. The Judeo-Christian cosmology[24] has been rather efficiently marginalized and is now regarded by many as a retrograde relic of a superstitious past. British literary critic George Steiner submits the following observations about the ideological and moral consequences of the collapse of Judeo-Christian influence in the West[25] (1974: 2):

This desiccation, this drying-up, affecting as it did the very centre of Western moral and intellectual being, left an immense emptiness. Where there is a vacuum, new energies and surrogates arise. Unless I read the evidence wrongly, the political and philosophical history of the West during the past 150 years can be understood as a series of attempts — more or less conscious, more or less systematic, more or less violent — to fill the central emptiness left by the erosion of theology.[26] This vacancy, this darkness in the middle, was one of "the death of God" (remember that Nietzsche's ironic, tragic tonality in using that famous phrase is so often misunderstood). But I think we could put it more accurately: the decay of a comprehensive Christian doctrine had left in disorder, or had left blank, essential perceptions of social justice, of the meaning of human history, of the relations between mind and body, of the place of knowledge in our moral conduct.

Viktor Frankl, a German psychiatrist and Nazi concentration camp survivor, calls this phenomenon the "existential vacuum". He writes (1959/1971: 168, 169-170):

> … man has suffered another loss in his more recent development: the traditions that had buttressed his behavior are now rapidly diminishing. No instinct tells him what he has to do, and no tradition tells him what he ought to do; soon he will not know what he wants to do. More and more he will be governed by what others want him to do, thus increasingly falling prey to conformism. … Let us think, for instance, of "Sunday neurosis," that kind of depression which afflicts people who become aware of the lack of content in their lives when the rush of the busy week is over and the void within themselves becomes manifest. Not a few cases of suicide can be traced back to this existential vacuum. Such widespread phenomena are not understandable unless we recognize the existential vacuum underlying them. This is also true of the crises of pensioners and aging people.

Postmodern propaganda asserts that after secularization had taken place in the West, "religion" left the public sphere and this place has since remained largely empty. The typical mantra, confidently chanted by enthusiastic devotees of the Enlightenment, is that "Science has rendered religion superfluous." But is this truly the case? Can the question of finding meaning for one's existence be so easily set aside? One hears people talk about individuals going through an experience of "a loss of faith", but not a word is said about what has been **gained** in this conversion processus. When social science researchers assure us that no society can do without ideologico-religious systems, one must wonder if the space formerly occupied by Christianity may now be occupied by a system of beliefs of a new kind, a system of beliefs denying its religious character and function. This obviously demands that we re-examine the definition of religion, but we will come back to this issue later on.

In the postmodern world, orthodox answers to fundamental questions are often considered inadequate, deficient. It is precisely for this reason that the issue of the meaning of life arises in such a brutal way. Awareness of this void cannot be explained away as a passing mood swing. In the early twentieth-century, our elites assured us that science would lead us towards infinite progress, but this dream has turned out to be an illusion. In Europe, many placed their faith in socialism and the hope that the dictatorship of the proletariat would make us all comrades, but this dream also fell into grotesque and tragic ruin. Only the void left by a dysfunctional and incoherent worldview remains.

A number of symptoms of the Western ideological void can be detected in everyday life. At times, the West looks to the East to find lost meaning. Perhaps shamans, Zen masters or gurus will come to our rescue. Perhaps Feng Shui devotees will lay out our homes auspiciously in order to protect us from the convergence of negative Qi energies! At other times, the West raises its eyes to the stars to read its future in the horoscope, if not, then to await wisdom coming from higher civilizations in another galaxy. And if that doesn't work, let us pop quartz crystals in our refrigerators and in our jeans in hopes of enjoying better health! So if formerly, in Catholic countries, after buying a new car devout Catholics would often place a statue of Mary[27] on the dashboard, nowadays ex-Catholics may set up a politically-correct fetish, an Ojibwa Dreamcatcher, in its stead. And on our computers we install SETI@ home, in the remote hope that Someone will speak and the meaning of it all will be explained to us… The West is adrift.

For those with no hope of finding a job in a scientific field, the scientific materialism of the modern elites did not fulfil its promises. Student movements of the 1960-70s were, to a large extent, a revolt against this ideology and this way of seeing life. Progress had to wait… Artists again seem to have greater insight. **Logical Song**, by the progressive rock band SuperTramp, initially looks at the world's beauty, seen through the innocent eyes of a child but, as time goes on, with the alienated and cynical eyes of the adult world, a cold and empty world, the logical offspring of materialism. The song goes on to ask (1987):

At night, when all the world's asleep,
the questions run so deep,
for such a simple man.
Won't you please, please tell me what we've learned.
I know it sounds absurd,
but please tell me who I am.

This song puts the finger on a critical issue. The cold and austere universe of materialism, which characterized the modern old guard and deeply influenced the West in the twentieth-century, has been found lacking, insufficient. If the significant universe amounts to nothing more than matter, how does one justify or understand love? Isn't love then little more than an illusion, produced by erratic hormonal cycles or the random trajectory of molecules?

The belief systems proposed by our modern elites have been seen to lack satisfactory answers to a great number of basic questions about the meaning of life. Looking for a way out, the masses have sought to the left, to the right. Modern utopias were optimistic, rational and pathetic... as corroborated by statements from one of the most respected twentieth-century intellectuals (Sartre 1980: 59):

> What I think, is that, when man exists authentically and completely, his relationship with fellow humans and his manner of being will attain what one could call humanism. That is, it will be the manner of being of man, his relationships with his fellowmen and his manner of being in itself. But we are not there yet. You could say rather that we are submen, i.e. beings not fully formed, a state, perhaps, we may never even reach, but towards which we strive.*

While the reservations mentioned by Sartre here seem reasonable, on the other hand his optimism and hopes appear rather misplaced. What can you say? Another child of the same generation, British journalist Malcolm Muggeridge,[28] has considered another way out of this dilemma (1988: 147):

> It has never been possible for me to persuade myself that the universe could have been created, and we, homo sapiens, so-called, have, generation after generation, somehow made our appearance to sojourn briefly on our tiny earth, solely in order to mount the interminable soap opera, with the same characters and situations endlessly recurring, that we call history. It would be like building a great stadium for a display of tiddly-winks, or a vast opera house for a mouth-organ recital.

Religion, Reincarnated

> *The statement that religion is present in non-specific form in all societies and in all "normal" (socialized) individuals is, therefore, axiomatic. It specifies a religious dimension in the "definition" of individual and society, but is empty of specific empirical content.*
> *(Luckmann 1970: 78)*

The postmodern West no longer identifies with a structured and easily recognizable ideologico-religious system. Many individuals now seek meaning in culture and the arts. In broad terms, culture performs not only an aesthetic role for modern man, but has also become the source of **meaning**, a role played in centuries past by religion and its derivative cultural expressions.[29]

The stark contrast between the new ideologico-religious practices of the masses and those of the elites should come as no surprise. Rather than participating in traditional religious rites, our elites may attend a play or a concert, while the masses go to a movie, a music concert or a football game.[30] Rather than daily prayer, some will check their horoscope in the newspaper. The consolation and inspiration formerly found in religion are sought for today in diverse artistic or cultural expressions. Priests and clergy have been replaced by media personalities. In mass culture, one encounters rock 'n' roll stars, talk-show hosts, the morning-man, etc. The elites however, seek their new ideological clergy among astrophysicists, intellectuals and prominent arts personalities such as poets and musicians. In this context, the ultimate motivation, the search for meaning must remain concealed, subliminal. But in reality, such behaviour is inevitable, hardwired into the human condition. David Porush, professor of literary studies at Rensselaer Polytechnic Institute, observes that in the domain of postmodern fiction, the search for meaning, a coherent religion, has become increasingly explicit (1994: 571):

> Long habits of associating transcendence with essentializing beliefs (mistakenly), and essentializing beliefs with intolerant and destructive movements to exclude and expunge alternatives, have made us blind to our own inadmissible tendencies and yearnings, effaced and buried in our own essentializing denial. "Metaphysics" is the bad word of postmodern academia. "Religion" is unthinkable. Yet, if we attend to this late postmodern cybernetic literature and our own irrational pronouncements about the visions and yearnings it has induced in us, it

becomes clear that our most interesting literature is slowly leading us, willy-nilly, into considerations of matters that were recently worthy only of contempt or marginalization in academia:[31] that there may be more here than a mere babble of words, more than a relativizing ethos, more than congeries of bodies, energy, and information unfolding blindly in space and time.

So the cat is slowly coming out of the bag. Myths are always replaced by new myths. This process is inherent in the development and legitimation of any social endeavour, of any civilization. It is inevitable, inescapable. Examining the seminal Enlightenment essay, **The Social Contract** by Jean-Jacques Rousseau, Albert Camus made the following instructive remarks (1951/1978: 114-115):

> The Social Contract is, primarily, an inquiry into the legitimacy of power. But it is a book about rights, not about facts, and at no time is it a collection of sociological observations. It is concerned with principles and for this very reason is bound to be controversial. It presumes that traditional legitimacy, which is supposedly of divine origin, is not acquired. Thus it proclaims another sort of legitimacy and other principles. The Social Contract is also a catechism, of which it has both the tone and the dogmatic language. Just as 1789 completes the conquests of the English and American revolutions, so Rousseau pushes to its limits the theory of the social contract found in Hobbes. The Social Contract amplifies and dogmatically explains the new religion whose god is reason, confused with nature, and whose representative on earth, in place of the king, is the people, considered as an expression of the general will.

Postmodern man is fragmented and this is reflected in his worldview. American sociologist Thomas Luckmann has pointed out (1970: 98-99) that, in the same way the individual in the West is free to shop where he likes to get his groceries or clothing, in ideologico-religious terms the individual is free to hit the ideologico-religious market and shop for ideas and concepts and cobble together his own custom-made, individualized religion. Under postmodernism, all options are open, nothing is excluded. Unwittingly, we have become sophisticated religious syncretists.

The postmodern worldview also postulates that the individual is the measure of all things. All transcendent, pancultural moral rules or standards are rejected. Absolutes are of no use to us. Discussing this topic, a reporter once remarked that it is not surprising that we are so fascinated by criminals and serial killers. Such outlaws push their individualism to the extreme limit. Satisfying their instincts/needs becomes their only real ethic, regardless of the consequences to others. But if, as postmodernism asserts, everyone has his or her own 'truth', when interests are in conflict, this leads to a stalemate. In this context, real discussions or debates, cannot take place. And why is that? Where can one find a common ground to sort things out and arbitrate conflicting interests? This has been disallowed. To which benchmark or Standard would you refer to separate truth from various subjective opinions? All we have left to sort out such matters are little more than power struggles and emotional manipulation, played out behind a ridiculous charade called "tolerance". Those in power attempt to marginalize other ways of looking at things. And if necessary (or desirable), alternate views can be stifled through legal means. Recognized minorities can claim their rights while highlighting the oppression of the majority. An excellent marginalization strategy is to label the assertions of the opposite party as 'hate speech'. Once this label has been applied, then there is no room for discussion. Game over. Critics of the consensus are then recognized by all for the heretics they truly are.

In the academic context, professor Edward Veith examines the postmodern perspective and its influence on the establishment of university programs (1994: 57-58):

> These new models tend to be adopted without the demands for rigorous evidence required by traditional scholarship. If Eurocentricism is a fault, one would think Afro-centrism would be similarly narrow-minded. If patriarchy is wrong, why would matriarchy be any better? But these quibbles miss the point of postmodernist scholarship. Truth is not the issue. The issue is power. The newer models *empower* groups formerly excluded. Scholarly debate proceeds not so much by rational argument or the amassing of objective evidence, but by rhetoric (which scheme advances the most progressive ideals?) and by the assertion of power (which scheme advances my particular interest group, or more to the point, which is most likely to win me a research grant, career advancement, and tenure?).

In the postmodern context, rights claimed by the individual may even threaten the State. At a protest staged against the Gulf War in 1990, among the demonstrators a mother asserted emphatically that no war could justify her son having to die. If this message is deconstructed, it implies that the individual is then the supreme value to which all others must submit.[32] Yet there remains a question: where does the supreme value of the individual come from? Who endorses this value? The individual himself? That would be both embarrassing and ridiculous. Or is this just a dark joke played on us by an indifferent universe? Discussing surrealism, Camus explored the grim side of individual liberty, breaking free of all restrictions or constraints (1951/1978: 93):

> Surrealism did not rest there. It chose as its hero Violette Noziere or the anonymous common-law criminal, affirming in this way, in the face of crime, the innocence of man. But it also was rash enough to say— and this is the statement that Andre Breton must have regretted ever since 1933 — that the simplest surrealist act consisted in going out into the street, revolver in hand, and shooting at random into the crowd. Whoever refuses to recognize any other determining factor apart from the individual and his desires, any priority other than that of the unconscious, actually succeeds in rebelling simultaneously against society and against reason.[33]

Before the individual's rights and aspirations, even the State must stand silent. Its authority, its demands, with respect to the individual, are rejected as arbitrary and unjust. In many cases, the State is viewed as acceptable only if it acts to support and guarantee individual rights. Desire and irrational urges are at the heart of the postmodern worldview. Morality and cosmology are then subservient to this central reality. Everything else about postmodernism amounts to little more than the chameleon's changing colours.[34] Perhaps the environment is the closest postmoderns can come to in terms of a deity to which all must submit.

In the past, the West lived in a unified world, a world where variations of Christianity or Judaism gave meaning to all aspects of life. But in the wake of the growing influence of the Enlightenment, materialism and other derivative schools of thought, this unity has vanished. Life is segmented into zones or compartments where specialized ideologies reign. This gives rise to a form of schizophrenia rather characteristic of postmodernism. In this context, it is not surprising that many people will state that they identify with a traditional religion on a personal level, but if you look at their professional or public life, their behaviour and thinking is deeply moulded by a materialist or postmodern worldview.

Ideological Schizophrenia

This was a world where gods and goddesses could cross the garden or atrium at any time, to no one's surprise (not even an alleged atheist like Lucretius). Where wonders, omens, divination, apparitions, angels, devils, miraculous cures — the stuff of fairy tales in our view — are seen as just part of ordinary (as well as political) life. This universe is inhabited, inside and out, on a day-to-day basis by the invisible, where the supernatural is normal and epiphany, commonplace. Such untrammelled religion — preceding the proposal of a "religious field", in a circumscribed area — where the ordinary casually mingles with the fantastic, where there are no border crossings or customs bureaus, may still be experienced in sub-Saharan Africa or Haiti.*
(Debray 2004: 6)

The power and influence of ideological schizophrenia in the West is due to the division of life into private and public spheres (each with its own, supposedly symbiotic, worldviews). This dichotomous concept leads to individuals living in two worlds. Though the individual must submit to postmodern ideology in the public sphere (in his professional life), in his private life, he is free to entertain the most exotic, strangest beliefs he likes, as long as he has the decency to express them elsewhere. Dichotomous thinking has, for a long time, haunted the West. We find this view first in Plato, where the rational/spiritual world is opposed to the terrestrial/carnal/emotional/sensual world. Ascetic medieval thought as well as the monastic movement, for example, are rooted in this conception. Many Christian thinkers, such as Augustine and Thomas Aquinas (who opposed divine grace and the natural world), modified and heavily invested in these concepts and ensured them a long life in the West. More recently, this dichotomy reappeared in the thinking of René Descartes, where it is expressed in terms of spirit/mind/emotions/desire as opposed to a deterministic and mechanical world of matter.[35]

The German philosopher Immanuel Kant proposed concepts such as liberty/self which he viewed in contrast to the deterministic world of Newtonian mechanics. Closer to our times, we encounter a widespread dichotomy opposing, on the one hand, religion/arts/values/emotions and, on the other, science and reason. Since the Enlightenment, many have attempted to construct an all-encompassing scientific and rational worldview, but morality, creativity, love and many other things have typically eluded such efforts. The Sixties Generation asked "What about love?" and right-ly so. Against this backdrop, the eighteenth-century Romantic movement may be viewed, to a large extent, as a protest against the gloomy, bleak world of science. As Debray previously pointed out, in the process traditional [Christian] religions have been pushed into a cultural ghetto, that of the private life.

But this has not always been the case, even in the West. Originally science made no grand cosmological claims and did not attempt to propose an explanation of EVERYTHING. Cosmological concerns were typically left to Christian theology. It must be under-stood that the expectation that science should also provide cos-mological answers to the question of origins is the direct result of the Enlightenment. Initially science was born and developed in symbiosis with the ideological-religious system of the time, that is to say, the Judeo-Christian worldview. In most cases, early genera-tions of scientists saw their work as a religious quest, endeavouring to explore the thoughts of God in the empirical world. This attitude did not completely disappear even in the twentieth-century. For example, Albert Einstein[36] once justified his rejection of quantum mechanics by saying "God does not play dice!".[37] Since science was born in a symbiotic relationship with the Judeo-Christian world-view there was, at that time, no need to provide a "scientific" expla-nation, justifying ethics and other features unique to humans. This is the result of Enlightenment influence, which needed to use sci-ence to produce cosmology (an origins myth) and, subsequently, a total explanation of life, a religion.

In the field of the anthropology of religion, up until the 1970s, religion was typically defined in terms opposing it to sci-ence.[38] This fed the typical stereotypes: "Science is empirical, reli-gion is metaphysical; Science is rational, religion is emotional; the domain of Science is the natural world, that of religion, the super-natural world,[39] and so on..." But with further study, anthropolo-gists recognized the need to admit that this dichotomous approach to culture, though typical in the West, is not universal. It breaks down in many non-Western cultures and anthropologists realized the mistake of attempting to force other cultures into this mould. Most non-Western cultures have a unified, integrated perspective of reality, where moral wisdom and empirical knowledge are not thought of in terms of opposition.[40]

The Western ideological-religious schizophrenia, expressed in the private/public dichotomy, sometimes leads to crisis situations where postmoderns do not know which "personality" to express, which principles to apply. For example, in San Salvador, after the January 2000 earthquake disaster, a journalist noted that some of the sites he visited were so disturbing that he did not know whether he should go on doing his job or stop and help the desperate people around him. What an ethical dilemma! Should he behave like a journalist or as a human being? For postmoderns, these are challenging questions. How does one decide? The personal/professional dichotomy appears on many levels. The most classic case (as well as the most trivial) is probably the Canadian politician who, when asked to state his position on the abortion issue, replies: "Personally I'm against it, but[41]..." A rather stark contrast is produced when this schizophrenia is compared to the attitude of the eighteenth-century British MP, William Wilberforce, who was a leader of the movement for the abolition of the slave trade throughout the British Empire. In a letter to Alexander, Emperor of France, Wilberforce advocated the abolition of slavery in France and, as such, justified this request by explicitly referring to his religious beliefs (1822):

> It is our belief that in this crowd of exiles, and the return of peace brought to their homeland, religious sentiment should prevail, and we firmly believe that all religious and virtuous men should be favourable to our cause. This cause is indeed that of any man who has not entirely broken the moral and intellectual ties that bind him to the Supreme Being and has not renounced the doctrine of a God who rewards the just and punishes evildoers.*

Criticising the slave merchants' hypocritical and incoherent 'religion', Wilberforce observed (1822):

> There is something more shocking still that appears before the enlightened mind, that is a daily and practical denial of God's providence, coldly and systematically defying his revenge, by the pursuit of a commerce recognized as the most manifest violation of his laws. While the most obstinate atheist can be enlightened, the worst criminal, repent and be forgiven, what shall we say of such men who, recognizing divine authority and the enormity of their crime, claim however that this flagrant crime, while cruel, is too lucrative to be abandoned?*

Can political initiatives then be explicitly justified by reference to religion in the twenty-first century West? Such an attitude has now become simply inconceivable! Excepting perhaps the United States[42], nowadays traditional religious beliefs are routinely marginalized and excluded from the public sphere. Inevitably this mind-set contributes to postmodern religion's dominance and ideological monopoly in public life as well as insuring the marginalization of traditional religions,[43] which have been relegated to the private sphere.[44] Postmodern religion then is primarily a community-focused religion, with rare exceptions, occupying the centre of public institutional life. It embraces and allows for many individual idiosyncrasies and tolerates other religions, as long as they are compatible with postmodern core beliefs (i.e.: rejection of the absolute truth concept). Any religion, claiming universal truth, must accept ghettoization and exclusion from public institutions. This is the root cause of the so-called "culture wars" in the United States.

The schizophrenia of the modern mind, inhabited by parallel forms of logic (rooted in parallel mythologies), has been cleverly analyzed by Kurt Vonnegut in his novel **Mother Night**. Such schizophrenia is more common than one might think. In his novel, Vonnegut uses the concept of the cuckoo clock in Hell, where individuals use one form of logic in one context and, another form in a different context. The characters in the novel then slide from one logic to another without ever grasping the contradictions involved. In the context of the novel, this is brought up in a discussion on Nazi ideology, but there is reason to think it has much wider applications (Vonnegut 1961: 162-163):

> I have never seen a more sublime demonstration of the totalitarian mind, a mind which might be likened unto a system of gears whose teeth have been filed off at random. Such a snaggle-toothed thought machine, driven by a standard or even substandard libido, whirls with the jerky, noisy, gaudy pointlessness of a cuckoo clock in Hell. The boss G-man concluded wrongly that there were no teeth on the gears in the mind of Jones. You're completely crazy, he said. Jones wasn't completely crazy. The dismaying thing about the classic totalitarian mind is that any given gear, though mutilated, will have at its circumference unbroken sequences of teeth that are immaculately, that are exquisitely machined. Hence the cuckoo clock in Hell keeping perfect time for eight minutes and thirty-three seconds, jumping ahead fourteen minutes, keeping perfect time for six seconds, jumping ahead two seconds, keeping perfect time for two hours and one second, then jumping ahead a year. The missing teeth, of course, are simple, obvious truths, truths available and comprehensible even to ten-year-olds, in most cases. That was how a household as contradictory as one composed of Jones, Father Keeley, Vice-Bundesfuehrer Krapptaer, and the Black Fuehrer could exist in relative harmony. That was how my father-in-law could

contain in one mind an indifference toward slave women and love for a blue vase. That was how Rudolf Hoess, Commandant of Auschwitz, could alternate over the loudspeakers of Auschwitz great music and calls for corpse-carriers. That was how Nazi Germany could sense no important difference between civilization and hydrophobia. That is the closest I can come to explaining the legions, the nations of lunatics I've seen in my time.

No doubt Albert Speer, Hitler's chief architect and the Nazi governments' top civil servant, would agree with Vonnegut's analysis as he made the following comments on the abdication of public conscience among members of the Nazi party under Hitler's rule (1970: 33):

> The ordinary party member was being taught that grand policy was much too complex for him to judge it. Consequently, one felt one was being represented, never called upon to take personal responsibility. The whole structure of the system was aimed at preventing conflicts of conscience from even arising. The result was the total sterility of all conversations and discussions among these like-minded persons. It was boring for people to confirm one another in their uniform opinions.
> Worse still was the restriction of responsibility to one's own field. That was explicitly demanded. Everyone kept to his own group—of architects, physicians, jurists, technicians, soldiers or farmers. The professional organizations to which everyone had to belong were called chambers (Physicians Chamber, Art Chamber), and this term aptly described the way people were immured in isolated, closed-off areas of life. The longer Hitler's system lasted, the more people's minds moved within such isolated chambers. If this arrangement had gone on for a number of generations, it alone would have caused the whole system to wither, I think, for we would have arrived at a kind of caste society. The disparity between this and the *Volksgemeinschaft* (community of the people) proclaimed in 1933 always astonished me. For this had the effect of stamping out the promised integration, or at any rate of greatly hindering it. What eventually developed was a society of totally isolated individuals. For although it may sound strange today, for us it was no empty slogan that "the Fuehrer proposes and disposes" for all.

In the postmodern era, where beliefs are compartmentlized, meaning is deconstructed and postmoderns manage the public sphere, individuals must find meaning on their own and develop their personal worldviews as best they can. Some find meaning in environmental activism. Others become capitalists and find meaning in two dominant values, production and consumerism. Others become social activists and a political project becomes the centre around which their lives revolve. This was common in the early twentieth-century (particularly in Europe), but rarer now. In an attempt to put their worldview into action, others go into the arts and seek meaning in aesthetic and artistic expression. Since the only truths recognized by postmoderns are individual, the large-scale political projects of the twentieth-century have lost almost all their powers of attraction.[45] Would you die for the Revolution? Hell no, we won't go! In the twenty-first century, our highest "spiritual" aspiration is to attain the rank of postmodern grand master, that is to say, the accomplished consumer...

The Invisible Church

> *But the flock will come together again and will submit once more, and then it will be once for all. Then we shall give them the quiet humble happiness of weak creatures such as they are by nature. ... They will marvel at us and will be awe-stricken before us, and will be proud at our being so powerful and clever, that we have been able to subdue such a turbulent flock of thousands of millions. They will tremble impotently before our wrath, their minds will grow fearful, they will be quick to shed tears like women and children, but they will be just as ready at a sign from us to pass to laughter and rejoicing, to happy mirth and childish song. Yes, we shall set them to work, but in their leisure hours we shall make their life like a child's game, with children's songs and innocent dance. Oh, we shall allow them even sin, they are weak and helpless, and they will love us like children because we allow them to sin. We shall tell them that every sin will be expiated, if it is done with our permission, that we allow them to sin because we love them, and the punishment for these sins we take upon ourselves.*
> *(Dostoyevsky 1879/1933: 268-269)*

> *Of all tyrannies, a tyranny sincerely exercised for the good of its victims may be the most oppressive. It may be better to live under robber barons than under omnipotent moral busybodies. The robber baron's cruelty may sometimes sleep, his cupidity may at some point be satiated; but those who torment us for our own good will torment us without end, for they do so with the approval of their own conscience.*
> *(C. S. Lewis 1947/2002: 292)*

Few would dispute the fact that over the course of the nineteenth- and twentieth-centuries the Christian religion suffered great setbacks to its social influence in the West. In France, a secular perspective became dominant by the eighteenth-century, in the English-speaking world, this occurred later. That Western society is now secular, largely without traditional religious influence is common knowledge. But what about in practice? Has religion actually been done away with? Has it vanished as Enlightenment thinkers had prophesied? Is it possible that in a sense, as Steiner pointed out previously, this is an illusion. Perhaps a more subtle shift has occurred, is this just new wine in old wineskins? It is said that nature abhors a vacuum. Though proven false in the world of physics, in religious or ideological terms, there is good reason to believe it true.

In the present situation, perhaps what we face is not an absence or eradication of religion, but rather the appearance of a new form of religion, a religion with no explicit creeds, no visible temples or cathedrals and with no well-known religious leaders. In actual fact, it owes much of its power to its invisibility. Social anthropologists have from time to time observed such phenomena in societies dominated by syncretism[46], but the implications of such observations are rarely explored in the Western context. In Sub-Saharan Africa, the local religion is often implicit. Since syncretistic societies tend to avoid developing grand doctrinal edifices or a formal set of rituals, one encounters much fluidity in matters of doctrine and ritual.[47] This explains certain facts noted by French anthropologist Marc Augé (1974b: 12):

> One can certainly say that in most African societies, no fully formulated and complex ideological system is ever proposed. It is simply referred to in specific circumstances, particularly when interpreting misfortune, illness or death, providing the elements of representation necessary to allow understanding.*

If we are open to the idea that the West has become dominated by an invisible religion, then one must face the logic leading to the presence of a new class of religious elites. In the West one generally associates church and religion, that is, a system of beliefs linked to a consecrated building used by a community of believers assisted and/or directed by some form of clerical hierarchy. In addition, in common sense language, religion and the supernatural are stereotypically linked. But when considering postmodern religious elites, such links are no longer relevant. First of all, the new religious elites are not part of easily identified communities. Secondly, they typically do not refer to a divinity or to concepts referring to gods of some sort. Is it still legitimate then to speak of religious elites? No doubt the majority of these individuals would energetically protest that their activities or attitudes are not "religious" in any shape or form. We should expect no less… To follow the argument here, it must first noted that some religions, such as Theravada Buddhism[48] for example, do not necessarily refer to a deity. Religion then does not demand a reference to supernatural beings of some sort or even a supernatural dimension. American anthropologist Clifford Geertz has proposed a definition of religion that goes so far as to delete the reference to the supernatural, commonly associated with religion. Geertz's definition is as follows (1973: 90):

A religion is (1) a system of symbols which acts to (2) establish long-lasting moods and motivations in men by (3) formulating conceptions of a general order of existence and (4) clothing these conceptions with such an aura of factuality that (5) the moods and motivations seem uniquely realistic.

If we indeed accept such a definition of religion, then it becomes entirely justifiable to consider our postmodern elites as religious elites, but this leaves us with a religion with no name. For want of a better term, we will be content here with the expression 'postmodern religion'.

But such a small change in a definition opens up a huge can of worms in the postmodern context. If postmoderns actually have a religion, what are its doctrines? Can one define it without immediately falling into stereotypical comparisons with the Middle Ages or the nineteenth-century? Other anthropologists have since followed Geertz's lead and dropped any reference to the supernatural in their definitions of religion though they diligently avoid exploring the implications of such a move in the West. In short, one of the main functions of a religion or an ideologico-religious system is to answer four very basic questions about the human condition:

- Where do we come from?[49] / Why do we exist?
- What is the source of human alienation?
- How do you establish rules governing interaction between individuals?[50]
- How do you reduce (or abolish) human alienation?[51]

In the West, it turns out that postmodern elites are in fact attempting to address these issues as well as set themselves up as authority figures. Another feature of this religion, distinguishing it from traditional religions, is its invisibility. It does not knock on your door, does not host any recognized pilgrimages and does not distribute tracts in the streets to make converts. It has no visible places of worship or any notorious 'TV evangelists'. To a very large extent, it propagates its presuppositions and doctrines through the activities of the postmodern elites. Their recruitment methods are then implicit, invisible.

In his essay **The Dust of Death**, British author Os Guinness contrasted Christianity and Hinduism regarding their methods of recruitment and proselytization and wrote (1973: 229-230):

The difference between the ultimate intolerance of the East and the intolerance of Christianity can be illustrated as follows: Christianity stands across a man's path like a soldier with a drawn sword saying "choose or refuse", "life or death", "yes or no"; the choice and the consequences are extremely obvious. The subtlety of Eastern religion is that it enters like an odourless poison gas, seeping under the door, through the keyhole, in through the open windows so that the man is overcome without his ever realizing there was any danger at all.

Biblical Christianity differs from Hinduism and many other Eastern religions by demanding a raising of **conscious** awareness, a formal conversion (usually expressed in ritual of some kind). This requires a reasoned decision. Hinduism, on the other hand and, much like the postmodern religion, currently dominant in the West, does not require a deliberate conversion. It is typically content with the following strategy: to constantly undermine the assumptions of its target audience and portray its own presuppositions as 'normal', 'enlightened', 'cool', etc.. Even a rock can be reduced to dust by the waves that lap on it relentlessly. On this subject, Guinness observed (1973: 230):

In Rishikesh I shared a room at the ashram with a friend of Fredrico Fellini. This man reminded me ad nauseam that he was still very much an atheist and an Italian and not a Hindu. But after only a week with him, I could see that all his views of man, morality and life were thoroughly Hindu in timbre, though not in name.

Much like Buddhism and other syncretistic religions, postmodern religion does not openly seek to convert, but to rather to influence, to quietly slip in its assumptions, while at the same time marginalizing other belief systems. This religion does not demand a moment of decision involving an explicit conversion ritual. The process is largely implicit, unconscious. When a transition from one belief system to another occurs, this process is typically referred to as a conversion. The individual abandons his prior assumptions/ beliefs and acquires others to build his new worldview, his new identity as well as principles guiding his behaviour. Sometimes this can be a tumultuous and dramatic process or, to use Christian terminology, a Damascus Road experience, but this is the exception. Typically, conversion is the result of a long process with one or more triggering events exposing the failings of the former ideologico-religious system. An objective examination of the conversion process almost always brings to light residues of influence of the previous belief system, even many years after conversion has taken place. It is interesting in that it is commonly held that a Christian or a Jew adopting a modern or postmodern belief system is said to have 'abandoned the faith' or has 'lost his/her faith'. The expression is odd as it underscores only what has been set aside, but is silent about that which has been gained or adopted... The fact that this process has two faces is evaded and denied. Perhaps, regarding the destination of this path, silence is golden...

Postmodern religion differs from traditional religions in that it is acquired, not through public initiation rites or memorizing a catechism or creed, but through manipulative coercion and by daily contact with the surrounding culture, absorbing the assumptions communicated until behaviour aligns with propaganda. Two institutions play a major role in this process: public education and popular culture.

Though traditional religions are usually associated with a visible community (that is, a group of people visibly gathered, in a church or other place of worship, a place with distinctive architecture), in the context of the postmodern religion, this visible characteristic has been dropped. However, it should be noted that since postmodernism is an invisible religion, places of assembly and worship do exist, but they too are invisible.[52] Places of worship in the postmodern religion turn out to be the various social institutions where postmoderns tend to congregate. This will be discussed at length in the following pages. It is in these institutions that the highest concentration of postmodern devotees can be found. Moreover, popular culture provides many other places of worship: music shows, movies,[53] Oscar awards ceremonies, in France, the Palm d'Or movie awards, football/soccer games,[54] Nobel Prize awards, etc.. A gathering always involves ritual in some form and ritual involves religion (and its concepts). In this regard Marc Augé notes (1982: 318-319):

> ... ritualistic logic is related not only to material and ideological domination between communities. It is the source of all collective behaviour that may convey to communities, irrespective of the principle of their constitution, a consciousness, perhaps ephemeral, of their identity and in Durkheimian terms, their sacredness. In modern societies, social gatherings are neither exclusively, nor primarily religious in the narrow sense. Economic life, trade unions, political and, more importantly, sporting events give rise to the largest mass events. One could also mention large gatherings at pop concerts. These diverse gatherings

... lend themselves well to Durkheimian analysis in that the enthusiasm generates embodied representations (celebrities, stars), some more abstract (the Party or football club) or more symbolic (colours, animal figures), which are packaged in various ways (T-shirts, posters, pennants, caps) and constitute the basic materials of a fragmented worship characterized by its totemic formulation.*

Among Artificial Intelligence's (AI) most ardent proponents as well as with followers of the posthuman movement,[55] cyberspace has come to be the central (virtual) place of worship and utopian hope. In this regard, David Porush notes (1994: 555):

> The strong utopianism with which many are anticipating cyberspace, and the consistency with which cyberpunk fiction depicts transcendent or metaphysical occurrences there, suggest to me that cyberspace has become to our postmodern culture, with more than rational force, a sacramental architecture — even though it does not yet exist, quite. Like most sacramental architectures, cyberspace is prefigured as a site for the initiation or control of apocalyptism, where at some time in the future revelations from places beyond rational or material experience will occur. ...
> In short, the intersection between the transcendent world and this one has always created or required an architecture that ultimately restructures society itself. Or better, perhaps we should say this: humans inevitably feel that a certain architecture is needed to summon the transcendent into this world. The reverse is also true: when the correct architecture is constructed, (we feel) the transcendent will be compelled to inhabit it willy-nilly: "Build it and they will come" For postmoderns, cyberspace is it. We are no more free of this metaphysical impulse than are the Zinacatecos.

French media specialist Régis Debray ironically notes (2004: 2): "'Beliefs' are always views entertained by others or those that the speaker has discarded. At present, all we believe is certain". In the following pages we shall examine influential groups in the West regarding their place in the postmodern religion. For example, we shall consider science experts regularly appearing on TV or radio. What is their function? Is it conceivable that our elites can play an ideological-religious role and, if so, how do they fulfil this function? There is reason to believe that a critical issue for these scientists is integration, that is to say, scanning science's latest discoveries and framing them to a target audience in terms that are consistent with the dominant worldview. This process, beyond the initial intent of educating the public about science, implies/ includes the ultimate goal of reassuring the postmodern faithful that science legitimizes their system of beliefs and that it is cloaked in scientific aura. When media gatekeepers choose individuals destined to become scientific talk-heads, it must be understood that the individual's performance or prestigious degrees, though necessary, are not the bottom line. What really matters is that these individuals are actually true believers[56]. It goes without saying that another scientist, with even greater accomplishments, but who is not a 'believer', will not fit the bill.

Typically the ideologico-religious role played by intellectuals goes unnoticed, but some do manage to make the connection. Kim Pournin, a journalist with the French *Le Figaro* newspaper, gives us a cynical view of the work and influence of renowned psychoanalyst, Jacques Lacan (2004):

> From 1953 to 1980, the psychoanalyst Jacques Lacan (1901-1981) made a huge show of his Seminar, theatrically exploiting his voice, gestures and persona. In Sainte-Anne, at Ulm, then at the Pantheon, his teaching became more obscure as it became more popular. Admittedly, this deprives our Freudian Gongora and his labours of any structure and gives his work the abrupt aura of a Rosetta stone, but it does not conceal the clerical cliquishness of his manner: submission to the master, benedictions, excommunications... They are watching, the fanatics, devotees and other world-weary women, as Jean-Francois Revel would say. In the last years of his pontificate, they filled seats in lecture halls, where our man pronounced his sermons.*

Pournin's tone here is darkly ironic, perhaps offered in jest, but it nevertheless hits the nail on the head in pointing out Lacan's ideological role (and that of many others of lesser fame, it goes without saying). British Sociologist Eileen Barker, observing the immense prestige acquired by science in the middle of the twentieth-century, produced a fascinating study (1979) on the ideological (or cosmological) role played by scientists in the origins of life debate. Barker took the novel tack of examining scientists as a priesthood, exploiting the aura of science and enhancing the prestige of worldviews promoted by various groups.

Regarding media, is it conceivable that one of the gathering places of the 'elect' centres in multinational media corporations[57] and in national TV channels in left-leaning countries? But does the Right evade this phenomenon? Not at all. The invisibility of these religious elites is ensured by the convenient myth of 'media neutrality' and the fact that they all have another, official job, while their largely subliminal ideological influence is wielded in their recognized field of activity.

It should be noted that the 'invisibility' of the postmodern religion is linked to the fact that individuals in each elite group play (as actors in a play may be required to do at times), two roles, a professional/visible role alongside an ideological/subliminal role. The professional role provides a reliable alibi, a smokescreen ensuring concealment/denial of the latent ideological role, provided, of course, that some restraint is exercised when censoring or marginalizing opposing perspectives. This leads us to the ideological and religious role of superior court judges in the developed nations of the West. In a context where traditional religions are largely excluded from public institutions, judges may now establish for all what is good or evil. Among scientists, for example, we can easily think of elite organizations playing critical roles such as the Académie française in France, the Royal Society in England or the National Academy of Sciences[58] in the US, as well as other granting agencies which researchers depend upon for research funding.[59]

Regarding education, who has the most influence? This question leads logically to ministries of Education in Western nations[60] as well as the universities that train such individuals. These groups all have a dominant influence on the content of educational programs. Each of the groups mentioned above has its own hierarchy and keeps watch over its territory. Obviously, from time to time, territorial disputes will arise between these groups, each attempting, when opportunity arises, to extend its influence (for example, when the media sometimes attempts to play a judicial role).

The public education system produces individuals with professional skills and qualities of use to the postmodern ideological system. Should individuals going through the education system preserve innermost convictions other than postmodern they will nonetheless acquire, as by osmosis, the necessary reflexes and flexibility to compartmentalize their perspective and store their non-postmodern beliefs in the closet of their 'private life'. Of course educational systems are not ruthless factory lines[61] and individuals with beliefs contradicting the postmodern religion may nevertheless work through the system and find a job. But when this occurs, the system still has defence mechanisms and filters. Dissidents can expect to earn an honest living, but will have to accept a rather marginal existence in ideological terms. They will never gain (short of serious blunders by system gatekeepers) positions of real influence. Such positions are earmarked for true believers of the postmodern religion or, at the very least, for individuals that have learned how to 'appropriately' compartmentalize their beliefs and behaviour.

Getting a Hearing

> *Law can reign, in fact, in so far as it is the law of universal reason. But it never is, and it loses its justification if man is not naturally good. A day comes when ideology conflicts with psychology. Then there is no more legitimate power. Thus the law evolves to the point of becoming confused with the legislator and with a new form of arbitrariness.*[62] *Where turn then? The law has gone completely off its course; and, losing its precision, it becomes more and more inaccurate, to the point of making everything a crime.*[63] *Law still reigns supreme, but it no longer has any fixed limits. (Albert Camus 1951/1978: 131)*

Civilizations find their basis in a worldview, and the judicial systems developed by such civilizations express, in practical terms, inter-relational principles implicit in that worldview. In a court case, neutrality should, in theory, exist when sorting out evidence offered by the diverging parties, but when we consider the judiciary as a whole, in ideological terms neutrality is impossible. Formerly, it was common in Western democratic systems to consider that the role of the judiciary at its highest levels was to apply the law as established by the elected government to which it is bound. But over the course of the twentieth-century in most Western democracies, the superior judiciary has slowly abandoned this view, particularly in the case of Superior Court judges. As a result, supreme courts in several countries increasingly have taken on the role of defining or shaping the law along postmodern lines. One notices supreme courts invalidating existing laws and/or exploiting their broadened powers to reinterpret such laws (which comes down to the same thing). This is not an ideologically neutral situation, but amounts to the imposition, by judicial measures, of a morality with its basis in the postmodern worldview. A door has been opened.

The late nineteenth- and early twentieth-centuries saw the growing influence, in legal circles, of the modern/humanist old guard. As a result of this infiltration, the concept of justice itself has changed. If, at one time in the West it was considered that the basic principles of the law had to be based in the absolute and were fixed for all time, we now find other considerations affecting the expression and practice of law. Consequently, the establishment of justice is conceived of as based not in any absolute, but linked rather to statistical, sociological factors and legitimized by what is perceived by the elites to be "customary", "enlightened" or "normal" in the context of a postmodern, multicultural and pluralistic society. To justify such changes in practice, the concept of progress is often invoked. Societies and attitudes must be "progressive". This new view of justice is usually expressed by referring to individualistic values rather than community-based values. Issues such as abortion, relaxed divorce laws and children's rights all appeal to such a rationale. The euthanasia debate is also expressed in terms of individual rights, that is to say, the individual's "right" to die with dignity, typically veiling the State's interests in such matters.

Having observed this change in religious (some may prefer the term "ideological") allegiances among our legal elites, one may ask how these changes have been implemented? If we examine mechanisms used by the elites to establish postmodern morality within the legal system, the situation in the West varies considerably from one country to another. Here are a few examples:

- The Declaration of the Rights of Man and of the Citizen (France)
- The Canadian Charter of Rights and Freedoms (Canada)
- The Constitution and Bill of Rights (United States)

In the United States, legal judgments framed in terms of the new moral order have usually been handed down by appeals to the constitution. In postmodern states, cases involving legal precedent often provide a useful opportunity to advance the new postmodern moral order and render decisions in harmony with postmodern ideology. Note that cases involving legal precedent are but one tool among others that can be used to introduce postmodern influence. It goes without saying that ordinary law enforcement occupies most of the lower court judges workload, but as one works up through the legal system to the supreme courts, the expanded powers of these institutions provide favourable opportunities making it possible to reinterpret the law or to repeal existing laws, that is laws that have come to be considered "reactionary" or "intolerant". This is obviously a long and more or less random process. Since judges cannot directly modify the laws in the books they must wait until an appropriate case is brought to their attention.[64] Judges of course do not have the power to rewrite the law, but given their right to review the law, this distinction becomes relatively meaningless considering their stranglehold on the actual day-to-day administration of justice.

In Canada, the introduction of the Charter of Rights and Freedoms in 1982 provided a useful mechanism with which to reshape the legal system. In an address beginning the 2003-2004 court year in Quebec courts, Quebec Chief Justice Michel Robert noted (in Balassoupramaniane 2004):

> We've evolved from a system where parliamentary supremacy was practically unlimited … to a regime based on constitutional supremacy in which both the powers of Parliament and the powers of legislatures are limited by respect for rights and freedoms guaranteed by Article 1 of the Charter. In such a system, the court's mission has broadened considerably and the judiciary has become as important as the executive and legislative powers. The courts have now become instruments of governance themselves. Several controversial issues, especially those that divide the population, are often partially or completely resolved by the courts rather than by governments. [For example], the legalization of abortion [was decided] by the Morgentaler verdict and same-sex marriages have already been the subject of five judgments. It is difficult to imagine a fundamental question that has not been addressed by the courts: capital punishment, euthanasia, pornography, assisted suicide, mercy killing, freedom of expression in commercial advertising, rights of detainees to vote, the status of political parties funded by state resources and the list goes on.*

In the Canadian context, one may consider the Charter of Rights and Freedoms as a kind of law above the law. In the West, if legal elites are seen as promoters of postmodern religion, by what process is this done? Before answering this question, one must note that legal elites have always played an ideologico-religious role, since the law always has moral implications. Ethics, as well as concepts of good and evil, are never pulled out of a magician's hat. They are always rooted/based in a worldview. Furthermore, it should be noted that the Western legal system has long existed in a symbiotic relationship, in terms of basic principles, with the dominant worldview of the time, which was influenced by the Judeo-Christian worldview.[65]

To some extent this long-standing symbiotic relationship with the Judeo-Christian worldview has actually rendered the ideological dimension of the judicial system neutral and invisible. Over time, Judeo-Christian legal concepts came to be considered "natural" and were taken for granted in the West. That said, there never was, at any time, a total dominance of the judiciary by Christianity because the legal system varies according to geographical and cultural contexts in addition to harbouring residual legal concepts from pre-Christian societies, of which Roman law is but one example. Inevitably, one can observe features of a country's judicial system that are clearly linked to its history and particular cultural context. Having said that, the Judeo-Christian worldview has often played a key role in shaping the legal system in the West. This reflects a societal choice. It should be noted that even in the Middle Ages, Christian influence on the legal system has never been comprehensive or consistent. Moreover, the Judeo-Christian worldview provides basic legal principles, but makes no particular demands on how to resolve the details of human interaction. Though the Ten Commandments condemn theft, the Bible, for instance, does not specify what sentence to hand down to a con artist that has defrauded an old lady out of $40,000. In the case of Islam, the situation is different, as the integration of the judiciary (and politics) by religion is generally much more thorough and far-reaching.[66] In this regard, British anthropologist Raymond Firth remarked (1981: 589):

> But from the central postulate of God as the supreme, ultimate, blinding reality come propositions about man as the servant of God, about nature as symbols reflecting the divine reality, and about the law (Shari'a) as expressing the will of God and covering all aspects of human life. It is a neat and logical faith. For Muslims, there is no ultimate distinction between divine law, and human law. So every act, including every political act, has a religious dimension and should have a demonstrable religious sanction.

Christianity is generally content to address general principles, the value of human life for example. In the eighteenth-century, Christians in England struggled to outlaw slavery. Later in the nineteenth-century, many anti-slavery activists in the United States were motivated by Christian religious views.[67] It is no accident that slavery was first abolished in nations under Reformation influence[68]. In the twentieth-century, where residues of racist influence still persisted, another Christian, Martin Luther King was in the forefront of the fight against black segregation.

An article published by Larson and Witham (1999) in Scientific American examined the religious beliefs of American scientists. The authors found that atheism among scientists is more common than in the general population, but they noted that in elite institutions such as the National Academy of Sciences (NAS), the proportion of atheist respondents was much higher yet. In these elite groups, atheists form an overwhelming majority. If a comparable study were done regarding the ideological and religious beliefs of Superior Court judges in the West[69], one may wonder if the results would not be, to a large extent, similar... and that we would discover that devotees of the modern or postmodern religions form an overwhelming majority there too.

Though the selection process of judges is important, in the final analysis the critical issue is the ideological motivation of the judges themselves during the course of their activities and particularly when handing down decisions. Some conservatives have focused much attention to the judicial selection process, but in our opinion this is only one aspect of the situation and typically ignores the deeper question about the new powers of judges to rescind or reshape the law.

During the twentieth-century most legal elites abandoned their previous implicit support of the Judeo-Christian heritage. Initially judges promoted the modern or humanist worldview, and of late, the postmodern worldview. This institutional ideological and religious shift has taken place, in most cases, without any real input from society. Often it is driven by a gradual process of substitution where, generation after generation, "old-fashioned" players are replaced by individuals with more progressive or modern outlooks. Ideological commitments on the part of our legal elites are typically ignored, if not vehemently denied, but at relaxed peer events, such matters can be broached with less ambiguity or hypocrisy. For instance, during a speech at a benefit banquet honouring a colleague, attended by other lawyers, Québec Chief Justice, Michel Robert, noted (2003: 11-12)

> C. G. is a deeply moral man, I say moral, not moralistic or preachy. The morality emerging from his opinions, is not specifically religious,[70] but rather has a humanistic foundation characteristic also, despite the centuries separating them, of the works of Erasmus, the Dutch-born philosopher.

Obviously judge Robert is not discussing a colleague's personal opinions here, but rather his legal opinions, that is to say his court decisions.[71] It is odd to note that the ethical schizophrenia demanded of politicians (who have to separate their private and public beliefs into watertight bulkheads) need not apply to Superior Court judges. Robert's statements make it clear that a judge's private (ideologico-religious) beliefs also affect his or her judgments in court. In this situation there is clearly no separation of "church" and state and the conveyed subliminal message conveyed is that such a state of affairs is desirable and normal. Though for specific cases, there may be several views on the merits of the positions of Superior Court judges in the West, there can be no doubt about the ideologico-religious motives behind many decisions. It appears that those concerned very rarely recognize such motives, but rules are made to be broken. Concerning the role played by supreme court judges, Judge Michel Robert states (Schmitz 2004: 1):

> In a sense, we have become the new priests of civil society, as we make decisions about gay marriage, euthanasia and abortion. We hand down decisions on highly controversial issues with intrinsic moral content and very broad moral implications. We have become the instruments of governance in the broadest sense. We now define the socio-economic basis of society.

The evolution of legal decisions over the twentieth-century in the West must not be viewed in isolation, but rather in the context of their ideological and religious basis. And if one commits to this logic, then one must wonder where it will lead. It is understandable though that some may think it best if this question were not raised…

Postmodern religion now dominates the public square and tolerates no rivals. An article by American law professor Stephen L. Carter (1989) discusses the process of appointing U.S. Supreme Court judges. Carter proposes the hypothetical case of a judge applying for a position at the U.S. Supreme Court, a judge openly displaying beliefs deemed "religious".[72] The article examines the obstacles and various exclusion mechanisms that such a candidate (whose politically correctness is regarded as insufficient) may encounter in seeking such a position. It is very important to keep in mind that this process (and the exclusion mechanisms on which it is based) has two aspects; what it seeks to exclude and what it attempts to promote and protect… Of course this article deals with the American context, but elsewhere, even taking into account variations of the different legal systems in the West, the end result will be generally comparable. In most Western countries, the process of selecting judges to supreme courts involves an [implied] evaluation of the candidate's professional ideological perspectives while at the same time ensuring conformity in judges' ideological positions. And once installed, to which side will they lean in making their decisions? In most cases there is little point in guessing...

Among the politically correct, when it comes to entrusting important tasks or filling a critical position, one can instinctively recognize "open-minded" or "progressive" individuals. To begin with, their intellectual and professional production will speak volumes. Do they quote the *right* authors, look at the issues from the *proper* perspective, use *appropriate* terminology and arrive at *acceptable* conclusions? It is much the same in everyday life, in a bus or subway, for example, when looking over another passenger's shoulder, quietly reading a book or magazine, one can sometimes guess or recognize (within a certain margin of error), by assessing the content or title, if one is dealing with someone with a compatible outlook, a nonentity or an ideological opponent.

The process by which Supreme Court judges are chosen is then a critical moment in the life of a democracy because it determines which individuals will gain access to positions of great influence as well as allowing the public [in a limited fashion] to examine the players ideological convictions. Undoubtedly in the West each country develops its own idiosyncrasies regarding this process. The Canadian situation differs from that in the United States. Among Americans, candidates for Supreme Court judge positions are first nominated by the president, but this choice must be ratified by the Senate Judiciary Committee, a committee which, depending on the unfolding political situation, may not necessarily favour the presidential choice. Standing before this committee, judges must answer questions about their integrity, professional qualifications and ideological convictions. Following these hearings, the Senate then votes on whether to confirm the candidates or not. "Inconveniently" this process happens to be open to public view. In recent years, some candidates have been questioned in connection with their positions on the issue of abortion.[73]

In Canada, the process is left to the Prime Minister's discretion, who may take into account recommendations made by the Minister of Justice. As is the case in other countries, candidates for the Canadian Supreme Court must meet certain professional requirements. Candidates submit their applications to an advisory committee, which later makes its recommendations to the Prime Minister. The Prime Minister takes the final decision. Note that when this process meets the ideological and religious expectations of the parties involved one should expect them to zealously argue that the process is entirely neutral and vital to insure the independence of the judiciary, etc. If some may suspect that these observations imply some form of conspiracy mongering, let them rest easy. Converging interests are amply sufficient to achieve the desired results.

In the course of the 2003-2004 session of the Canadian Parliament a proposal was tabled regarding the appointment of Supreme Court judges and expressing the hope that the process be made more open, that is, subject to review by elected MPs rather than being the Prime Minister's sole fiat. This suggestion was not enthusiastically received. Some interveners seem to consider it a major "concern" that candidates for posts at the Supreme Court of Canada could be subjected to scrutiny by elected officials. To protect the status quo, it is expected that they categorically deny that the process involves any impartiality,[74] bias or subjectivity. For example, professor of law Alain-Robert Nadeau, in an article entitled **Democratization or Witch Hunts*** noted (2004):

> To begin with, the very idea that the process of appointing judges to the Supreme Court should be made more "democratic" is incompatible with the independence of the judiciary.[75] … My view is that the idea of examining judges' ideology before their appointment to the Supreme Court would undermine the independence of the judiciary and would result in witch hunts rather than a democratizing of the political system.*

So perhaps in less refined terms the message is: "Get your filthy paws off this process and mind your own business! We have everything under control." And if such reprimands aren't heeded, then any serious questioning or process that could shed light on the ideological and religious commitments of current (or potential Supreme Court judges, will be thoroughly discredited by all means possible. In this view, it seems expressions such as "witch hunts" are then never too overstated nor too strident… Canadian member of Parliament, Richard Marceau, thought it somewhat strange that a judge should expect to avoid a review process which is par for the course for others involved in the government system (2003: M288, 13:25):

> It is important for Canadians to know about the beliefs and values of the men and women who are making these decisions that are foundational to our society. You see, Madam Speaker, you and I can be held to account, as can everyone in this chamber. Every four years or so, I am

held to account by means of an election. My beliefs and values are scrutinized, and sometimes frankly it is not too pleasant. But I am in the little league of important decisions. A justice of the Supreme Court[76] is a virtual unknown, yet he or she can trump government and Parliament and send society off in directions in which legislators do not necessarily want society to go, i.e., same-sex marriage, legalized marijuana, election laws, aboriginal rights, et cetera. Once he or she is appointed, he or she is completely immune from scrutiny and accountability.

Another Canadian MP, James Lunney, commenting on the motion proposed by Marceau, made the following remarks (2003: M288, 19:30):

> It is an issue that Canadians are indeed concerned about. There was a huge public outcry in British Columbia, for example, because judges failed to respond to child pornography with the John Robin Sharpe case and refused to prosecute any child pornography cases. People were outraged because of that. People have an understanding that it is the role of Parliament to make the laws. It is the role of police to enforce the laws, and it is the role of judges to do the sentencing and to settle disputes where those arise. ... There have been so many issues where this judicial activism has gotten out of hand. We see it now in the issue of defining marriage. Recently the courts have been telling Parliament that it needs to change its marriage laws. We have another court in British Columbia coming to the same conclusion, that the government must respond because society has changed. The courts are telling us that society has changed. We recognize that this is not what society expects of judges. It needs to be fixed.

Perhaps some will argue that many of these complaints are "religiously motivated" and in some cases this may be quite true. But there is a flip side to this coin and that is, if we consider the cases of individuals who **do not** complain about the activities of these judges (or about the selection process that puts them in place), then we must conclude that their indifference and acceptance of the changes initiated by such judges are equally religiously motivated. It is misleading (or dishonest) to state that only certain positions on such matters are ideologically or religiously neutral. The attitudes and behaviour of those who do not complain about the selection process for judges can be understood only in relation to their prior ideologico-religious commitments. But, except in very rare circumstances, postmoderns will at all costs avoid discussing the influence their personal presuppositions, or the worldview that underlies them, have on their initiatives or opinions. No doubt institutional objectivity would suffer from such admissions... This ensures that the official discourse is shielded from any serious critique or comparison. One observes then, in the current legal environment, a marginalization of any discourse motivating its initiatives with reference to a moral order other than postmodern. Regarding the situation in the United States, Charles Colson notes (1996: 34):

> Writing the decision for the Ninth Circuit Court of Appeals in Compassion in Dying v. Washington, which overturned a state ban on euthanasia, Judge Reinhardt slammed the door on people "with strong moral or religious convictions," as he put it. "They are not free," he wrote, "to force their views, their religious convictions, or their philosophies on all the other members of a democratic society."

Seeing postmodern states deny the existence of transcendental, universal, law, a law taking precedence over edicts of the State, logically one must concede that Supreme Court judges are now the ones defining what good and evil means both for society and postmodern religion. No doubt Judge Reinhardt's attitude towards religion (Christianity) is widespread in the postmodern West. But there is reason to wonder what would have happened if judges with such attitudes had presided over courts in the eighteenth and nineteenth centuries. The question arises: Is it reasonable to believe that Wilberforce and other co-belligerents in the anti-slavery movement would have reached their goals, taking into account the fact that they explicitly and unambiguously justified their opposition to slavery by referring to the Judeo-Christian beliefs that motivated their initiatives?[77] Certainly, if their activism had been ruled out for the same reasons as those outlined by Judge Reinhardt, then one must face the grim alternate reality in which slavery would be a bare fact of life in the present-day West.[78] This would mean in practical terms that in all likelihood our bus drivers, garbage men, janitors or daycare workers would be, as was the case in ancient Rome and Greece, slaves, chattels of the elite. Economic interests certainly are no stranger to us and have been used, in all time periods, to rationalize all forms of injustice.

2 / Vivisecting the Patient

The more the universe seems comprehensible, the more it seems pointless.
(Steven Weinberg 1977: 154)

Such, then, was the state of my imaginative life; over against it stood the life of my intellect. The two hemispheres of my mind were in the sharpest contrast. On the one side a many-islanded sea of poetry and myth; on the other a glib and shallow "rationalism." Nearly all that I loved I believed to be imaginary; nearly all that I believed to be real I thought grim and meaningless.
(C.S. Lewis 1955: 170)

Over the course of the twentieth-century the vast majority of Western elites were influenced by a materialistic cosmology enhanced by the prestige of empirical science. The old guard of our modern religious elites is therefore almost exclusively materialistic. Their propaganda implies the equation science = truth. In their view, science has become the ultimate epistemological point of reference. In social terms, such authority can be compared to that once enjoyed by the Pope or the Bible. Since WWII, however, a new guard of postmodern elites has gradually gained influence and territory.

To better understand the contrast between the old modern elites and the new postmodern elites, it should be noted that the late nineteenth-century and the first half of the twentieth was an era of certainties and truths. This was an era dominated by identifiable, polarized, political ideologies. One could be a fascist, communist, anarchist, capitalist, Maoist, etc. Modern man claims that history has meaning and that this meaning is found in the concept of progress.[79] Moderns told us that progress would certainly lead us to a technological paradise or, failing that, to the classless society foretold by Marx. The modern religious perspective rejects the Judeo-Christian perspective on important issues and in particular sees science as the source of truth rather than in some form of Revelation. As a result, modern ideologies all claim the prestige of science as assurance of their truth. The modern worldview does share one thing with the Judeo-Christian worldview both agree that there is such a thing as Truth[80] though they strongly disagree about where Truth can be found. Modern ideologies are then supposed to be scientific, materialistic, with a basis in empirical data. Such beliefs have deeply penetrated the educational system in the West.

But the second half of the twentieth-century witnessed a gradual erosion of the collective political and ideological certainties that so passionately fired the imaginations of previous generations. The Berlin Wall is no more. China is now capitalistic, not in political terms perhaps, but economically, something unimaginable in the 1970s. Postmodern man has dumped these grandiose social projects. Collective utopias are *passé*. Leading the way in his novel, **The Rebel**, Albert Camus offered, after the Second World War, a few defiant, cynical observations (1951: 177):

All modern revolutions have ended in a reinforcement of the power of the State. 1789 brings Napoleon; 1848, Napoleon III; 1917, Stalin; the Italian disturbances of the twenties, Mussolini; the Weimar Republic, Hitler. These revolutions, particularly after the First World War had liquidated the vestiges of divine right, still proposed, with increasing audacity, to build the city of humanity and of authentic freedom. … The prophetic dream of Marx and the over-inspired predictions of Hegel or of Nietzsche ended by conjuring up, after the city of God had been razed to the ground, a rational or irrational State, which in both cases, however, was founded on terror.

Events of the last half of the twentieth-century have done little to contradict these observations… The Left, the Right, if one now looks beyond the labels and the rhetoric, it is often difficult to distinguish one from the other. Whereas formerly the Left/Right divide was contrasted by deeply held economic/political views, today, following the drift toward postmodernism, this cleavage tends to centre on questions of morality, sexuality and reproduction. Each seems trapped in its own variations on political correctness. In terms of belief, we live in a postmodern era, an era where, to a large extent, traditional ideological cleavages are mitigated and explicit certainties have been discarded. In politics, more often what matters now is not real debate, but image and marketing issues. Such issues must not be overlooked.

That said, one must not think the educated postmodern generation to be irreligious, lacking any ideology, but rather they prefer their religion in diffuse, adjustable and non-circumscribed forms. They particularly reject rigid creeds and explicit manifestos. Flexibility is the keyword. The grandiose social movements and collective utopias of the past have lost their glamour. The present generation has little faith in Revolution. From the Left, disillusioned by the fall of socialist ideologies and communist regimes, postmodernism has arisen, rejecting all grand narratives. Meaning and ideology are no longer collective. They are now based in the individual, on his or her preferences, tastes or fantasies. Postmoderns tend to break away from the old Right/Left categories and ask: "What's in it for me?". Political parties have become self-serve institutions. Postmodern religion then is custom-fitted to the client's preferences. As they say: "The customer is always right!" Postmoderns reject the idea that History has a meaning and that this meaning is "Progress". Postmoderns view the concept of progress as just one grand narrative among many others. It is seen as a by-product of Western culture and there is no reason to believe it need be applied to other societies or cultures.

The fall of the major twentieth-century ideologies has had an unintended result, postmoderns are **very** quiet about their core beliefs. Whereas modern beliefs, 'catechisms' and metaphysical pre-suppositions were explicit, out in the open for all to see,[81] in the postmodern context, things are different. Postmoderns keep their beliefs cool in a safety deposit box, far away from prying eyes and any serious questioning. There is a striking contrast between the pre-modern attitude, where assumptions were explicit, "in your face," and the postmodern attitude where assumptions are to a large extent implicit,[82] unacknowledged and unconscious. That the individual is the final architect and guarantor of postmodern religion certainly contributes to the sublimation of creeds, as everyone (potentially) has a creed of their own.

These are times of great religious promiscuity. We accept the legitimacy of all and of any religion. We are sophisticated syncretists.[83] Contrary to views found in Dawkins or Hitchens, among devotees of the postmodern religion, the great monotheistic traditions are not necessarily a phenomenon to abolish or eliminate, but their universality is inevitably rejected as well as any real right to speak in the public square (and affect public policy). Postmoderns then have no qualms in exploiting monotheistic religious symbolism and jargon. Followers of the postmodern religion consider traditional religious expression permissible, but on condition that it accepts its marginalization, relegated to "its place" in the private world. Moreover, it is possible to package secular postmodern discourse with Christian jargon and symbols emptied of their content.[84] This ensures that the illusion of tolerance is maintained.

Regarding modern beliefs, postmoderns sometimes commit heresy in the eyes of their philosophical ancestors, as they attack the special status of science. In effect, postmodern relativism leads to questioning that ultimately dissolves the supposedly impenetrable wall between science and religion. A prototype of this "heretical" critique of science's privileged status appeared in views proposed in the 1970s by the eccentric (and somewhat anarchistic) philosopher of science Paul K. Feyerabend (1924-1994). Feyerabend wrote (1975/1979: 295):

> ... science is much closer to myth than a scientific philosophy is prepared to admit. It is one of the many forms of thought that have been developed by man, and not necessarily the best. It is conspicuous, noisy, and impudent, but it is inherently superior only for those who have already decided in favour of a certain ideology, or who have accepted it without ever having examined its advantages and its limits. And as the accepting and rejecting of ideologies should be left to the

individual it follows that the separation of state and church must be complemented by the separation of state and science, that most recent, most aggressive, and most dogmatic religious institution.

Of course Feyerabend has always been tolerated among academics as long as no one took him too seriously.[85] Now given the importance of science in terms of media presence and cosmology in the West, it should come as no surprise that observations such as the one above remain little known to the general public. Director Stephen Spielberg is a fairly typical example of the new postmodern religious elites. Several of his films proclaim that wisdom comes, not from reason or science triumphant, but from extraordinary beings from far away galaxies. Such beliefs are now served up by popular movies such as **ET, Close Encounters of the Third Kind, Contact** and television series like **Taken**. Postmoderns consider that the triumphant rationalism of the first half of the twentieth-century must be discarded. We now find many postmodern intellectuals among the new cultural elites. To all accounts, modernism, cold and rational, has failed.

The late Stephen Jay Gould, a palaeontologist and Marxist, was certainly a very colourful character and may be considered a transitional case between these two worldviews. At times he is the stalwart apostle of the Enlightenment, bravely defending reason and the achievements of empirical science against creationist 'heresies'. But in other circumstances, he developed the NOMA concept,[86] which concedes that religion can have authority and play a legitimate role in the world of morality, while science holds the monopoly of its epistemological authority in the physical/empirical world. Note that in his spare time, one of Gould's hobbies was singing[87] devout Christian works such as **The Creation** by Joseph Haydn. Gould coolly responded to any intimation of double-mindedness that (2000) "I embrace Haydn's Creation text for its moral and aesthetic qualities, while regarding its factual inaccuracies as quite irrelevant and beside the point." This is precisely in the logic of NOMA. Another transitional figure that can be considered is the Canadian philosopher of science Michael Ruse. A convinced Darwinist, Ruse (2005) nonetheless believes that in the context of the origins debate, religious involvement may have its uses.[88]

Others, such as British zoologist Richard Dawkins, a faithful representative of the old materialistic guard, obviously have little respect for such compromises. In his essay, **A Devil's Chaplain**, Dawkins complains (2003: 154):

> Why has our society so meekly acquiesced in the convenient fiction that religious views have some sort of right to be respected automatically and without question? ... If I want you to respect my views on politics, science, or art, I have to earn that respect by argument, reason, eloquence or relevant knowledge. I have to withstand counter-arguments. But if I have a view that is part of my religion, critics must respectfully tiptoe away or brave the indignation of society at large. Why are religious opinions off limits in this way? Why do we have to respect them, simply because they are religious?[89]
>
> (2003: 150) Theologians, if they want to remain honest, should make a choice. You can claim your own magisterium, separate from science's but still deserving of respect. But in that case you have to renounce miracles. Or you can keep your Lourdes and your miracles, and enjoy their huge recruiting potential among the uneducated. But then you must kiss goodbye to separate magisteria and your high-minded aspiration to converge on science.

In Dawkins' view, attempts to reconcile science and religion are impossible, a waste of time. But taking a wider view, chances are that within a generation or two, the power and influence of the old materialistic guard, of which Dawkins is an eminent representative, will be a thing of the past. In Europe perhaps this process may take a little longer, as the modern worldview's institutional base there is more entrenched. As in the case with royalty in England, one may expect that some members of the old materialist guard will remain at their posts, wielding symbolic power and prestige, long after the erosion of their real influence has occurred.

It should be noted that the "openness" of the new postmodern elites regarding religion, in fact, thinly masks the inconsistencies and shallowness of their relativist ideology. Can all religious or ideological discourses be equally true? If the answer is yes, then all "truths" are good, but none are actually true, that is to say universal. Loving, hating, healing, killing, gay or straight, maternal or paedophile behaviour, acting friendly or infuriating anyone crossing your path, how does one then distinguish between good or evil behaviour in the postmodern world? There is no room anymore for the Absolute. Recognizing this, would Hitler, Jesus, Stalin, Muhammad, Robespierre, Charlie Chaplin and Pol Pot then all be right? Do they all have their own "truth"? Why not? If there are no moral absolutes nor any overarching Natural Order, then society's moral standards become entirely arbitrary, to be constantly renegotiated depending on the outcome of power struggles in particular historical circumstances. Media and marketing methods then become powerful tools in this regard. A smug "critical perspective"[90] becomes an illusion.

Although there are areas of conflict, in the twenty-first century one does observe cohabitation, juxtaposition as well as symbiotic relations between modern and postmodern worldviews. Moreover, although theoretically postmoderns do attack science, in practical terms, technology still has its uses. Even postmoderns like DVD players, cell phones, the Internet and a cure for cancer or obesity would be nice. Although postmoderns pride themselves on their critical and analytical minds, some things still remain untouchable, taboo. Despite the fact that postmodern scholars zealously attack colonialism, patriarchy and other Western institutions, we should not expect from them anything like a serious deconstruction of the West's own dominant metanarrative, the theory of evolution, as it constitutes the logical basis for postmodern relativism. No one goes around shooting themselves in the foot. Any mention of another explanation of origins, of any other cosmology, could potentially undermine relativism. The postmodern assumption of the "fact" of evolution is then foundational as, in this context, there can be no pan-cultural, universal law.

The Sokal Affair[91] is a rather entertaining example of territorial conflict between moderns and postmoderns as it exposes differences in attitudes between the two groups. A physics professor at the University of New York, Alan D. Sokal, was in touch with colleagues in the social sciences who were followers of postmodern thought. The high-sounding claims, obscure language and lack of scientific rigour or logic of postmodern authors got on Sokal's nerves so he devised an experiment. Here is the problem he wanted to explore (1996b):

> So, to test the prevailing intellectual standards, I decided to try a modest (though admittedly uncontrolled) experiment: Would a leading North American journal of cultural studies — whose editorial collective includes such luminaries as Fredric Jameson and Andrew Ross — publish an article liberally salted with nonsense if (a) it sounded good and (b) it flattered the editors' ideological preconceptions?

Sokal then submitted an article to the Social Text journal. It was entitled **Transgressing the Boundaries: Towards a Trans-**

formative Hermeneutics of Quantum Gravity. His article was accepted and published in a special issue entitled Science Wars (1996a). Subsequently, Sokal exposed the hoax. This provoked quite a row. Although the postmodern perspective in this case came off rather badly, one of the issues linked to the Sokal Affair is the fact that many postmodern intellectuals referred to in this article (which included French intellectuals such as Derrida. Lacan, Irigaray and Aronowitz) had questioned or criticized the absolute/ pan-cultural nature of Western science. Of course members of the modern old guard viewed such critiques as heresy, to be put down as soon as possible. The first paragraph of the article by Sokal submitted to Social Text ironically ridicules those idiotic scientists, still accepting the old-fashioned idea that there is a real world outside the observer, a presupposition that is, incidentally, fundamental to Western experimental science.[92] There is good reason to believe then that the soap-opera saga of modern/post-modern conflicts is far from over...

This trend, this drift towards the postmodern perspective, takes different forms. For example, an anthropologist I met in the 1970s was, at the time, a zealous and devout Marxist and materialist. Today, in his free time, he initiates groups to out of body experiences. Basically he has become a shaman. I very much suspect that there are a few such "apostates" lurking in anthropology/sociology departments in most big Western universities. When "misguided individuals" question the basic assumption of the modern old guard, i.e. that science and reason must answer all the big questions in life, this stirs up strong and rather predictable emotions as an ideological monopoly is being attacked. This is the case with a review published by Fuller, the biographer of philosopher of science Thomas Kuhn. An old guard modern, Chet Raymo responded to Fuller in an article published in Scientific American (Raymo 2000: 105):

> Kuhn wrote: "The very existence of science depends upon vesting the power to choose between paradigms in the members of a special kind of community." Fuller has confidence in the intelligent good sense of ordinary folks and properly calls for *the right to be wrong*. But do statements such as *the universe is light-years wide, the earth is billions of years old, all life is related by common descent, organisms are composed of cells that contain double-helix DNA*, and so on really have no greater claim on *reality* than the Genesis stories of creationists or the popular consolations of astrology? If the answer is no, as Fuller comes danger-

Vivisecting the Patient

ously close to asserting, then most scientists would throw in the towel and get jobs flipping burgers.[93]

What, exactly, is this "catastrophe" that Raymo[94] alludes to here? If scientific discourse isn't something unique, leading us to Truth, then what shall we do? If science is of no help in answering the big questions, how should we then live? Should we declare a state of emergency? Should we all go out into the streets waving placards saying "The end of the world is near!" Some may view such issues as no laughing matter. Some may fear that such a crisis may initiate conversion to a different ideologico-religious system. Despite loud denials, modern man cannot totally avoid dogma. Just as medieval Inquisitors could invoke the flames of hell (and, if necessary, the fires of the stake) to defend their core beliefs, our modern (and postmodern) religious elites invoke, from time to time, the end of the scientific world against any heretics who dare question the modern scientific "truth" about origins. As a result, such heretics must then be marginalized/excluded, even if they may appear well intentioned or actually have empirical arguments and possess valid degrees in science.

In social terms, we often find postmodern religious elites gathered around social, environmental or political causes. They have charitable works of their own, their confessors (shrinks, fortune tellers or Tibetan lamas) and their cultural events. Like the Medieval Church, they have their saints, martyrs and religious processions. Darwin, for example, plays the role of prophet of reason and one may encounter works spouting his praises that compare favourably with the most devout hagiographic works.[95] Postmoderns have no lack of martyrs either. One can think of the environmental activist facing the chainsaw to avoid a tree being cut down, the struggles of the lesbian Muslim or the abortionist shot dead by a fanatic Pro-Lifer, the quadriplegic atheist astrophysicist, to the feminist enrolling into the infantry and gays dying of AIDS.[96] Among postmoderns the confessional has been replaced by the ritual of private confession with a shrink. Postmoderns also have the option of a communal confessional ritual, that is to say participation in a TV talk show where one's experiences, one's deepest emotions and vilest sins,[97] are exposed for all to see. In moral terms, postmoderns have at least one mortal sin: intolerance. They have their own missionary endeavours, such as doctors opening abortion clinics in ghettos or university professors engaged in applied anthropology in the Third World. Postmodern elites are elegant, well dressed, well educated and in interviews, dialogue is typically scripted and predictable, avoiding any serious questioning. Like the Medieval Church, our postmodern elites have power. And like Louis XIV, they are sought after by hordes of courtiers lured by their influence.

To understand the rise of the modern elites (now the old religious guard), in particular the growing influence of scientific elites in the nineteenth-century and their acceptance of new ideological roles, historian of science Robert Proctor made the following observations (1988: 12-13):

> By the second half of the nineteenth-century, the dramatic achievements of the experimental and theoretical sciences had brought a certain prestige to science. Science in the middle decades of the century becomes a major source of military, industrial, and economic strength. As a consequence, one sees a fundamental transformation in the political function of science. Science becomes increasingly a metaphor for the explanation of why things are as they are: people look to science to explain the origin of human character and institutions; science becomes an important part of ideological argumentation and a means of social control.

Total Science

> *It is absolutely safe to say that if you meet somebody who claims not to believe in evolution, that person is ignorant, stupid or insane (or wicked, but I'd rather not consider that). Richard Dawkins (1989)*

Western elites sometimes find it difficult to recognize a commonplace, but too easily forgotten truth, that is to say that science is limited. When experimental science was born in the West in the sixteenth and seventeenth centuries, these limitations were viewed as normal and acceptable. That science was incomplete and needed to refer to religion[98] to provide ultimate answers in matters cosmological as well as for moral laws was not considered shocking. Huge shifts have occurred in the social role played by science. Science is linked to a methodology permitting the exploration and study of observable processes. For example, if I drop a ball from a height of one metre, those present can observe its acceleration as well as its speed on impact. Anyone can redo my experiment and check my findings. Such an experiment can be repeated. And if others do not get the same results, then I will have to go back and redo my homework.

This in fact is the reason why the cold fusion process, which got a lot of attention in the late 1980s, was not the expected scientific and technological gold mine many had hoped it would be. Researchers had announced the discovery of a method to obtain nuclear energy, at room temperature! When other labs tried to replicate these experiments, disappointment followed. Those who tried to repeat the experiment did not obtain the same results. Had the initial claims been confirmed, there is little doubt that the discoverers would have been up for the Nobel Prize! Imagine, an inexhaustible form of eco-friendly and cheap energy! The moral of this story is that science deals with **observable** and **reproducible** processes. The rest is outside the domain of science (or should be). But science has gained such prestige that it exerts a quasi-irresistible attraction, seducing many ardent admirers among those who hope to exploit this prestige for their own mythical/ideological purposes.

When one looks back to the beginning of all things, we find ourselves reaching the limits of our means of observation, either at the macro level (the universe) or at the micro level (the subatomic world). Empirical data becomes harder and harder to come by. But more importantly, finding the means to repeat the processes that we are attempting to explain also becomes increasingly difficult. The closer we find ourselves to the limits of science, the greater importance we find our theories taking on (as well as the subjectivity involved in choosing their presuppositions) while (proportionally) the real influence of the available empirical data decreases.

It must be understood then that when scientists attempt to explain unique events that took place at the origin of time, they go beyond the limits of science, as these processes are no longer observable. Knowingly or not, they have left the field of empirical science and have begun to navigate the wild and wonderful world of myth and cosmology.

Of course things aren't always totally black and white, scientific research involves some grey areas. In geology, for example, one can study rocks, examine strata and discover new ore deposits. There is plenty of empirical observable data to check out and sort through, but one can neither observe nor replicate conditions that produced the strata or deposits which sometimes cover thousands of square kilometres, any more than biologists can observe the conditions that gave rise to the first living cell. Like the Battle of Waterloo or the fall of the Berlin Wall, these are unique events, no longer directly observable today. This leaves us with little more than nice "scientific" stories framed in the context of the dominant materialistic origins myth. This is the best we can expect. Of course, frankly asserting that the process of evolution involves storytelling is generally considered extremely irresponsible, if not heretical, but read this startling admission from the prestigious evolutionary biologist Ernst Mayr (1997: 11):

> Biologists have to study all the known facts relating to the particular problem, infer all sorts of consequences from the reconstructed constellations of factors, and then attempt to construct a scenario to explain the observed facts of this particular case. **In other words, they construct a historical narrative.**
>
> Because this approach is so fundamentally different from the causal-law explanations, the classical philosophers of science —- coming from logic, mathematics, or the physical sciences - considered it inadmissible. However, recent authors have vigorously refuted the narrowness of the classical view and have shown not only that the historical-narrative approach is valid but also that it is perhaps the only scientifically and philosophically valid approach in the explanation of unique occurrences. Of course, proving categorically that a historical narrative is *true* is never possible.

Now one should not reasonably expect Mayr and other disciples of Darwin to admit that evolution is just a story… To maintain the integrity of their worldview, materialists find it essential to rely on a loose definition of science, that is to say including things other than observable, repeatable processes. It must be understood that in philosophical or ideological terms, the adoption of a definition of science (either restricted or loose) is not a neutral question. In our modern/postmodern context, it is **always** linked to prior choices, by individuals or institutions, of an ideologico-religious system. In modern man's view, science must have all the answers. Referring to a loose definition of science becomes in fact necessary, unavoidable. Moderns find a restricted definition to be intolerable, and generally for unacknowledged ideologico-religious reasons. But there's more. One should then expect that any serious questioning of the loose definition of science will be firmly opposed in many research organizations since this is also linked to funding issues.

In 1975 Harvard entomologist and ant behaviour researcher E. O. Wilson, published **Sociobiology: the New Synthesis.** Wilson's theory is based on two principles. 1) Genetics generally determines the forms of hierarchy that we find in animal societies. Wilson believes there is no reason why this observation should not apply to men just as much as to ants. The individual's role is then assigned by natural selection. 2) Individuals behaviour is determined by a fundamental principle, transmitting one's genes as widely as possible. Thus, behaviour as diverse as slavery and altruism, wars between nations as well as gender inequality, are all explained by genetic determinism. Wilson's theory attempted to provide an evolutionary explanation for human attitudes, morality and behaviour. His theory provoked a firestorm of controversy, even drawing criticisms from a Harvard colleague, renowned palaeontologist Stephen Jay Gould. Proponents of Wilson's theory were accused of implicitly promoting racism and sexism. According to Gould and others, humans, having become cultural beings, are no longer solely determined by their genes. As a result, humans have escaped the normal evolutionary process and are no longer subject to evolution as it (still) applies to the animal world. If humans evolve, it is now along cultural lines rather than genetic.[99] Over time Sociobiology, as a theory, has come to be discredited, marginalized. For now, modern man can escape the spectre of rigid biological determinism, with all that it implies.

But more recently a new approach has taken over where Sociobiology left off. This school of thought is called **Evolutionary psychology**[100] and focuses on human behaviour and internal states. The fundamental concept is that human psychology is just as subject to natural selection as an organism's morphology. Evolutionary psychology involves the application of the theory of evolution to human psychology and it follows then that morality must be framed in terms that are compatible with evolutionary cosmology. Because Evolutionary psychology considers that man does not differ in any essential way from the animal world, as he is no less a product of evolution than any other organism, one finds many Evolutionary psychology studies comparing animal and human behaviour. From this perspective then, human consciousness and self-awareness are basically an illusion. In academia, those rejecting Evolutionary psychology sometimes condescendingly put down its promoters as "Darwinian fundamentalists".[101]

Evolutionary psychology often exploits a pedagogical device called the *exemplum*. Basically this involves taking an example of animal behaviour and using it to drive home a moral lesson, thus transmitting an ideologico-religious principle. Depending on the teacher's objectives, this moral lesson may be explicit or implicit. But such strategies are nothing new. Almost all religions as well as many ancient philosophers exploited this pedagogical device. The Bible, for example, in the book of Proverbs states: "Go to the ant, thou sluggard; consider her ways, and be wise" (Prov. 6: 6). Similar sayings are also found in books of Hindu and Arab wisdom. The *exemplum* is then an efficient method of packaging ideological information, propaganda. *Exempla* are generally used, not to illustrate some abstract truth, but to goad the faithful into action or, in other cases, to avoid their involvement in some evil action. The great world religions typically exploit *exempla* in a context where they can illustrate a law drawn from outside of nature, a moral law derived from their worldview. The choice of animal behaviour then is never arbitrary, but must serve objectives that are deemed acceptable by the worldview in question. In the context of Evolutionary psychology however there is no law outside of nature. This means that nature itself becomes the ultimate moral reference point. Selecting *exempla* then becomes completely arbitrary, as they are no longer determined by an explicit ideology or moral code. Such choices then have no real logic, save perhaps an opportunism tempered by certain marketing considerations. Public image issues can be important.

The French popular science magazine **Sciences et Avenir** had a special issue on Evolutionary psychology. This included an essay by philosopher of science Michael Ruse (2004) exploiting an *exemplum* and in fact made it his main argument. Beginning the article, Ruse notes that one of his students at the University of Florida is blind and comes to class accompanied by a guide dog. The dog serves her mistress in a fairly obvious way. Ruse then raises a series of questions about this dog: Is it a machine? Is it a moral being? These questions are then used as a pretence to present Ruse's beliefs about human nature. And what is the moral of Ruse's sermon? In this case he states explicitly: "My blind student loves and has moral concern for her seeing-eye companion. The canine companion loves and has moral concern for her mistress. We humans are not unique."[102] (2004: 66) It should be noted here that Ruse behaves more like a theologian developing his catechism/cosmology than as a philosopher. In the same issue of **Sciences et Avenir**, philosopher Elisabeth de Fontenay discusses nineteenth-century evolutionary thinking and makes explicit the ideological-religious purpose served by *exempla* in this context. She remarks (2004: 70): "They serve a specific function: that is to devalue man's lofty dignity by relativizing his language and reasoning skills, by denying him access to reality, truth and morality which set him apart from other animals and which is a subject of his pride." It must be stressed that such goals are of course not neutral, nor strictly empirical.

Does science then play a truly religious or ideological role? Stephen Toulmin, a philosopher of science with few illusions, observed (1957: 81):

> The Creation, the Apocalypse, the Foundations of Morality, the Justification of Virtue: these are problems of perennial interest, and our contemporary scientific myths are only one more instalment in the series of attempted solutions. So next time we go into an eighteenth-century library and notice these rows upon rows of sermons and doctrinal treatises lining the shelves, we need not be puzzled by them. Now we are in a position to recognize them for what they are: the forerunners, in more ways than one might first suspect, of the popular science books that have displaced them.

It should be noted that in the field of cosmology, speculation among twenty-first century astrophysicists about multiple universes (one also encounters the term "multiverse") has attained a high level of refinement, demonstrating wild flights of imagination that would put to shame even the most esoteric medieval Byzantine theologians. These theories begin with the observation that our universe seems endowed with all the features essential for life, as if this was the intent. The multiple universes concept weakens the strength of these observations by assuming that our universe is not unique, but is only one among a huge number of other universes, produced by some kind of "universe-producing machine". So is it then a coincidence that we happen to live in one that has precisely the characteristics for life? Some proponents of the multiple universes concept, including Martin Rees,[103] freely admit that these theories are not susceptible to empirical refutation as the universe creation process is not observable. Without a doubt this issue deserves more attention, as it offers a fertile and intriguing theological/cosmological field.

But isn't science's sole function to explore and describe the empirical world and no more? Doesn't adopting a scientific point of view mean dropping all issues of faith? British philosopher Mary Midgley explains that the development of science's cognitive structure, its way of looking at the world, requires metaphysical presuppositions (or unprovable beliefs) and these presuppositions, in turn, are inevitably linked to a worldview, a religion (1992: 57):

> Science can clash with religion if it — science — is in the business of providing the faith by which people live. Is it actually in that business? This kind of faith is not primarily a belief in particular facts. It is not what William James's schoolboy meant when he remarked,: 'Faith is when you believe something that you know ain't true.' **The faith we live by is something that you must have before you can ask whether anything is true or not.** It is basic trust. It is the acceptance of a map, a perspective, a set of standards and assumptions, an enclosing vision within which facts are placed. It is a way of organizing the vast jumble of data. In our age, when that jumble is getting more and more confusing, the need for such principles of organization is not going away. It is increasing.

Beyond such basic considerations, in the last ten years or so a curious phenomenon has emerged, that of scientists coming out of the closet and playing an increasingly explicit religious role. Bookstores are now loaded with countless works published by miscellaneous scientific gurus/hucksters offering their philosophy of life, their worldview. Works by authors such as Carl Sagan, François Jacob, Stephen Hawking, Jacques Monod, E. O. Wilson and many others are filled with exhortations and recommendations to "make sense" of the world, exhortations to rely on reason (or science[104]) to improve the human condition. Such authors present themselves as those who "know", as providers of wisdom. But materialistic science has never justified nor explained why humans should be obsessed with "making sense of life" in the first place. In general, these authors do not seek to explain such concerns. They simply assume "making sense of life" is a given and proceed to take us on guilt-trips if we do not buy into their own worldviews. Note that these elite scientists work within a symbiotic relationship with media. Mass media may or may not provide a platform to such scientists. What might be the media's interests in providing a platform to specific scientists? Obviously, such individuals must be experienced, competent scientists, recognized by their peers, Nobel Prize winners if possible, but above all they must deliver a kosher postmodern message. French philosopher J. - F. Lyotard made the following remarks on the interaction between science, media and the State (1979/1984: 27-28):

> Why do scientists appear on television or are interviewed in newspapers after making a "discovery"? They recount an epic of knowledge that is in fact wholly unepic. They play by the rules of the narrative game; its influence remains considerable not only on the users of the

media, but also on the scientist's sentiments. This fact is neither trivial nor accessory: it concerns the relationship of scientific knowledge to "popular" knowledge, or what is left of it. The State spends large amounts of money to enable science to pass itself off as an epic: the State's own credibility is based on that epic, which it uses to obtain the public consent its decision makers need.

The psychiatrist Viktor Frankl has observed a shift that has occurred during the twentieth-century in the role played by mental health professionals, a subliminal slippage, towards ideologico-religious functions (1959/1971: 183-184):

> More and more, a psychiatrist is confronted with questions such as: What is life? What is suffering after all? Indeed, incessantly and continually a psychiatrist is approached today by patients who confront him with human problems rather than neurotic symptoms. Some of the people who nowadays call on a psychiatrist would have seen a pastor, priest or rabbi in former days, but now they often refuse to be handed over to a clergyman, so that the doctor is confronted with philosophical questions rather than emotional conflicts.

This implies that psychologists and their like must not only treat neuroses, but enable the development of identity and give meaning to individual's lives. It would seem unrealistic to believe that other large institutions, such as the education system, escape this phenomenon. What about science then? If one allows some doubt about the popular/common-sense definition of science (which claims the "virginal purity" and absolute ideological neutrality of science), we must then admit the possibility that "science" has come to play an important ideological-religious role in the West. In modern societies, science has then acquired or usurped the role of bearer and guarantor of Truth,[105] a function comparable to that of medieval popes, presiding over the coronation of kings and emperors.

Media Mirages

> *.. man is surrounded on all sides: man and men, for we must bear in mind that different forms of media are not all directed at the same public. Those who go to the movie theatre three times a week are not the same as those who carefully read their newspaper. The instruments of propaganda target specific groups and all must be used in a combined fashion in order to reach as many individuals as possible. For example: a poster is a popular way to reach those who have no car. Radio messages are listened to by the in crowd. ... However, each method is specifically adapted to a particular form. Film as deals with human relations is a choice method for sociological, "atmospheric" propaganda, slow infiltration, promoting a progressive shift in a certain direction. Public meetings and posters on the other hand are the instruments of shock propaganda, intense and short-lived, leading to immediate action.* (Ellul 1962: 22)*

A worldview that integrates and makes sense of life's experiences is just as essential for the physicist doing research on interactions between quarks and leptons, as for the Orthodox Jew praying at the Wailing Wall, the Krishna disciple with his head shaved, chanting in the street, the old lady in her rocking chair listening to a televangelist while petting her cat or the New Age guru storing quartz crystals in his fridge. No one can do without a worldview. The process of individual identity development inevitably demands the adoption of a worldview, an ideologico-religious system. And since the individual[106] is rarely the carrier of a single unadulterated ideologico-religious belief system, one may consider his identity as the expression of the conflicting cosmologies cohabiting in his mind.

To understand the scope of the influence of the new postmodern religious elites, one must specifically consider the immense power of modern mass media. Like fish in water who do not know what water is,[107] postmodern man is surrounded on all sides by this influence and generally cannot recognize it. The philosopher Jacques Ellul made the following remarks on this matter (1954/1964: 21-22):

> It is the emergence of mass media which makes possible the use of propaganda techniques on a societal scale. The orchestration of press, radio and television to create a continuous, lasting and total environment renders the influence of propaganda virtually unnoticed precisely because it creates a constant environment. Mass media provides the essential link between the individual and the demands of the technological society.

The Truman Burbank character in **The Truman Show** movie, once aware of his situation, finds it necessary to behave in unpredictable ways in order to get a grasp of the limits of his artificial reality. This amounts to adopting a critical attitude when he is typically expected to swallow everything about his "reality" without question. The same applies in the postmodern context. Those who go with the flow, never escape. Always cynical, British journalist Malcolm Muggeridge regards the vaunted objectivity of the media as a myth. The media's "facts" are constructs (1978: 61-62):

> The ostensibly serious offerings of the media, on the other hand, represent a different menace precisely because they are liable to pass for being objective and authentic, whereas actually they, too, belong to the realm of fantasy. Here, the advent and exploration of visual material with the coming of the camera, has played a crucial role. This applies especially to news and so-called documentaries, both of which are regarded as factual, but which, in practice, are processed along with everything else in the media's fantasy-machine. **Thus news becomes, not so much what has happened, as what can be seen as happening, or seems to have happened**. As for documentaries, anyone who has worked on them, as I have extensively, knows that the element of simulation in them has always been considerable, and has only increased as making and directing them has become more sophisticated and technically developed. Christopher Ralling, a gifted BBC producer, in an article in the Listener, has expressed his concern about how documentary-makers tend more and more to venture into a no-man's-land between drama and documentary.

In postmodern terms, if media discourse must be considered a narrative, one must then ask then what this narrative is? What are its assumptions and from which grand narrative is it derived? Of course, postmodern elites have every reason to deny their ideological and religious role, as their power would inevitably suffer from such an admission.[108] The king and his courtiers cannot confess that he is naked. In the postmodern context, everything is filtered and "pre-digested". With little effort, media provides an illusion of multiple viewpoints and perspectives by cleverly packaging its production, packaging its production to fit the interests of population groups, educated or not, men or women, young or old, athletic or literature-lovers, etc.. Various containers, similar content. The seamless environment discussed by Ellul stifles critical thinking and ensures the conformism of the masses.[109] Art critic Suzi Gablik provides a pointed analysis of the development of the postmodern perspective (1984: 37):

> A person whose whole life is spent performing a few repetitive tasks becomes mechanized in mind; hardly ever breaking through the surface of his routine, he finds little opportunity to exert his understanding, judgement, or imagination. The critical faculties grow dull and perception is blunted, hardened by a crippling sameness. This sort of collective trance, with its automatic and reflex responses, usually remains constant: the conformist mind does not change, or grow with experience, unless something happens to disrupt it.

It is important to note that Social Anthropology suggests that all civilizations find their basis in a worldview, a religion. This is a lesson that followers of Mohammad have learned by heart. The French anthropologist Marc Augé, in an essay on paganism, has upended Geertz' approach to the definition of religion (that is, "Religion as a Cultural System") and observes that in fact it is useful to consider culture as a implicitly religious system (1982: 320):

> No doubt it would be rather difficult, though not entirely futile, to examine the subtle links between the varied, fragmentary symbolic practices that constitute an important part, in modern societies, of a form of religion, though lacking unified expressions of faith or worship. An endeavour of this sort involves an approach opposite to that of religious anthropology, particularly as defined by one of its foremost theorists, Clifford Geertz: "The anthropological study of religion is therefore a two-stage operation: first an analysis of the system of meanings embodied in the symbols which make up the religion proper, and, second, the relating of these systems to social-structural and psychological processes." (Geertz 1966, p. 42). Thus religion should be defined less as a cultural system as opposed to culture, understood in its most contrasted expressions, should be defined as a virtually structured and implicitly religious system.*

As a result it follows that in ideologico-religious terms there can be no entirely neutral cultural institutions, despite the fact that the institutions involved may deny any religious role or agenda.

Vivisecting the Patient

The Decline of the Materialist Empire

Vivisecting the Patient

Your question about the comet has drawn me into an odd meditation, it would seem that atheism is nearly a form of superstition almost as childish as the other. Nothing is indifferent in an order of things that a general law binds and controls, it seems everything is equally important. There are no large or small events. The Unigenitus constitution is as necessary as sunrise and sunset, it is difficult to blindly surrender to the universal torrent just as it is impossible to resist. Impotent or successful efforts are also determined. If I think I love you freely, then I am deluded. This cannot be. Oh what a fine system for ingrates! It maddens me to be caught in such a damned philosophy that my mind must approve, but my heart deny. I cannot bear that my feelings for you, and your feelings for me, should be subject to anything in the world, and that Naigeon would have them depend on the passage of a comet. I might even consider becoming a Christian just to promise to love you in this world as long as I live, and to find you, and love you again, in the next. It is a thought so sweet that it comes to no surprise that good souls believe it. If Ms. Olympe were about to die, she would tell you: "My dear cousin, don't cry, we'll see each other again." And so that is where your treacherous question about the comet has led me.*
(Denis Diderot, A letter to Madame de Maux[110], 1769/1963: 154-155)

Despite all my rage, I am still just a rat in a cage.
(Billy Corgan/Smashing Pumpkins: Bullet with Butterfly Wings 1995):

If in previous times one could hope for future salvation, a heaven where war, disease and all forms of alienation would be abolished, modern ideology has promised all these things, through reason and scientific progress, here in the present life. If in the past salvation was conceived as otherworldly, in the modern context one must look only to the present world. Excluding transient (and meaningless) fame, moderns have no hope in life after death. Materialist cosmology is one-dimensional and tedious. In the **Manifesto of Surrealism**,[111] Andre Breton dryly noted (1924): "This world, in which I endure what I endure (don't go see), this modern world, I mean, what the devil do you want me to do with it?"

In his essay **Grammars of Creation** (2001: 4-5), British literary critic George Steiner observed that the twentieth-century, as far as Europe and Russia was concerned, was not heaven on earth, but rather hell. Steiner notes that between August 1914 and the Balkan wars of the 1990s more than 70 million people died. While the First World War has inaugurated mechanized massacres, the Second introduced industrial extermination and the next generation experienced the terror of nuclear incineration. Obviously, wars, pestilence and famine are not phenomena unique to the twentieth-century. Such things have happened before. But the disintegration of the humaneness in this century bears a certain mystery.[112] This decay is not the result of barbarian invasions or external threats. Nazism, fascism and Stalinism all emerged from the social and administrative context of Western intellectual institutions and power centres. In the case of the Nazi Final Solution, there is a singularity, not in terms of scale, as Stalinism killed more people, but in terms of motivation. Nazis decreed that there was a class of individuals, including women and children, whose crime was simply to exist. The West has a dark side, but detecting its source seems problematic.

Steiner notes that the twentieth-century European disaster included another peculiar feature, it caused a regression of civilization.[113] The Enlightenment confidently predicted the end of torture by legal authorities and decreed that the revival of censorship, book-burnings and that even the burning of dissidents or heretics was inconceivable. The nineteenth-century took for granted that the development of education, accumulating scientific knowledge and increased opportunities to travel would bring an inevitable improvement of public and private morality as well as greater tolerance of political views. Each of these hopes proved false. The First World War then produced a shock, a great disillusionment for this generation, but it was a small matter if one considers what was to come… According to Steiner, one must recognize that education has actually shown itself unable to nurture compassion as well as resistance to the logic of hatred. But it is still shocking to see that a culture as refined and as advanced in artistic, scientific and intellectual terms as that of Germany collaborated so readily and actively with the sadist ideology of the Nazi State. It turns out that technocratic engineering may efficiently assist or remain indifferent to the call of the inhumane. Modern cosmology offers no intrinsic obstacle to such temptations. In this regard, French biologist Pierre-Paul Grassé notes (1980: 44):

> After the [1933] triumph of National Socialism, German science provided massive unconditional backing to the Führer. Anthropologists, geneticists, economists and lawyers began zealously serving their new master. [Grassé adds in a footnote at the bottom of the page [2] – PG]: German intellectuals' support to their Führer was substantial. During the

1933 referendum, statements by university professors were collected in one volume. Among the authors of these texts one encounters the famous philosopher Martin Heidegger, which is both surprising given the idealism that permeates his work and revealing of the mind-set that gave Hitler such a victory.*

Is it possible to develop a modern (that is to say materialistic) worldview that can give meaning to life with all its complexities? What has been the real contribution of the modern ideology[114] to History and culture in the West? Perhaps the time may be ripe for a full accounting...[115] No doubt some people have adopted the principles of the modern worldview and lived consistently within these principles, but there is reason to believe nonetheless that History establishes that materialism is, at least in moral terms, a deficient or dysfunctional worldview. The British anthropologist Ernest Gellner points out a few shortcomings of the Enlightenment's "reasonable ideology" (1992/1999: 86):

> It has a number of weaknesses, from the viewpoint of its use as a practical faith, as the foundation either for an individual life or for a social order. It is too thin and ethereal to sustain an individual in crisis, and it is too abstract to be intelligible to any but intellectuals with a penchant for this kind of theorizing. Intellectually it is all but inaccessible, and unable to offer real succour in a crisis... In practice, Western intellectuals, when facing personal predicaments, have turned to emotionally richer methods, offering promises of personal recovery, such as psychoanalysis.

Is the modern worldview is too bleak, too one-dimensional? Even in the nineteenth-century, some had foreseen its weaknesses. The British naturalist Alfred Wallace may be considered a precursor of this phenomenon. Wallace, although he was the largely forgotten co-discoverer of natural selection along with Charles Darwin, at the end of his life he abandoned a strict materialistic worldview and turned to spiritualism, the phenomenon of automatic writing, séances[116] and the occult. Another thinker foreshadowing the erosion of hard-core materialism is Julian Huxley, who in his essay **Religion without Revelation** (1927) reaffirmed the importance of religion, but, oddly, an explicitly materialistic religion. Understandably Enlightenment devotees politely and studiously ignored Huxley's initiative. The postmodern new guard, in particular the cultural elites, are attracted to divers forms of mysticism (New Age cults, the occult, Eastern and First Nations religions, etc.). This worldview challenges the dominant role of science in the West.

Postmodern religions are distinguished from the pagan[117] cultures of antiquity in that neo-pagan postmoderns reject the concept of a transcendent, absolute morality typically accepted by the vast majority of the pagan cultures of past millennia. Our elites are then, paradoxically, materialistic magicians. In the postmodern context, morality is reduced to an arbitrary aspect of reality, to be manipulated at will. But we will come back to this.

The ethical weaknesses of the materialist worldview may be perceived from several angles, but the well-known American materialist, Stephen Jay Gould, provides one of the most striking demonstrations of this fact. In the early twentieth-century, no self-respecting materialistic pundit would have admitted to finding any use for religion and would have rather reaffirmed his faith in a bright future where all medieval superstitions had been swept away by the inexorable progress of science and reason. But things change… In an essay entitled **Nonoverlapping Magisteria**, written partly in response to a papal statement acknowledging the scientific validity of the theory of evolution, Gould[118] confessed his admiration of papal wisdom and proposed a compromise position[119] regarding the respective authority claims of science and religion. Only a generation or two ago, such demeaning proposals would have been rejected out of hand by most self-respecting orthodox materialists and deemed tainted with "heresy".[120] Gould says (1997a: 18):

> The position that I have just outlined … represents the standard attitude of all major Western religions (and of Western science) today. … The lack of conflict between science and religion arises from a lack of overlapping between their respective domains of professional expertise - science in the empirical constitution of the universe, and religion in the search for proper ethical values and the spiritual meaning of our lives.

What could be considered the "respective domains of professional expertise" remains to be established, but the type of compromise put forward by Gould, better known as NOMA or **NO**noverlapping **MA**gisteria, assigns areas of exclusive authority for both science and religion. From members in good standing of the scientific materialist elite, one can hardly expect a more explicit confession (an involuntary admission, it goes without saying) of the moral defects of the materialist worldview, but some do go further. In an interview on ABC,[121] Richard Dawkins, despite having disagreed several times with Gould's positions regarding the mechanisms of evolution, oddly enough seems to reach rather similar conclusions about social/moral applications of Darwinian cosmology (Dawkins 2000):

> There have in the past been attempts to base a morality on evolution. I don't want to have anything to do with that. The kind of world that a Darwinian, going back to survival of the fittest now, and nature red in tooth and claw, I think nature really is red in tooth and claw. I think if you look out at the way wild nature is, out there in the bush, in the prairie, it is extremely ruthless, extremely unpleasant, it's exactly the kind of world that I would not wish to live in. And so any kind of politics that is based upon Darwinism for me would be bad politics, it would be immoral.[122] Putting it another way, I'm a passionate Darwinian when it comes to science, when it comes to explaining the world, but I'm a passionate anti-Darwinian when it comes to morality and politics.

From a Darwinian fundamentalist such as Dawkins, this is a rather startling and paradoxical admission. The logic of Dawkins' cosmology does not lead to such a position in an obvious manner, but taking into consideration marketing issues that have come to the fore since the Second World War (the trauma of the Holocaust), such an outcome is inevitable. At the end of the twentieth-century and early twenty-first, evolutionists rarely demanded much cosmological consistency in such matters. It should be noted that in the late 1970s and early '80s, Gould was deeply involved in the Sociobiology debate, a theory claiming that all human behaviour and social interaction can be explained by referring solely to genetics. Despite his opposition to this approach in the areas of politics and ethics, there is reason nevertheless to believe that Gould came to realize the cosmological and ethical consistency of the sociobiologist's position when viewed from a coherent Darwinian perspective. Such a realisation would have led Gould into an embarrassing intellectual stalemate as he had always opposed deterministic systems of thought. It is conceivable that in reaction to the Sociobiology controversy[123] Gould developed his NOMA concept, which in a sense legitimized religion, to find a way out of this predicament. It is ironic that, while mature Enlightenment thinkers insisted that religion must be gotten rid of at all costs, their heirs have found themselves forced to back away from such statements to avoid living in a world ruled solely by the Darwinian fight for survival!

France was one of the first Western nations to secularize on a large scale. Enlightenment derived forms of materialism, in one form or another, almost constitute a State religion in France. But at the dawn of the twenty-first century, signs of erosion have begun to appear. As such, we can think of the anti-cult law (May 30, 2001) passed in reaction, amongst other things, to the Ordre du Temple Solaire scandal.[124] This scandal exposed, both in Europe and in Québec (French Canada), the attraction of cults, even among architects, engineers and journalists; educated individuals that one would think quite "immunized" from the temptations of religion. Other European nations have also considered implementing similar anti-cult laws in order to protect Enlightenment ideological capital. It appears the faithful need reassuring... The March 2004 French law banning (Muslim) headscarves in schools and public places also comes to mind. Such laws are the expression of the dilemma posed by the growing presence of Islam in France, bringing to the fore unavoidable issues of social and collective identity. It is clear, in this context that the old materialist elites are off balance, a vulnerable position both demographically and ideologically as they find themselves forced to protect their influence by legal interventions. They no longer have the strength to counter these trends in terms of mere rhetoric or logic. So why not convert them? Well except for a few zealots such as Dawkins or Christopher Hitchens, the Enlightenment has largely lost its momentum with the masses.[125] Enthusiasm for the modern/materialist religion has faltered and here and there one encounters divers symptoms of its fragility/vulnerability.

In France, using the words "secular" and "religion" in the same sentence can be considered provocative. In the 1960s, the philosopher Régis Debray joined the Communist Party. He then moved to Cuba and followed Che Guevara to Bolivia, where he was arrested. He returned to France after his release from prison. Since then, his thinking has evolved. Already in 1981 with his essay **Critique de la raison politique** (Critique of Political Reason), Debray drifted away from an orthodox Marxist perspective by offering a critique of Western political ideologies, equating them to forms of religion.[126] In 2002, he signed a controversial government report (2002a) recommending a return of religion in public (secular) schools in France. This recommendation did not mean a return of catholic catechism classes (or teaching of the Koran by an Imam) in public schools, but rather allowed religion to be discussed in class as an object of study or, to be blunt, as a cultural artefact. Expressed in these terms, the intention appears to be to broaden popular culture as well as to provide a "vaccine" inoculating the French against the attractions of living religions. Debray remarks (2002b):

> It would seem that a secular perspective that would forbid this field of knowledge would be doomed to certain vulnerability, but well thought-out teaching methods might actually contribute to the promotion of secularism itself. It would then be a shame to give up information in this field to those who would distribute it beyond all scientific control,[127] as direct propaganda or unquestioningly.*

But many French would view such a "concession" to religion as unnecessary if not "excessive".[128] In their perspective, such a measure would be one step down on the slippery slope to the rehabilitation of religion. Some may also believe that the vaccine may actually have the opposite effect of that suggested by Debray. If the good old-time materialist catechism was fine for Dad, then sonny will live with it for a while yet too. In the English-speaking world, an effort has been made to improve the rather tarnished image of materialism. This has required a marketing rather than a polemic approach. As a result, the term "bright" has been coined to designate materialists and atheists, the last Jedi masters of the Enlightenment. This effort is supported by, among others, Richard Dawkins[129] Charles Simonyi professor For The Understanding of Science at Oxford. It seems vigorous action is now required to boost the Enlightenment's ideological ratings.

Meanwhile pop culture has turned to finding meaning in horoscopes and Native American dream catchers. Movies tell us that science and rationality may be useful, but that real wisdom will come from the stars (aliens). Amongst the masses, the materialist worldview has never had many convinced followers. Materialists were at the apex of their power and influence at the end of the nineteenth-century and in early twentieth-century, but promoters of the Enlightenment worldview, including existentialists, penetrated pop culture, especially in Europe, but in a circumscribed manner in most cases. Disney Studios, for example, has always been interested in magic. Hollywood has always had a market for horror, the occult and fantasy. The background message of these productions is "Beyond the banality of the material world, there is *something else*." Even in Europe, where the Enlightenment deeply penetrated culture and institutions, wizards, druids, devotees of radiesthesia and UFOs do a booming business. In literature, when science fiction tackles the question of the origins of life, in general it discards a purely materialistic view of origins. Typically it ends up evoking the intervention of some mysterious, if not mystical, phenomenon. As such, we can think of the movie **2001, A Space Odyssey** (1968, S. Kubrick). It is possible that, in terms of plot development, watching the slowly bubbling primordial soup for thousands of hours[130] may not hold as much dramatic appeal as bringing in a *deus ex machina*, an agent that can quickly save the story from its deadlock and produce life. "Let there be light!"[131] Oh well, you get the picture…

In the twentieth-century, the materialist elites' rise to power in the West coincided, in general terms, with the massive institutional penetration of the Darwinian cosmology. Since the Enlightenment, one of the deities much venerated by modern elites is Reason. For example, it is no coincidence that most twentieth-century French graphic novels (BD), featured heroes who are (besides being good-looking guys) champions of reason, the rational as well as superstition-busters. They are bright-eyed, the eyes of those who "know". Characters such as Tintin,[132] Spirou, Asterix and others come to mind. But where do Reason and a coherent materialist worldview lead us? Time passes, and by the late twentieth-century one observes the emergence of dissatisfaction and disillusionment. One encounters in the 1960s and 70s, for example, the romanticism and anti-rationalism of the hippy movement. Drugs even appeared, for a while, a refuge from soul-numbing grasp of Reason. Here are a few changes in attitudes over this period reported by British sociologist Eileen Barker (1979: 80):

> The science which had been heralded with such messianic zeal, began itself to contribute to its own demise — at least in its role of Provisor Absolute.[133] Science, especially, but by no means exclusively, to an increasingly vocal youth lacked something. It was incapable of reaching the transcendent heights of humanity. It reduced, it materialized, it objectified, it dehumanized. It understood quantity, not quality; it did not understand love. … The beauty of creation was lost in the destruction of Hiroshima. Auschwitz laughed at progress.

After WWII, beatniks rebelled against "the deification of rows of large houses with lawns and televisions and where everyone looks and thinks the same thing, at the same time." The rock group Cream echoed, with biting irony, the existential vacuum of modern ideology with the song **Anyone for Tennis?**[134] (1968). Another symptom of materialism's decline are proud materialists such as Francis Crick[135] (co-discoverer of the DNA molecule), cosmologist and astrophysicist Fred Hoyle,[136] who openly called into question the orthodox materialist explanation of the origins of life. Both argue that the difficulties of the abiogenesis concept[137] are such that we should look elsewhere for an explanation of the origin of life.

Although perhaps better known as professor of Medieval and Renaissance English, C. S. Lewis was also interested in philosophical issues. He suggested a problem with the materialist worldview that is not moral or existential, but intellectual. Lewis observed (1947/2002: 136) that a coherent materialist perspective[138] presupposes that the only significant causes are material and that laws determine all events in this world.[139] It follows logically that not only our physical growth, our sexuality, our hormonal reactions are determined by laws, but our cultural and intellectual achievements as well. Thus, biochemical or genetic laws determine even our very thoughts. While it may be considered in bad taste to point out such facts, the logic of the system inevitably leads to such a conclusion. And if one thinks of works such as Descartes' **Discourse on Method**, Darwin's **Origin of Species**, Picasso's **Guernica** or Marx' **Das Kapital**, the modern worldview's own logic leads to the conclusion that all these are nothing, but the consequence of natural laws.[140] One must then allow that they are the result, and no more, of reactions in the brain interacting with environmental circumstances. Lewis noted that the individuals concerned obviously do not perceive things this way. Such individuals obviously felt they were exploring things outside of themselves or freely expressing their individuality. They are also careful to claim personal credit for these works and, when possible, benefit financially from their publication. But if materialism is true, logic dictates that these impressions are an illusion and nothing else! Evolutionary psychology would state that such works are no more than an expression of our genes. Thus, those who accept the materialist worldview must also accept that all their cultural and intellectual production is just as rigidly predetermined the trajectory of a ball falling from the tower of Pisa. And if that is the case, why should such works be considered significant or taken seriously? At best, they may be deemed objects of curiosity, like odd patterns left by waves in the sand on the seashore. On this matter, here are a few comments by C. S. Lewis himself (1947/2002: 138):

> It is like that with naturalism. It goes on claiming territory after territory: first the inorganic, then the lower organisms, then man's body, then his emotions. But when it takes the final step and we attempt a

naturalistic account of thought itself, suddenly the whole thing unravels. The last fatal step has invalidated all the preceding ones: for they were all reasonings and reason itself has been discredited. We must, therefore, either give up thinking altogether or else begin over again from the ground floor. There is no reason, at this point, to bring in either Christianity or spiritualism. We do not need them to refute naturalism. It refutes itself.

One of the Enlightenment's most famous apostles of reason was well aware of this problem and seems to have found a way out. Descartes observed (1641/1907: med. IV, s. 17):

> ... for as often as I so restrain my will within the limits of my knowledge, that it forms no judgment except regarding objects which are clearly and distinctly represented to it by the understanding, I can never be deceived; because every clear and distinct conception is doubtless something, and as such cannot owe its origin to nothing, but must of necessity have God for its author — God, I say, who, as supremely perfect, cannot, without a contradiction, be the cause of any error;[141] and consequently it is necessary to conclude that every such conception or judgment is true.

In the modern context, obviously this door has been closed. On the other hand, Stephen Jay Gould's NOMA concept and fall of the Berlin Wall and various such events are striking reminders of the decline of hard-core materialism that had been so dominant in the twentieth-century. The twenty-first century was supposed to be the scene of the total victory of Science and Reason over religion and medieval superstitions, but things have not turned out as expected. The twenty-first century is "open" to religion, the spiritual, in all its forms. The postmodern perspective excludes neither Hinduism, firewalking, the occult nor pagan (pre-Christian) religions. That said, the West still seeks to escape the Absolute. In the present ethical, cosmological vacuum, this dearth of meaning, one should not be too surprised by the raw emotions that surround sexual issues in the West. Previously, this came into play with laws on divorce and pornography. At present, the hot issue is homosexuality and who knows what tomorrow?[142] Following the disintegration of Western modern religions, many find that only sex gives meaning to life. An erotic existentialism has taken its place in the marketplace of beliefs.

Outside the West, postmodern relativism is typically viewed as repugnant, and many seek refuge in Islam, sometimes even die-hard materialists of the past such as the Frenchman Roger Garaudy, who converted from Stalinist communism to Islam.[143] Elsewhere, in parts of Africa and South America, Christianity is booming. Obviously, it is too early to shout, "Materialism is dead! Long live Materialism", as here and there, in the West, one can still find a few zealous defenders of the purity of Reason and of reductionist views of Reality, but they are increasingly isolated. Is it possible that the end is near and some sense this? Time will tell. Perhaps de Tocqueville got it right regarding the phenomenon of the decline in belief (1840/1847: v.2 part 3, ch. xxi):

> Time, events, or the unaided individual action of the mind, will sometimes undermine or destroy an opinion [or belief], without any outward sign of the change. It has not been openly assailed, no conspiracy has been formed to make war on it, but its followers one by one noiselessly secede — day by day a few of them abandon it, until last it is only professed by a minority. In this state it will still continue to prevail. … The majority have ceased to believe what they believed before; but they still affect to believe, and this empty phantom of public opinion in strong enough to chill innovators, and to keep them silent and at respectful distance.

Since WWII the West has become subject to a peculiar form of schizophrenia. On the one hand, we see an insatiable thirst for the technological products of science, vaccines, jet travel, computers and the Internet, but on the other hand, we are less fond of the materialist worldview and of rationalist fundamentalism. The power of the old materialistic guard has suffered, in recent decades, slow, but steady erosion. That said, its institutional base[144] still plays an important protective role, otherwise its current situation would be much more desperate. Today, our postmodern religious elites are evolving and one observes a new trend, acknowledging the narrow-mindedness of the old modern guard and willing to allow some "room for religion".

New Religious Elites

> In ages of fervent devotion, men sometimes abandon their religion, but they only shake it off in order to adopt another. Their faith changes the objects to which it is directed, but it suffers no decline. The old religion then excites enthusiastic attachment or bitter enmity in either party; some leave it with anger, others cling to it with increased devotedness, and although persuasions differ, irreligion is unknown. (de Tocqueville 1835/1838: v.1 ch. IX, sect. vi)

A preliminary consideration of the new postmodern religious elites suggests they are composed of a majority of individuals with links to (and active in) the following four institutions:

- Mass media (print and electronic)
- The Supreme Courts
- The higher echelons of national educational institutions
- Media experts/scientists

Though these categories cover a lot of ground, a few qualifications are in order. It would actually be possible to reduce the new religious elites to three groups rather than four, as one could cynically observe that the existence of media experts/scientists is almost entirely dependant on media fiat. Even Nobel laureates whose achievements are recognized by their peers, but whose opinions or positions are not considered useful or "relevant" (relative to media interests) will be largely ignored by the media (and the public).[145] Typically, their public influence will be negligible. And if, moreover, a media-approved scientist crosses the invisible line, making statements contrary to media interests, i.e. things that some people do not want to hear, then his phone may stop ringing. He can go back to quietly working in his lab.[146] As a result, one could conceivably reduce the four influential groups listed above to just three, as the media experts/scientists group has no real independent existence outside of the media. They are first and foremost prestige spokesmen, giving weight to established media perspectives or, perhaps more cynically, talking heads. Of course some scientists have great standing in their field of research. As a result they can influence other researchers and, if they are teachers, several generations of students as well. This is real influence, but more circumscribed in its scope. Furthermore, scientific elites have in the past played a critical role in the initial development of modern religion and universities have served as incubators of new ideas. With respect to mass media, it is critical that attention be given to the activities and interests of those who have editorial power over the content that actually gets broadcast (as well as deciding **how** to present it, which can be as important as the content itself), that is to say those that have power to define program content, decide which sources will be trusted and sort out information that is deemed "worthy" to be run in the news.

It is important to emphasize that in the West these elites have largely replaced, if one considers the control they exert on contemporary epistemological, social and moral discourse, traditional religious clergy such as archbishops, bishops, priests and pastors. These new religious elites give birth to the ocean of information and cultural artefacts that condition the postmodern mind. Centuries ago, in ideological (and sometimes political) terms the Catholic Church ruled over Europe. Priests were regarded as intermediaries between God and men and had great control over cultural expression. Today, the media in particular play this role by serving as an (almost unique) intermediary between men and what we call "Reality". Furthermore, they shape and define what is considered a "normal person" in the West, a person with no traditional "religious beliefs", or more precisely, religious beliefs that do not conflict with the core dogmas of postmodern religion.

Of course some may ask if government agencies should not be included alongside the aforementioned groups. It must be conceded, in some contexts (especially in Europe), that it may be legitimate to add national trade union organizations or other powerful government agencies to this mix. As power centres, they attract thousands of followers of the postmodern religion, but generally, senior government officials find themselves, in terms of influence, followers of the other groups mentioned above. They are not at the forefront. In most cases, government agencies simply provide useful ideological foot soldiers, putting into practice concepts and strategies developed elsewhere. When changes to the legal system are introduced, government bodies may occasionally play a more active role than the legal elites. In the present context, it seems that in general the media have claimed the largest share of power and influence. But these circles of influence remain dynamic and can change over time.

It should be noted that in the French-speaking world, intellectuals as a class are a very influential group and, as such, could be included in the class of experts and gurus, depending on how connected they are to mass media.[147] Some owe their influence to scientific research achievements, others to their cultural and literary creativity. In the English-speaking world, overlooking a few exceptions, outside academic circles, intellectuals rarely enjoy such cult followings. Few are known to the general public. Beyond pop culture stars, the most influential people are probably less known, seated, not in front of the camera, but behind. They are few in number. They are the sentinels, the gatekeepers, those who decide what is deemed "acceptable" and what is not. They routinely filter the events and perspectives and determine what gets broadcast into the major news or cultural networks. They are the ones who determine what is "relevant". And this simple power is enormous. But such observations must be qualified; this power is by no means absolute (as in Orwell's **1984**), but it still has huge potential to channel and mould lines of thought. Such power to influence should never be underestimated. In the final analysis, one could say that these gatekeepers have a hand on the rudder, but do not control where the wind blows…

One could push the analysis further, revealing that each of the groups mentioned above has its own sub-mythology, its exclusive heroes or demigods, and high priests. Media, for example, fosters the myth of the objective journalist, dispassionately weighing facts, dispelling ignorance, seeking the truth about particular events, a truth suppressed by large evil corporations. In educational circles, one finds the myth of the great scientist or teacher sharing his knowledge and freeing the masses from prejudice and superstition. In legal circles, one encounters the mythical brave and altruistic lawyer, seeking justice and defending the rights of the lowly outcast.[148]

Vivisection was once practiced with the objective of exposing to direct observation hidden structures in a living organism, but forgoing anaesthesia. Needless to say, since vivisection is a rather painful procedure for the object of study, it may draw the strongest protests from the patient, especially if the latter does not agree with the usefulness of the operation. In our present context then, one must expect the strongest protests and denials from the subjects of our study.

3 / The Phantom Creed

Tony saw himself as a thinker and he wanted to share his thoughts with me, but even he found it difficult to reveal to me, and sometimes to himself, his basic beliefs, the structure which supported and surrounded him. We do not display our set of basic beliefs any more than we display our skeleton. Yet, just as our skeleton determines whether we spread our fine bones in the shape of a hand or a wing, whether we stand upright or pad along on all fours, so our beliefs determine whether we shall act upon the world with mastery, or soar freely and confidently through life, or stand upright against life's buffeting, or plod through life's weary ways. We do not state some of our beliefs, or even bring them to mind, since we regard them as totally obvious and axiomatic. We hide our beliefs from others to prevent them from laughing at our childish faiths, or belittling our deepest fears, or chiding our foolish optimism. Or simply not understanding what was being told. (Rowe 1982: 15)

Tragedy [theatre] has often seemed to me the school of nobility; theatre, the school of good manners and I dare say that these things, which we look upon only as amusements, have been more useful to me than books.*
(Sophronie in Voltaire 1761)

In a journalism textbook entitled **Rhetoric Through Media**, Gary Thompson (1997: 23) remarks that myth is usually implicit and present just below the visible surface of all that surrounds us. It is probably impossible to live without myths. The idea that we can be totally free of them is likely one of our most cherished postmodern illusions. If you want reasonably balanced social interaction, it is important to recognize the myths that surround us as well as the fact that myths are not things only afflicting or subjugating "others".

But what if one had the bad manners to actually ask a doctor performing abortions, a gay activist advocating gay marriage or a geneticist proposing to clone humans, "How do you justify your behaviour or position? How do you define good and evil? And to which worldview, cosmology or religion do you refer in proposing this definition?" Since postmodern religion is typically subliminal and implicit, such a question would no doubt be received in puzzled silence by most or in some cases by a categorical rejection of the question's premise: "This has nothing to do with religion, it's just common sense!" Such reactions are to be expected. Postmodern thought is profoundly ambivalent. To be perceived as "religious" is often viewed as a form of "contamination", to some extent as the violation of the mind's "virginity". Of course this is a vestige of modern gut reactions. In order to keep the postmodern worldview well out of view, postmoderns will pontificate about the convergence of progressive ideas and offer nebulous gibberish about the necessity of individual "self-fulfilment" or the noble task of destroying old metanarratives. David Porush, commenting on the sci-fi novel **Snow Crash** by Neal Stephenson, offers insights that have great bearing on postmodern culture. These remarks expose both postmoderns' hypocrisy as well as their search for meaning (Porush 1994: 570):

> The inability of Snow Crash to confront its own metaphysics, the spiritual transcendence it conjures only to banish, comes from the fashionable unwillingness to grant any credence to narratives of metaphysics, even while so much of postmodern culture apparently yearns for it (as the literature and pronouncements about cyberspace persistently hint). We can understand this reluctance, not just on the basis of Stephenson's proud heritage from a clan of itinerant hard scientists and engineers, nomad rationalists, but as part of our more general suspicion of mystical ideas. After all, as controlling, essentializing, and privileged discourses, metaphysical constructions have done much harm throughout history,[149] and therefore seem most worthy of resistance and radical

The Phantom Creed

skepticism. Yet the turn has been taken: either we are only primitives disguised as rational postmoderns and we are fooling ourselves, or we are trying to tell ourselves something that we are trained to ignore.

In postmodern rhetoric, the term "religion" often takes on a negative connotation. And even when this is not the case, most find it impossible to apply it to their own beliefs. Postmodern conditioning reinforces the view that only others have "religious beliefs". But to maintain the illusion of "neutrality", of being able to "get along without religion", many intellectuals continue to appeal to a convenient, rather obsolete nineteenth-century definition of religion, which, by a curious coincidence, excludes postmodern religion. There is a strange irony in the fact that our elites are quite skilled in the task of analysing and deconstructing other metanarratives, but find that exposing their own core beliefs and dogmas to view involves quite another level of difficulty. The media typically demand that adherents of traditional religions involved in the public sphere immediately come clean and expose their worldview for all to see. No "hidden agendas"! This domain must be kept "disinfected", free of "contamination". To do so, views must be categorized and, when necessary, marginalized. Epidemics of the mind cannot be allowed to run free… But then again, this is not such a big deal. On the flip side of the coin, just out of view, postmoderns quite happily exploit secondary religious artefacts, symbolism and aesthetics. Ambivalence is the rule. Perhaps such cultural parasitism is indicative of a lack of creativity, a decline in imagination.

Like moderns, most postmoderns view serious ideological introspection as a painful, boring and ultimately "useless" procedure. But those who nonetheless might want to assess whether they are in fact influenced by postmodern religion, can begin the process by asking questions such as: Where do I get the beliefs to which I adhere, beliefs that influence my attitudes and guide my behaviour? What is their source? Do the same beliefs guide my professional and my private lives? Which authorities or social institutions seem to me to be the most trustworthy? One should take care not to respond too quickly to such questions. A little time for serious thought is useful. If one of the three previously named elite groups turns out to be a major ideological source, then there is good reason to believe that postmodern religion is the dominant influence. Moreover, if other postmodern institutions are identified as a source of belief as well then it is quite likely that we are a convinced follower of the postmodern religion as, to a large extent, postmodern devotees draw their beliefs from their cultural environment. But serious ideological introspection is typically viewed as "too difficult" and our sources of influence will be exposed only with great difficulty. Individuals who have travelled a self-conscious and persistent path of search for meaning in life are the exception, as this can be costly in social terms. Buying into mainstream thinking does simplify things.

Postmodern religion is peculiar in that, unlike many religious cults, it does not knock on doors, does not distribute tracts in the streets to recruit converts and does not have its own "evangelists" on TV begging for money. It does not publish catechisms or explicit creeds,[150] as this would result in exposing its core beliefs to the light of day, for all to see. And this would allow comparisons. Over time, postmodern religion has gained access to centres of power allowing it to impose its progressive worldview on the masses. The masses have to swallow this day after day after day… The State is of course a powerful magnet. It is an important place of worship for postmodern elites. The State is their ideal tool and, to some extent, a critical instrument of salvation.[151] Postmodern evangelists do not have to beg for money on TV, they need only apply for government grants to ensure the operations of their various agencies and associations. Getting involved in debates, winning arguments, persuading the masses to convert, discussing issues before the public is too tedious and even actually unnecessary when power centres are controlled. Ideally, converts to the postmodern religion will be unaware of this influence, but in most situations converts will say what the postmodern elites want to hear. When the conversion process is complete, a convert's thoughts and behaviour take place within the parameters set by postmodern elites and go no further.

In epistemological terms, the modern religion is heir to the Judeo-Christian worldview in that it also asserts that there is an epistemological standard, a concept of truth. Of course, modern religion has sought truth, not in some sacred writing or in statements emanating from some ecclesiastical hierarchy, but in scientific discourse, in empirical and positivist knowledge[152]. Few are aware that the modern assertion of an epistemological standard opens a door that may lead to a New Inquisition and modern forms of censorship. Arthur C. Clarke, a noted author and fairly typical representative of the modern perspective, offered, in one of his sci-fi novels, a vision of a tolerant and wise utopian society that would thrill many of our goodthinking elites as well as the most zealous Inquisitors of the Middle Ages. The scene unfolds on a distant planet in the galaxy and broaches the thorny matter of what parts of humanity's cultural heritage had to be dropped by early space settlers before they left for the stars (Clarke 1986: 115):

> A thousand years ago, men of genius and goodwill had rewritten history and gone through the libraries of Earth deciding what should be saved and what should be abandoned to the flames. The criterion of choice was simple, though often very hard to apply. Only if it would contribute to survival and social stability on the new worlds would any work of literature, any record of the past, be loaded into the memory of the seedships. The task was of course, impossible as well as heartbreaking. With tears in their eyes,[153] the selection panels had thrown away the Veda, the Bible, the Tripitaka, the Qur'an, and all the immense body of literature — fiction and nonfiction — that was based upon them.[154] Despite all the wealth of beauty and wisdom these works contained, they could not be allowed to reinfect virgin planets with the ancient poisons of religious hatred, belief in the supernatural, and the pious gibberish with which countless billions of men and women had once comforted themselves at the cost of addling their minds.

Is it conceivable that the Inquisition may have inspired such "tolerance"? Of course, although the physical annihilation of heretics can no longer be contemplated since the fall of the Third Reich and the Iron Curtain,[155] our postmodern elites have other means to impose their worldview, means that generally maintain at least a semblance of tolerance. While Communists and Nazis often persecuted and sought to physically eliminate followers of other religions/ideologies, capitalists have typically tolerated other groups when they seemed useful in one way or another. Postmodern tolerance accepts everything except… that which calls into question the core assumptions of the postmodern elite's religion.

Given the syncretistic presuppositions of the Western postmodern religion, one cannot exclude this leading, someday, to a synthesis of elements drawn from the scientific cosmology allied with occult practices.[156] Welcome to the era of multimedia superstition! Parallels could be drawn between religious views of our own time and those prevailing in the last days of the Roman Empire. In particular, syncretistic attitudes[157] are commonplace in both times. It is true that some segments of society remain(ed) impervious to syncretism in both periods, but if one considers the big picture, syncretism is a widely accepted and characteristic attitude of both eras. This attitude allows, in a short time frame, great shifts in ideo-logico-religious beliefs.

All ideologico-religious systems involve a set of fundamental assumptions, doctrines or dogmas. This set may be explicit, visible to all, as is the case of a creed or a catechism or it may be implicit[158] as is the case with the postmodern religion. Here is a (perhaps incomplete) list of assumptions/beliefs at the heart of the postmodern ideologico-religious system:

- Any suitable origins myth may be integrated into the postmodern cosmology as long as it does not conflict (or can be suitably amended) with the following assumptions/beliefs.[159]
- Humans are the result of evolutionary processes.
- Humans are part of nature and can claim no special status.
- Human nature is not fixed, but is in constant evolution, subject to natural, cultural and political forces.
- Since there is no such thing as a divine Lawgiver, no moral system should be considered absolute or universal.
- The concept of Truth is at best a cultural construct with no independent or universal existence.[160]
- Because there is no such thing as absolute Truth, all religious concepts, despite their contradictions, should be considered worthy of attention and respect (religious relativism).
- Reason is not the only path to knowledge; the irrational is a possible and legitimate way.[161]
- The material world is **not** all there is. It is only one aspect of reality and the supernatural (in **all** its forms) is worthy of attention.
- Western superiority and the concept of Progress must be rejected.[162]
- As a result, in ethical/moral terms postmoderns can adopt whatever behaviour or attitude they like as long as they (or their community) consider these a source of fulfilment[163] (moral relativism).
- Salvation is found in individual self-fulfilment,[164] this is the ultimate goal of any society or individual pathway.[165]
- Sex is an important means of salvation.[166]
- Anything pleasurable may contribute to the individual's development and his self-fulfilment/salvation
- Ridding one's self of guilt feelings contributes to the individual's development and self-fulfilment/salvation.
- Individuals should be autonomous (free of any constraint) to pursue self-fulfilment.
- Reality is a construct.[167] Identity and reality find their basis

The Phantom Creed

in language.
- Since the individual's development is the ultimate good and taking into account that there is no universal ethical or moral system regarding sexuality, no one has the right to judge the sexual urges or behaviour of others however strange or "vile" they may appear.[168]

Among these presuppositions (or beliefs), the central value of the individual is key.[169] The individual's desires and needs are beyond any norm or social value. They come first. Postmoderns hate constraint; they hate to be deprived of their elbowroom. The pursuit of autonomy is then viewed as fundamental, a "right". Another presupposition, derived from the first, is, in moral terms, the rejection of any absolute (relativism). While postmodern cosmology is quite open and does not forbid the admission of miscellaneous deities into its pantheon, it should be noted that such deities could never pass at postmodern security checkpoints if they happen to carry along in their luggage a definitive or absolute morality.[170]

With the materialist old guard, it should be noted that any explanation of origins involving Intelligence outside nature would be automatically excluded.[171] Debate on such questions is impossible as this is a non-negotiable article of faith. If a critical observer finds exposing the assumptions or structure of postmodern thought elusive this should come to no surprise, as one can see how difficult it is for Aldous Huxley, a transitional case between modern and postmodern belief systems, attempting (somewhat unconvincingly) to set up a "Truth" and explain the principles at the heart of a "proper way of looking at things", that is to say, to frame his utopian society or explain how to resolve the deep problems of the human condition[172] (1958/2007: 112):

The value, first of all, of individual freedom, based upon the facts of human diversity and genetic uniqueness; the value of charity and compassion, based upon the old familiar fact, lately rediscovered by modern psychiatry — the fact that, whatever their mental and physical diversity, love is as necessary to human beings as food and shelter; and finally the value of intelligence, without which love is impotent and freedom unattainable. This set of values will provide us with a criterion by which propaganda may be judged. The propaganda that is found to be both nonsensical and immoral may be rejected out of hand. That which is merely irrational, but compatible with love and freedom, and not on principle opposed to the exercise of intelligence, may be provisionally accepted for what it is worth.

From the first sentence one can tell that the lesson of Auschwitz has been learned. But Huxley then resorts to optimistic clichés and avoids the fundamental question raised by the socio-political catastrophes of the twentieth-century. An accusing finger points at the modern worldview. Though raised by strict materialists, Huxley is a precursor of postmodernism.

The world's great religious traditions, which developed over many generations and founded civilizations, all involve a core of basic assumptions shared by their followers. But these same religious traditions also exhibit, from within, a variety of communities and currents of thought in which areas of interest, habits and rituals and secondary beliefs[173] may differ widely. In the case of Islam, for example, believers are divided into three major branches[174]:

- Sunnis,[175] who are divided into different sub-groups: (Malekism, the Hanbali, the Shafi'i, the Hanafi)
- Shiism
- Kharidjites (less common than the first two)
- Sufis
- Wahhabis[176]
- The Mutazila
- Nation of Islam[177] (U. S.)

Although a highly centralized hierarchy governs the Catholic Church, it nonetheless accommodates a large range of groups and movements with diverse focuses and interests. Here is no doubt an incomplete list:

- Jesuits
- Capuchins
- Dominicans
- Carmelites
- Franciscans
- Oblates
- Opus Dei
- Marist Brothers
- Ursulines
- Christian Brothers
- Benedictines
- Knights Templar
- Chartreux
- Cistercians
- Scholastics
- Récollets
- Trappists
- Catholic Sisters

Much the same could be said of the countless Protestant churches and denominations. Of course postmodern religion is not immune to this phenomenon and, beyond a core of shared assumptions, one can identify many varying (and sometimes contradictory) expressions of the postmodern perspective. As we can see, many postmodern movements and schools of thought focus on sex as a means of salvation:

- Movement for divorce liberalization
- The Pro-choice movement (abortion)
- New Age movement
- The Posthuman movement
- Animal Rights activists
- Environmental Extremists[178]
- Evolutionary Psychology
- The Gay Pride ideology
- Defenders/promoters of pornography
- Lesbian Feminism
- Paedophilia sympathizers
- Biotechnology Ethics consultants
- Postmodern scholars (particularly in the Social Sciences)
- The Ecumenical movement
- Movement against the physical punishment of children (either in school or at home)
- Death with dignity movement

Of course the term "movement" is used very loosely here. For the purpose of our present discussion it should be noted that the associations and schools of thought listed above include not only individuals working for a cause[179] directly linked to formal organizations, but also others active in certain causes, who are not identified with any structured or formally recognized organizations. We must also add that since these movements or schools of thought are not explicitly religious, they may not be exclusively composed of postmodern devotees. Given the implicit nature of the postmodern religion, it is legitimate to maintain some cynicism even in cases where supporters of such movements loudly claim to belong to a religious tradition other than postmodern. It should be noted, that despite their being classed as postmodern, some of the movements listed above may retain more or less significant residues of modern influence. This is the case, for example, with the movement for divorce liberalization that took off in the first half of the twentieth-century and played a pivotal role between modern and postmodern periods.

As we have seen, the postmodern worldview boasts an amazing variety of forms of self-expression. This should come to no surprise as all major world religions spontaneously foster a comparable assortment of ideological and institutional expressions once they reach a certain level of dissemination (branching out into divers cultures) and exceed a critical mass of converts.

What Use is a Cosmology?

> The whole modern episteme, that which took shape toward the end of the 17th-century and still serves as the positive base of our knowledge, has framed man's singular mode of being and the possibility of empirical understanding. This whole episteme was linked to the disappearance of Discourse and its monotonous reign, to the downfall of language on objectivity's side and to its multiple reappearances.*
> (Foucault 1966: 397)

> As time goes on and experiences pile up, we make a greater and greater investment in our system of labels. So a conservative bias is built in. It gives us confidence. At any time we may have to modify our structure of assumptions to accommodate new experience, but the more consistent experience is with the past, the more confidence we can have in our assumptions. Uncomfortable facts, which refuse to be fitted in, we find ourselves ignoring or distorting so that they do not disturb these established assumptions. By and large anything we take note of is pre-selected and organised in the very act of perceiving. We share with other animals a kind of filtering mechanism, which at first only lets in sensations we know how to use.
> (Mary Douglas 1966/79 pp. 36-37)

The cosmology of an ideologico-religious system plays a key role. Cosmology gives structure and meaning to human existence. In its development, its assumptions give distinct shape to human behaviour, from the most admirable forms of altruism to the most despicable racist and genocidal prejudices. It provides the conceptual framework of reality. It renders reality thinkable. It justifies actions, behaviours. However, a cosmology does not dictate what clothes a teenager will wear in the morning or what career to choose. Its task is to establish the benchmarks of existence, what are the cosmos, humans, good and evil. The American lawyer Phillip Johnson notes (2002: 105) that in the postmodern West the materialistic cosmology is the dominant metanarrative, the foundation of our institutions of higher education; but this metanarrative remains implicit, unspoken. Reduced to its simplest form, it states: "In the beginning subatomic particles appeared along with the impersonal laws of physics. Somehow these particles became complex matter, living organisms. And these organisms first conceived religion and deities, but then discovered evolution." Despite the postmodern elites rise to power, this origins myth retains much of its force and influence. In this context, once the Divine Lawgiver has been discarded, a relativistic cosmology inevitably follows. Anyone can develop their own morality. No one answers to a higher power.

As noted above, postmoderns have abandoned the grand social utopias. At the heart of the postmodern perspective, the dominant themes are now the individual, his self-fulfilment, desires and rights. The twentieth-century buried the grand collective political projects. All that remains is the individual and his sexual, artistic, ideological and professional impulses and ambitions. His salvation is found in self-fulfilment. Anything that constrains the individual finds itself opposed to the postmodern perspective. This is the perfect worldview for eternal teenagers.

In the twenty-first century, the three groups mentioned in the previous chapter (media, educational and judicial elites), collectively give form to and propagate the postmodern religion in the West. These groups define concepts such as good and evil. It would be difficult to overestimate their influence and power.[180] They are the ones that establish postmodern taboos, prescribe and prohibit certain behaviours or attitudes. Their power lies in particular in the fact that they are the ones that determine, for postmodern man, what is "significant" (and deserving of mention), whether in political, economic, ideological or cultural terms. They also define what should be considered "insignificant" (and thus worthy of being ignored, silenced or, if necessary, censored...). They ask the questions, but never answer questions themselves. To a large extent they control the context of discourse in the public square. This power however is never absolute, as if this were to occur, from that moment on their ideology would risk becoming clearly visible to all. If they decide that a social issue must be addressed in one way and not another, information supplied to the public must then be filtered appropriately. And in promos for TV news shows, we are assured: "If something important happened today, we covered it!" But this is easily arranged when one has the power to establish or control what is "important" and what is not. The end product of this system is a discourse that overall is rather uniform, conforming to a set pattern, as the Russian writer Alexander Solzhenitsyn discovered while a refugee in the United States (1978):

> Such as it is, however, the press has become the greatest power within Western countries, exceeding that of the legislature, the executive, and the judiciary.[181] Yet one would like to ask: According to what law has it been elected and to whom is it responsible? In the Communist East, a journalist is frankly appointed as a state official. But who has voted Western journalists into their positions of power, for how long a time, and with what prerogatives?
>
> There is yet another surprise for someone coming from the totalitarian East with its rigorously unified press: **One discovers a common trend of preferences within the Western press as a whole (the spirit of the time), generally accepted patterns of judgment, and maybe common corporate interests, the sum effect being not competition but unification.** Unrestrained freedom exists for the press, but not for readership, because newspapers mostly transmit in a forceful and emphatic way those opinions which do not too openly contradict their own and that general trend.

It should be remembered that these words were written at a time when the Soviet Union and Communism were part of reality and if the Soviet regime is now a thing of the past, media power in the West has not decreased.[182] Like Solzhenitsyn, British journalist Malcolm Muggeridge considers that media conformism is indicative of a pattern of thought or ideology, and such conformism makes media discourse quite predictable (1978: 91):

> There is something, to me, very sinister about this emergence of a weird kind of conformity, or orthodoxy, particularly among the people who operate the media, so that you can tell in advance exactly what they will say and think about anything. It is true that so far they have not got an Inquisition to enforce their orthodoxy, but they have ways of enforcing it which makes the old thumbscrews and racks seem quite paltry.

Of course to even become aware of the conformism[183] noted by the two previous observers, it is essential to have a previously adopted coherent perspective contrasting with or opposing the postmodern perspective. Otherwise, the whole phenomenon will slip under the radar... Everything's fine. Nothing to report. The process of controlling and deconstructing meaning is actually quite simple, but very effective (as it operates behind the scenes, out of view). Information sources that address a question in an "appropriate" manner will be entitled to speak and be treated positively, with no demeaning filters. No serious criticism will be made of such positions; no in-depth analysis examining the consequences of the assumptions involved in such perspectives will be made. In producing literary criticism of a postmodern writer, for example, one will hear that the author has produced a work with "fast-flowing, graceful and intelligent drama" and that "the narrative goes beyond virtuosity offering a deep reflection about life, the Other and art itself". On the other hand, when it comes to works based on the traditional worldview (or institutions identifying with it) then the gloves come off. The scalpel comes out and the implicit assumptions and beliefs will be exposed for all to see, while the assumptions of works by postmodern artists or personalities will rarely be subjected to any serious critical examination or questioning.[184]

When a cultural phenomenon conflicting with the postmodern worldview appears it would seem that the most effective marginalizing strategy would not be to give battle, but rather simply to ignore it. However should an artistic or cultural speaker dare question some aspect of postmodern ideology (even when demonstrating the same literary quality as the previous one), these features become defects. This marginalization method is simplicity itself. They will describe his work (if they actually condescend to speak of it…) as a mess, badly written and full of inconsistencies. To marginalize a movie or a play expressing ideas displeasing to postmodern ears, a few well-chosen vague negative comments will often do the trick. For example: saying that the cast is second-rate, actors trapped in annoying mannerisms, with a sloppy script, saddled with poorly designed, nightclub lighting, bland music and dialogue that is humdrum, false and absurd. Such methods of marginalization are, in most cases much more effective than any open opposition or censorship, which would clearly expose the fact that the content of this work is intolerable **because** it questions postmodern dogma. Postmodern censorship is never acknowledged.

Instruments of Power

> Don't you see that the whole aim of Newspeak is to narrow the range
> of thought? In the end we shall make thoughtcrime literally impos-
> sible, because there will be no words in which to express it. Every
> concept that can ever be needed will be expressed by exactly one
> word, with its meaning rigidly defined and all its subsidiary meanings
> rubbed out and forgotten. [...] The Revolution will be complete when
> the language is perfect. Newspeak is Ingsoc and Ingsoc is Newspeak.
> (Orwell 1949/1984: 46-47)

> We do not talk to say something, but to obtain a certain effect.
> (Josef Goebbels in Riess 1956: 130)

Towards the mid-twentieth-century, two American ethnolin-
guists, Edward Sapir and Benjamin Lee Whorf, worked on Native
American languages. Sapir hypothesized that different language
groups have their own distinct way of looking at the world.[185] In
their view, language then does not just passively reflect reality, but
each language shapes and frames reality in its own original way.
Each language therefore offers a perspective on the world. For
example, among the Hopi of the American Southwest, language
has no time markers; time is not considered as flowing. For example,
the word "day" has no plural form. Among the Canadian Innu, there
are different words for several types and colours of snow while, for
the average North American, there is just one kind of snow and it is
always white. Therefore according to the Sapir-Whorf hypothesis,
language to some extent determines how we perceive the world
around us.[186] Taken to the extreme, this hypothesis would imply that
specific languages are our only access to reality and as a result
translation or communication from one language to another would
be impossible. However, in the real world translation is done on a
regular basis despite the difficulties such a task entails.[187] Although
this hypothesis is not accepted in its extreme form, it does highlight
the power of language to shape the thinking of its speakers.

In the postmodern context, it should be noted that in the
hands of our elites, language is more than a means of communication: it is a plastic, malleable tool. Using language as a tool, attempts
are made to channel thought in certain directions and, moreover,
to prevent some undesirable developments in others. Supporting

abortion, for example, is not expressed as "promoting the killing of unborn children", but rather as advocating "control over one's own body" and adopting a "pro-choice" perspective. What is "harassment", "homophobia", "intolerance", "compassion" or being labelled "reactionary"? What is a "left" or "right-leaning" individual? These terms are empty shells into which almost any content may be dumped. If you are told, "I love you"[188] this statement can mean many things.[189] On the other hand, being told "I hate you", is typically less ambiguous…

Terms such as "tolerant" or "intolerant" are extensively used in postmodern rhetoric, but originally the term "tolerate" had a much more physiological meaning. In this regard, Griffiths notes (2002: 31):

> The transitive form of the verb has as its root meaning (as also is true of the Latin *tolerare*) "putting up with" or "enduring" or "bearing something unpleasant." This meaning survives when we say that some trees tolerate drought better than others, or that some people can tolerate a surprising amount of suffering. A minor extension of this fundamental sense makes it possible to use the verb to denote the action of permitting or letting be something unpleasant or undesirable. I can, in this sense, tolerate your pipe-smoking so long as you don't do it in my car. Or, I tolerate my allergies because I find that attempting to medicate them away is worse than allowing them free rein. In all these cases, what is tolerated is something unpleasant or incorrect or improper or otherwise difficult. The substantive "toleration" then denotes the action (and the theoretical commitments that inform such an action) of putting up with or permitting or letting be some pattern of action or belief found by those practicing toleration to be false (if a belief) or improper (if an action).

Of course language is always changing, evolving. Since the seventeenth-century the word "tolerate" has come to refer primarily to political and religious beliefs. In English-speaking countries, the term has become associated with the art of legislation, ensuring that the State and its citizens be tolerant of religious practices and beliefs with which they disagree. The philosopher of science Karl Popper, in his book **The Open Society and Its Enemies**, evokes an often overlooked paradox that is part of postmodern thought: "We should therefore claim, in the name of tolerance, the right not to tolerate the intolerant."[190] The inherent contradiction of such a sentence clearly exposes the potential futility of terms such as "tolerant" or "intolerant". Like the term "gentleman" (addressed by C. S. Lewis below), it has become little more than a term of approval, or in this case, disapproval and censorship. If one deconstructs the "intolerant" concept and its use by postmoderns, using the term regarding one's fellow man, and stripped of ambiguous rhetoric, it usually means nothing more than: "I do not like your views and think society should force you to shut up!"[191] In postmodern language, the term "intolerant" has become a form of accusation, mud slung in the face of an ideological enemy. It targets those who are viewed as having no right to speak. In one case, as in the other, these terms are too easily used.

As used by postmoderns, accusations of "intolerance" parallel witchcraft accusations in medieval times.[192] Those accused of being "intolerant" are then considered as polluting or defiling the social order as they challenge the dominant ideas. They are the new heretics. As British anthropologist Mary Douglas points out (1966/1979: 113):

> A polluting person is always in the wrong. He has developed some wrong condition or simply crossed some line which should not have been crossed and this displacement unleashes danger for someone.[193] Bringing pollution, unlike sorcery and witchcraft, is a capacity which men share with animals, for pollution is not always set off by humans. Pollution can be committed intentionally, but intention is irrelevant to its effect — it is more likely to happen inadvertently.

In the postmodern era, the "intolerant" individual is a perfect fit for the heretic concept. He gets little more respect than do terrorists or rapists. Ironically, he is the proscribed individual, one that must be silenced and cannot be "tolerated". The development of labelling terms such as "intolerant" is characteristic of postmodernism. Such language use has precedents in the twentieth-century and involves the attribution of pejorative labels. One might as well sew Stars of David on the coats of the individuals involved…[194] In modern discourse, the term "fascist" has been similarly exploited. The historian Karl Dietrich Bracher notes in this regard (1969/1995: 645):

> … the "fascist" epithet is used with much enthusiasm by the left, as much to designate all of the right as well as rival left-leaning organisations. This is due to the fact that this term says nothing about their content or their claims, as soon as one goes beyond the specific historical context and Italian terminology.*[195]

Writing in the 1970s, the philosopher Francis Schaeffer made the following comments regarding this type of language use in the West and as it relates to the issue of abortion (1994 vol. V: 344):

Language itself is a subtle indicator and a powerful tool. Think of the deliberate changes in language that have been used to soften the stark impact of what is actually happening. Abortion is merely the "removal of fetal tissue," or "discontinuing" or "termination" of pregnancy. Childless couples are now "child free," a term that subtly establishes children as an unwanted burden. Language has power. The language we use actually forms the concepts we have and the results these concepts produce. Think of the Nazi use of the name *The Charitable Transport Company for the Sick*[196] for the agency conveying people to the killing centers. But let us not be naive. Exactly the same language power is being used when the unborn baby is called "fetal tissue".

Physician and biochemist Leon Kass made the following observations regarding the use of language to modify assumptions and expectations at the end of the twentieth-century (2004: 88):

At one time, in debates about abortion and contraception, slogans such as "Every child should be wanted" were used. However, this may lead us to perceive a child, not as a gift that we must take care of and cherish, but as a being existing to satisfy our own desires. Increasingly, the child is viewed as a condition for the parent's self-fulfilment. This is a deep change that I have observed in recent decades in the United States.*

Controlling the meaning of words is important, but controlling the **context** of social discourse is equally important, as the American philosopher Peter Kreeft demonstrates (1999: 141):

Isa: … You relativists are like the Communists: you always pretend to be the party of the people, while you really scorn and despise the people's philosophy.

Libby: It sounds like sour grapes to me. You're complaining because we're winning.

Isa: No, I'm complaining because you're lying. For a whole generation now your small minority of relativistic elitists who somehow gained control of the media have been relentlessly imposing your elitist relativism on popular opinion by accusing popular opinion — I mean traditional morality — of elitism, and of imposing *their* morality! It's like the Nazi propaganda saying Germany was victimized by Poland.

When a perspective becomes dominant, it can safely eliminate definitions of terms that are deemed "unsuitable". In an essay, C. S. Lewis explored an example of changes over time in the meaning of the English word "gentleman", contrasting the original, very practical and economical, meaning (that is, an individual of English nobility with a coat of arms and estates) to its modern, more diffuse or emotional usage (1943/1977: 10):

> When a word ceases to be a term of description and becomes merely a term of praise, it no longer tells you facts about the object: it only tells you about the speaker's **attitude** to that object. (A "nice" meal only means a meal the speaker likes.) A "gentleman", once it has been spiritualised and refined out of its old coarse, objective sense, means hardly more than a man whom the speaker likes. As a result, "gentleman" is now a useless word.

As a result the prestige of the word "gentleman" has been exploited while emptying it of its original contents. All that remains is an empty shell, a mask for unacknowledged emotional issues. Postmodern language involves many terms that have little function other than to denote major Western institutions' approval or disapproval of certain views or perspectives. Ivan Illich has commented on this phenomenon and uses the term "plastic-word" to describe such language techniques (in Cayley 1992: 253-254):

> A plastic word has powerful connotations. A person becomes important when he uses it: he bows to a profession which knows more about it than he does and he is convinced that he is making, in some way, a scientific statement. A plastic word is like a stone thrown into a conversation — it makes waves, but doesn't hit anything. It has all these connotations, but it does not designate anything precisely. Usually, it's a word which has always existed in language but which has gone through a scientific laundry and then dropped back into ordinary language with a new connotation that has something to do with what other people know and you can't quite fathom. Pörksen puts *sexuality*, for instance, into the category of amoeba words — or *crisis* or *information*.

A similar phenomenon commonly occurs in postmodern discourse. In the media, the term "intolerance" is used in similar contexts to terms such as "sectarian", "fundamentalist" or "extremist"; that is to say, serving primarily as an instrument of marginalization, used to silence proponents of perspectives that offend postmodern elites. Much the same could be said of the term "fundamentalist". Originally, this term referred to an individual attempting to develop a coherent, integrated worldview, that is to say attempting to behave consistently within his cosmological assumptions. One may then encounter Catholic fundamentalists, communist fundamentalists, materialistic fundamentalists, Nazi fundamentalists and postmodern fundamentalists. But when the media use this term it becomes essentially a negative label, categorizing someone (typically a Christian[197] or Moslem) voicing views disapproved of by the media elites. Because the "fundamentalist" has rejected postmodern relativism, postmoderns then consider him a heretic, a pariah, an outcast. And yet, in a sense, everybody is a fundamentalist.[198] All, despite their contradictions, seek coherence,[199] integrating cosmology (their most basic beliefs) and daily life, belief and behaviour.

Law professor Butler Shaffer remarks (2005) that in the postmodern political context the term "extreme" as in "extreme" right or its derivative "extremist" are used to force discussion into postmodern categories. Creating a collective consciousness allows the State, or other major social institutions, to keep the masses in line. The concept of compromise, so useful in economic and social transactions, is put to use in debates on policy positions in a way that marginalizes positions based on coherent philosophical principles.[200] In a culture of collective consciousness, once a perspective has been labelled "extremist", it can no longer be voiced in the public square. It is, for all intents and purposes, eliminated from further discussion, no matter how rigorously empirical, rational or philosophical it may be. It thus becomes surrounded by fear and suspicion. Outside of the postmodern Church there is no salvation… Non-postmodern individuals are then rendered impotent, though not mute, as no one will listen unless these critics bow down to the ideologico-religious powers that be. Shaffer notes that this does not imply that views, labelled as "extremist", will necessarily be empirically, rationally or philosophically based. What matters is the fact that, rightly or wrongly, such views are considered "problematic" for the "efficient" management of political systems, as they introduce variety and complexity in discussions and, as a result, undermine the simplistic certainties upon which the postmodern consciousness rests. Herd-thinking makes things much easier.

On an Internet forum, I "virtually" met a participant claiming that a website he had visited was, in his opinion, "biased". This participant did not seem aware of the fact that all speech is a priori biased and implies a perspective, a way of seeing things as well as value judgments. Thus, the term "biased" is misleading, in fact meaningless, but from another point of view, this term is significant because, like Lewis' discussion of the term "gentleman", it tells us something important about the person using the term. Though this term tells us little about the website in question, it does provide us with accurate information about how the website was **perceived** by the participant confirming that the web site's "bias" did not mesh very well with his own bias.[201]

The euthanasia concept[202] illustrates a change of meaning that both initiates and reflects changing social attitudes. Originally, this term only applied to ordinary health care services[203] provided to the dying. But over time things change (Universalis Encyclopaedia 2003; entry: Euthanasia):

> Not until the late nineteenth-century ... did the term euthanasia take on a new meaning: to provide a gentle death (the old definition), but [with the added concept of] deliberately ending the patient's life. And this is now the predominant meaning in public opinion in Western societies.*

The Nazis exploited euphemisms[204] with great sophistication as an ideological weapon, which resulted in perverse language stripped of meaning. The term "Final Solution", for example, originally had a fuzzy connotation, disguising the actual intent, that is to say, genocide carried out on an industrial scale. In the context of postmodern discussions on euthanasia, one often encounters the phrase "living (or dying) with dignity". It goes without saying that a deconstruction of the term "dignity", as used by postmoderns, reflects a shift that is both ideological and semantic. Whereas the phrase "live with dignity" formerly dealt with individuals facing the difficulties and trials of life with courage and perseverance, in the postmodern context it typically describes individuals who decide to act to end their life (and suffering). The concept of euthanasia is also extended to health care administrators as they act in order to kill[205] a person suffering under their responsibility, as well as ending the administrators' own psychological suffering (as witnesses to another's suffering).

In the postmodern context, examples of language control by the media abound. A common media buzzword is the term "homophobia", which is usually linked to the postmodern concept of "tolerance". Although this term is a neologism, oddly postmoderns typically avoid defining it. Perhaps all could agree, for example, that the term "homophobia" could legitimately describe:

- Physically attacking an openly gay (homosexual or lesbian) individual.
- Any statements that would encourage others to physically attack an openly gay individual.
- Any insult demeaning the person of an openly gay individual.

But generally the concept of "homophobia" has a broader meaning. In common usage the terms "homophobic" and "homophobia" go well beyond such matters. Usually, homophobia also (and especially) focuses on:

- Any criticism or serious questioning of gay ideology.

But what's going on here? This is rather strange. While the majority of modern democratic states have made free speech a fundamental right, this implies that individuals are free to criticize Catholic, Protestant, American, fascist, Muslim, feminist, Palestinian, Jewish, communist or socialist views. Why then should it be "illegitimate" or "unacceptable" to criticize gay ideology? Why should this view be "protected" from the natural selection of ideas and opinions that takes place in the public square? Why seek special status for this ideology? This implies that everyone else should be "tolerant" towards the gay ideology, but gay ideology "evangelists" are under no obligation to return the favour... Some would even go so far as to make "homophobia" a "hate crime". Why do we suddenly find ourselves facing an implicit/hypocritical form of censorship applied to any serious debate in the public square? Such a tactic would likely attract the admiration of imams seeking to silence any critic (in a comic strip or elsewhere) of Islam. Why chop someone's head off when you can shut them up? But regarding the concept of "homophobia", perhaps all we have here is misunderstanding and in actual fact only "goodthinkers" are now entitled to real freedom of expression. This is a question that remains to be cleared up.

Like witchcraft accusations in the Middle Ages, charges of "homophobia" are too easily made as this notion is a very effective weapon of ideological marginalization. The "homophobia" concept includes the combining form "phobia" implying that those questioning homosexual behaviour "fear" or "hate" homosexuals. Orthodox postmodern propaganda leads to the conclusion that such an individual then has an irrational "fear" of homosexuals. It follows that such a critic has a "problem" and problems can be treated... The term "homophobic" then transforms the critic of gay ideology into an "unbalanced" person, someone subject to "unreason" and "phobias". Of course one may be compassionate towards "homophobes" (and have them "referred"), but you cannot listen to them. One cannot take a demented person seriously, though they may be feared. This is in fact a phenomenon discussed by the postmodern scholar Michel Foucault.[206] Such a tactic is extremely effective in marginalizing, silencing, discrediting and excluding critics. Framing a debate in such a way is a very powerful ideological weapon as it can be used to eradicate any criticism of homosexuality. The homosexual is then, by definition, always the "victim" and critics of gay ideology[207] are always narrow-minded, reactionary, intolerant, phobic, irrational aggressors. The State (and other major social institutions) develops knowledge and the cosmological categories of language defining "normality". The constraints imposed on language by postmodern religion are quite effective in labelling certain attitudes as taboo, to be avoided.

In the postmodern context, it can be observed that imposing constraints on individual's sexual freedom is now considered serious heresy, an object of condemnation and zealous politically correct browbeating. How strange! The media often portray current critics of homosexuality in a manner bearing comparison to that of the homosexual in Victorian times: a suspicious, repulsive and evil being. How ironic! Each time period seems to have its own heretics and witch hunts.

In a time of ideological confrontation, postmodern elites do not openly and directly challenge traditional concepts drawn from the Judeo-Christian worldview such as family or marriage, for example. They may say, quite sincerely, that they are "profamily", but take care to empty this concept of all its traditional content and replacing it with postmodern content.[208] In this context, if traditional definitions of marriage or the family are deemed "inconvenient", it is pointless to attack them openly. One need only to redefine these concepts and the end result will be much the same... This is much more effective than a frontal attack. Such an approach avoids much needless debate as well as time-consuming confrontations of ideas where one would have to justify one's assumptions and give an account of one's cosmology. Oddly enough, the naturalist Charles Darwin well understood this principle and put it to use in the promotion of his theory. He had accurately grasped the contradiction between his theory and the literal interpretation of Genesis that had dominated the West for almost two millennia. Darwin advocated a discreet, indirect approach, avoiding open confrontation. In a private letter[209] to his son George, then studying at Cambridge, he wrote (in Himmelfarb, 1959/1968: 387):

> Lyell is most firmly convinced that he has shaken the faith in the Deluge &c far more efficiently by never having said a word against the Bible, than if he had acted otherwise. … I have lately read Morley's Life of Voltaire & he insists strongly that direct attacks on Christianity (even when written with the wonderful force & vigour of Voltaire) produce little permanent effect: real good seems only to follow from slow & silent side attacks.

Regarding the power of language to shape the meaning of concepts, Ernest Gellner noted (1992: 63): "Indisputably, it is the case that concepts do constrain. Concepts, the range of available ideas, all that is suggested by a given language, and all that is inexpressible in it are part of the machinery of social control in any given society." If one considers language control processes presently exploited by major Western institutions, the French philosopher Jean-François Lyotard makes the following observations (1979/1984: 17):

> In the ordinary use of discourse — for example, in a discussion between two friends - the interlocutors use any available ammunition, changing games from one utterance to the next: questions, requests, assertions, and narratives are launched pell-mell into battle. The war is not without rules, but the rules allow and encourage the greatest possible flexibility of utterance.
>
> From this point of view, an institution differs from a conversation in that it always requires supplementary constraints for statements to be declared admissible within its bounds. The constraints function to filter discursive potentials, interrupting possible connections in the communication networks: there are things that should not be said. They also privilege certain classes of statements (sometimes only one) whose predominance characterises the discourse of the particular institution: there are things that should be said, and there are ways of saying them. Thus: orders in the army, prayer in church, denotation in the schools, narration in families, questions in philosophy, performativity in businesses. Bureaucratisation is the outer limit of this tendency.

While interviewing French intellectual Jacques Derrida, Samuel Weber points out that media's ideological power also consists in presupposing itself as a prerequisite to knowledge and understanding (in De Vries & Weber 2001: 75):

> The media, as we concretely experience them, tend to naturalize their social and historical specificity. A technological structure that "naturalizes" itself may seem paradoxical, but the anecdote just recounted demonstrates how it works: "If you can see anything at all, it is because we allow you to. And we only allow you to see anything insofar as you

accept your 'freedom to choose' among the commodities our advertisers[210] offer you." Otherwise, you will be deaf and blind, for lack of anything to see and hear. This is a side of the much-vaunted "multimedia" that seems often neglected, but that is surely part of its reality today.

While Weber's statement above pertains mainly to media's commercial interests, it is entirely appropriate and useful to apply this observation elsewhere and extend it to the media's claim to provide the basis and condition of knowledge and moral thought in postmodern societies.[211] This is particularly true in light of the massive quantities of material produced as well as the control exerted by electronic and print media over basic categories of thought in the West. At present only the Internet is out of postmodern control, but for how long?[212]

Media Behavioural Patterns

> Structure within a story means that everything that occurs within the story follows a preexisting plan, that is, an order with a purpose. One of the rules in effective filmmaking is that everything that happens in a movie has to have a purpose. From what a person eats to what is going on in the background—all are precisely ordained by writer and director to communicate character, plot and theme. There can be no arbitrary events. Anything that does not advance the story must be thrown out.
> (Godawa 2002: 64)

> ... to live is, in itself, a value judgment. To breathe is to judge.
> (Camus 1951/1978: 8)

The media's usual knee-jerk reaction, when facing a speaker daring to challenge fundamental postmodern tenets, appears to be inevitable marginalization. Of course hostile behaviour or attitudes need not come to the fore when issues of lesser importance are on the table. In such circumstances the legitimacy of religious discourse and "free speech" will be left unquestioned, but when real confrontation between postmodern politically correct dogma and someone challenging postmodern core beliefs occurs, various marginalization techniques may come into play. This is what anthropologists call a taboo reaction or pollution behaviour. Mary Douglas describes this in her classic book **Purity and Danger** (1966/1979: 36) "In short, our pollution behaviour is the reaction which condemns any object or idea likely to confuse or contradict [or *contaminate*] cherished classifications." We will come back to this concept later on, but that said, if a non-postmodern participant in public debate is involved in a minor news story with no serious repercussions for the postmodern worldview, it is unlikely this individual will become the target of the behaviour discussed below.

First things first. Where is the nexus of media power? In our view, it is found at the initial stage of the process: in the choice of topics to be discussed, in the initial sorting of information and selection of information sources, in setting priorities, in decisions relating to how a subject will be discussed and the contextualization of debates. Media power is therefore expressed in the selection of information, in the form it is given, in providing a broad framework in which people think, in deciding which questions will be asked and those which will be ignored. Thus, the media controls not only the entry and exit of information, but also the context of its presentation. Of course this does not result in absolute power, but we think it would be very naive to underestimate such power. It should be added that selection of information of some kind is inevitable. This is not at issue here, but having said that, the popular and naive concept of the media as a "virginally pure", neutral transmission channel must be rejected.

In day-to-day life, when the media attempt to ensure the "quality" (ideological uniformity) of their production (marginalizing "undesirable" content while keeping up appearances of "impartiality"), several strategies can be put to use. Here are some measures that may be of use, for example, in setting up a pre-recorded interview with a critic of the postmodern religion:

- Take care to expose the critic's ideological commitments.[213]
- Use the critic's statements or arguments selectively.[214]
- Eliminate the critic's strongest and most credible arguments or material from the edited version.
- Quote the critic's weakest arguments.
- Quote the critic's actual statements, but out of context.
- When possible, link the critic to persons, perspectives or organizations deemed "heretical", "intolerant", "fanatical", "extremist" or "racist".
- Allow more time for interviewees supporting postmodern religion to call the critic into question.

- Discuss the critic's academic or professional achievements if they can be questioned.
- If the critic's academic or professional achievements cannot be questioned, ignore them.

These are some of the available techniques that can be used when the need arises. In the context of a live interview, things cannot be played as loosely. To neutralize an ideological adversary, questions need to be scripted in a tighter fashion, though at times it may be useful to let things slide just by asking banal, emotional, empty questions instead of engaging in a serious discussion.

Note that these strategies are designed to undermine the critic's credibility. Once a critic's credibility is destroyed, he may talk as much as he likes. In fact once this is accomplished, when he speaks, he also discredits any others associated with his position. This can have its uses. In general terms the way in which a critic of postmodernism will be treated may vary, depending on several factors amongst which:

- The significance of the issue discussed;
- The relative weight of the organization that the non-postmodern debate participant represents;
- The size of the media organization hosting the debate or exchange;[215]
- Specific prejudices of the media representative involved;
- Is the non-postmodern debate participant well known[216] to the general public?

Though the media system does not publicly exclude journalists with non-postmodern religious beliefs, it does demand they keep a "flexible outlook", which means that when there is a significant conflict between the postmodern perspective and a traditional religious position, they must look at the issues from a postmodern perspective (or, at very least, learn to shut up). If traditional religion can keep the subservient place that postmodern elites have so generously assigned it to, then everything will be fine. The renowned linguist, social activist and major spokesman for the left, Noam Chomsky observed (1988: 304):

A propaganda model also helps us to understand how media personnel adapt, and are adapted, to systemic demands. Given the imperatives of corporate organization and the workings of the various filters, conformity to the needs and interests of privileged sectors is essential to success. In the media, as in other major institutions, those who do not display the requisite values and perspectives will be regarded as "irresponsible," "ideological", or otherwise aberrant, and will tend to fall by the wayside. While there may be a small number of exceptions, the pattern is pervasive, and expected. Those who adapt, perhaps quite honestly, will then be free to express themselves with little managerial control, and they will be able to assert, accurately, that they perceive no pressures to conform. The media are indeed free - for those who adopt the principles required for their "societal purpose." There may be some who are simply corrupt, and who serve as "errand boys" for state and other authority, but this is not the norm. We know from personal experience that many journalists are quite aware of the way the system operates, and utilize the occasional openings it affords to provide information and analysis that departs in some measure from the elite consensus, carefully shaping it so as to accommodate to required norms in a general way. But this degree of insight is surely not common. Rather, the norm is a belief that freedom prevails, which is true for those who have internalized the required values and perspectives.

The main advantage in controlling the context of expression is that open censorship, eliminating or silencing one's ideological adversaries, is unnecessary. Controlling the context of expression has the same effect and allows keeping up the media's facade of "tolerance". A truly win-win situation… Censorship therefore exists in the postmodern context, but in a hypocritical, unrecognized and unadmitted form. Such censorship silences critical discourse (from non postmodern sources) and uses it for its own purposes. As part of an essay on propaganda (dealing with political forms of the modern religion, exploiting mass media), Jacques Ellul pinpointed the need for integration, for a total answer,[217] which is actually at the heart of the religious impulse (1973: 11):

… propaganda cannot be satisfied with partial successes, for it does not tolerate discussion; by its very nature, it excludes contradiction and discussion. As long as a noticeable or expressed tension or a conflict of action remains, propaganda cannot be said to have accomplished[218] its aim. It must produce quasi-unanimity, and the opposing faction must become negligible, or in any case cease to be vocal. Extreme propaganda must win over the adversary and at least use him by integrating him into its own frame of reference. That is why it was so important to have an Englishman speak on the Nazi radio or a General Paulus on the Soviet radio.…

When the media marginalizes a work or viewpoint, it can obviously afford to give some credit to the enterprise or school of thought it is attempting to denigrate. This helps veil the implicit censorship with a certain nobility, a contrived "openness". To obtain the desired effect, in parallel with more substantive criticisms, one may also "generously" give credit to such works on minor, trivial matters. As the saying goes: Damned by faint praise!

In our time, the postmodern church has become the norm, the Establishment.[219] In social terms, it provides the reference point most people will ever have with which to judge whether beliefs or prejudices are "biased", "narrow-minded", "progressive", "reaction-ary", "tolerant", "fair", or "extreme". This applies just as well to political, ethical, cultural or other issues. At times the media (discreetly) presents themselves as saviours, come to deliver us from chaos and give meaning to our lives. A BBC World Service self-promotional clip, introducing a radio news program, stated: "In a world awash with information [ocean sounds in the background], in a world of confusion and contradictions, BBC Television and BBC World Service makes sense of it all!" How modest…

Oddly enough, Social Anthropologists know in fact that it is a religion's role to provide a total explanation to the big questions of life, that is to say, to produce a narrative/discourse that attempts to give meaning to **everything**. Such an admission by media proves beyond a shadow of a doubt that the role that it has taken upon itself far exceeds (and has for a long time now) that of a "neutral provider of information". Control over the context of information transmission in mass media has a hidden advantage, as ideological opponents are automatically put in the position of aggressors, a position of imbalance. An individual espousing a postmodern perspective naturally benefits from a more favourable reception. His access to media will be facilitated[220] though of course subject to the vagaries of changing media interests and needs. The goodthinking elites' ideology is then characteristically cloaked in an aura of academic, legal or journalistic "objectivity". Media personalities then typically play two personas, private/professional. Depending on the level of responsibility exercised by the individual (and the particular circumstances in which he finds himself), the ideological aspect of his role may vary.

Presuppositions providing the basis for social or ethical stances taken by postmodern elites typically remain hidden, implicit, both for the audience and often even to their authors. There is some irony in the fact that Orwell explored this phenomenon in his novel **1984** (1949/1984: 174):

A party member is required to have not only the right opinions, but the right instincts. Many of the beliefs and attitudes demanded of him are never plainly stated, and could not be stated without laying bare the contradictions inherent in Ingsoc. If he is a person naturally orthodox (in Newspeak, a *goodthinker*), he would in all circumstances know, without taking thought, what is the true belief or the desirable emotion. But in any case an elaborate mental training, undergone in childhood and grouping itself round the Newspeak words *crimestop*, *blackwhite*, and *doublethink*, makes him unwilling and unable to think too deeply on any subject whatever.

In evaluating the ideologico-religious commitments of a member of the postmodern elite, given the syncretism prevailing in the West, it would be unwise to rely on public statements or religious affiliation. Ultimately, such judgements demand close scrutiny of the individual's life history or access to his curriculum vitae. When it comes to an individual's true beliefs, actions speak much louder than words. Examining causes a person has gotten involved in or given time to, provides a much more precise picture of the individual's real ideological commitments (even if these may contradict explicit ideological statements or references to other worldviews that may hold great emotional importance in the individual's private life). No doubt, the postmodern elites' hold on power depends, to a great extent, on maintaining a facade of objectivity and neutrality. Exposing postmodern core beliefs to the light of day inevitably requires considerable effort. Who has the courage or the means to demand it?

In a culture that has largely rejected the concept of absolute truth as the basis for culture or civilisation, we find ourselves in a situation where there is no way to distinguish between information and propaganda. Everything is contaminated. In a manual for journalism students, Gary Thompson raises the question of how to define propaganda, an issue he both addresses and avoids… In the postmodern West, Thompson notes (1996: 199):

> The idea of propaganda exists in contrast with something else — the truth, perhaps. It's propaganda if it's false, if it's an attempt to influence how you think, and so forth. But we've seen that media texts are always an attempt to influence how we think: *The truth* is always selected and arranged for us in a shape that conforms to our expectations of it, which in turn have been created for us by the culture at large. Seen in this way, all communication would be propaganda: You cannot get outside of interests — your own as well as those of a text's producers — in order to measure its degree of truth.

If the concept of truth is dead, then all we have left is propaganda, nothing more. In the context of the postmodern cosmology, given the presuppositions of this belief system, such a conclusion is inevitable. But most postmodern institutions would have too much to lose if their core beliefs were to be seriously examined and exposed for all to see. What are the chances that major Western institutions would recognize their ideologico-religious function in postmodern society? Their neutrality and credibility would suffer. In some cases the bottom (financial) line is where this would hurt the most though. Presumably the ability of an individual or institution to acknowledge the system's ideologico-religious role is inversely proportional to their degree of commitment to this system of thought. If an individual's (or institution's) degree of commitment to this system of thought is absolute, then there is little chance that they could question the system's neutrality or admit its religious role.

In their reporting and in documentaries, the media, despite their much-touted "objectivity", widely express implicit or explicit value judgments on attitudes or behaviours. For example, scandals are often the media's bread and butter.[221] But what is a "scandal" in the first place, if not the violation of some moral code? It goes without saying that a scandal has significance only if a person has violated a universal moral code. But if there is no such thing as a universal moral code and nothing is forbidden, then logically nothing should scandalize us. Focusing attention on a "scandal" makes an implicit value judgment. Furthermore, we are told, more or less explicitly, that criticism of sexism, racism or gay ideology is forbidden. Forbidden, but why? Can such questions be seriously discussed? From which morality does the media draw such moral reprobation or sanctions? Which cosmology provides the basis for media judgments and "moral outrage"? Postmodern circles generally observe a studied silence on the ideological basis of their value judgments. If such matters were seriously and publicly addressed, postmodern elites would find themselves forced to reveal the ideologico-religious basis of their discourse and give an accounting. Their facade of objectivity would crumble. Their true role would be exposed to new awareness and to criticisms. No doubt the current situation has its advantages.

On a day-to-day basis, information sources addressing current issues in an "unsuitable" manner will find themselves "neglected" by the media. There is certainly no need to bring up accusations of "censorship" here, as one of the simplest and most effective tools available to the media is simply to ignore an "unsuitable" social phenomenon, intervener or opinion. This is a rather elegant solution, because if the media ignores a phenomenon, does it exist? If an abortion protest rally draws 140,000 people, but is not covered by the press, did it really occur? If a tree falls in a forest and no one is there to hear it, will it make a sound? When an issue or intervener cannot be ignored, one can always add more experts to the exchange, diluting any serious criticism. As a last resort, burying the audience in a confusion of opinions is always a useful option. For example, electronic media regularly calls on a multitude of experts and consultants of all kinds: astrophysicists, art historians, biologists, psychologists, sociologists, anthropologists, lawyers, etc. But typically one will not encounter individuals advancing a coherent critique of postmodern religion. To maintain this state of affairs, one need only check the source… If, on the other hand, an interview is actually done with someone challenging tenets of postmodern religion and does so in a convincing and logical fashion, then to avoid the more disagreeable fallout one can simply edit such material out of the interview and focus on excerpts where the interviewee seems less convincing or stumbles in his arguments.[222] Paradoxically, in the West it is very useful to gain access to "victim" status. Victims have the right to speak; they have rights and can make claims against others. They can demand JUSTICE! Obviously such status is not awarded on a whim, but in the long term is assigned by the highest authorities. However, such observations are not entirely novel. René Girard commented that (1999/2001: 161):

> Above one of the portals of many medieval churches is a great angel holding a pair of scales. The angel is weighing souls for eternity. If art in our time had not given up expressing the ideas that guide our world, it would rejuvenate this ancient *weighing of souls*, and citizens would have a *weighing of victims* sculpted over the entrance of our parliaments, universities, courts of law, publishing houses, and television stations. Our society is the most preoccupied with victims of any that ever was. Even if it is insincere, a big show, the phenomenon has no precedent. No historical period, no society we know, has ever spoken of victims as we do. We can detect in the recent past the beginnings of the contemporary attitude, but every day new records are broken. We are all actors as well as witnesses in a great anthropological first.

The dominance of postmodern media elites sometimes leads to conflictual, paradoxical situations. This occurs when, for various reasons, an event (or person) questioning the postmodern worldview cannot be ignored, that is to say is already known to the public or represents a well-known institution. In journalistic jargon, "it must be covered". If such events were not covered, sooner or later accusations of censorship would come to the fore. This is problematic because, although all ideologico-religious systems seek to marginalize critics, postmodern religion claims to be "in favour of" freedom of expression, but of course not just any freedom of expression... On the other hand, leaving free rein to an "unsuitable" perspective may give credence to a reviled position. Nevertheless, using one's imagination, there is always a way out of such dilemmas.

One can, for example, choose to cover the event, while eliminating any fact or comment giving credibility to the excluded perspective and focusing attention on anything marginal, irrational, outrageous, etc. among supporters of the despised position. The journalist commissioned by a media institution (and the research on which he relies) therefore provides the filter, an intermediary. While avoiding any appearance of censorship, nevertheless advocates of despised perspectives cannot be allowed to freely express themselves. This would pose too great a threat to the elites' ideological perspective. Barring stupid errors, this rarely happens. In general, the invisible work of editing efficiently silences those who do not parrot the goodthinker party line. In all cases, one must begin by sorting the information and determining what will be retained (and brought to public attention), and, secondly, what will be consigned to oblivion.[223] But since the system is informal and to some extent uncoordinated, the procedure is not flawless. As a result, from time to time, lapses do occur. In **Purity and Danger**, Social Anthropologist Mary Douglas explores the marginalization and exclusion process which applies just as much to household products as it does to desirable/undesirable concepts, events, cultural/ideological products, which are the raw material for media or academic production (1966/1979: 160):

> To deal with **dirt** first. In the course of any imposing of order, whether in the mind or in the external world, the attitude to rejected bits and pieces goes through two stages. First they are recognisably out of place, a threat to good order, and so are regarded as objectionable and vigorously brushed away. At this stage they have some identity: they can be seen to be unwanted bits of whatever it was they came from, hair or food or wrappings. This is the stage at which they are dangerous; their half-identity still clings to them and the clarity of the scene in which they obtrude is impaired by their presence. But a long process of pulver-

izing, dissolving and rotting awaits any physical things that have been recognised as dirt. In the end, all identity is gone. The origin of the various bits and pieces is lost and they have entered into the mass of common rubbish. It is unpleasant to poke about in the refuse to try to recover anything, for this revives identity. So long as identity is absent, rubbish is not dangerous. It does not even create ambiguous perceptions since it clearly belongs in a defined place, a rubbish heap of one kind or another.

The invisible process of information sorting out and re-formulation is of paramount importance because in this way media gains tremendous power of moral and cultural intimidation, channelling lines of thought. This process can take many forms, some of them amusing, as in the following anecdote, described by British journalist Malcolm Muggeridge on his first day at work at the Manchester Guardian newspaper (1979):

> I remember my first day I was there, and somehow it symbolizes the whole experience. I was asked to write a leader — a short leader of about 120 words — on corporal punishment. At some head-masters' conference, it seemed, words had been spoken about corporal punishment and I was to produce appropriate comment. So I put my head into the room next to mine, and asked the man who was working there: "What's our line on corporal punishment?" Without looking up from his type-writer, he replied: "The same as capital, only more so." So I knew exactly what to tap out, you see. That was how I got into the shocking habit of pontificating about what was going on in the world; observing that the Greeks did not seem to want an orderly government, or that one despaired sometimes of the Irish having any concern for law and order; weighty pronouncements tapped out on a typewriter, deriving from nowhere, and for all one knew, concerning no one.

When events or sources are not in conflict with postmodern core beliefs, they encounter fewer obstacles to being covered. The basic question is not to determine how effective this process of channelling thinking is, but whether it is indicative of ideological intent. The educated postmodern man or woman, with no external, coherent ideological or religious allegiance and unattached to any community, is most vulnerable to this influence. They have no outside reference point that would enable them to advance any substantive criticism.[224] They cannot "think outside the box". All they have left are fleeting emotional reactions and vague memories of cultural traditions of the past. In this connected generation, the more "plugged in" one is (in the age of the omnipresent gadget), the more likely one will be determined by and subject to media terms of belief! In a dialogue[225] about absolute moral laws, Kreeft has noted that the rejection of absolute moral law in the West led to an unintended consequence, the absolute conformity of the masses and the end of any serious social criticism[226] (1999: 74-75):

> **Libby**: … We liberals are always the progressives, and we're the relativists. You conservatives are always the absolutists. You've got it all backwards.
> **'Isa**: No, you have it backwards. If you're a relativist, that means you think values are relative to cultures, right?
> **Libby**: Yes…
> **'Isa**: So you have no universal law, no higher law, no higher standard than culture, right?
> **Libby**: Right. We don't claim to have a private telephone line to heaven, like you.
> **'Isa**: So you can't criticize your culture, then. Your culture sets the standard. Your culture creates the commandments. Your culture is God. "My country right or wrong." That doesn't sound like progressivism to me. That sounds like status quo conservatism.
> **Libby**: You're confusing me. You make everything stand on its head.
> **'Isa**: No, you do. Or your media do, and you've been suckered by them. It's a big lie; it's pure propaganda. If you just stop and think for yourself for a minute, you'll see that it's really just the opposite of the media stereotypes. Only a believer in an absolute higher law can criticize a whole culture. He's the rebel, the radical, the prophet who can say to a whole culture, "You're worshipping a false God and a false good. Change!" That's the absolutist; and that's the force for change. The Jews changed history more than anyone because they were absolutists — the conscience for the world, the Jewish mother who makes you feel guilty about not calling her, not calling on God, not praying. Or guilty about vegging out in front of the TV instead of going out and getting an education and getting a job and changing the world.
> **Libby**: Not fair! The relativist is for change too.
> **'Isa**: But he has no moral basis for it. All a relativist can say to a Hitler is, "Different strokes for different folks, and I like my strokes and I hate yours." The absolutist can say, "You and your whole society are wrong and wicked, and divine justice will destroy you, inescapably, unless you repent." Which of those two messages is more progressive? Which one is the force for change?
> **Libby**: OK, there is a problem here: How does a relativist generate moral passion for changing a culture without a natural law above that culture? I guess…

Oddly enough, one finds an echo of Kreeft's remarks in Albert Camus. Discussing Hegel's thought, Camus observes (1951/1978: 142-143):

> One of Hegel's commentators, Alexandre Kojève, of left-wing tendencies it is true, but orthodox in his opinion on this particular point, notes Hegel's hostility to the moralists and remarks that his only axiom is to live according to the manners and customs of one's nation. A maxim of social conformity[227] of which Hegel, in fact, gave the most cynical proofs. Kojève adds, however, that this conformity is legitimate only to the extent that the customs of the nation correspond to the spirit of the times — in other words, to the extent that they are solidly established and can resist revolutionary criticism and attacks. But who will determine their solidity and who will judge their validity?

Has deficient, incoherent logic become a virtue? In general, the media can easily stifle any criticism or serious questions.[228] If a politician or other public figure is found to be "displeasing", it is sometimes possible to destroy his professional credibility and render him impotent.[229] This can be accomplished by putting a magnifying glass on any negative issues or scandals, to portray him as an incompetent or an "intolerant extremist".[230] He then wakes up to find himself discredited, deprived of expression, struck dumb. Veith calls our attention to another marginalization strategy which may appear more "tolerant", that is, to push any discourse based on an absolute, out of the public square, into the "private world" (Veith 1994: 148):

> Dominant ideologies have often dealt with religious minorities by sealing them off into self-contained ghettos. Reducing religion to just another subculture is a way to marginalize Christianity, to silence its arguments ("You pro-lifers are just trying to force[231] your religion onto other people.")

Religious discourse targeted by such techniques thus finds its "freedom of expression" restricted to the private sphere. It must then learn to stay in "its place".[232] The public square has become off-limits. Ironically, this is often accompanied by strident calls for "tolerance" as the elites conjure up ghosts of minorities who might be "offended" by the targeted speech.

This marginalization process is particularly evident in the context of the origins debate. As a cosmology, evolutionary orthodoxy dominates the intellectual and institutional scene in the West, but postmodern elites must stay alert in order to maintain their cosmological monopoly in education. In French-speaking communities, there is little or no debate on origins. Centralization of the media and educational system makes it very difficult if not impossible for individuals in French-speaking communities to leave the trenches and challenge orthodoxy. In the United States and English-speaking nations generally, the situation is different, that is to say rather heated, as criticisms of the evolutionary cosmology are numerous and vocal. Court cases heard in the U. S. on the issue of allowing criticism of evolution in schools are commonplace. Advocates of the theory of evolution must then refine their strategies. In 2001, the NCSE[233] issued a note suggesting various methods of promoting the evolutionary position in the media. It proposed that its readers to send letters to the editor in the print media. Among the methods proposed, we note in paragraph 6 (Mendum 2001):

> Slant your letter towards the newspaper's style. Do not attack the creationists' right to advocate their beliefs when you write to a liberal paper — you might even want to include a statement that you support their freedoms of speech and religion, *when they are exercised outside of the science classroom.*

This is a rather instructive statement. It would appear that creationists have the "right" to criticize, to dissent, but only outside of science classes, where it counts… In short, "You still have the right to speak, but only in your quaint little ghetto." In actual fact, such vestigial "free speech" is bogus. And nothing is said about the ideologico-religious role played by the theory of evolution,[234] not a word. Postmoderns then "nobly" grant others a right to dissent, but it is a fake, empty right. Critics of evolution are then encouraged to learn to stay in "their place", as did (for a time) Jews in the Warsaw ghetto. Such strategies follow common epidemiological principles. During an infectious outbreak, it is crucial to keep the disease in quarantine until it has run its course. But there are also "infections of thought". If "diseased" thought patterns are isolated, in the long run they become ineffective and die out. Obviously, censorship is a strong word, raising emotional reactions that recall the Inquisition or Nazi book burnings. These are vivid images, but not relevant here. Postmodern censorship is different. It is implicit, "tolerant". It wears a benevolent, accomodating mask. It has properly grasped a lesson learned by Mao long ago (1957):

> We intend to use the policy of "opening wide" to unite with the several million intellectuals and change their present outlook. As I have said

above, the overwhelming majority of the intellectuals in our country want to make progress and remould themselves, and they are quite capable of being remoulded. In this connection, the policy we adopt will play a big role. The question of the intellectuals is above all one of ideology, and it is not helpful, but harmful to resort to crude and heavy-handed measures for solving ideological questions.[235]

In the context of orthodox concepts on origins, it is of course essential to ensure both that the evolutionary ideological monopoly remain in place in the education system, while at the same time maintaining the illusion of "tolerance". On the political front, in the United States, the elites cleverly wield the postmodern clause of the Separation of Church and State. Initially, this clause was drafted to protect religious practices by preventing the State from favouring a particular Christian church, as was common practice in Europe in the eighteenth-century when the American Constitution was written. Today, the postmodern elite (and its postmodern Dominicans, ACLU lawyers) exploits this clause when postmodern presuppositions are seriously attacked and excludes traditional religious discourse from any public debate.[236] Although the deliciously cynical Aldous Huxley seems to have misjudged the circumstances that would bring our new religious elites to power, in general he seems to have quite accurately anticipated our present situation in **Brave New World Revisited** (1958/2007: 393-394):

> Under the relentless thrust of accelerating overpopulation and increasing overorganization, and by means of ever more effective methods of mind-manipulation, democracies will change their nature; the quaint old forms — elections, parliaments, Supreme Courts and all the rest — will remain. The underlying substance will be a new kind of non-violent totalitarianism. All the traditional names, all the hallowed slogans will remain exactly what they were in the good old days. Democracy and freedom will be the theme of every broadcast and editorial — but democracy and freedom in a strictly Pickwickian sense. Meanwhile the ruling oligarchy and its highly trained elite of soldiers, policemen, thought-manufacturers and mind-manipulators will quietly run the show as they see fit.

Confronted with modern or postmodern aspirations for unlimited freedom, a cynical perspective is probably most realistic. Although Huxley foresaw many aspects of our current situation, it is unlikely he would have recognized the current state of affairs, as the forces involved are not linked to big government, but rather to informal associations and converging interests. No need to conjure up dark conspiracy theories, only factions whose activities are based in converging ideological and religious interests, ensuring the system's coherence. A critic daring oppose postmodern religion, whether in political, economic, ideological or cultural terms, must initially expect to be ignored and, if this is not feasible, then attacked, his credibility questioned, maligned and find himself marginalized. The more his questions disturb the postmodern elites, the more aggressive their reaction. His influence (potential or actual) undermines postmodern elites' ideological monopoly.[237]

Even in a context of official "tolerance", censorship can be tempting and may reappear under a new guise. It is odd to note when marketing the postmodern religion and facing a challenge by a speaker identified as "religious" or Christian, a recurring theme is the oppressively religious period of the Christian Middle Ages. It is important to understand here that in ideological terms modern, as well as postmodern religions are both reactions[238] to the Judeo-Christian worldview.[239] And to justify this ideological break, a dark past has its uses.[240] One could claim that the mathematician Bertrand Russell has proposed the canonical version of this metanarrative (1957: 20):

> It seems to me that the people who have held to it [Christianity] have been for the most part extremely wicked. You find this curious fact, that the more intense has been the religion of any period and the more profound has been the dogmatic belief, the greater has been the cruelty and the worse has been the state of affairs. In the so-called ages of faith, when men really did believe the Christian religion in all its completeness, there was the Inquisition, with all its tortures; there were millions of unfortunate women burned as witches; and there was every kind of cruelty practiced upon all sorts of people in the name of religion.

Oddly enough, David Hume, though admired by Russell, makes distinctions ignored by Russell and in some ways challenges modern stereotypes. In his essay **Of Superstition and Enthusiasm**, Hume discusses two trends in the Christian religion that he considers under the terms "superstition" and "enthusiasm" (1748/1910):

> My third observation on this head is, that superstition is an enemy to civil liberty, and enthusiasm a friend to it. As superstition groans under the dominion of priests, and enthusiasm is destructive of all ecclesiastical power, this sufficiently accounts for the present observation. Not to mention, that enthusiasm, being the infirmity of bold and ambitious tempers, is naturally accompanied with a spirit of liberty; as superstition, on the contrary, renders men tame and abject, and fits

them for slavery. We learn from English history, that, during the civil wars, the independents and deists, though the most opposite in their religious principles; yet were united in their political ones, and were alike passionate for a commonwealth. And since the origin of Whig and Tory, the leaders of the Whigs have either been deists or profest latitudinarians in their principles; that is, friends to toleration, and indifferent to any particular sect of Christians: While the sectaries, who have all a strong tincture of enthusiasm, have always, without exception, concurred with that party, in defence of civil liberty. The resemblance in their superstitions long united the High-Church Tories, and the Roman Catholics, in support of prerogative and kingly power; though experience of the tolerating spirit of the Whigs seems of late to have reconciled the Catholics to that party.

But the dark icon of anti-progressive and evil Christianity is still an indispensable part of postmodern mythology. The most useful and most referred to symbol in this regard, when reacting to traditional religion, is of course the Inquisition. There is no doubt that Christians have things to be ashamed of, but it is worth observing that the demonized Middle Ages is a rather efficient way to silence any reciprocal criticism of the modern worldview,[241] its consequences, values and ideals. What about the ideological sources of the Gulag, the Laogai,[242] and the scientific racism[243] of the Final Solution? Does anyone really care? Regarding these matters, much serious self-examination remains to be done, but can this be accomplished by those who share the same cosmology, the same presuppositions?

Additional evidence pointing to the fact that the modern is primarily a reaction to the Judeo-Christian worldview is the corpus of anticlerical journalism and literature in the West, particularly in French-speaking nations. In France, this genre goes back to the eighteenth and nineteenth centuries, while in Quebec it is mainly a twentieth-century phenomenon, reaching its peak during the Quiet Revolution (1960-1970). Obviously, this genre loses its critical importance once modern elites have gained control over the major social institutions in their respective countries. Once the opposition is effectively marginalized, the need for such polemic literature is no longer felt. In English-speaking nations, the genre sometimes takes the form of polemical debates or, more typically, satire.

The Structure of Scientific Monopolies

> Science, on the other hand, is characterised [by Horton] by an 'essen-
> tial scepticism'; ... Such a study reveals that, while some scientists
> may proceed as described, the great majority follow a different path.
> Scepticism is at a minimum; it is directed against the view of the
> opposition and against minor ramifications of one's own basic ideas,
> never against the basic ideas themselves. Attacking the basic ideas
> evokes taboo reactions which are no weaker than are the taboo reac-
> tions in so-called primitive societies. (Feyerabend 1975/1979: 297-
> 298)

Modern mythology presents the scientist as always neutral and objective, a devotee of empirical knowledge and, in the course of his research, evaluating all possible hypotheses, avoiding any bias. All in all, he is a "spiritual" being, living above common passions. In the best medieval tradition, he is an ascetic. Like the Stylite in ancient times, sitting on top of his column, he looks down on human life from his lofty vantage point. He is an apostle of reason, a bearer of light, one who knows. He is the destroyer of idols, taboos and superstitions. He is a shaman, a guru confidently showing the way to salvation; that is to say, to knowledge, gnosis and progress. This is the essence of modern discourse in relation to the scientist. But as noted above by Feyerabend, sometimes there is a flip side to this coin. Early positivists claimed that science must be free of all metaphysical presuppositions, but to be coherent this also requires excluding the metaphysical presupposition or statement that science must be free of all metaphysical presuppositions. This is an interesting conceptual paradox/trap.

Physicist Frank Tipler published a study (2003) discussing the peer review process in science journals. This process begins when a scientist submits an article reporting experimental results or a note expressing a view to a science journal. The first objective of peer review is to eliminate technical or methodological errors, plagiarism or duplication of experimental results already produced by other scientists. Tipler relates a little known fact, that none of the three major essays published by Albert Einstein in 1905 (one of which earned him a Nobel Prize) were subjected to the peer review process. At the time, almost all submitted papers were published. Of course things have dramatically changed since then. David Goodstein, Cal Tech professor of physics, notes (2002):

Peer review is not at all well suited, however, to adjudicate an intense competition for scarce resources such as research funds or pages in prestigious journals. The reason is obvious enough. The referee, who is always among the few genuine experts in the field, has an obvious conflict of interest. It would take impossibly high ethical standards for referees to fail to use their privileged anonymity to their own advantage, but, as time goes on, more and more referees have their ethical standards eroded by receiving unfair reviews when they are authors. Thus the whole system of peer review is in peril. Editors of scientific journals and program officers at the funding agencies have the most to gain from peer review, and they steadfastly refuse to believe that anything might be wrong with the system. Their jobs are made easier because they have never had to take responsibility for decisions. They are also never called to account for their choice of referees, who in any case always have the proper credentials. Since the referees perform a professional service, almost always without pay, the primary responsibility of the editor or program officer is to protect the referee. Thus referees are never called to account for what they write in their reviews. As a result, referees are able, with relative impunity, to delay or deny funding or publication to their rivals. When misconduct of this kind occurs, it is the referee who is guilty, but it is the editors and program officers who are responsible for propagating a corrupt system that makes misconduct almost inevitable. This is the kind of misconduct that is, I fear, rampant in all fields of science, not only biomedical science.

Of course such matters take place in a context governed by the Darwinian publish or perish principle. This system has developed to such an extent that in some fields, researchers are assigned a rating based on their research and publication productivity. This rating may affect their office size, research budget, even the mere existence of their job… But competition among scientists affects not only available space in prestigious science journals or access to research funds, it also involves competition between schools of thought. Sir Fred Hoyle, world-famous English astronomer whose cosmological concepts and theories on the origin of life have been the target of censorship, refers to the process of how ideas get filtered out in scientific publications (in Horgan 1995: 47):

Science today is locked into paradigms, … Every avenue is blocked by beliefs that are wrong, and if you try to get anything published by a journal today, you will run up against a paradigm [or model], and the editors will turn it down.

But it must be admitted that this is not a common situation, for the simple reason that few scientists actually submit articles challenging dominant paradigms and that not all fields of study tolerate competing paradigms (or theories). In an interview in palaeontology discussing the extinction of animal species in past geological eras, Stephen Jay Gould notes (in Glen 1994: 261):

I think orthodoxy[244] is enormously supported. In fact, I would make an argument — and I think that anyone who argues against this is not being quite honest — that institutions, universities in particular, are very conservative places. Their function is not — despite lip service — to generate radically new ideas. There's just too much operating in tenure systems and granting systems, in judgmental systems — usually older upon younger people [with] the pretenure needs to conform.

The philosopher of science James Barham has examined the restrictions and pressures contributing to suppress critical thinking in academia with respect to the reigning theory in biology (2004: 184):

I think the worst censorship we all face is internal — the fear of departing from the path approved by our peers. No matter how powerful the arguments against a viewpoint, it is very difficult for them to really register with us as long as we are living within a milieu in which alternatives are simply unthinkable. I no longer worked in the Academy, but I had been intellectually reared in it, and I remember well the intense discomfort I felt when it first occurred to me that the only solution to the problems with metaphysical Darwinism was to take teleology seriously.

When tectonic plate theory[245] became popular in the 1960s, some geologists complained that this new theory was being imposed in their field with rather inexplicable zeal. For example, up until 1983, a popular science book published by American geologist Donald Baars was sold in U.S. national parks. The author wondered if this theory was not more metaphysics than geophysics. He shares the following comments (1983: 217-218, 219):

The concept of the New Global Tectonics may be likened to a new religion; since hard facts are lacking, if one is not a believer one is considered an atheist with regard to the many theories and interpretations of the clergy, the oceanographers and geophysicists. Many of the concepts are plausible and exciting, and sometimes they fit the hard geologic facts. Many times, however, they are contradictory and totally incongruent with known geologic facts, at which time the facts are ignored. With enough faith, every known earth event is compatible with the religion, especially with respect to oceanography. On land, however, where outcrops and fossils abound, it is often extremely difficult to be a follower. The entire doctrine may in time be proven true, it may be completely disproven by geologists, or a compromise may be reached. I prefer to think the last possibility is likely.... [Baars describes some examples of contradictions.] It would require another book to argue fully the pros and cons of plate tectonics theory. It is obvious at this point that I have not been totally converted to the religion. That is a matter for individual preference. You are free to believe as you wish, but please, don't send missionaries.

When apostles of materialism defend the theory of evolution's ideological monopoly in the education system, claiming that this theory is "a fact", this turns out to be a very effective immunization strategy who's first purpose is shielding their theory from serious criticism. This is reminiscent of observations made by French sociologist and philosopher Jacques Ellul in connection with the phenomenon of propaganda (1954/1964: 370):

> Propaganda technique, moreover, creates a new sphere of the "sacred".[246] As Monnerot put it: "When an entire category of events, beings, and ideas is outside criticism, it constitutes a sacred realm, in contrast to the realm of the profane." As a result of the profound influence of the mechanisms of propaganda, a new zone of the forbidden is created in the heart of man, but it is artificially induced, in contrast to the taboos of primitive societies. When there is propaganda, we are no longer able to evaluate certain questions, or even to discuss them. A series of protective reflexes organized by technique immediately intervene.

Re-examined Fetishes

> An interdiction is addressed to the hero. (Definition: interdiction. Designation Y.) 1. (Y1) "You dare not look in this closet" (159)
> (Vladimir Propp 1928/1968: 27)

Galileo Galilei is one of the most revered figures in the modern religion's pantheon. Moderns sing praises of his development of the heliocentric theory of the solar system and his courageous opposition to the Inquisition. Galileo is seen as the ultimate archetype of opposition to obscurantism and religious prejudices rooted in an unscientific and authoritarian Christianity. A modern "martyr"[247] in the war between science and religion, Galileo is an icon around which revolve many modern stereotypes.[248] According to modern mythology, he was the first to give us a taste of the "forbidden fruit" of knowledge. But is this the historical Galileo or a repackaged version, a vehicle for modern prejudices or political correctness? Is the claim made that science is necessarily incompatible with religion true? Would the real Galileo stand up please? What would Galileo himself have to say about science and belief in God? Regarding the capacity of reason and logic involved in the study of mathematics, Galileo himself made the following comments (1632/1953: 103-104):

> I say that as to the truth of the knowledge which is given by mathematical proofs, this is the same that Divine wisdom recognizes; but I shall concede to you indeed that the way in which God knows the propositions of which we know some few is exceedingly more excellent than ours. Our method proceeds with reasoning by steps from one conclusion to another, while His is one of simple intuition. ... I conclude from this that our understanding, as well in the manner as in the number of things understood, is infinitely surpassed by the Divine; but I do not thereby abase it so much as to consider it absolutely null. No, when I consider what marvellous things and how many of them men have understood, inquired into, and contrived, I recognize and understand only too clearly that the human mind is a work of God's, and one of the most excellent.

In his letter to the Grand Duchess Christina (1615), Galileo justified the importance of direct observation and experimentation in his theories by stating:

> I do not feel obliged to believe that the same God who has endowed us with senses, reason and intellect has intended to forgo their use and by some other means to give us knowledge which we can attain by them. He would not require us to deny sense and reason in physical matters which are set before our eyes and minds by direct experience or necessary demonstrations.

Examples of such thinking, among scientists of the period, are commonplace. Johannes Kepler (1571-1630), the famous seventeenth-century German astronomer, discoverer of the elliptical orbits of the planets, rejected the old heliocentric Ptolemaic system. In **De fundamentis astrologiae certioribus** [Concerning the More Certain Fundamentals of Astrology], he observed (1601: thesis xx):

The chief aim of all investigations of the external world should be to discover the rational order and harmony which has been imposed on it by God[249] and which He revealed to us in the language of mathematics.

Kepler did groundbreaking research on the solar system. He was also aware of the materialistic outlook and rejected it in his scientific works. In **De nova stella in pede Serpentarii**, Kepler wrote (in Anonymous 1879: 210):

This star has God for its author, not chance, which is nothing. Nature has produced this star, that is to say, it comes from God, the author of nature. That the appearance of this star is attributed to the ordinary course of nature, it is nonetheless a result of God's initiative in determining the time and place of the apparition. What then is chance? It is the most detestable idol, which is nothing else than contempt of the supreme and omnipotent God, and for the work of his hands, a very perfect World, an idol whose soul is but a blind and reckless motion, whose body is infinite chaos. It is a sacrilege to attribute omnipotence and Creation to chance and eternity, things that belong to God alone.*[250]

Regarding the typical eighteenth-century scientist, the French Encyclopaedia Universalis observes (2003, entry on: Carl Linnæus):

With Linnaeus, as is the case with Newton, faith is not an obstacle to science. Religious conviction sanctions scientific research, it provides the presupposition of the unity and harmony of creation. That said, scientific discourse is nevertheless autonomous, implementing elements of rigorous positivity.*

Linnaeus (1707-1778) is considered the founder of modern natural history and the author of a classification system still in use in biology today. In his **Oratio de Telluris habitabilis incremento** [Discourse on the Increase of the Habitable Earth], Linnaeus notes (1744/1972: 29-30):

1. Not only divine Scripture, but also sound reason teaches us that we must look with amazement on the machine of the universe produced and created by the hand of the infinite Artist.
2. Indeed, nothing exists without cause and the idea of an endless succession of secondary causes is repugnant to a healthy mind. The First infinite, most perfect Cause, must put an end to the causal series.
3. Contemplate our very selves; consider all the animals and insects, think of the plants. These Works leave us in amazement and no human or limited art can imitate them. Neither art, nor genius can even imitate a single fibre of the endless tissues that make up each body. The smallest filament, in fact, shows the Finger of God and the Artist's signature.*

Since Linnaeus' time, advances in genetics have increased rather than weakened our amazement at the works found in nature. Actually, we have discovered further levels of complexity that Linnaeus or even Darwin could not have imagined. In the field of physics, few can rival Isaac Newton's (1642-1727) accomplishments. On this matter, Pierre Thuiller explains how Newton's work finds its basis in assumptions derived from the Judeo-Christian cosmology (1972: 46-47):

> Over time, Newtonian physics has emerged as the archetype of true scientific research, detached from religious or metaphysical speculations. But in fact, Newton based his work on Christian beliefs, linking the order found in nature to the intelligence of the Creator. The second edition of **Mathematical Principles of Natural Philosophy** is explicit: "This most beautiful system of the sun, planets, and comets, could only proceed from the counsel and dominion of an intelligent and powerful Being.... This Being governs all things, not as the soul of the world, but as Lord over all; ... He endures for ever, and is every where present; and by existing always and every where, he constitutes duration and space."*

Blaise Pascal, who lived from 1623 to 1662, was a mathematician, physicist, writer, theologian and philosopher. At a young age he developed an interest in science. By twelve, he had discovered on his own several theorems appearing in Euclid's Elements, a classic work in geometry. At the age of eighteen, he invented and marketed a calculating machine, a forerunner of today's computers, which was put to use for administrative and scientific tasks. He made many scientific and mathematical discoveries amongst which, the laws of atmospheric pressure and hydrodynamics, the arithmetical triangle and the hydraulic press. He did important research in the field of probability and in geometry was responsible for important studies on cones (one published when he was only sixteen). As an author, he wrote the **Pensées** and the **Provincial Letters**. In computer science, the Pascal programming language was named in his honour. In Pascal's view, the Christian God is more than a First Cause, as some ancient Greek philosophers and many deists among Pascal's contemporaries may have claimed. In his **Pensées**, he wrote (1670: s. VIII: 556):

> The God of Christians is not a God who is simply the author of mathematical truths or of the order of the elements; that is the view of heathens and Epicureans. He is not merely a God who exercises His providence over the life and fortunes of men, to bestow on those who worship Him a long and happy life. That was the portion of the Jews.

But the God of Abraham, the God of Isaac, the God of Jacob, the God of Christians, is a God of love and of comfort, a God who fills the soul and heart of those whom He possesses, a God who makes them conscious of their inward wretchedness, and His infinite mercy, who unites Himself to their inmost soul, who fills it with humility and joy, with confidence and love, who renders them incapable of any other end than Himself.

An influential nineteenth-century scientist, James Clerk Maxwell (1831-1879), was a Scottish physicist and author of the electromagnetic theory of light, also did work on kinetic theory and proposed the famous Maxwell's demon paradox in thermodynamics. Like many scientists of his time, he saw no contradiction between his Christian worldview and scientific research. Here is a prayer found in his personal effects:

O Lord, our Lord, how excellent is Thy name in all the earth, who hast set thy glory above the heavens, and out the mouths of babes and sucklings hast perfected praise. When we consider Thy heavens and the work of Thy fingers, the moon and the stars which Thou hast ordained, teach us to know that Thou art mindful of us, and visitest us, making us rulers over the works of Thy hands, showing us the wisdom of Thy laws, and crowning us with honour and glory in our earthy life; and looking higher than the heavens, may we see Jesus, made a little lower than the angels for the suffering of death, crowned with glory and honour, that He, by the grace of God, should taste death for every man. O Lord, fulfil Thy promise, and put all things in subjection under His feet. Let sin be rooted out from the earth, and let the wicked be no more, Bless thou the Lord, O my soul, praise the Lord.

Before the twentieth-century, this symbiotic relationship between science and Christianity was the norm, but since then the Enlightenment and modern propaganda have "buried" it, keeping such facts out of view. Despite this rejection of the Judeo-Christian cosmology by the modern perspective we sometimes bump into revealing slips in serious scientific texts, expressing strange implicit cosmic expectations. In these texts, we find the physical universe described using adjectives such as "hostile" or "indifferent". Now if one accepts materialistic cosmological assumptions, this raises a question: why should the universe appear to us as "hostile" or "benevolent"? British philosopher Mary Midgley examines the following statements by Steven Weinberg and Jacques Monod in relation to the universe as well as the implicit expectations that these Freudian slips reveal (1985: 87):

First, there is the tone of personal aggrievement and disillusion, which seems to depend, both in him and Monod, on failure to get rid of the animism or personification, which they officially denounce. An inanimate universe cannot be *hostile*. To call it that is to reproach it for not being the divine parent of earlier belief. Only in a real, conscious human parent could uncaringness equal hostility. Weinberg's mention of farce seems meant to imply the malicious callousness of such a parent, perhaps of one who leads a child on to expect affection and then rejects it. Monod seems to express the same unreasonable disappointment when he says that man lives on the boundary of an alien world, a world that is deaf to his music and as indifferent to his hopes as it is to his sufferings or his crimes. Certainly if we expect the non-human world around us to respond to us as a friendly human would, we shall be disappointed.

How is it that one finds amongst modern elites, even the most zealous and coherent, an irrepressible urge to anthropomorphize the universe, to give it personality and intentions? In the modern cosmological context, such expectations are incoherent, inexplicable. But in actual fact these lapses reveal once again the ideological function played by science in the postmodern West and oddly enough take us back to a primitive view of the cosmos, as described by anthropologist Mary Douglas (1966/1979: 86-86, 88):

> So here is another way in which the primitive, undifferentiated universe is personal. It is expected to behave as if it was intelligent, responsive to signs, symbols, gestures, gifts, and as if it could discern between social relationships.... The Golden Bough is full of examples of an impersonal universe which, nevertheless, listens to speech and responds to it one way or another. So are modern field-workers' reports.... To sum up, a primitive world view looks out on a universe which is personal in several different senses. Physical forces are thought of as interwoven with the lives of persons. Things are not completely distinguished from their external environment. The universe responds to speech and mime. It discerns the social order and intervenes to uphold it.

It should give us pause to consider these residues of anthropomorphism discovered in the modern context, a cosmology dominated by the rational and the material. These slips of the tongue (or keyboard) seem to be symptoms, but of what?

4 / Rites of Passage

Danger lies in transitional states, simply because transition is neither one state nor the next, it is undefinable. The person who must pass from one to another is himself in danger and emanates danger to others. The danger is controlled by ritual which precisely separates him from his old status, segregates him for a time and then publicly declares his entry to his new status. Not only is transition itself dangerous, but also the rituals of segregation are the most dangerous phase of the rites.
(Douglas 1966/1979: 96)

The postmodern elite's ideologico-religious power is typically implicit, but when power must be handed down to a new generation of leaders, it becomes more exposed to view. In any regime, the transfer of power is always a critical time. The election of a Supreme Court judge in a Western nation, for example, is typically an obscure bureaucratic process of little interest to the average citizen. This is unfortunate because this procedure can effectively marginalize individuals with politically incorrect views, and thus constitutes a powerful tool ensuring the ideologico-religious conformity of important Western institutions. This recalls, for example, Clarence Thomas' appointment as Justice to the U.S. Supreme Court in 1991. His previous public pronouncements on abortion[251] were the object of much scrutiny and controversy and almost cost him his job. Following one's accession to such a position, individuals must expect to come under pressure to insure they do not "defile" the status quo. Elsewhere in the West, this process is much less transparent. As a result such issues[252] are kept out of the view of the general public.

Malcolm Muggeridge (1903-1990) worked in the British media (print and electronic) for many years and felt that although the selection of candidates for positions of influence in the media does not involve explicit censorship or overt pressure to comply, the end result is nevertheless entirely predictable in ideological terms (1978: 51-52):

> From the lowest dregs of the media, like *Penthouse* or *Forum*, to the dizzy heights of Radio 3 lectures on Milton's politics or Dante's imagery, from *Steptoe and Son* and *Upstairs Downstairs* to Clark's *Civilisation* and Bronowski's *Ascent of Man*, through the whole media gamut, there runs a consensus or orthodoxy which is, within broad limits, followed, and in some degree, imposed. Certainly, any marked deviation other than in terms of eccentricity — the 'Alf Garnett' syndrome, for instance — is at some point, or by some means, disallowed. At the same time, there is every reason to believe that this happens of itself. People are not hand-picked for this or that job because they fall in with the consensus. Nor are they, in any way that I know of, pressurised to fall in with it in the course of their work. All the same, they are consensus-orientated, if not fixated. One way and another, I know a lot of people working in the media; on newspapers, magazines, in news agencies, in radio and television, and believe me, I should have the utmost difficulty in naming more than a handful whose views are not absolutely predictable on matters like abortion, the population explosion, family planning,[253] anything whatever to do with contemporary mores, as well as aesthetics, politics

and economics, who will not say more or less the same thing in the same words about say Nixon, or Solzhenitsyn, or apartheid, or Rhodesia.

Certainly the conformism pointed out by Muggeridge can be found far beyond the newsroom. Perhaps some may wonder, will explaining the widespread phenomenon of political correctness in the postmodern world inevitably lead to invocations of conspiracy theories? Is the present situation the result of collusion or back-room arrangements between these groups? Should we invoke a conspiracy by mysterious postmodern shadow organizations? As a matter of fact, this would be pointless. The logic of the phenomenon is actually quite banal. In his essay **Manufacturing Consent**, Noam Chomsky (with Herman) relates this question to ideological positions in media (1988: xii):

> We do not use any kind of *conspiracy* hypothesis to explain mass-media performance. In fact, our treatment is much closer to a *free-market* analysis, with the results largely an outcome of the workings of market forces. Most biased choices in the media arise from the preselection of right-thinking people, internalized preconceptions, and the adaptation of personnel to the constraints of ownership, organization, market and political power. Censorship is largely self-censorship, by reporters and commentators[254] who adjust to the realities of source and media organizational requirements, and by people at higher levels within media organizations who are chosen to implement, and have usually internalized, the constraints imposed by proprietary and other market and governmental centers of power.

Though in the context of their study, Herman and Chomsky are more concerned with political and economic issues, their observations are just as relevant in regard to broader ideologico-religious attitudes taken by media institutions. The question then arises: how does one ensure the succession of postmodern ideological elites in the context of an invisible religion? Like the choice of a cardinal or pope in the Catholic Church, the issue of an informal process of "natural selection" for candidates at the highest ideological levels of power among Western postmodern elites may be of some interest.

Given the informal and a priori invisible nature of this process, it would be unrealistic to expect a seamless, monolithic structure. In the media's day-to-day activities, a leak sometimes appears in the dike and unfiltered information gets broadcast, challenging the consensus. But such problems are quickly solved; as there are safe-guard mechanisms making sure things quickly get back to "normal". In any case, too much media uniformity would be boring[255] and would soon draw attention to and expose the reality of the situation. Chomsky comments (1988/2003: xii):

> It is well known and one can even argue that this is part and parcel of the institutional critique presented here that different media domains retain a limited autonomy, that certain professional and personal values influence media production, that the general political line is not always fully followed and that media can even allow itself a few deviations — some reports questioning the dominant view. It follows that some dissent can cover embarrassing or "inappropriate" events. The system needs to demonstrate that it is not monolithic, while at the same time ensuring that these marginal discrepancies do not interfere with the official consensus.*[256]

We offer here a critical view of media power, but this should not be construed as some sort of itch for a settling of accounts, nor the symptom of a more or less veiled desire to see media become subject to some 'conservative agenda'. As pointed out by Noam Chomsky, media plays an important role in the West, not only as a disseminator of information, but also as a check to state, corporate and even ecclesiastical power.[257] Chomsky observes (1988/2003: 298):

> We quite agree with Chief Justice Hughes, whom Lewis also cites, on "the primary need of a vigilant and courageous press" if democratic processes are to function in a meaningful way. But the evidence we have reviewed indicates that this need is not met or even weakly approximated in actual practice.

Like Chomsky, we think the media's social role as a watchdog of democracy is important relative to other major Western institutions, but that said, one must not overlook the fact that traditional (print) and electronic media now form a very powerful independent social institution, often serving its own economic, political or ideologico-religious interests. It would be perversely naïve to view the media as "neutral". In a context of buyouts and mergers, one finds fewer and fewer players in this field, a multinational corporation can accumulate huge market share and control traditional media as well as firms in entertainment and as a result media power becomes an even more critical issue. The State is no longer the only major social player. In the twenty-first century one should consider media (ignoring any distinction between news producers and pop culture producers) as the West's most powerful ideologico-religious institution.

One may also encounter a certain narrowing of views, when considering the expression of critical thinking in science. This conceptual homogenization occurs when the dominant scientific institutions consolidate what they deem "conventional wisdom". In his essay **Hunting Down the Universe**,[258] Michael Hawkins, astronomer at the Royal Observatory (Edinburgh), openly admits that this occurs in the field of astrophysics (1997: 29):

> Indeed, it takes almost suicidal courage to leave the herd and challenge the authority of the astrophysical establishment. Typically, papers expressing genuinely new ideas are refused publication by referees of reputable scientific journals on the ground that they undermine the generally accepted principles of physics. Those who persist in writing such papers are usually sidelined from the astronomical community by their peers.[259]

If one considers the American scientific community, an article by Larson and Witham (Scientific American, 1999) explores a related phenomenon. These two researchers[260] repeated a survey of American scientists by asking them questions about their ideological and religious views, for example, if they believed in the afterlife or in the existence of a personal God who hears prayers. A similar survey done in 1916 revealed that about 40% of scientists believed in the existence of God. Larson and Witham were surprised that when the survey was repeated in 1996 and 1998, the percentages were nearly the same. In a second stage, the researchers asked the same questions, but this time to a group of elite American scientists in the prestigious National Academy of Sciences (NAS). Among NAS members, 95% defined themselves as atheists or agnostics. This indicates that though among ordinary scientists, belief in God is already lesser compared to the overall U.S. population (where about 90% said they believe in God), when approaching the highest levels of scientific power and prestige, the modern religion[261] becomes utterly dominant and the marginalization of "undesirables", more efficient. Since the system is informal, a priori invisible, it is not necessarily omnipresent or monolithic and some "non-kosher" individuals may still manage to find their way inside this elite group. But such occurrences are not disastrous as generally such individuals learn to keep a low profile, keeping their beliefs to themselves for fear of offending modern or postmodern colleagues (and possibly see their research grants or careers affected). In an interview, one of the scientists questioned by Larson and Witham explained (1999: 91):

> In research universities, 'the religious people keep their mouths shut,' Stark says. 'And the irreligious people[262] discriminate. There's a reward system to being irreligious in the upper echelons.' Stark suggest that perhaps more NAS members are religious than think it politic to admit.

There is little reason to expect this situation to be much different elsewhere. In Europe, for example, it should be noted that modern religion has penetrated the culture quite deeply and for this reason large segments of the population have discarded the Judeo-Christian worldview, much more so than is the case in America. In Europe there now is a gulf between empirical science and theology and the latter cannot claim to influence the former. A German participant in an Internet forum on origins found the creationist view encountered in America strange, even incomprehensible. On this matter, he made the following comments:

> In Germany, Science and Christianity have reached a kind of concordat, a gentleman's agreement. Both groups ask (and answer) different questions and thus get along quite well. The pastor who taught me the Bible, before my confirmation, openly acknowledged the many contradictions and other problems in the Bible. I accepted it all without flinching, because in any case here Christianity is primarily a social matter.[263] One is a Christian because everyone else is.

This comment underscores the fact that in Europe, Christian churches have, over time, learned to keep "their place", and not trespass outside of the ghetto they have been so generously provided with. In Europe, the NOMA concept, developed by S. J. Gould (1997a), appears not as a hypothetical or potential arrangement, but as an efficiently enforced *fait accompli*. Note that when the modern ideologico-religious system became dominant in the West over the nineteenth and twentieth centuries, one subsequently encounters in all major religious traditions (Judaism, Christianity, Islam, etc.) influential figures and movements that have attempted to develop a syncretistic fusion of monotheistic moral principles with the materialistic cosmology, seeking thereby to appropriate its "scientific" prestige. The intent behind such syncretistic mergers was to avoid total capitulation to materialistic cosmology. These compromises have attempted to reduce intellectual and social tensions among monotheists confronted with a dominant and apparently irrefutable belief system. Such mergers obviously come with a price, a loss of coherence in the monotheistic system, but for those involved, a lesser evil compared to going for broke and taking a chance and losing all the aesthetic and moral benefits of traditional religion.[264] This strategy involves a secondary benefit, borrowing residual prestige from the dominant ideologico-religious system. As a result, one encounters theologians, rabbis or imams to whom labels such as "modern", "tolerant", "open", "liberal" or "progressive", may apply. In each of the major world religions one then observes influential figures[265] and schools of thought that have contributed or are contributing to such syncretistic mergers between monotheism and the modern belief system.

	Influential Figures	Schools of Thought/Movements
Judaism	Abraham Isaac Kook	Sionism, Reformed Jews
Christianity	Schleiermacher, Bultmann, Kierkegaard, Barth, Heidegger, Tillich, Teilhard de Chardin	Biblical Higher Criticism, God is dead theologians, Jesus Seminar
Islam	Khaleel Mohammed, Irshad Manji[266]	Kemalism (Mustafa Kemal or "Ataturk ")

When attempting to get postmodern elites to acknowledge the existence of filters used against candidates influenced by the Judeo-Christian worldview[267] as revealed by Larson and Witham, one encounters great reluctance to examine or admit such matters as this would call into question scientists' proverbial "openness". When asked about this by Larson, the philosopher of science and passionate defender of evolution, Michael Ruse, responded (see text in italics) with a certain ambivalence (Larson & Witham 1999: 93):

> Yet as an early member of the modern historical school of science, he cannot but see social factors influencing both disbelief among biologists and membership selection in the NAS. Do great minds tend to turn atheistic or do such academies welcome only atheists? *'It is a bit of both,'* Ruse says. *Overtly religious members would doubtless feel tension, especially if their beliefs were theologically conservative.*

One observes that scientists challenging the dominant cosmological perspective will be defined (or at least treated) as "unbelievers" by the system. As a result, they will then play a structural role similar to that of an individual accused of witchcraft in so-called "primitive" societies. In **Purity and Danger**, anthropologist Mary Douglas notes (1966/1979: 102):

> These people are none of them without a proper niche in the total society. But from the perspective of one internal sub-system to which they do not belong, but in which they must operate, they are intruders. They are not suspect in their own system and may be wielding the intentional kind of powers on its behalf. It is possible that their involuntary power to do harm may never be activated. It may lie dormant as they live their life peacefully in the corner of the sub-system which is their proper place, and yet in which they are intruders. But this role is in practice difficult to play coolly. If anything goes wrong, if they feel resentment or grief, then their double loyalties and their ambiguous status in the structure where they are concerned makes them appear as a danger to those belonging fully in it. It is the existence of an angry person in an interstitial position which is dangerous, and this has nothing to do with the particular intentions of the person.

One wonders if Isaac Newton, Blaise Pascal or Louis Pasteur were to come back, would they be welcome (and allowed to voice their explicit Judeo-Christian beliefs) in present-day elite postmodern scientific institutions such as the Royal Society or the NAS? Clearly, the selection process is at work not only at the highest levels of scientific research, but also in graduate studies. At this point, selection is sporadic, but still present. The choice of a thesis topic may have much influence on the type of relationship between the student and accreditation agencies as well as on chances of finding a job later on. Of course, an empirically oriented thesis topic, far from theoretical conflict zones and not calling into question important postmodern doctrines or dominant schools of thought, will cause less tension. But even in this context, the private beliefs of the candidate, if known, can add an implicit element of tension to the process.

When it comes to influential positions in a prestigious institution, the "natural selection" process becomes more rigorous.[268] This involves a paradox. The official view of course asserts that the ideological aspect of the selection process does not exist. When soldiers go to war, camouflage is used to make them invisible or difficult to see. In the same way numerous subterfuges (generally unpremeditated) will be placed at the postmodern system's disposal, ensuring that the marginalization of undesirable candidates will appear "accidental", a series of coincidences, the inevitable workings of a hierarchical system. Inevitably, it will be claimed, with much conviction, that only unbiased professional or administrative criteria are involved, even if the long-term results of the process clearly demonstrate otherwise.

A scientist who has learned to be "flexible" with his personal beliefs poses no threat to the system. He will be left in peace and may find his place. But the rigorous selection process undergone by candidates for positions of influence underscores the ideological implications of the scientist's role, both as teacher influencing generations of students and as a potential media personality (reaching an even wider audience).[269] It must be conceded that most scientists do not reach positions of great influence and therefore are never subject to such pressures or demands. In postmodern society, media scientists play a shamanic role, a role comparable, in general terms, to that of a priestess[270] of Delphi in ancient Greece, consulted to gain access to sacred knowledge. Obviously such comparisons will seem over-blown or exaggerated to some readers, but in anthropological terms the media scientist provides us with revelations from our civilization's highest epistemological authority, science. He provides our civilization the closest it has to Truth. Yes, a small word, but its influence is hard to overestimate. In this regard, the philosopher of science Larry Laudan observes (1988: 337):

> We live in a society which sets great store by science. Scientific *experts* play a privileged role in many of our institutions, ranging from the courts of law to the corridors of power. At a more fundamental level, most of us strive to shape our beliefs about the natural world in the "scientific" image. If scientists say that continents move or that the universe is billions of years old, we generally believe them, however counterintuitive and implausible their claims might appear to be. Equally, we tend to acquiesce in what scientists tell us not to believe. If, for instance, scientists say that Velikovsky was a crank, that the biblical creation story is hokum, that UFOs do not exist, or that acupuncture is ineffective, then we generally make the scientist's contempt for these things our own, reserving for them those social sanctions and disapprobations which are the just deserts of quacks, charlatans and con-men. In sum, much of our intellectual life, and increasingly large portions of our social and political life, rests on the assumption that we (or, if not we ourselves, then someone whom we trust in these matters) can tell the difference between science and its counterfeit.

If one were to repeat the survey done by Larson and Witham, but targeting social scientists instead, chances are good that views derived from the postmodern religion would be more dominant in this field. Compared with modern influence, no doubt that the degree of postmodern influence may vary from one field of study to another as well as from one social institution to another. Again, it seems legitimate to postulate the hypothesis that exclusion of traditional religions will be greater as one nears the core of elite institutions and positions giving greater mainstream media access. Among legal elites (such as Supreme Court justices), evidence suggests that the postmodern religion is dominant.

How the Game is Played

> ... since there is anyway no God and no immortality, the new man may well become the man-god, even if he is the only one in the whole world, and promoted to his new position, he may lightheartedly overstep all the barriers of the old morality of the old slave-man, if necessary. There is no law for God. Where God stands, the place is holy. Where I stand will be at once the foremost place... 'all things are lawful' and that's the end of it! (Dostoyevsky 1879/1933: book XI chap. ix)

> "Don't you believe in God?" she asked him. On Rambert's admitting he did not, she said again that "that explained it." "Yes," she added, "you're right. You must go back to her. Or else what would be left you?" (Camus 1947/1991: 208)

> They feed on the sins of my people and relish their wickedness. And it will be: Like people, like priests. I will punish both of them for their ways and repay them for their deeds. They will eat but not have enough; they will engage in prostitution but not flourish, because they have deserted the LORD. (Hosea 4: 8-10 NIV)

A little-known sci-fi novel entitled **The First Men** by author Howard Fast was published in the 1960s.[271] The narrative begins with an exchange of letters between a soldier and his sister, Jean Arbalaid, who is conducting child development research. Generous grants finance the research and Harry, the soldier, gets to travel around the world in search of unusual cases of child development, in particular children raised by animals. His sister Jean concludes that given the circumstances of their development, these children are hindered in their psychological development. A child raised with wolves becomes, in effect, a wolf. A child raised with baboons becomes a baboon. But the story takes another turn and the idea is proposed that this being the case, at the other end of the spectrum, there must also be children with above average intelligence who are held back in their development by being raised with normal (less advanced) human families. A project is then developed proposing to raise gifted children in a loving, ideal environment, that is a protected, isolated and controlled environment (Fast 1967: 21):

> We shall teach them **the truth**, and where we do not know the truth, we shall not teach. **There will be no myths, no legends, no lies, superstitions, no premises and no religions**. We shall teach love and cooperation and we shall give love and security in full measure. We shall also teach them the knowledge of mankind. During the first nine years, we shall command the environment entirely. We shall write the books they read, and shape the history and circumstances they require. Only then, will we begin to relate the children to the world as it is. … We are simply taking a group of very gifted children and giving them knowledge and love. Is this enough to break through to that part of man which is unused and unknown? Well, we shall see. Bring us the children, Harry, and we shall see. (emphasis added)

The first two sentences are of course laughably contradictory. Is it possible to speak of "truth" while at the same time avoiding any (conscious or unconscious) reference to a religion, ideology, worldview or myth? According to modern ideologico-religious thought, education is an important means of salvation, the path to utopia and progress. Following the French philosopher Jean-Jacques Rousseau, modern religion assumes mankind's innate moral sense, its basic goodness,[272] despite the fact that such assumptions are violently contradicted by twentieth-century geopolitics and daily headlines. Along with the concept of progress, the idea of man's innate goodness was one of the major (implicit) doctrines of the modern ideology that dominated the nineteenth and twentieth centuries.

A materialist perspective has its uses in science as it offers an framework[273] where one can study the law-like behaviour of nature to determine the boiling point of water, that of tungsten, the trajectory of Pluto around the Sun or of an electron around an atomic nucleus or the influence of free radicals on cardiac function. Using the scientific approach, one can obtain detailed information about the physical and biological world around us, develop bombs and invent ever more powerful computers, but if we look to the materialistic worldview (and its many derivatives) in order to identify standards with which to govern interaction between human beings, it offers no answers. Since the Enlightenment, the modern West has rejected the constraints of a Creator proclaiming absolute moral law, but if one looks at the logic of this rejection, it is clear that modern man faces profound contradictions as a result. Moderns demand to conduct their lives as they see fit, ensuring that no celestial busybody will breathe down their necks and tell them how to think or behave. Any absolute rule, in moral terms, is viewed as an intolerable constraint, to be gotten rid of at any cost. However humans cannot live long without any rules at all. One then arrives at a situation where the rules guiding interaction between humans are made, but have little basis other than arbitrary social convention.

In the West, the theory of evolution provided the origins myth legitimating this rejection of the divine Lawgiver. The theory is ideally suited for this purpose, a "natural selection" one could say and fulfils very specific ideological needs. Is it a coincidence that all copies of **The Origin** were sold out on the first day of publication? Maybe not. The publication of **The Origin** coincided precisely with a decisive change in religious and cosmological views in the nineteenth-century. A demand therefore existed for a credible materialistic origins myth.[274] Darwin himself was confronted with the consequences of his theory and the issue of morality in a materialistic world. In his autobiography, Darwin reflected on morality and offered the following thoughts (in Nora Barlow 1958: 94):

> A man who has no assured and no present belief in the existence of a personal God or a future existence with retribution and rewards, can have for his rule of life, as far as I can see, only to follow those impulses and instincts which are the strongest or which seem to him the best ones. A dog acts in this manner, but he does so blindly. A man on the other hand, looks forwards and backwards, and compares his various feelings, desires, and recollections. He then finds, in accordance with the verdict of the wisest men, that the highest satisfaction is derived from following certain impulses, namely the social instincts. If he acts for the good of others he will receive the approbation of his fellow men and gain the love of those with whom he lives; and this latter gain undoubtedly is the highest pleasure on this earth. By degrees it will be more intolerable to him to obey his sensuous passions rather than his highest impulses, which when rendered habitual may be almost called instincts. His reason may occasionally tell him to act in opposition to the opinion of others, whose approbation he will then not receive; but he will still

have the solid satisfaction of knowing that he has followed his inner-most judge or conscience.[275]

But what about in the real world? Does human behaviour confirm Darwin's views? Yes, yes, modern religion claimed that Reason would lead us to "enlightenment" and "progress", but weren't Hitler,[276] Pol Pot and Stalin all reasonable, consistent men, if one takes in consideration the premises of their respective cos-mological assumptions? Now if some apply the label "monster" to such individuals, is it possible that their intent might be to bury affinities between their own cosmology and that of these infa-mous twentieth-century political leaders? Is this a gratuitous assertion? Simone Weil made in this regard, a rather unambiguous comment (1949: 240):

> Hitler's entire life is nothing but the putting into practice of that conclusion. Who can reproach him for having put into practice what he thought he recognized to be the truth? Those who, having in themselves the foundations of the same belief, haven't embraced it consciously and haven't translated it into acts, have only escaped being criminals thanks to the want of a certain sort of courage which he possesses.

The "monster" label, as applied to Hitler and others like him, appears then to be considered "necessary" by some as they find it too offensive to seriously contemplate the logical consequences of cosmological consistency. Darwin, and his followers after him, sug-gested the hypothesis that morality is an evolutionary develop-ment, linked to adaptations to social life. But that leaves a lot unsaid, as based on the same premises it is just as consistent to say that a serial killer has also developed his own forms of adaptation to social life in that he takes steps (that seem appropriate to him) to satisfy his own particular impulses and needs. All this revolves around the more or less broad definition of the term "adaptation" that one is willing to admit. Such statements will obviously appear "offensive" and unjustified at first glance, but we will get back to this later on.

Evolutionary cosmology tells modern man: "You are the cul-mination of processes that have taken place for billions of years. Chance is your Father. Chaos is your mother. You are alone in the universe. Your destiny is to establish order as you see fit.[277] You can dispose of things in any way that seems right to you. No one will object to your demands. Natural laws will be your only limitation, but as your knowledge grows, one day your power will be absolute and even nature must submit to you." To this prophecy, one might add: "But you must know that if you can not attain the position of the dominant organism in your environment, know that the power of others[278] over you will also be absolute." Discussing values (and implicitly ethics) and the moral attitudes associated with them, the mathematician, philosopher and renowned atheist Bertrand Russell expressed the strict empiricist view, a commonplace in the early twentieth-century (1935/1997: 230-231):

> Questions as to "values" — that is to say, as to what is good or bad on its own account, independently of its effects — lie outside the domain of science, as the defenders of religion emphatically assert. I think that in this they are right, but I draw the further conclusion, which they do not draw, that questions as to "values" lie wholly outside the domain of knowledge. That is to say, when we assert that this or that has "value," we are giving expression to our own emotions,[279] not to a fact, which would still be true if our personal feelings were different.

It should be noted that Russell's position is fully consistent with materialist cosmology. As a result, moderns reject any knowledge that is not empirically based and deny its validity or value. Beginning with materialist presuppositions, here are a few conclusions arrived at by the great Austrian logician Ludwig Wittgenstein, in his **Tractatus** regarding moral codes (1921/1922):

> 6.4 All propositions are of equal value.
> 6.41 The sense of the world must lie outside the world. In the world everything is as it is and happens as it does happen. In it there is no value — and if there were, it would be of no value. If there is a value which is of value, it must lie outside all happening and being-so. For all happening and being-so is accidental.
> What makes it non-accidental cannot lie in the world, for otherwise this would again be accidental. It must lie outside the world.
> 6.42 Hence also there can be no ethical propositions. Propositions cannot express anything higher.
> 6.421 It is clear that ethics cannot be expressed. Ethics is transcendental. (Ethics and Æsthetics are one.)[280]

Wittgenstein is of course in agreement with Russell. In this context, morality finds itself without a firm (empirical) basis. As a result, it finds itself discredited, dumped in with the irrational and matters of taste. Other Western thinkers have given thought to this question whose conceptual genealogy can be traced back at least to David Hume. He seems to have been the first, in his **A Treatise of Human Nature**, to note that it is impossible to draw any ethical obligations from strictly empirical observations. Expressed differently, that which **is** cannot determine in any way what **ought** to be. No logical connection can be established between the two. This is known as the is/ought paradox. The question is: Is it possible to draw a moral rule from what is empirically observed? Hume observed (1740, Book III: part 1, s. 1):

> In every system of morality, which I have hitherto met with, I have always remarked, that the author proceeds for some time in the ordinary way of reasoning, and establishes the being of a God, or makes observations concerning human affairs; when of a sudden I am surprised to find, that instead of the usual copulations of propositions, is, and is not, I meet with no proposition that is not connected with an ought, or an ought not. This change is imperceptible; but is, however, of the last consequence. For as this ought, or ought not, expresses some new relation or affirmation, it is necessary that it should be observed and explained; and at the same time that a reason should be given, for what seems altogether inconceivable, how this new relation can be a deduction from others, which are entirely different from it. But as authors do not commonly use this precaution, I shall presume to recommend it to the readers; and am persuaded, that this small attention would subvert all the vulgar systems of morality, and let us see, that the distinction of vice and virtue is not founded merely on the relations of objects, nor is perceived by reason.

If, as modern religion asserts, empirical science is the ultimate epistemological authority and has no control over morals, it is logical to suggest, as do Hume, Russell and many others after them that morality, as it is without empirical basis, does not exist or, if it exists, has no real meaning beyond subjective preferences.[281] The silence of the universe becomes deafening... To say that only empirical observation is valid, as do most consistent materialists, is itself a metaphysical hallucination, as the statement itself has no basis in empirical observation. But these authors are good boys and generally do not have the ferocious courage or consistency of the Marquis de Sade,[282] who pursued materialist logic to the end, making a telling remark about murder (1795/1965: 329-330):

> What is man and what difference is there between him and other plants, between him and all the other animals of the world? None, obviously. Fortuitously placed, like them, upon this globe, he is born like them; like them, he reproduces, rises, and falls; like them he arrives at old age and sinks like them into nothingness at the close of the life span. Nature assigns each species of animal, in accordance with its organic construction. Since the parallels are so exact that the inquiring eye of philosophy is absolutely unable to perceive any grounds for

discrimination, there is then just as much evil in killing animals as men[283], or just as little, and whatever be the distinctions we make, they will be found to stem from our pride's prejudices, than which, unhappily, nothing is more absurd.

If in actual fact man has no immortal soul, if he is just one of the many animals that evolution has produced,[284] if he is just a walking piece of meat, why not butcher him? Why should that be "wrong"? And when the events of history offer power to an individual sharing the cosmological assumptions of Sade, the Final Solution and the Gulag become totally natural, consistent results. Within the framework of this fierce logic, the death of six million Jews in death camps and sixty million in the Soviet gulag appear little more than the boring details of History. Nothing to move us to raise our voices in indignation at the oppressors. Nothing either to foster our compassion for the victims. Indifference is the rule... As long as we are not targeted ourselves of course. Darwin, though a soft-spoken and well-connected English gentleman, despite dealing with the scruples of Victorian society nonetheless in a private letter clearly expressed the ruthless logic of his worldview when applied to concrete social circumstances (Darwin 1887: II):

> Lastly I could show fight [sic] on natural selection having done more for the progress of civilization than you seem inclined to admit. Remember what risk the nations of Europe ran, not so many centuries ago, of being overwhelmed by the Turks, and how ridiculous such an idea now is? The more civilized so-called Caucasian races have beaten the Turkish hollow in the struggle for existence. Looking to the world at no very distant date, what an endless number of the lower races will have been eliminated by the higher civilized races throughout the world.[285]

Nowadays who would dare express themselves so brutally saying: "eliminated by the higher civilized races throughout the world"! It is obvious that military power seems to be the only criteria establishing "superiority" in Darwin's view here. Such "compassion", such "benevolence"... In this regard, Nietzsche chimes in even more ruthlessly (1901/1967: 142):

> Through Christianity, the individual was made so important, so absolute, that he could no longer be sacrificed: but the species endures only through human sacrifice — all "souls" became equal before God: but this is precisely the most dangerous of all possible evaluations! If one regards individuals as equal, one calls the species into question, one encourages a way of life that leads to the ruin of the species: Christianity is the counter principle to the principle of selection. If the degenerate

and sick ("the Christian") is to be accorded the same value as the healthy ("the pagan"), or even more value, as in Pascal's judgement concerning sickness and health, then unnaturalness becomes law.... The species requires that the ill-constituted, weak, degenerate, perish: but it was precisely to them that Christianity turned as a conserving force; it further enhanced that instinct in the weak, already so powerful, to take care of and preserve themselves and to sustain one another. What is "virtue" and "charity" in Christianity if not just this mutual preservation, this solidarity of the weak, this hampering of selection?

One may find a grim echo of such "compassion" in Marx and Engels (in Camus 1951/1978: 235):

Engels, with the approval of Marx, dispassionately accepted this prospect when he wrote in answer to Bakunin's **Appeal to the Slavs**: "The next world war will cause the disappearance from the surface of the globe, not only of reactionary classes and dynasties, but of whole races of reactionaries. That also is part of progress."

Unfortunately the twentieth-century offered power to some who held such views and provided us with many demonstrations of such "progress". But doesn't the blood of the "kulaks" and many other counter-revolutionaries that died in the Gulag or the Chinese Laogai cry out for justice against those who made such statements? And if one turns to the postmodern worldview, although it is in part a response to the barbarities of the twentieth-century and to the ruthless logic of the modern religion and though it exploits the language of "tolerance", nothing is really resolved in ethical terms as it remains trapped in the same cosmological logic when it states that each individual[286] must develop his or her own morality. Therefore, all moral systems are equivalent, that of Amnesty International as well as that of Idi Amin Dada, Pol Pot, Stalin or the neighbourhood paedophile killer. If one compares the Judeo-Christian and materialist worldviews regarding their view of man, the contrast is stark. C. S. Lewis wrote in this regard (in Green & Hooper 1979: 204):

There are no ordinary people. You have never talked to a mere mortal. Nations, cultures, arts, civilisations — these are mortal... But it is immortals whom we joke with, work with, marry, snub, and exploit... Next to the Blessed Sacrament itself, your neighbour is the holiest object present to your senses.

According to the Judeo-Christian worldview, human beings, regardless of race, IQ test results, presence or absence of physical defects, presence or absence of a stock portfolio, have an inestimable value. The reason is simple because for the Jew or Christian a human's value is fixed once and for all given that men and women are made in the image of God. Moderns however have long since discarded such concepts. Russell, Wittgenstein and other moderns ruthlessly argue that since moral rules cannot be determined scientifically, morality is nothing more than the expression of the transient emotional states of the individuals promoting it.

In discarding the concept of an absolute law (and, of course, the related concept of a divine Lawgiver), the need to understand the sources of human behaviour remains. In the context of a materialist cosmology, since the human race is conceived of as produced solely by natural laws, as a result humans become slaves/subject to these same (biological and/or social) laws of nature. There is no escape. The need to explain and understand human nature cannot be avoided and only a cosmology can provide the reference points and assumptions needed to develop a coherent view of man. Determinism, in one form or another, becomes inevitable and biological determinism constitutes a fully consistent solution for understanding man within this cosmology. In **Mein Kampf**, Hitler addressed the issue and stated (1925/1941: 234):

> ... man will then never fall into the lunacy of believing that he has now really advanced to the position of master and lord of Nature, which the conceit of a semi-education brings about so easily, but he will then understand all the more the fundamental necessity of the working of Nature, and he will realize how far also his existence is subjected to these laws of the eternal battle and struggle in an upward direction. We will then feel that, in a world in which the planets circle around the sun, where moons ride around planets, where power alone is always the master of weakness and forces it into obedient service or else breaks it, there can be no special laws valid for man.[287] For him also the eternal principles of this ultimate wisdom apply. He can try to comprehend them, but he will never be able to free himself from them.

In the deterministic view, one can defend homosexual activity for example by claiming it is genetically determined[288] (the homosexuality gene). If one agrees with this logic, then one must accept that other less desirable forms of social behaviour such as paedophilia or Hitler's or Stalin's genocidal activities may also be defended and "tolerated" for the same reasons. Why accept the logic in one case and not in another? Might this be an "offensive" question? Probably, but if the logic of postmodern religion and the resulting consequences are too painful to postmodern awareness, they will be more easily set aside and forgotten by our generation.[289] Morality then finds itself reduced to nothing more than an ad hoc, arbitrary convention decreed by our elites on behaviours that, at present, serve (or disserve) their interests. In the postmodern setting, if one takes the case of a man whose wife was raped or a mother whose child was abducted, abused by a paedophile and found dead two months later, why should such individuals not yield to the urge to take the law into their own hands? Why rely on a transcendent, state-administered justice? Why should such a justice system, so slow, often so incompetent and biased in favour of the rich, have priority over that dealt by the individual? What justifies this priority? Postmoderns are content to let such questions remain unanswered and fall into oblivion.

In the West, a pathetic illusion reigns in major social institutions. There one encounters ethical judgments proclaimed with great authority, but never accompanied by any attempt at making their cosmological infrastructure or foundation explicit. This involves the implicit claim that it is possible to address ethical issues in the abstract, in a "neutral" fashion, in a vacuum so to speak, but there is a fundamental error here. Ethics is always rooted in a cosmology and has its basis in a worldview, a religion. Whether this link is recognized or not changes nothing. Avoiding such discussions or ignoring this fact does not change anything either. However one must understand the historical circumstances that explain this attitude on the part of our major social institutions. As we have previously noted, for centuries Christianity was the dominant worldview in the West,[290] sinking deep roots in the culture and as a result it was taken for granted that ethics, in its fundamental principles, was built largely on the Christian worldview.[291] Thus there was no felt need to establish the foundation of ethics, or to justify it. The whole matter of ethics was typically uncontroversial. Our postmodern elites have conveniently kept such habits, avoiding any discussion of the basis for ethics within their own worldview.

Today the situation is quite different. Explicit Judaeo-Christian views are typically derided if not despised in most influential Western social institutions. There is no reason to expect that technocrats will base their ethics on the Judaeo-Christian worldview. In this context it is then not only unwise, but also dishonest for bioethics experts to make grandiose pronouncements without very explicitly indicating which cosmology or religion provides their basis and justifies their opinions and recommendations. It would certainly put things in a different light if they did. But since many people have careers that depend on this illusion of "objectivity", it is perhaps inevitable that these issues will remain buried in the closet of post-modern consciousness for a long time yet. Professional "objectivity" demands this... And after all ethics consultants have to make a living too!

Medical Protocols and Fatal Distinctions

This was the political and social setting in which the stereotype of "the" Jew evolved and gained currency. The image of the "typical" Jew found in popular literature, even by such liberal authors as Gustav Freytag (Soll und haben [Debit and Credit]; 1855) and Wilhelm Raabe (Der Hungerpastor [The Hunger Pastor]; 1862), was not at all racially conditioned, a fact which later made it possible for many a good German who did not accept racist doctrines passively to accept Nazi anti-Semitism. Even in the preracist stereotype, the Jew was thought to be incapable of creativity and spirituality. He was the embodiment of everything negative which, under the heading "civilisation", was counterposed to the higher value of true culture". This discord between the inner "soul" as the basis of culture and superficial "intellect" as the embodiment of civilisation spelled the end of culture, according to the widely accepted ideas of Chamberlain and Spengler. The growing conflict between the reality of an industrial urban world and the poetic glorification of rural virtues, of the simple life, of irrational life forces, was linked to the repellent figure of the urban, commercial Jew. (Bracher 1970: 36)

Abandon all hope, ye who enter here. (Dante, Divine Comedy)

Consider the case of Dr. Eduard Verhagen, head of paediatrics at the Groningen University Medical Centre (Netherlands). Dr. V is a doctor at the vanguard of postmodern thought. He feels it is his duty to provide all available care to his patients, but when dealing with a patient for whom the most advanced medical technologies can offer no help, he says it would be better if doctors had the (legal) option to end such lives. These patients and their intractable pain are considered cases involving suffering with no hope of alleviation by medical means. In this regard, Dr. V has petitioned the legal authorities of the Netherlands requesting that euthanasia become an accepted, public practice, rather than illegal or condemned (in public opinion). He has also developed a protocol (Verhagen 2005a) providing a list of criteria or medical conditions that can be consulted by doctors to determine which patients should be treated or left to live and others which... One of the arguments offered by Dr. V in favour of such practices is (in Sheldon 2005: 560) "It's time to be honest. All over the world doctors end lives discreetly, out of compassion."

What exactly does this assertion mean? Would it be more meaningful or have more weight if it had been expressed in the following manner: "Let's be honest. All doctors in the world kill people, discreetly and with compassion. In fact, a survey conducted over a period of ten years, funded by the World Health Organization, found that all doctors in the world deliberately kill at least two patients per year." Or would the assertion be less credible if the reality behind Dr. V's statement was in fact: "Last year two doctors killed a patient deliberately. One was Dr. V, aided by a colleague." But this leads to a further question: Can one really come to a decision on such weighty issues based solely on statistical, bean-counting data? Certainly not. What kind of civilization makes such life and death decisions based on how many beads end up on one side or other of an abacus?

The obvious intent behind Dr. V's original statement is to mould the attitudes and behaviour of his fellow citizens. Taking this into account, the statement must be deconstructed, that is to say, consider it a moral or moralizing discourse and, as noted earlier, all moral discourse is anchored in and refers to a cosmology. But in our case, to which cosmology does Dr. V refer? What is the epistemological (or spiritual) authority referred as a justification of his claim? Certainly not Jehovah or Allah. He does not invoke Buddha, Voodoo spirits, Baal or the demi-gods of sports stadiums either. Nor does Dr. V invoke the teachings of Joseph Smith, of Zarathustra, the Upanishads, Ron Hubbard or the Urantia Book. No, Dr V is a modern and he has no moral compass other than empirical and social reality, the materialist cosmology[292] ultimately. The logic of his argument leads to the following conclusion: if a phenomenon or behaviour exists, then it is legitimate.[293]

This demands some reflexion. If a social phenomenon or behaviour can be demonstrated to exist, does that make it legitimate or acceptable? To understand the logic of Dr V's argument, one needs only to change the context of its expression. Following the logic of his statement, would we be more inclined to accept the following statement: "We must be honest, police officers around the world on a regular basis kill[294] the people they arrest, but discreetly and with compassion?" Even if it this were found to be confirmed by the facts, who in their right mind would accept the implicit legitimizing inference of such an argument? Would anyone accept it as a "moral argument"? Why then should such arguments be more acceptable coming from the mouth of a doctor and than from a police officer?

Of course, many historical or social facts can be adduced without in any way legitimizing the behaviour or attitudes involved. Dr. V's argument is then very poor, as it could quite legitimately be used to legitimize the behaviour of serial killers, paedophiles or genocidal despots. Consistency and coherence are things that most men aspire to, but they do not always like what they find once they reach their destination.

In general, the death penalty is applied only to the worst criminals. From a legal standpoint, the individuals targeted by Dr. V's protocol, people living with little hope, have done nothing to feel guilty of. They have committed no crimes. But from a postmodern perspective are they guilty on other levels? It is conceivable, for example, with respect to their families or to society, that these patients are guilty, because their suffering, viewed within the context of the postmodern ideologico-religious system (which states that this life is the only life and death is annihilation), is deemed empty? The temporal and emotional investment demanded of parents in the lives of these "hopeless children" is also considered to be in vain. These patients bring to light the fact that in the postmodern religion, some people will never find "salvation", as in most cases they are unable to enjoy the pleasures of sex, to consume and produce. Deprived of these faculties, the individual's life is considered "meaningless". Thus, relatives of such patients often agree with calls for euthanasia, as they too have accepted postmodern assumptions.[295] These patients expose, with their bodies, the limits of human existence. These patients are also "guilty" in regards to their doctors as they reveal/expose, in their bodies, the limitations of medical science and scientific progress. This is their "crime". Their very existence is a challenge to postmodern religion and to "tolerance". After all, what do we do with heretics? It seems it would be best, for "the greater good", to terminate them rather than have to deal with such physically and morally troubling issues.

In the postmodern context, the term "compassion" is typically empty, though it comes with nice packaging. Meilaender (2002: 28) examines the contrast between the ancient notion of sympathy and the postmodern concept of "compassion". He notes that sympathy involves a willingness to share the suffering of others and to enter the darkness of sorrow. The postmodern concept of compassion, on the other hand, means the will to oppose suffering itself. Postmodern "compassion" works at a distance and does not attempt to get close to the suffering. It involves the rejection of suffering (as well as those who suffer[296]) rather than attempting to find meaning in this experience. Since this cosmology promotes the individual's will as an absolute, suffering contradicts its principle of self-fulfilment. Suffering does not make sense in this context. It must be gotten rid of, at all costs…

No doubt this deconstruction does not exhaust the subject. What are the motives behind statements such as those of Dr. V? It would be revealing to explore this question. In this regard, an alert psychologist or psychoanalyst could examine Dr. V's underlying motivations. Possibly a look at his biography could tell us more about his views. Pursuing this matter, an economist might shed light on the financial constraints affecting the administration and medical practice in a health institute in the Netherlands (taking into account an aging population, etc.) Such factors can influence positions such as those taken by Dr. V. The subject is fertile. That said, the rhetoric used by the defenders of the Groningen protocol is steeped in high sounding moral and ethical terminology (Verhagen 2005b: 2355):

> The Groningen protocol was designed to motivate physicians to adhere to the highest standards of decision-making and to reduce hidden euthanasia by facilitating reporting. The protocol requires that all possible palliative measures be exhausted before euthanasia is performed. This requirement might do more in mobilizing the availability of palliative care services than the current situation of unreported practice.

Another aspect of Dr. V's statement ("It's time to be honest. All over the world doctors end lives discreetly, out of compassion.") is its inclusion of an implicit request addressed to society for approval and support. Implicitly, it is assumed that it is not "normal"[297] that physicians should be forced to euthanize patients in a clandestine fashion, in a legal grey area. Because physicians are important, prestigious people, all their activities should be supported or at least performed with society's complicity. The approval he seeks would allow euthanasia practices, which Dr. V assumes to be universal, to come out of the closet. Of course, we must believe Dr. V about all this.

On a subliminal level, these doctors are saying: "In actual fact we demand the death of these diminished people, these people with little hope, but we do not want to bear the responsibility or suffer the blame that would be associated with such acts, even on the basis our own medical code of conduct.[298] We do not want to have to deal with a guilty conscious, or disturbed sleep." But it is important to note that this request is part of a larger invisible conversion process to the postmodern religion, which involves the imposition, presupposition-by-presupposition, belief-by-belief, of a new ideologico-religious system. This conversion process though is implicit, not explicit, and avoids the open confrontation of the imam issuing a fatwa demanding the assassination of critics of Islam or that of the televangelist exhorting his listeners to "accept Jesus as Saviour". The postmodern conversion process carefully avoids such open and unambiguous confrontation and in particular moments of awareness that would expose it for all to see. Debates on abortion as well as on homosexuality and gay marriage, just to name a few, are also part of this covert ideologico-religious transformation process.

Although eugenic concepts such as "inferior or superior races" are now condemned in the West, variations in physical and intellectual capacity nonetheless exist between humans and if one has only the Darwinian cosmology as a reference point (where "fitness" is a critical issue), it is not inconsistent to consider these differences as significant or decisive. It is ironic that the only obstacle to the widespread application of such logic is the Judeo-Christian concept stating that all men are made in God's image and therefore deserving the same respect. The new postmodern eugenics is no longer expressed with tainted terms such as "more or less pure races",[299] but nonetheless remains caught in the same logic demanding an assessment of humans based on their (actual or potential) intellectual, economic or physical contribution to life and their capacity for "self-fulfilment".

Relativity and Relativism

> *But of course you must understand that rules of that sort, however excellent they may be for little boys — servants — and women —and even people in general, can't possibly be expected to apply to profound students and great thinkers and sages. No, Digory. Men like me who possess hidden wisdom, are freed from common rules just as we are cut off from common pleasures. Ours, my boy, is a high and lonely destiny. (Lewis 1955/1970: 18)*

> *Thrasymachus, suppose I say that you have proved that you are right, that you have convinced me that morality is only a man-made thing, but I am going to bow down to it anyway and worship it as if it were the voice of God, and I will feel guilty whenever I transgress it, and I shall teach others to do the same. What would you say about me then?"*
> *"That you are a fool, Socrates. And a lying fool at that."*
> *"So, I would then be* **wrong***? Really wrong?"*
> *"Uh-oh. There's that word again."*
> *"See? If, as you hold, there is nothing right or wrong but thinking makes it so, then I think it's not really wrong to be dishonest and lie and to teach that to others, then it's not really wrong. So why are you so 'judgmental' against me now for my being 'judgmental'? Why are you preaching if you have no faith? " (Kreeft 1996: 77)*

In **Esthétiques de la postmodernité** (or Postmodern Æsthetics), Caroline Guibet-Lafaye[300] reviews and establishes reference points shedding light on the context of postmodern art as it has developed. Guibet-Lafaye draws our attention to some of the implications of postmodernism, implications affecting not only art, but ethical and moral reflection in the postmodern context as well (2000: 4):

The dissolution of the grand narratives [in the West] and their proposed standards, the downfall of modernist illusions have resulted in a growing empowerment of the individual. The end of the grand narratives opens the door to individualism. The rejection of reason, as a universal [principle], sets up the individual as the ultimate purpose of everything. Individualism expresses and coincides with the trend towards heterogeneity and plurality, which are specific to postmodernism. It values differences and peculiarities, and the equivalent legitimacy [of all statements]. The demand for increased freedoms and rights reflects the empowerment of the individual. The dissolution of traditional values is replaced by a single value, "our right to decide for ourselves what we want." This freedom of choice entails, ultimately, the right to choose our own criteria of truth. The dissolution of traditional values is also that of metaphysical values. Postmodern individualism rejects any imposed values or authority[301] as well as any norms.*

Postmodern societies promote "tolerance". Tolerance of views and tolerance of biological impulses. "Judging" others is prohibited. It is forbidden to forbid... Anthropologists and ethnologists were among the first to go to bat on this matter. The appropriate technical expression in the social science in this regard is "cultural relativism". This concept, which had its heyday before World War II, involves the rejection in principle of any imposition of one group's values (typically Western) on individuals of another cultural group (as well as on more marginal groups in the West). This implies that, in their original cultural context, all legal codes and ethical systems are equivalent. No nation or people can claim to possess a concept of good and evil that is absolute, universal or superior to others. This attitude obviously applies to Western colonial activities during the eighteenth and nineteenth centuries as well as to missionary groups seeking to advance the cause of Christianity, but there is no reason, in logical terms, to avoid extending this principle to other matters as well. With such views, the anthropologist doing fieldwork for example in a tribe deep in the jungle is also supposed to refrain from making any value judgments at all on the rules of interaction between individuals in non-Western societies.

But even in social science research, things don't always go as planned. Circumstances sometimes lead to a crisis, exposing the deep contradictions between various postmodern assumptions, contradictions that typically go unnoticed. Here is an instructive example. While doing fieldwork,[302] anthropologists rely on informants to provide insight into the culture under study. But some informants are more knowledgeable than others and these are called key informants, serving as experts that the researcher consults on a more frequent basis to understand deeper aspects of this culture that is so different. In this context, relationships of sympathy and friendship often form between the researcher and the informant. This is the case in the quote below. In this particular situation, the authors did fieldwork among the Sambia of Papua New Guinea and the informant is a woman designated by the pseudonym "P". In this context, the rules governing interaction between humans in the society under study shed light on prob-

Rites of Passage

lems that arise when applying a coherent relativistic view to the real world. (Herdt et al. 1990: 200):

> In P.'s case, we wondered, before we left the Valley, whether, when her husband died, some of the men, within the bounds of their customs, would kill her for being an uppity, disruptive female. Was it our business to prevent her murder, and in doing so, inflict on these people our alien morality? When we decided, to hell with it — we were going to protect her by warning them not to kill her or even beat her senseless — **we knew we were indulging ourselves**. In doing so, we perhaps saved her but pushed our friends one step further on the road to unforeseeable cultural change. (emphasis added)

For the anthropologist or the postmodern that has bought into the relativistic revelation, questioning or "judging" customs or cultural practices outside the West becomes, to some extent, heresy, behaviour subject to censorship by the anthropological community, taboo behaviour to be avoided. Under the anthropological community's (unwritten) rules of behaviour, the authors acknowledge their "guilt". But there are two levels of relativism. The first is explicit and targets, in actual fact, beliefs or practices regarded as having little value by the relativist. This relativism primarily focuses on beliefs the relativist does not share, namely those of others! As we have seen in the example above, circumstances may unmask such lazy relativism and expose the non-relative assumptions underlying postmodern cosmology. Hard-core relativism, that is to say absolute relativism, is little more than a theoretical concept. Regarding relativism's two faces, C. S. Lewis noted (1943/1978: 22):

> Their scepticism about values is on the surface: it is for use on other people's values; about the values current in their own set they are not nearly sceptical enough. And this phenomenon is very usual. A great many of those who 'debunk' traditional or (as they would say) 'sentimental' values have in the background values of their own which they believe to be immune from the debunking process.

If one carefully examines the quote by Herdt above, it is clear that these anthropologists fully realized they were violating an implicit taboo in social anthropology, that is to never change or challenge the customs or values of a society that they are studying. But Herdt et al state they dared to defy the relativistic taboo and proceeded to impose their Western values. What then is the source of such postmodern snobbery and moral superiority? In the final analysis, this must be linked to leftovers, residues of a worldview long rejected. Given the dominant cosmological presuppositions in Darwinian discourse, it is then totally incoherent to talk about behaviour that is not "natural". Everything is natural (if it occurs). That the authors mentioned above freely admit to having "indulged themselves" in warning the men of the valley not to attack the woman (referred to as "P"), highlights the fact that they recognize (at least at a subconscious level) that their relativism renders such an intervention or judgment unjustifiable. As a result, their intervention/judgment becomes completely irrational, as it cannot be motivated or justified in the cosmological context in which they operate. Their only reference point regarding moral ethics is a reaction, for the most part emotional, to a particular situation. But social pressure[303] and the erosion of time can easily overturn such a reaction.[304] Unless reinforced, ethical emotions eventually dissipate and indifference sets in. Like the wind, it is soon gone. But one should not get too worked up about such matters. The statements above do not specifically target Herdt et al, as there is strong evidence that the average relativist, either in the field or in everyday life, behaves much the same way.[305]

Cultural or moral relativism, in feminist anthropology, leads to a similar ethical cul-de-sac. Real dilemmas appear. In many non-Western cultures the subordinate status of women is often seen as natural or normal and a rebellious woman can be publicly beaten by her husband. In this case, one may ask: "Do we have the right to preach the "Good News" of the Western feminist perspective of gender relations to non-Western societies?" If the answer is yes, then this course of action must be justified. One should be aware of the fact that this involves the sacrifice of the cultural relativism concept. And if one sacrifices cultural relativism, on what basis does one justify this rejection? If some consider it necessary to impose a universal value on non-Western societies, to which cosmology will one appeal to justify this recourse? Are women's rights truly universal and absolute or, as assumed by relativistic postmodern religion, legitimate only in their original cultural context? This is no small matter. Can Western postmodernism, which asserts the principle of relativism, consistently oppose for example, excision rites performed on young girls in Africa or the sex trade involving minors in Thailand or elsewhere? If these practices are to be opposed, on what moral basis can this be done while avoiding incoherence in logical and cosmological terms? There is no lack of sticky questions.

Conceptions of human rights find their basis in a society's moral code and a society's moral code in turn finds its basis in the cosmology of this society. In ideologico-religious terms, everything is connected. It is interesting to note that in the West, where the Judeo-Christian worldview was dominant for so many centuries, this resulted in a situation where morality was taken for granted, set in stone so to speak. But as Hume pointed out morality is never "given" or "natural". Ethics becomes possible, for societies and individuals, when they have, (more or less consciously) committed to and invested in a cosmology. In a study on relationships between the West and Islam, Ernest Gellner explores another facet of relativistic schizophrenia. He notes that absolutes promoted non-Western societies are effortlessly tolerated by postmodern elites, but in their own backyard, it is another matter entirely (1992/1999: 84):

> The relativists in turn direct their attack only at those they castigate as *positivists*, i.e. non-relativists within their own Enlightened tradition, but play down the disagreement which logically separates them from religious fundamentalism [Islam]. Their attitude is, roughly, that absolutism is to be tolerated, if only it is sufficiently alien culturally. It is only at home that they do not put up with it.

There is another aspect to differing reactions among postmoderns to assertions of the absolute, inside or outside the West. At face value, this schizophrenia will seem incomprehensible, even irrational, unless one considers the fact that modern and postmodern belief systems are largely reactions to the Judeo-Christian heritage.[306] This explains rather well the different attitudes noted by Gellner. In relation to other major world religious traditions, one might even actually consider these two currents (modern and postmodern) as Christian heresies, given the many residual Judeo-Christian concepts they carry around in their cultural baggage (some of which we have pointed out, here and there, in this text). In their attitude vis-à-vis Christianity (and Judaism at times) both, in different ways, pursue Voltaire's famous phrase: « Écrasez l'infâme! ».[307]

If one considers modern and postmodern ideologico-religious systems primarily as reactions to Christianity,[308] this observation explains the contrasting attitudes among postmodern elites in the West towards Islam and Christianity. With blunt irony Gellner adds (1992/1999: 73-74):

Next, there is a movement which denies the very possibility of extra-neous validity and authority. Admittedly, it is specially insistent in this denial, when the contrary affirmation of such external validation comes from fellow-members, non-relativists *within their own society*. Relativist pudeur and ex-colonial guilt expiation on the other hand inhibit stress-ing the point to members of *other* cultures. The absolutism of *others* receives favoured treatment, and a warm sympathy which is very close to endorsement. (…) The relativist endorses the absolutism of others, and so his relativism entails an absolutism which also contradicts it. Let us leave him with that problem: there is no way out of it.

The contradictions and paradoxes of relativism are issues of interest not only to philosophers and anthropologists, but give rise to very serious questions on the international stage. Several post-modern scholars consider, for example, the concept of human rights as little more than a Western construct, the product of a particular historical context.[309] The implications of this a view for organizations advocating women's rights in the world are signifi-cant. In the Muslim world, this issue is a particularly thorny one. Many societies influenced by Islam reject the requests/demands of Western agencies promoting women's rights by saying they have their own criteria to handle gender issues (Sharia law) and as a result are not accountable to Western morality. In the 1970s and 80s, the Afrikaner regime in South Africa defended apartheid using similar logic. It argued that apartheid practices were legitimate in the South African culture and in this context there was no need for imposed foreign concepts. A rather postmodern attitude…

In the West, the concept of human rights has a long tradition which is embodied in the British Magna Carta, the French Revolution's Declaration of the Rights of Man and of the Citizen or the principles of the American Declaration of Independence. In nations where Islam is dominant, the law usually[310] relies instead on the Koran and the standards set by the utterances and example of the Prophet. State policy is therefore directly rooted in cosmology. It should come to as surprise then that based on these sacred texts, Muslim states defend their own customs as legitimate. In fact, they are just being consistent within their worldview and demonstrate their desire to protect these supreme values. Attempts to separate religion and law in Muslim states, in order to marginalize the reli-gious texts, are viewed as impossible by many. Islam recognizes no other law than its own as the Sharia legal code is an integral part of this system of religious and moral rules.[311]

Except for the situation in France,[312] as noted by Gellner, Islam is not usually the target of marginalization by elites in the West, which is consistent with postmodern discourse on traditional religious institutions. It is certainly not the target of restrictions or marginalization as is the case of non-Muslim religions in Islamic countries.[313] In a worst-case scenario, non-Muslim religions in Islamic countries are actively persecuted; at best, their activities are subject to various administrative restrictions. Proselytizing is generally illegal. Given these conflicts in values when postmodern culture collides with other cultures, how can one avoid saying (implicitly or explicitly, it does not matter) to others that Westerners have the Truth and others must submit to our conception of things as superior or better, particularly the Western (postmodern) perspective on gender relations! Faced with this kind of paradox, the following is a solution proposed by postmodern organizations regarding the status of women in Iran under the ayatollahs. Kristin J. Miller[314] notes (1996):

> Women in Iran suffer human rights abuses at the hands of their government every day. While the international community has attempted to hold Iran accountable under international law, those attempts have failed. The Iranian government argues it is not bound by international law because its culture and religion permit Iran to treat women according to its own standards. This comment proposes a solution that incorporates aspects of both universalism and relativism to lessen Iran's violations of women's human rights. This solution, the grass roots method, combines universalist ideals with relativist strategies in order to give universalism cultural legitimacy in Iran.

How ironic that one should play the relativistic game, exploiting local beliefs, but all the while with the avowed aim of promoting absolutist objectives! In marketing terms, this approach is wickedly cunning. The bottom line is in fact to assert absolute values by resorting to astonishing, high-sounding hypocrisy to avoid this becoming too obvious. This leads to a paradox, a trap, from which few, even among the great, can extricate themselves. In this regard, for example, French philosopher Jean-Paul Sartre found himself in an impasse both grotesque and tragic[315] (de Beauvoir 1981: 551-552):

> S. B. - What do you think about Dostoyevsky's statement: "If God does not exist, anything goes." Do you agree?
> JP S. - In a sense, I can see what he means, and in the abstract it is true, but in another sense I can see that to kill a man is bad. It is inherently, absolutely bad, bad for another man [to do so], but of course it is not

bad for an eagle or a lion, but bad for a man. I consider, if you will, morality and man's moral activity as an absolute in the relative.*[316]

But faced with such hazy, uncertain ethical principles, reality imposes its own laws, typically economic. Google is, at the time of writing, the most popular search engine on the Internet. It has had a reputation of avoiding questionable business practices such as pop-ups, banners and other forms of conspicuous and irritating advertising. In September 2002 the Chinese government, concerned about Internet access in China to documents critical of its policies, blocked access to Google. Representatives from Google immediately contacted the Chinese government and four days later access was restored. At least this seemed to be the case. Journalist Josh McHugh notes (2003: 133) that following this event, a Chinese web surfer doing a Google search on "Falun Gong" or "human rights in China" would be directed to a page of apparently normal search results, except that if the user actually clicked on a link, a government-approved page would be offered to him instead of the sought-for page or he might simply be denied access to Google for an hour or two (with possibly a note added to his state police file?). When McHugh asked Sergey Brin, Google's co-founder, if this was a coincidence, Brin's only response was to say that Google hadn't changed anything on its servers. Right...

When dealing with human rights issues in China, most Western countries adopt a realpolitik approach (fully consistent with the postmodern religion) where access to the Chinese market dictates policy. Measures against human rights violations in China are generally limited to minor protests made through diplomatic channels. None of the G8 nations are seriously considering sanctions similar to the economic boycott declared against South Africa in the 1980s in relation to the apartheid system. The fear that competitors might get into China first and pick up lucrative contracts quickly silences any scruples with regard to political and religious human rights violations in that country. The mantra is endlessly repeated that the Chinese market is too important... In **The Rebel,** Camus[317] explored some of the consequences of relativism, which are at the heart of the postmodern religion (1951/1978: 5):

> But, for the moment, this train of thought yields only one concept: that of the absurd. And the concept of the absurd leads only to a contradiction as far as the problem of murder is concerned. Awareness of the absurd, when we first claim to deduce a rule of behaviour from it,

makes murder seem a matter of indifference, to say the least, and hence possible. If we believe in nothing, if nothing has any meaning and if we can affirm no values whatsoever, then everything is possible and nothing has any importance. There is no pro or con: the murderer is neither right nor wrong. We are free to stoke the crematory fires or to devote ourselves to the care of lepers. Evil and virtue are mere chance or caprice.... Finally, we may propose to embark on some course of action, which is not entirely gratuitous. In the latter case, in that we have no higher values[318] to guide our behavior, our aim will be immediate efficacy. Since nothing is either true or false, good or bad, our guiding principle will be to demonstrate that we are the most efficient — in other words, the strongest. Then the world will no longer be divided into the just and the unjust, but into masters and slaves. Thus, whichever way we turn, in our abyss of negation and nihilism, murder has its privileged position.

I suppose one should nonetheless be grateful that in general postmoderns are rarely very coherent in their beliefs. In the postmodern context, how does one justify calls for "tolerance"[319] (which implies a vague love or at least respect for those whose opinions or behaviours differ from those of the majority) while rejecting any absolute moral law? If good and evil are strictly relative matters, questions that only the individual can decide, how can one even demand tolerance of others? What is the basis for this demand? This is a fundamental issue. Why should it be said that tolerance is "necessary" in society? In other words, in the name of which absolute principle does one demand that the intolerant abandon their intolerance?[320] We find ourselves floundering in the most absolute contradictions! Kreeft notes (1994: 74) that relativism leads to an embarrassing inconsistency. The relativist claims that no culture can claim to be universal or superior to others. Strangely, relativism finds itself in opposition to all the cultures of Antiquity (as well as many contemporary ones) that rejected postmodern relativism. Yet, on the other hand the West, which accepts relativism, implicitly declares itself (and its ideological serfs) superior to these cultures[321].

Not surprisingly, in the nineteenth-century Dostoyevsky had already foreseen the difficulties involved with developing ethics in the context of a materialistic cosmology. In his novel **The Possessed**, Dostoyevsky perceived (before Russell and Wittgenstein) the inability of the empirical to produce ethics as well as the ideological role to be played by science later on in the West (1872/1971: 257):

Reason has never been able to define good and evil or even to separate good from evil, not even approximately;[322] on the contrary, it had always mixed them up in a most pitiful and disgraceful fashion; as for science, its solutions have always been based on brute force. This was particularly true of that half-science, that most terrible scourge of mankind, worse than pestilence, famine, or war, and quite unknown till our present century. Half-science is a despot such as has never been known before. A despot that has its own priests and slaves, a despot before whom everybody prostrates himself with love and superstitious dread, such as has been quite inconceivable till now, before whom science itself trembles and surrenders in a shameful way.

It would be an understatement to allow that the twentieth-century has massively confirmed Dostoyevsky's views. If one explores ethical thought within the framework of postmodernism, inevitably the question must be asked: "If nature is often cruel, why would we not be as well?" In the West, the dilemma is how to build a system of rules with which to manage human behaviour (that is to say a moral code) in the context of a materialist cosmology and, particularly, in a coherent materialist context? On what basis can this be done?

To better understand the challenges faced by a coherent relativist, let's look at a hypothetical situation. Suppose you are an eccentric person, taking a peculiar pleasure in torturing and maiming people aged between 40 and 50 years (with no preferences regarding sex or sexual orientation). Suppose you justify the pleasure you derive from this kind of behaviour on the grounds that it is programmed in your genes, imposed by social conditioning and that there is no way you can change this pattern. You claim: "In my case these activities are essential for my physical and psychological equilibrium. If my instincts dictate that I interact with others using physical violence, assaulting or maiming other human beings,[323] what's wrong with that? Why should anyone oppose me? If there is no God establishing good and evil, if there is no absolute moral law, who can dare say that such behaviour is "wrong"? Who can dare dictate to me what is wrong? Why should someone else's concepts of right and wrong be rammed down my throat if I'm fine with mine? In fact, I do not recognize any god, imposing his law on all humans. Yes, the State may use force to impose its values on me, but circumstances change and who knows? Perhaps one day I may get to impose my own..."

Rites of Passage

In an article published in Newsweek magazine on the origin of evil, Sharon Begley (Wall Street Journal Science Editor) offered some comments on the psychological development of serial killers and sociopaths (2001: 32-33):

> Goldberg, who has studied killers and sociopaths, argues that the seeds of evil are sown early in life. If a child suffers extreme neglect or cruelty, especially from a trusted friend or beloved relative, the result is often shame and humiliation: "I was not worthy of love from those I love most." Those feelings, if not countered by compassion from others in the child's world, can grow into self-contempt so profound that the only way to survive is to "become indifferent to other people, too" says Goldberg. "I may not be worthy, but neither is anyone else". Someone who hates himself projects that hatred onto his victims. He "puts his hated self in the shoes of the victim, then tortures and kills that person," Simon explains.

And if one should try to reason with or reform the sociopath, such individuals may well reply: "Why should I consider that the ethical system that other people have made up should be superior to mine since their system has never been of any use to me? Why should someone else's ethical scruples be imposed on me? On what basis? Is the true basis for your 'moral argument' that ultimately society (using the State) will use brute force if I don't curtail my natural impulses?"[324] On the other hand, if science a priori excludes ethical and moral issues and the gods are dead or asleep on their thrones, what can we do in moral terms, other than imitate nature? Why should I bother to listen to those who tell me to act on the basis of a hypothetical "common good" (especially if I am in a strong position to ignore them)? To this kind of moral discourse the sociopath may well reply: "Get off my back with your moralizing about the 'common good' or that I should think about my contribution to the survival of the species. Has society or my species ever expressed any interest in me? Why should I care about them? Let's just say I have my own personal definition of 'society'.[325] As far as I'm concerned, I've evolved beyond morality." Of course defenders of postmodern morality may say something to the effect that Nature (or evolution) has made us "moral/ethical beings". As an example of postmodern theological statements this is of some interest, but empty in terms of logic, as unless one were to evoke an absolute biological or genetic determinism,[326] nature's power on individual behaviour is entirely fictitious. One might as well talk bring up the influence of the stars. Explaining everything and nothing...

When dealing with the chaos of one's impulses, relativism is a comforting doctrine, but it is hardly admissible when dealing with historical data, for example, the development of the Gulag Archipelago by Lenin and Stalin, the Killing fields in Cambodia under Pol Pot or the Nazi Final Solution. Do coherent relativists really exist or are they just fictional characters found solely in academic folklore? In principle, such mythical individuals could be stripped of everything they have, as on what basis could they claim universal rights (property, respect, happiness or life) against the wishes or demands of others? In real life, when a relativist finds himself robbed or injured by a large corporation or a government, his relativism quickly evaporates. Someone sold him a defective product, he was promised a pension that will not be paid out? Well, he will cry out loud and clear: "I demand Justice!" But what concept of justice is he talking about? Why, all of a sudden, is his concept of justice no longer relative or strictly personal? What has happened to logic?

It is ironic to observe postmoderns continuing to rant about the "intolerance" of major religions such as Judaism, Christianity and Islam, because religions dare proclaim an absolute moral code. But in turn, one may wonder if postmodernism will not result in even greater intolerance. If one considers the radical relativism of this system, one ends up in a situation where each individual's moral concepts are incommensurable,[327] where there no longer exists any common ground that all could agree on. Thus one ends up with brutal intolerance either on the interpersonal level or, at best, between ethnic groups. This leads to a return to tribal society. To each (and each community) its own ethical bubble, an airtight bubble. Therefore, one can no longer refer to (without hypocrisy, conscious or not) "fair play", the Torah or even to "common sense". All references to an absolute will provoke this kneejerk reaction: "You have no right to judge me! Don't ram your rules or your morality down my throat!". All that is left are games of emotional influence, manipulation and, ultimately, pure power struggles. I can/will impose my morals and my will on others because I have a bigger stick/better paid lawyer/marketing consultant/cannon/nuke, etc. The anthropologist Ernest Gellner points out some of the consequences of relativism (1992/1999: 49-50):

> Relativism *does* entail nihilism: if standards are inherently and inescapably expressions of something called culture, and can be nothing else, then no culture can be subjected to a standard, because (*ex hypothesi*) there cannot be a trans-cultural standard which would stand in

judgement over it. No argument could be simpler or more conclusive. The fact that this entailment is valid does not mean that people must in fact, psychologically, also become nihilists if they are relativists. The argument is not refuted by the fact that our author is sympathetic to relativism *and* has his own standards which he upholds with firmness. We cannot legislate against inconsistency, and have no wish to do so. The existence of a contradiction in a given mind does not refute the argument. But there are some of us who are influenced and bothered by cogent inferences, and have some little difficulty in accepting premiss A and rejecting conclusion B, if (as most emphatically happens to be the case here) A does indeed entail B...

Freedom and the Conversion Process

Every religion is to be found in juxtaposition to a political opinion which is connected with it by affinity. If the human mind be left to follow its own bent, it will regulate the temporal and spiritual institutions of society upon one uniform principle; and man will endeavor, if I may use the expression, to harmonize the state in which he lives upon earth with the state which he believes to await him in heaven. (de Tocqueville 1835/1838, vol. I, ch.IX, sect iv)

Thought slowly follows its logical course, like a river seeking the sea. (Anonymous)

Civilizations find their basis in belief systems (in at least one), in a religion. Once adopted, a religion will thereafter have, if it is dominant for at least a couple of generations, a profound influence on the subsequent development of institutions, practices and attitudes of the societies that have adopted them.[328] In this section, we propose a hypothesis regarding the influence of religion on culture. We will examine the possibility of a link between how salvation[329] is understood, that to say **conversion** to a particular religion, and the development of freedom of expression in the press, in academia and in politics in a society dominated by a particular religion over a period of several generations.

The conversion process is both a socialization process (an individual joining a new community) and a cognitive process (where one replaces certain presuppositions, beliefs and dogmas by others). The overall objective? To transform the unbeliever into a believer. In social terms, the convert leaves one community of beliefs (and practices) for a new one. Often, but not always, the convert undergoes a ritual to mark his adoption by the new community as well as his new belief in a different cosmology and its linked ethical principles. In the ancient world Jewish proselytes abandoned pagan polytheistic beliefs and began complying with the laws of Moses and the worship of one God. In the modern context, a convert to Stalinist communism would reject capitalism and fascism, would join the Communist party and dedicate himself to the revolution and the teachings of the Prophet Marx and Saints Engels, Lenin and Stalin. This is a central dimension of any ideologico-religious system. From the birth of an ideologico-religious system, inevitably the question must be addressed: How does one recruit new converts, bring in the crowds and stem defections?

And when conversion goes the "wrong way", that is to say leading to an ideologico-religious system that the observer does not share (a process designated by the term "apostasy"), a variety of control mechanisms kick into action to restrain the misled individual. Basically, it comes down to the old carrot and stick principle: "Get back on the right path, there's still time, it would be better if you did. If not, you'll have to face the consequences." The emphasis is on a fait accompli, "You've become associated with questionable and dangerous practices and beliefs. The time to act is now." An interest in unorthodox views [that is to say, false beliefs, heresy in fact] will be treated as unhealthy, a passport to downfall and hellfire. Someone tempted by apostasy will be viewed as a victim, if not a fool, a naïve, misinformed person... If things go too far, the possibility of being "kicked out of the tribe," excommunication, may be evoked (though expressed more or less clearly) — "You're hanging out with heretics... You'll lose your privileges you know?"

In the first chapter (p. 26) we examined the contrast between Christian and Hindu belief systems using a metaphor of the soldier and toxic gas. Both approaches are clearly forms of proselytizing, but forms of proselytizing of a different kind. Both involve a different perspective on the conversion process. In the case of Christianity and the Protestant tradition, particularly among Evangelicals,[330] conversion is viewed as legitimate only when it is freely chosen, unrestricted and linked to an conscious, personal, reasoned deci-sion. The baptism of Infants (before the age of reason) is thus reject-ed. The conversion of an adult may involve circumstances where emotion plays a role, but this is a secondary aspect. The most important issue is real freedom of choice.

Alongside what we noted above with respect to attitudes toward conversion, another assumption with far-reaching social consequences is a religion's attitude towards the state and political power. In historical terms, Christianity did not immediately iden-tify with the State or with a geographic area, as was the case with Islam. Another issue is that Christianity's initial expansion was not driven by military conquest, rather by preaching and persecution. The Christian church of the first three centuries was largely a per-secuted underground movement, attracting the poor, slaves and refugees.[331] The Early Church did not identify with the State, as this relationship was generally tense if not hostile.[332] Christ's claims to the effect that "My kingdom is not of this world" (John 18: 36) or "Give unto Caesar that which is Caesar's and unto God what is God's" certainly contributed to this distrust, but also gave legiti-macy to the idea of a secular, non-Christian or secular State. Another attitude differing from that of Islam, many early Christians rejected military service as a legitimate occupation. Moreover, the writers of the epistles recommended that Christians be submitted to civil authority, at a time when none of these authorities were Christian and who, in some cases actively persecuted Christians (Titus 3: 1; 1Peter 2: 13). The result of this recommendation was to ensure the independence of the state.

When the Emperor Constantine adopted Christianity in 312 AD, things changed dramatically. The Church-State relationship became much closer, symbiotic even. Subsequently, depending on particular circumstances, the Catholic Church dominated or was dominated by political powers.[333] Among the Greek or Russian Orthodox, the relationship to the State was more often character-ized by a situation of symbiosis/submission[334] (involving a relation-ship where the emperor or sovereign was considered the "protector of Christianity"). Examining policies regarding conversion in the eastern provinces of the Russian Empire, historian Paul Werth observed that Orthodox missionary activities followed the Russian military conquest of the seventeenth-century in the eastern prov-inces. Another wave of State-supported missionary activities occurred during the nineteenth-century. Werth notes (2000: 499):

But because these "conversions" had depended on coercion and material incentives, the attachment of the "converts" to Christianity was demonstrably weak, and their Christian status thus remained above all a formal and legal one, forcibly upheld by the Russian state.[335]

A territorial conception of religion thus developed in much of Christianity. In the Middle Ages, the Western Church was at times financed by the state. As a result, kings had great influence on the choice of bishops and cardinals in their lands. Constantine's conversion created a precedent. In the following centuries, as Europe was evangelized it became customary, after the conversion of a sovereign to Christianity, that the people would follow their leader, in his new religion, with little debate. Individual choice was then largely removed, overshadowed. Conversion to Christianity then largely became a social issue, a matter of cultural identity and not a personal decision, as had been the case during the first centuries of Christianity. When the controversy with the Donatists[336] erupted, Augustine (354-430 AD) took the step of advocating the use of force to ensure their return to the Catholic Church. Centuries later, this precedent opened the door to the Inquisition. Subsequently, a deeply entrenched conversion and acculturation pattern developed whereby an individual born in a Catholic (or Orthodox) culture, marked by the ritual of baptism at birth, was automatically considered Catholic (or Orthodox).

In Latin America, the Catholic Church pursued this pattern. To give just one example, in Spanish territories, which later became the State of New Mexico, Catholicism was forced on the Pueblo Indians. In 1680, they revolted and the Spanish were expelled. The Spanish retook the territory in 1702, but from that point on took a more conciliatory view towards Pueblo beliefs and practices. To avoid sanctions against ancestral beliefs, Pueblos combined Catholic rituals with their own cosmology. This "solution" was replicated, with some local variations, in most of Latin America where Catholicism is now dominant, that is to say, the forced conversion of conquered peoples and subsequent syncretism. In France, a similar situation prevailed until the Revolution. The St-Bartholomew's Day Massacre[337] is a clear example of this territorial view of religion. The rising power of the Protestant Huguenots threatened to destabilize the established equation of one nation = one religion. Protestants, in turn, often had no recourse other than to take refuge in the territory of princes favourable to their cause, replicating the Catholic territorial pattern. In medieval

Europe, Jews were generally the first to bear the brunt of this territorial attitude to religion where expulsion often followed the confiscation of property and persecution.

Among Catholics (as well as with Lutherans and Anglicans), the practice of baptizing children before the age of reason eventually became an indispensable element in the system. As a recruitment practice, the effectiveness of such an approach makes it rather irresistible. All one has to do is rely on reproduction within the community as well on the subsequent acculturation/education of children. The problem of existential crises and the escape of potential members are thus largely avoided. The individual's free choice is of little concern in this context, excluding perhaps exceptional cases, such as the conversion of adults from another, non-Catholic, culture. Although this model may be defended by stating that "the individual always has the choice to stay or leave," the fact remains that before the individual has any chance to understand the implications of what Christianity entails, he is already identified, by those around him, as a Catholic, Anglican or Lutheran Christian. In practical terms, individual choice has been done away with.

Historically, one can very briefly trace the timeline for the requirement of freely chosen adult conversion (and opposition to infant baptism[338]) among various dissident Christian groups, who in the early days of the Reformation, often paid for their stand with blood or exile. Among these, one finds the Waldensians, Anabaptists, Mennonites, Puritans, Quakers, German Pietists, Moravians, and (later on) Baptists, Methodists and other groups identifying with the evangelical movement. It is important to understand that freedom of choice and of conscience was won primarily on the religious front before such things were heard of in the political sphere.

In nations where the Evangelical view of Christianity sunk deep roots, it became taken for granted that the conversion process, becoming a Christian, required a free choice on the part of the individual. Regarding this influence, we note that the Protestant principle of the priesthood of all believers broke down[339] castes within Christianity and exerted an anti-hierarchical influence. Patterns of government in Reformed Churches, managed by elders[340], helped establish democratic attitudes and habits in the West. Moreover, in the nineteenth-century, this anti-hierarchical influence eventually led to the abolition of slavery.[341] The social contribution of the Judeo-Christian worldview to Western civilization, particularly under the influence of the Reformation, is substantial (Gariépy 1999):

> ... the priesthood of all believers is a central proposal brought forward by the Reformation and led to the break with the Church of Rome. With the priesthood of believers, there are no intermediaries between man and God, nor any sacred people, places or institutions. Thus, no man can establish himself as guardian of the temple, as a unilateral, authoritarian or infallible[342] holder of power or knowledge. This core Protestant doctrine led to the rejection of all absolutism, totalitarianism, of any system of submission binding the conscience. Protestantism recognizes pluralism and the diversity of personal approaches, as opposed to systems based on submission and power and it seeks the establishment of collegial organizations avoiding hierarchical authority in religious matters. Finally, unlike rigid Roman dogma that was rejected by the Reformation, Protestantism is a movement that constantly calls believers and organizations to revise their positions and not simply to reproduce traditional ways of doing things.[343]*

But let's get back to religion's attitude towards the State and political power. In the case of Islam, the Catholic Church in the Middle Ages[344] and several modern ideologies including communism and fascism, the State is seen as an essential instrument of the ideologico-religious system. Religion and State are synchronized, united. From this (religious) drive was born the modern totalitarian state. The means of control may vary of course. In some cases, indirect influence suffices; in others it involves direct and absolute control. Total identification between state and religion can lead to significant social crises. France, which saw the rise of Richelieu, and Germany with its state religion, Lutheranism, later experienced "la Terreur"[345] and Nazism. Heaven and Hell came down or arose on earth... Of course there is no simple cause and effect relationship. Other factors also come into play, but at this stage, it appears that in the long term a religion's attitude toward Church and State can profoundly influence a society's political patterns of behaviour. Note that strong identification of religion with the state often introduces a territorial aspect, that is to say that within a territory belonging to a state or religion, believers will have special status and other groups (defined as unbelievers) will tend to be subject to special taxes, restricted rights and red tape, if not attempts at forced conversion. Middle East historian Eliezer Cherki explains the geographical and cultural views of Islam (2001):

Islam views the world as divided into two: *Dar al-Islam* and *Dar al-Harb*.[346] The first term refers to territories where Islam has political power, even if it is a minority and if all the citizens are not Muslims. *Dar al-Harb*, "territory of war" is the rest of the world that Islam has a duty to conquer by perpetual war or *jihad*. There is no difference between the countries that make up Dar al-Harb; people and property in these territories are Mubah, "permitted", at the mercy of Muslims [and can be plundered and killed].

Now let us consider the relations of Muslims with the people of *Dar al-Harb*. Idolatrous tribes have no choice: conversion or extermination, but men only — women become slaves. For the peoples of the Book, that is to say Jews and Christians, the alternative is somewhat better, conversion is not imposed, but submission to [Islamic] political power is demanded. This submission typically takes the form of the *jizya*, a tax levied only on non-Muslims that was used over the centuries, along with war booty, to endow the "treasure trove of the Muslims." It is also reflected in other outward signs of humiliation, which enforce an inferior status that appears to be almost an obsession to Muslims. In exchange for this submission, *dhimmis* are entitled to the protection of the various Islamic powers (Sultan, Qaid, etc..), allowing them to live in Islamic countries. This contract can only be broken by the revolt of the *dhimmis* against their masters and, even more so if the *dhimmis* want to take over, in any manner whatsoever, a land belonging or that belonged to Islam.*

Discussing conversion to Islam under Ottoman rule in the nineteenth-century, Selim Deringil examines the fluctuating role played by compulsion (2000: 547):

To convert is to change worlds. This can be done voluntarily or involuntarily. In the spectrum ranging from the proverbial "conversion at the point of the sword," to the completely sincere and intellectually committed act, the gradations of conviction and motivation are almost infinite. They range from the conscious act of a Polish aristocrat who took refuge in the Ottoman Empire and accepted Ottoman service in the 1830s, to those Christians in Damascus who converted to save their lives during the riots of 1860. But there is also that grey area, the small insults of everyday life: being referred to as *mürd* rather than *merhum* when you die, not being allowed to wear certain colours or clothes, not being allowed to ride certain animals. These little barbs, endured on a daily basis, these must have been the basic reason for many a conversion to Islam.

Compulsion does not always take the form of death threats, but sometimes shows a softer, more reasonable face, that of the haggling merchant or the religious state bureaucrat. His role is to reward the faithful and punish the recalcitrant. Social and economic restrictions are thus a form of religious persuasion, less violent, but potentially more effective in the long-term than naked physical threats. Note that the pressures of everyday life can also erode religious passion and proselytizing zeal. For example, it seems that in the past some caliphs discouraged the over-zealous conversion of dhimmis, because the *jizya*, the tax to which they were subject (unlike ordinary Muslims), had become an essential source of income.

The relationship between religion and politics was a central concern for Frenchman Alexis de Tocqueville. As a young lawyer, he left France in 1831 travelling in the United States to study the prison system. At the time, Europe (and France in particular) had seen 50 years of revolutions, wars and incessant turmoil. After his return to Europe, he wrote on the American prison system and then produced a more detailed study of the American political scene entitled **Democracy in America**. The first volume of this essay was published in 1835. Ethics and political science professor at the ENAP,[347] Yves Boisvert wrote on the subject (1999):

> In de Tocqueville's view, the presence of religion[348] at the heart of the customs of the American people was the source that helped further the healthy development of democracy. The influence of the religious spirit on behaviour, he said, leads people to use their freedom wisely, without abusing it. He also seems to believe that the American people, this people of faith, will become a beacon for the young European democracies.... Tocqueville believed that democracy had a future if the societies who adopted it knew how to organize themselves. With this in mind he left for America to see if it might have practical lessons to offer Europe. There, he soon realized that the democratic genius of the American people was to have organized a society on the basis of a separation and interdependence of public spaces. Thus, American society seems to be a harmonious coexistence between religious, civil and political society. Tocqueville therefore postulates a direct link between the moral qualities of a people, the quality of social dynamism and the quality of democracy. This link then enables the development of a real will to live together and a desire to work together.*

It is somewhat surprising that de Tocqueville, though Catholic, understood the dangers of a relationship between religion and state that had become too close, too symbiotic. De Tocqueville wrote (1840/1847: Book 4, ch. V):

Nor do I hesitate to affirm, that amongst almost all the Christian nations of our days, Catholic as well as Protestant, religion is in danger of falling into the hands of the government. Not that rulers are over-jealous of the right of settling points of doctrine, but they get more and more hold upon the will of those by whom doctrines are expounded; they deprive the clergy of their property, and pay them by salaries; they divert to their own use the influence of the priesthood, they make them their own ministers — often their own servants — and by this alliance with religion they reach the inner depths of the soul of man.

Of course, excessive intimacy between religion and secular power can just as easily be the result of a political will to control religion as the other way around; that is to say a religious perspective that sees the State as an instrument of salvation or a way to initiate utopia on earth. The end result is, for all practical purposes, the same. The state becomes an instrument of religion (or vice versa). Criticism of the state (and its policies) therefore becomes a critique of the sacred order. Early Protestants briefly attempted such a State-Religion fusion in Geneva under Calvin,[349] but such experiments were quickly dropped. In the Islamic world, the attitude which sees the State as an essential tool of religion, was, until recently, almost universal (though suffering a period of decline in the 20th-century). A secular state in a nation with an Islamic cultural heritage is difficult to imagine and, in practice, is subject to constant tension and inner contradictions.[350]

If we examine the case of Hinduism, where being born into a caste leaves a permanent mark on an individual's identity, many questions also arise. Can an untouchable (or *Dalit*) possibly accede to the Brahmin caste in this life? Can untouchables "convert" to an upper caste by some means? Is the only way open, that of finding their way through successive reincarnations (samsara)? Can they expect some form of salvation in this life or only in future reincarnations?

Of course none of the major world religions reject the free conversion of an adult, but having said that not all religions demand this particular form of conversion. Within the Islamic world, for example, voluntary conversion is just one of many possible forms of conversion. In the modern context, it is fine if people freely convert to Islam, but historical data indicates that the free choice of converts to Islam is neither significant, nor critical. In the first century of its existence, most of Islam's expansion took place, not by means of missionary activity, but on the geopolitical front, through military conquests, Jihad.[351] That said, this statement must be qualified, as jihad does not automatically lead to mass conversions.

Many present-day Muslims argue that the Koran forbids forced conversion. For example, it is understood that in an Islamic state the People of the Book (Jews and Christians) may retain and practice their religion provided that this is done in a discreet manner, with little pomp. Typically non-Muslim religious groups must adapt to a semi-clandestine existence. A priori, Islam and the Muslim should always dominate. This is the reward of the righteous, those who obey the divine law. For example, it is permissible for a Muslim man to marry a Jew or a Christian. In these situations, the children will remain Muslim. On the other hand, a Muslim woman cannot marry a Jew or a Christian, because this would imply that the woman would be subject to her husband and it would be an abomination to see a Muslim subject to a *dhimmi*. The *dhimmi* retains the right to practice his religion, but it is understood by all that his status is lower than that of the Muslim convert.

Obedience to God's law, the Sharia, is the bottom line because it is the ultimate duty of a Muslim. The means by which conversions to Islam are obtained is not important. If the *dhimmi* is "under protection", logically this implies that others are not... In the Qur'an, the conversion of pagans/polytheists is discussed in sura 9. This sura indicates that polytheists are entitled to a warning, followed by a period of four months during which they may reflect on the proposal to accept Islam. If they refuse to convert,[352] here is what the Qur'an ordains (Mohammad, sura 9: 5):

> And when the sacred months are passed, kill those[353] who join other gods with God wherever ye shall find them; and seize them, besiege them, and lay wait for them with every kind of ambush: but if they shall convert, and observe prayer, and pay the obligatory alms, then let them go their way, for God is Gracious, Merciful.

Perhaps this uncompromising attitude towards non-Muslims resisting conversion to Islam has its source in sura 9: 9-12 which states, regarding infidels:

> They sell the signs of God for a mean price, and turn others aside from his way: evil is it that they do! They regard not in a believer either ties of blood or faith; these are the transgressors! Yet if they turn to God and observe prayer, and pay the impost, then are they your brethren in religion. We make clear our signs to those who understand. But if, after alliance made, they break their oaths and revile your religion, then do

battle with the ring-leaders of infidelity — for no oaths are binding with them that they may desist.

While we find that in Islam the means by which converts are made is of little consequence,[354] it should also be noted that Islam calls for severe punishment, even death, of those who leave Islam for another religion or for a Muslim who dares to criticize it publicly. In this regard, Deringil observes (2005: 550):

> The issue of apostasy from Islam (*irtidad*) is a particularly thorny one. The commonly accepted belief among Muslims is that the apostate (*mürtedi*) is liable to execution according to the Sharia. The highly respected S,eyhülislam of the sixteenth-century, Ebu's Su'ud Efendi, was unequivocal in his *fatwa* on this matter: "Question: What is the S,er'i ruling for a dhimmi who reverts to infidelity after having accepted Islam? Answer: He is recalled to Islam, if he does not return he is killed." A major recent study on Ebu's Su'ud has also drawn the picture in rather stark lines: "The penalty for the male apostate is death. Before the execution... jurists grant a three day delay. If, during this period, the apostate repents and accepts Islam he is reprieved... An apostate, in fact lives in a legal twilight. If he migrates and a judge rules that he has reached the realm of war, he becomes legally dead." This ruling is also the basis of what some authors have called "neo-martyrdom." The "neo-martyrs" are men and women who "turned Turk" for various reasons, but then repented and publicly declared themselves Christians. "The Turkish law was explicit and their doom, if they persisted, was certain."

In the West generally, Muslims tend to voice less extreme views, but the situation in nations where Islam is dominant is quite different. What of someone rejecting Islam in Saudi Arabia[355] or Sudan? Do even individuals with an Islamic background living in the West dare to criticize Islam in public? What about the fatwas and death threats against Salman Rushdie and other less well-known individuals who have dared criticize the Prophet or his law? Is it an exaggeration to say that by all indications Islam is a religion that one may freely adopt, but which one cannot so freely leave? In the West, to ward off criticisms of Islam, Muslims often refer to sura 2: 256 which states "Let there be no compulsion in religion. Now is the right way made distinct from error. Whoever therefore shall deny Thagout[356] and believe in God — he will have taken hold on a strong handle that shall not be broken: and God is He who Heareth, Knoweth." But does this work out in the real world?

Freedom House is an organization publishing a yearly report[357] on freedom of the press in the world (Karlekar 2003). All nations are analyzed. If one sets aside, within this report, the analysis of countries where Islam is dominant, there is one constant: the greater the influence of Islam, the greater the restrictions placed on media. That a political system is explicitly Islamic, that is to say fundamentalist, does not seem to significantly influence the results. What matters is the dominant influence of Islam (both in historical and cultural terms) within a nation. Making a living as a journalist in an Islamic country is sometimes dangerous and, in the best of times, subject to harassment, restrictions and self-censorship. In Iraq, for example, under Saddam Hussein, a journalist questioning a decision by the president or a minister (considered an "insult"), could face the death penalty. When considering the Freedom House report on press freedom worldwide, we note that journalists in countries under Islamic influence must take into account two more or less implicit prohibitions:

- Never criticize Islam.
- Never criticize the State[358] (or the leaders) of the country where the press organization resides.

In societies with an Islamic tradition, since it is taken for granted that the state is identified with Islam, a critique of the state, is then viewed as an implicit criticism of Islam and, as such, is inadmissible. Al Jazeera, the CNN of the Muslim world, situated in Qatar, is considered the freest and most cutting edge of media organizations in the Islamic world. But can Al Jazeera disregard the two prohibitions above? In the 2003 report on press freedom published by **Freedom House**, one need only to check out the observations on Qatar (2003: 127-128). Many Islamic nations have a government department or censorship agency whose explicit purpose is to monitor the media for any unorthodox views, either in political or religious terms.[359] That said, the Islamic world is not monolithic and in some countries with an Islamic background where other (typically Western) influences are more pronounced (or the influence of Islam on the state has diminished) freedom of expression may increase. However for the coherent Muslim, a state in a country with a Muslim majority that does not enforce Sharia Law will be considered illegitimate or suspect, as Allah's revealed law is the only legitimate law. When examining the Freedom House report one observes that several countries where Catholicism is dominant are also found in the "Not Free" category, that is to say that press freedom is subject to restrictions and censorship. On the other hand, traditionally Catholic nations that, over the course of the twentieth-century, have seen Catholic influence marginalized or replaced at the institutional level by modern influences, have a higher press freedom rating. Such data confirm our hypothesis so far. Considering political freedom, we can expect similar consequences.

But what about the postmodern West? Like Catholicism, Buddhism and Islam, the postmodern religion does not concern itself much with whether conversion to its belief system is voluntary or due to pervasive, manipulative propaganda. As a result, its attitude regarding freedom of expression and democracy is affected. Like Buddhism, postmodern religion typically gains a foothold by the transmission of implicit assumptions rather than by direct confrontation or debate. Examining the views of French philosopher Jacques Derrida, Catherine Halpern highlights (perhaps unconsciously) a very useful contrast between modes of conversion (and ideological promotion) among moderns and postmoderns (2005: 52):

> There are many ways to rebel. Burning one's bridges is one way of course. One then becomes a revolutionary; no compromise, no doubts, no in-betweens. A clean break is made with the past. But there is another way, just as efficient: subversion. This involves undermining [ideas] from the inside, an almost invisible process. One then recycles codes, conventions and the [cultural] heritage by displacing [meaning], imperceptibly at first, by pitting the rules against themselves. The result is new, unorthodox, but deriving its meaning both from difference and from the likeness to that with which it finds itself in contrast.*

The postmodern religion avoids confrontation, the moment of decision and it offers no explicit conversion rituals. Through exploiting of mass media, it takes hold, and society's basic beliefs are manipulated by means of a gradual process of modification and infiltration. The postmodern conversion process is implicit, unconscious and primarily targets control of social institutions rather than convincing individuals. Moreover, the postmodern religion also sees the State as an essential tool to establish its Holy Order. As a result, the State must be dominated by postmodern elites. In this context, the separation of Church and State essentially becomes a concept applicable to others. Despite its claims to "equality" and "tolerance", this trait makes the postmodern religion fundamentally undemocratic. And when postmoderns political hopes are frustrated, an escalation of rhetoric ensues. Recall, for example, the attitude of some U.S. Democrats who viewed the outcome of the 2004 presidential election as "criminal"... simply because the election results did not reflect the aspirations of postmodern elites. This exposes a crisis in democracy, as the democratic system requires that citizens accept the fact that they cannot all achieve their political aspirations in every election.

On the other hand, a phenomenon contributing to the anti-democratic tendency may be observed in the postmodern media's insistence, particularly in Quebec, that it speaks "on behalf of the people" and faithfully report its views, while polls and surveys consistently contradict such claims. On this subject French philosopher J. - F. Lyotard bluntly acknowledges (1979/1984: 53) "It should come as no surprise that the representatives of the new legitimacy of the people are also the actual destroyers of the people's traditional knowledge.[360] [Common] people are now viewed as minorities or potential splinter movements whose destiny can only be unprogressive."* One thus observes the attitude that people must be convinced and put on the "right path", one individual at a time. One means of insuring conformity is rhetoric to the effect that "everyone" already believes or accepts certain things anyway. In fact, one could almost say that the ruling elites in the West demand individual conversion, or at least nominal assent, to a certain way of looking at things.[361]

The concept of salvation in the postmodern ideologico-religious system, that focuses on individual self-fulfilment, finds itself opposed to a basic principle of democracy, interest in the community. The decline of the political ideologies that dominated the twentieth-century is certainly linked to this preoccupation.[362] In an article on Vaclav Havel, a political prisoner and former Czech president, journalist Paul Berman offered the following provocative and enlightening statements (1997: 36):

> It is fine and good to speak about human rights, laws, constitutions, non-governmental organizations.... The world is full of countries that adopt the best of constitutions and proclaim the rights of man from here to the horizon, yet fail to achieve very much democracy. And why is that? It is because democracy requires a certain kind of citizen. It requires citizens who feel responsible for something more than their own well-feathered little corner; citizens who want to participate in society's affairs, who insist on it; citizens with backbones; citizens who hold their ideas about democracy at the deep level, at the level that religion is held, where beliefs and identity are the same.

In **The Condition of Postmodernity**, David Harvey notes a weakness of the postmodern perspective. With the rejection of universals, one is tempted to think regionally, which ultimately leads to narcissism. In discussing the political consequences of postmodernism, Harvey makes the following point (1989: 351):

> At worst, it brings us back to narrow and sectarian politics in which respect for others gets mutilated in the fires of competition between the fragments. And, it should not be forgotten, this was the path that allowed Heidegger to reach his accommodation with Nazism, and which continues to inform the rhetoric of fascism (witness the rhetoric of a contemporary fascist leader like Le Pen).

In the postmodern West, the individual (or community) finds itself established as the source of all morality. Since God is no longer the guarantor of morality, the State (through its legal elites) is assigned the heavy responsibility of deciding between individual and regional moralities.[363] When facing disasters or the hard knocks of life, postmoderns do not have the reflex, as would an individual influenced by the Christian heritage of the Middle Ages to take on the role of the penitent, self-questioning and repenting in sackcloth and ashes. Under the same circumstances, postmoderns typically take on the role of the victim that has seen his human rights violated. Victims never need self-examine themselves.[364] A victim is never held accountable for what he has done. Since in the postmodern conceptual framework the gods no longer play a significant role, the individual must then take his demands to the State. The State then leads the individual to his salvation, that is to say to self-fulfilment. Inevitably as moral issues are sorted out (which is now the State's responsibility in the West), this will be done on the basis of postmodern principles. This leads to a new form of State-Church fusion. Considering the interaction between law and moral implications of the abortion debate, John Garvey underscores the new role played by legal institutions and law in the postmodern context (1981: 360):

> Law has confused the issue profoundly but that is to be expected in a democracy, where law becomes the common ground of argument. The problem is that by a kind of idolatrous leap law becomes not only the common ground (since we accept no other common authority) but the source of all judgment, the only standard, as if law's function were not to reflect justice but to create it. Discussions about abortion frequently lead to the question, "Should people be allowed, or forbidden, to have abortions?" The implication is that what is forbidden for legal

reasons is bad, and what is allowed is good, and the overlap between law and justice happens so neatly, with such thorough congruence, that the question becomes a matter of what can or should be imposed upon people by the state. Law and morality embrace, wisdom is equated with legislation, and Cæsar is lord over all.

But in postmodernism, isn't such a result inevitable? Since in the West morality finds its sole basis in culture or local communities, one can expect that under the reign of postmodern elites the needs and interests of state structures will become the sole and exclusive reference points in establishing ethics. From this point on, one may expect a more or less gradual deterioration of human rights on the international scene, because, logically, in postmodern eyes the concept of human rights can be nothing more than the product of Western civilization. It is ironic that postmodern elites, whose numbers are swollen by refugees from leftist movements of the 60s and 70s, should end up, by the logic of their belief system, as Harvey noted above to the far right of the political spectrum.

Until now, the West has taken for granted that human rights are a set of legal and moral rights owed to every human being. As such they find their basis in a universal principle, that of the equality of all men. In the postmodern context however, this claim falls into a void. Imposing a Western concept of human rights on the rest of the planet is viewed as an unacceptable form of ethical and ideological imperialism. At most, postmoderns will admit that human rights may be a legitimate concept in the West, but will add that there is no reason to expect this be the case elsewhere. In the postmodern context, the rejection of universals also entails the rejection of any quest for freedom in political terms, as projects of national liberation and democracy are linked to universals such as the equality and dignity of all humans.

Politics and cosmology have always been intimately related. Cosmology provides us with clues about what a real human is and politics is just the attempt to develop and implement ways to achieve this objective. Despite the many advantages of the concept of human rights, postmodern ambivalence in this regard is entirely understandable given the assumptions of its cosmology. Their system's logic therefore constrains postmoderns to challenge concepts that have proven their worth in the social and political arena, concepts providing the basis for much of our political life. Fukuyama observes in this regard (2002: 217):

So, despite the poor repute in which concepts such as natural rights are held by academic philosophers, much of our political world rests on the existence of a stable human "essence" with which we are endowed by nature,[365] or rather, on the fact that we believe that such an essence exists.

In the communist belief system, from the moment one accepts the principle that class membership[366] defines consciousness, capitalists become oppressors to be opposed, marginalized and eliminated when possible. The conversion of a capitalist is impossible. Outside of the working class, there is no salvation.[367] From this observation, one notes in the case of classic communism (e.g., USSR, China, Vietnam, etc..), as is the case with Islam, a strong identification between the ideologico-religious system and the State.[368] This identification then violently rejects any criticism of the government or its decisions or any criticism of the ideologico-religious system that the state represents. In countries under communist rule, freedom of the press, freedom of thought and political freedom are typically very limited. One's thinking must follow the path prescribed by the dominant ideology, otherwise sanctions may be applied to the recalcitrant and unrepentant. In socialist regimes in the West, class membership has not been seen in such a defining way. The assumption that class membership defines consciousness has been dropped. As a result, freedom of religion and political freedom are viewed as permissible to varying degrees (persuasion then relies on manipulation rather than physical violence). A society built on a form of voluntary socialism (one that one can freely leave or disavow) then becomes conceivable. But the prohibition against the criticism of such religious states should come as no surprise if one takes into account Ellul's remark noted above in our discussion of the phenomenon of propaganda which establishes a new form of the sacred, that is to say speech immune from criticism or any serious questioning (1954/1964: 370).

With the Nazis, salvation is found in the genes, in race. Even among the so-called "higher races", there are defects, individuals with defective genes, who must be either isolated or eliminated. It should be noted that Nazism did not appear ex nihilo, with no intellectual or cultural origins. The concepts of superior and inferior races were well accepted in Germany before the advent of Nazism. In the early twentieth-century, the German elite had heavily invested in Darwinism and the Eugenics/Social Darwinism movement. Adherents claimed, based on the Darwinian principle of struggle for survival and survival of the fittest, that individuals whose disabilities could degrade the race (if they reproduced) should be put aside. A renowned German eugenicist Alfred Hegar, Professor of Gynaecology at the University of Freiburg, asserted in an article (1911: 80-81) that just as we consider it expedient and acceptable to eliminate criminals, since keeping them in prison is a burden on society and they represent a danger to it, why not eliminate the mentally or physically handicapped for the same reasons? Hegar claimed that the disabled are indeed a burden to society and, at the genetic level, their reproduction represents a danger to the race, which would then risk degeneration. Richard Weikart notes that Hitler's thinking was not isolated, but was nurtured by and participated in a widely accepted and dominant current of thought in the West (2004: 225):

> It seems unlikely that we will ever know the exact sources of Hitler's worldview. However, by examining Hitler's mature worldview and comparing it with the views of other leading scientists, physicians, professors, and social thinkers, it is apparent that social Darwinist racism, evolutionary ethics, and eugenics were not idiosyncratic views of radical "pseudoscientific" thinkers on the fringes. Even if Hitler imbibed the ideas from crass popularisers, the popularisers had derived these ideas from reputable scholars. Though not uncontested, they were mainstream ideas of respectable, leading thinkers in the German academic community. Many biologists and anthropologists at major universities, as we have seen, embraced ideas about racial inequality, racial struggle, eugenics, and euthanasia similar to Hitler's views. This helps make intelligible the willingness of "ordinary Germans," and even more so, leading physicians and scientists, to actively aid and abet Nazi atrocities.

Since the postmodern religion does not involve an explicit conversion ritual and, as is the case with Islam, the free choice of the convert is of no concern when obtaining recruits, one should not be surprised by its intolerance [cf. quote by J. Bouveresse in the last pages of this chapter, discussing reactions to criticism by postmodern elites]. Furthermore, the Dutch anthropologist Bob Scholte examines issues raised by postmodern relativism, questions having to do with the consequences of postmodernism regarding political and critical thinking in the social sciences (1980: 80-81):

> ... how do we choose between alternative paradigms?[369] Is such a choice a mere question of tossing a coin? ... How do we 'steer clear between the Scylla of historical (and cultural) relativism... and the Charybdis of ideologization through utopian historicism (or syntagmat-

ic reification)?' ... We need to develop a paradigmatic position which is not only contextual, comparative and perspectivistic but one which is also discontinuous, critical and evaluative. We have to confront, in other words, the fact that 'the reflexive assimilation of a tradition is something else than the unreflected continuation of a tradition.' (...) But how?

(Scholte 1983: 264) ... it seems to me that there are few if any compelling options that would transcend the specific circumstances of the social sciences at any given time and be founded on trans-cultural values to which anthropology should at all times be committed. Admittedly, the political and moral cynicism that attends a thorough, consistent relativism also seems intellectually irresponsible and politically impotent. Horkheimer's warning must certainly be taken to heart, especially since it quite accurately describes the institutional compromise made by many intellectuals: "Well informed cynicism is only another mode of conformity. These people willingly embrace or force themselves to accept the rule of the stronger as the eternal norm".

True critical thinking in the postmodern context, dies for lack of oxygen. On what would it be based? Typically it is only used to discredit utterances of non-postmodern thought. From this point of view, it leaves us with little more than the study of postmodern tribes,[370] smug conformity to fads and the whining and frustration of those who find their plans for self-fulfilment not meeting expectations. Critical thinking becomes impossible since, as Gödel's theorem pointed out long ago, logically a point of reference outside the system is required. And such a universal reference point is precisely what the postmodern belief system rejects. So where does the West get its concept of justice? The issue has enormous implications for the validity of the activities of organizations such as the UN and Amnesty International, for example. On what basis can one justify imposing a Western concept of justice or the right to dissent on other societies? Why should we be offended if other nations do not share our views on justice and equal rights? Why is it that Westerners are scandalized by the practice of slavery, female circumcision or the sati ritual,[371] in which a Hindu widow commits suicide (more or less voluntarily) to accompany her deceased husband in death? What are the cosmological assumptions driving these reactions among Westerners? Which metanarrative justifies them? If one chooses to avoid these questions, then perhaps we might as well get it over with, take our Ritalin® and recite (with sedated smiles) our postmodern catechism...

Despite calls for "tolerance", when social factions with conflicting interests promote differing opinions in the public arena in the postmodern West, reconciliation is impossible, as there is no longer any common ground. There is no basis for it in the postmodern context. When the dust settles, the group whose views best fit the postmodern religion (and the changing interests of its elites) may expect to gain access to circles of influence (media and legal circles first, then politics) to get their views heard, and without any real debate.[372] Only others need learn the art of tolerance. But what about the Truth? Don't get your hopes up... Ultimately, only those with no connections to circles of power find themselves under the obligation to be tolerant. In the postmodern era, when one has access to spheres of influence, "tolerance" is a matter of concern for others. Ultimately the concept of "in/tolerance" is empty. Its primary use seems to be to frame moral discourse, to establish the limits of what can be said/heard and enable the transmission (and implicit imposition) of postmodern cosmological assumptions.

And what will the fate of the new heretics be, those who dare question postmodern orthodoxy? Will it be torture, the stake or exile? Of course not. The torments reserved for postmodern heretics are rather marginalization, loss of credibility, influence and, if necessary, their jobs. The greater the heretic's potential influence, the greater the resources marshalled against him.

It would be futile to expect to resolve here an issue as complex as the broad (political and cultural) influence of a religion's attitudes towards the conversion process and the State. We will content ourselves with offering the above to the reader's attention as a preliminary, potential hypothesis. It goes without saying that the principle advanced here, postulating that ideologico-religious systems have a very real impact on individual freedom and social life, will be considered inadmissible by those devoutly adhering to postmodern relativist assumptions which postulate that beliefs and practices can be interchanged with no serious consequences.[373]

Intellectual Matters

Rites of Passage

> 1. All formal consistent systems likely to formalize within themselves the arithmetic of integers, will be incomplete.
> 2. No formal consistent system, capable of defining the arithmetic of integers, can prove its own consistency.
> (Kurt Gödel)

> There is clear evidence that certain operations of certain animal bodies depend upon the foresight of an end — and — the purpose to attain it. It is no solution of the problem to ignore this evidence because other operations have been explained in terms of physical and chemical laws. The existence of a problem is not even acknowledged. It is vehemently denied. Many a scientist has patiently designed experiments for the purpose of substantiating his belief that animal operations are motivated by no purposes. He has perhaps spent his spare time in writing articles to prove that human beings are as other animals so that "purpose" is a category irrelevant for the explanation of their bodily activities, his own activities included. Scientists animated by the purpose of proving that they are purposeless constitute an interesting subject for study.
> (Alfred North Whitehead 1929/1958: 16)

Previously we briefly discussed the Alan Sokal affair. A physics professor at New York University, Sokal was repelled by the verbose and shoddy work produced by researchers influenced by postmodern thought in academia. For his own amusement, he devised a cunning hoax targeting a prominent academic journal. To set the trap, he wrote an article (framed in accord with scholarly conventions) on quantum mechanics (Sokal 1996), an article brimming with high-sounding technical terms, but pushing totally bogus concepts. The objective was to verify whether it would be possible to get such an article published in a journal of postmodern studies while flattering the publishers by using buzzwords common to this kind of literature. Well Sokal's scam worked! But a firestorm ensued when he exposed the hoax. On the Sokal Affair, Peter Berkowitz, professor of political science, points out (1996: 15):

> What is truly troubling about the "cultural" or "critical" study of science as it tends to be carried out in universities today is what is troubling about postmodernism in general. By teaching that the distinction between true and false is one more repressive human fiction, postmodernism promotes contempt for the truth and undermines the virtue of intellectual integrity. Those who have never performed an experiment

or mastered an equation can, therefore, enjoy a sneering superiority based on the alleged insight that science is a form of literary invention distinguished primarily by its outsized social cachet.

Even a superficial reading of postmodern academic works will inevitably encounter the assertion that meaning and knowledge are products of human culture and that all meaning has its basis in the prejudices and passions of its authors. Such meaning can obscure reality and typically serves the interests of the elite. Science itself has little hope to escape this universal deconstruction, but this is only one aspect of postmodern discourse. If one examines it more thoroughly, one must point out an even more important assumption: the claim that all principles of morality and even reason are no more than social constructs. On this matter, Berkowitz adds (1996: 15):

> Time and again postmodern critics have used this eminently debatable opinion to discredit, with a single blow, the literary, scientific and philosophical achievements of the West.[374] Moreover, they have drawn comforting democratic and egalitarian inferences from the principle that morality and reason are human constructs or creations, a principle that actually fits far more comfortably with the anti-democratic and inegalitarian conclusions that nothing is true, everything is permitted and justice is the advantage of the stronger.

In the postmodern cosmological context the deconstruction of language tirelessly pursues its path. If one takes the step of deconstructing the concept of reality, that is, the empirical world, a world independent of the observer, as defined by Western science since the sixteenth-century, this step will call into question an assumption at the heart of experimental science itself.[375] On the concept of a real world, the American novelist Philip K. Dick offered the following remarks (1978/1985):

> But I consider that the matter of defining what is real — that is a serious topic, even a vital topic. And in there somewhere is the other topic, the definition of the authentic human. Because the bombardment of pseudo-realities begins to produce inauthentic humans very quickly, spurious humans — as fake as the data pressing at them from all sides. My two topics are really one topic; they unite at this point. Fake realities will create fake humans. Or, fake humans will generate fake realities and then sell them to other humans, turning them, eventually, into forgeries of themselves. So we wind up with fake humans inventing fake realities and then peddling them to other fake humans. It is just a very large version of Disneyland. You can have the Pirate Ride

or the Lincoln Simulacrum or Mr. Toad's Wild Ride — you can have *all* of them, but none is true.

If the real world finds itself reduced to an arbitrary Western construct, where does this lead? What might be the impact on science? As such, Gellner notes (1992: 93):

> Quite probably, the break-through to the *scientific miracle* was only possible because some men were passionately, sincerely, whole-heartedly concerned with truth. Will such passion survive the habit of granting oneself different kinds of truth according to the day of the week?

If, however, reason and logic are no more than arbitrary cultural conventions, such a statement brings into question the whole concept of the university, a haven for universal knowledge, which is, ironically, usually the postmodern's favourite refuge. The debate on the consequences of the Sokal Affair that we have briefly examined here goes beyond the motivations or competencies of the editors of **Social Text** and leads to a re-evaluation of the legitimacy of postmodern discourse itself. In France, the real scandal was having dared challenge the postmodern perspective as a whole (along with some of its most illustrious representatives). This led to a rather brutal self-examination, which forced postmoderns to justify the basis and the value of their views. Unsurprisingly there was a furious response to Sokal's challenge. The philosopher Jacques Bouveresse (College de France) made a comment related to the Sokal Affair, raising a matter of great importance, the attitudes of postmoderns in relation to any serious criticism of their views (1998):

> Deeming any criticism to be a kind of attack on freedom of thought and expression is also, I think, a relatively new way of doing things. In the past philosophers who are now among the most renowned in the history of philosophy had to withstand attacks at least as harsh as those led by Sokal and Bricmont. Generally these philosophers did not consider it beneath them to respond, even when the criticisms were based on fairly typical forms of misunderstandings. None of them it seems, at least, considered that a sufficient response might be simply to claim that the critics were undermining intellectual creativity or were seeking to exercise a form of repression, as they say, "thought police". Hence the question: How and why have we come to this, to a place where the right to criticize, which means the right to criticize anyone, including the most famous, influential or the most well-connected media gurus, has ceased to be regarded as something taken for granted, and where criticism is almost automatically identified with a repressive urge?*

Is this is the true face of postmodern "tolerance"? If this keeps up, postmodern imams will be soon be pronouncing fatwas against their "infidel" critics... Or as the compassionate Queen of Hearts would say: "Off with their heads!"... Historian of science Jean-François Gauvin notes on the Sokal affair (2000: 4):

> The publication of Sokal's article demonstrated a very important point: the legitimacy of postmodern writing is measured by the prestige of the authors cited and not by the intrinsic rigour of its contents. This approach takes us back to medieval scholasticism, which itself was replaced and repudiated by science in the seventeenth-century.*

Groping for an Anchor

Desire is the larval stage of an opinion. (Author unknown)

In the book of nature are written... the triumphs of survival, the tragedy of death and extinction, the tragi-comedy of degradation and inheritance, the gruesome lesson of parasitism, and the political satire of colonial organisms. Zoology is, indeed, a philosophy and a literature to those who can read its symbols.
H. G. Wells (1893)

Postmodern elites today assume a large share of the responsibility of resolving thorny issues such as the definition of human life. When does it begin? When does it end? Who deserves to live, who doesn't? That these elites should do so without invoking any particular deity does not change the fact that in these matters they now play critical ideologico-religious roles in the West. They also sit in large numbers on bioethics committees[376] in hospitals, making decisions on the maintenance of abortion services and elaborating protocols that could be adopted to terminate, in an "acceptable manner", services offered to individuals housed in chronic care facilities.

These elites offer long lists of diplomas and their professional track records are impressive, but in actual fact, all this is irrelevant. The decisive issue, ultimately, is the ideologico-religious system they serve, but that very system is typically concealed, even to them. They are also the ones that, overwhelmingly, set policies on euthanasia, suicide assisted (or initiated) by a physician, the legalization of stem-cell research, the commercial exploitation of abortion by-products, etc. Given the rapid development of biotechnology, opportunities for their intervention are endless...

All this raises many questions: Since morality always involves a reference to cosmology, how does one establish morality in the postmodern context? How will postmodern cosmology determine the interventions of our elites? In moral or ethical terms, if nature is our sole reference point or benchmark, when considering the definition of life why stop at abortion? Why not also accept infanticide, euthanasia, paedophilia or eugenics? Why not sterilize society's less productive individuals? Nothing in nature forbids such initiatives. The only thing postmodern cosmology (referring to nature) teaches us is that the powerful prevail, the strong dominate the weak, those who adapt, survive and those that do not, don't (or serve as food for those that did adapt). This is what nature teaches. And if the assertion that there must be something beyond nature (God?) is considered "religious" (and as a result automatically excluded from any serious public discussion) then where will one find an authority or standard which could challenge what some call "progress" or "the inexorable advance of science"? How then will one determine whether a scientific endeavour should be considered a "moral or social advance"? What broader cosmological benchmark will serve to determine the legitimacy of "scientific progress?" In the absence of a coherent response, one is left with only the irrational, arbitrary and class interests of our elites.

In his book **The Descent of Man**, Charles Darwin reflected on the question of the origin of morality in humans. He wrote (1871: 73-74):

> If, for instance, to take an extreme case, men were reared under precisely the same conditions as hive-bees, there can hardly be a doubt that our unmarried females would, like the worker-bees, think it a sacred duty to kill their brothers, and mothers would strive to kill their fertile daughters; and no one would think of interfering. Nevertheless the bee, or any other social animal, would in our supposed case gain, as it appears to me, some feeling of right and wrong, or a conscience.... In this case an inward monitor would tell the animal that it would have been better to have followed the one impulse rather than the other. The one course ought to have been followed: the one would have been right and the other wrong...

Though this may offend the true believers, Darwin is indulging in magical thinking here. Organisms originally led by nothing but instinct are suddenly transformed, with no plausible explanation, into beings with an "inward monitor" and are now above their passing impulses, endowed with an external reference point, concepts of good and evil. Though such a conclusion[377] was probably quite appealing to optimistic and naïve Victorian minds, one must ask where do these concepts come from and from what cosmology are they drawn? Who will be the founder of this animal religion to which Darwin refers? Fairy tale writers can get their protagonists out of trouble by waving a magic wand (or invoking a *deus ex machina*), but as a scientific argument, this is not acceptable.

Postmodern cosmology, rejecting any moral absolute (and the Judeo-Christian cosmology's divine Lawmaker[378]), leaves us with no reference for establishing ethics other than nature itself. Regarding male - female relationships, this perspective was been taken up by an author who did not fear to say out loud what others barely dared to think to themselves, namely Donatien Alphonse Francois, the Marquis de Sade... (1795/1965):

> If then it becomes incontestable that we [men] have received from Nature the right indiscriminately to express our wishes to all women, it likewise becomes incontestable that we have the right to compel their submission, not exclusively,[379] for I should then be contradicting myself, but temporarily. It cannot be denied that we have the right to decree laws that compel woman to yield to the flames of him who would have her; violence itself being one of that right's effects, we can employ it lawfully. Indeed! Has Nature not proven that we have that right, by bestowing upon us the strength needed to bend women to our will?

Because framing the question of morality in this manner may be undesirable for marketing purposes, it remains unlikely that our elites would publicly recognize their philosophical kinship with de Sade despite the fact that they share the essence of his cosmology, that is, his materialism, his rejection of moral absolutes, his rejection of a divine Lawgiver and they also appeal to nature as a moral guide.[380] An explicit reference to Nature as a moral benchmark has at times led to great controversy as well as a marketing crisis for postmodern thinkers. For example, if genes program men to be stronger than women, within the logic of modern or postmodern cosmology this implies that men are fully justified in dominating women as de Sade claimed. The legal equality of the sexes would then be a mistake in need of correction. Some researchers in

Sociobiology have explored these implications, but in so doing provoked a huge firestorm!

In 2000, biologists Randy Thornhill and Craig Palmer published their essay **A Natural History of Rape: Biological Bases of Sexual Coercion**. In this book they argue that rape is not just evidence of male domination of the female, it is also a strategy allowing men to pass on their genes when more conventional sexual negotiations fail. In short, rape then is not viewed as a pathological act or an assault, but rather as an evolutionary adaptation maximizing the transmission of the male's genes to future generations. The authors state (Thornhill & Palmer 2000: 190-191):

> We fervently believe that, just as the leopard's spots and the giraffe's elongated neck are the results of eons of past Darwinian selection, so also is rape. Human rape arises from men's evolved machinery for obtaining a high number of mates in an environment where females choose mates. If men pursued mating only within committed relationships, or if women did not discriminate amongst potential mates, there would be no rape.

Of course Thornhill and Palmer took care not to excuse or support rape, but that did not stop the cries of outrage, criticisms and protests from many social scientists as well as feminists.[381] The authors were accused of "ignoring the data," and their ideas were denounced as "lacking scientifically as they cannot be tested" and much more. Consistency is sometimes a painful road to walk. It should be remembered at this point is that though evolution does not necessarily lead to such a prospect, but neither does it explicitly exclude[382] such developments. Attempting to assuage their critics, Thornhill and Palmer note in their book (2000: 191-192):

> It is entirely clear, however, that rape is centered in men's evolved sexuality.... The human females who out reproduced others and thus became our ancestors were people who were highly distressed about rape.

If one attempts to sort out issues in the postmodern era, few moral anchor points are available. One solution is to take an anthropological approach, by referring to behaviour found in other societies. If, for example, homosexuality is observed and accepted in other societies, then the conclusion can be drawn that this fact legitimizes the same behaviour in the West. But such an approach involves a serious defect. If homosexuality is legitimized in the West by studies in the social sciences arguing that it is practiced in various non-Western societies, then one must follow the logic and concede that other behavious such as infanticide,[383] euthanasia, violence against women, slavery and even genocide should be also be considered legitimate, as these too have been accepted and practiced in known human societies. Unless one recognizes the nihilism at the basis of this kind of "ethical discourse", these principles lead to a dead end. In the materialist cosmology, reality is reduced to the empirical world and if nature is the ultimate reality, it is pointless and incoherent to talk about "unnatural behaviour", because nature just **is**... It includes everything and cannot be "against" itself or judge itself. This being the case, it is pointless to talk about "good" or "evil", for nature embraces all that exists (or may exist). There can be no outside reference point.

It should be understood that postmoderns are not "immoral" per se, but one might more appropriately say they have their own morality. That said, in the absence of a fixed anchor point, their morality is inevitably fluid, in constant evolution. Over sixty years ago, C. S. Lewis presciently described the postmodern dilemma as well as that of a cosmology entailing an unfixed moral order, with little basis beyond the fleeting impulses of its elites (1943/1978: 38):

> The Conditioners, then, are to choose what kind of artificial *Tao*[384] they will, for their own good reasons, produce in the Human race. They are the motivators, the creators of motives. But how are they going to be motivated themselves?
>
> For a time, perhaps, by survivals, within their own minds, of the old 'natural' *Tao*. Thus at first they may look upon themselves as servants and guardians of humanity and conceive that they have a *duty* to do it *good*. But it is only by confusion that they can remain in this state. They recognize the concept of duty as the result of certain processes which they can now control. Their victory has consisted precisely in emerging from the state in which they were acted upon by those processes to the state in which they use them as tools. One of the things they now have to decide is whether they will, or will not, so condition the rest of us that we can go on having the old idea of duty and the old reactions to it. How can duty help them to decide that? Duty itself is up for trial: it cannot also be the judge. And 'good' fares no better. They know quite well how to produce a dozen different conceptions of good in us. The question is which, if any, they should produce. No conception of good can help them to decide. It is absurd to fix on one of the things they are comparing and make it the standard of comparison.

As Lewis points out, in effect it is unlikely that the sole moral reference point for postmoderns is nature, though nature is commonly evoked as a justification. Ultimately "moral management" from a postmodern perspective comes down to the impulses, desires and interests of the postmodern elite class itself. Within this framework, anything can be promoted or be disapproved. One then should not expect consistency from postmoderns beyond the short term. In democratic regimes, one does find among the elites a residual sensitivity to public opinion and this somewhat mitigates their impulses, but history shows that public opinion can be managed quite easily if a little time and effort are invested.[385] The arbitrariness of moral/ethical issues becomes the norm. Because there is no transcendent moral reference point, one need only to gravitate to positions of power (and learn how to exploit ideological marketing in its various forms) to mould public opinion into a more "open", more "progressive" form and to impose one's perspective and one's values. Morality is therefore imposed by means of gradual media and cultural manipulation, by changes in the legal system and by pure force of law if necessary. Perhaps someday, even biotechnology may be put to work in such endeavours.

The materialist cosmology, which is generally shared by the modern and postmodern religions, obviously has its uses in eliminating puritanical constraints regarding sexuality. But the flip side is that this also opens the door to ethical and moral nihilism. To avoid having to come clean on such matters, moderns and postmoderns resort to different solutions/strategies including:

1. Moral catastrophes, such as the Holocaust, that have been justified by this cosmology are relabelled as "abuses" of modern ideology.[386]
2. In one's discourse, reject absolute law, but bring in a look alike (such as the common good).
3. Claim that morality or ethics are the result of natural selection (and social life).
4. As a last resort: appeal to a NOMA principle (recognizing a limited legitimacy of the older monotheistic religions).

It should be noted that the primary concern directing these strategies is not the development of a coherent system of thought, but rather product image, that is dealing with ideological marketing issues. These strategies are then side issues, just as caulking may be used to plug a breach in a ship's hull, but contributes nothing to its actual structure. As for the third point above, asserting that morality is "natural", that is to say a product of natural selection, this claim fails to take into account that **everything** affecting survival is a factor in selection and not just those appearing to contribute to a hypothetical "common good"... From the perspective of selfish gene theory, for example, it would be entirely consistent to consider the behaviour of a serial killer as a form of "natural selection", that is proceeding to remove genes seen to be competing with his own. As a result, the behaviour of a serial killer can be understood as well as legitimized in the modern context. At least, in terms of logic at least there would be no inconsistency in doing so.

The proposal in point 4, referring to the NOMA concept proposed by S. J. Gould, will appear as irresponsible to those still espousing the modern worldview, if not a desperate "solution" to the moral problem, but in a postmodern context this proposal becomes quite coherent as well as legitimate. That said, traditional "religion" then preserves its freedom of expression, inasmuch as it does not forget how to behave and keep "its place". If it submits to these constraints, it will then retain its freedom as long as it avoids any serious questioning of the basic assumptions of the postmodern cosmology.

In the West, two opposing principles have shaped political power over the centuries. For a long time monarchical government was legitimized by the divine right of kings. Because of the divine sanction involved, this principle admitted no limit to royal power. Typically in Catholic nations, religious and political powers were closely linked, and both tended towards absolutism. In nations under Reformation influence, the divine right principle gradually fell into disfavour as the principle of **Lex Rex** became dominant.[387] This principle states that since Law is first of all established by God, it stands above all, even above the highest human authorities. Its authority is supreme and, therefore, no temporal power can be considered absolute. Consequently, it is considered as a fundamental principle that no one should be viewed as above the law, not even the king. In this context, common people could therefore refer to the rule of law if a king abused his powers.

This strongly contrasts with the postmodern view. Calling on a transcendent law obviously becomes futile as ultimately only the power of the state and the uncontested, privileged positions of our elites justify the law in our time. On the other hand, in practice, persuasion[388] in all its forms is the method of choice to keep up appearances as well as ensure the compliance and subjugation of the masses. For these reasons a return to the principle of the privilege of divine right, the undeniable power of kings in some form, would once again be conceivable, although marketed by means of persuasion rather than violence. Is it possible that, in an unexpected form, a prediction made by Aldous Huxley has become true in our time (1958/2007: 260)?

> The future dictator's subjects will be painlessly regimented by a corps of highly trained social engineers. "The challenge of social engineering in our time," writes an enthusiastic advocate of this new science, "is like the challenge of technical engineering fifty years ago. If the first half of the twentieth-century was the era of the technical engineers, the second half may well be the era of the social engineers" — and the twenty-first century, I suppose, will be the era of World Controllers, the scientific caste system and Brave New World. To the question: *Quis custodiet custodes* — Who will mount guard over our guardians, who will engineer the engineers? — the answer is a bland denial that they need any supervision. There seems to be a touching belief among certain Ph.D.'s in sociology that Ph.D.'s in sociology will never be corrupted by power. Like Sir Galahad's, their strength is as the strength of ten because their heart is pure — and their heart is pure because they are scientists and have taken six thousand hours of social studies.

Invoking a transcendent moral standard or reference point in the postmodern era is condemned. As a result, inter-ethnic conflicts, for example, will tend to degenerate, because there no longer is any transcendent value that one can evoke to bridge the gap between two groups if urges for aggression or vengeance are not subordinated to other, more peaceful, urges. Why attempt reconciliation? One is left with only power plays and possibly *lex talionis*: an eye for an eye and tooth for tooth. This is what distinguishes the great moral debates of the nineteenth and twentieth centuries. Just like the current pro-choice position in the abortion debate, in the eighteenth-century being pro-slavery was the dominant politically correct position. In this time period there was no reason to be ashamed of being a slave owner, prominent figures had them. Thomas Jefferson,[389] humanist and respected politician, is one example among many others. But what distinguishes the debate over slavery in the eighteenth and nineteenth centuries and the abortion debate in the twentieth and twenty-first century is that the West of past centuries still admitted, at least implicitly, the existence of a transcendent standard judging individual behaviour as well as that of nations. Of course agreement wasn't always possible on all points, but it was still possible to discuss which position was closest to this standard because it was accepted by the majority. In our postmodern societies this is no longer the case as the very existence of such a standard is rejected, reducing it to an arbitrary cultural construct at best. Discussions of moral issues in the public arena often end with someone yelling "Don't ram your morality/theology/religion down my throat!" End of discussion. Since real debate is no longer possible, then matters must be resolved by the high-powered lobbying of political, media and legal contacts. This is where the real power lies in the postmodern era.

Although Western postmodern elites reject moral absolutes, this does not mean that they must abandon the use of traditional moral language. Like Hitler, the consummate politician exploiting religious language when he found it ideologically or politically expedient to do so,[390] our elites also know how to use moral language when it serves their interests. It all comes down to marketing...

When adopting a cosmology involving embarrassing/irritating ethical outcomes, coherence tends to become an objective with much lower priority. Though they reject moral absolutes, when their personal or corporate interests are threatened or violated, our postmodern elites will immediately play the role of the shocked, righteous and indignant victims and (as long as the crisis lasts) suddenly acting as if they believed in a transcendent morality. Admittedly, as far as the media are concerned, nothing pumps ratings (or the sales of tabloids) like a juicy scandal. Inevitably moral language will remain in use even if there is no real basis for it in the postmodern religion. From a marketing perspective, it is very profitable to continue to do so. Auschwitz and the Gulag, which exposed the consequences of the modern religion, cannot be considered great selling points. C. S. Lewis compares this situation to someone wanting to sit between two chairs, yet expecting he will never fall to the ground (1943/1978: 44):

> We have been trying, like Lear, to have it both ways: to lay down our human prerogative and yet at the same time to retain it. It is impossible. Either we are rational spirit obliged for ever to obey the absolute values of the Tao, or else we are mere nature to be kneaded and cut into new shapes for the pleasures of masters who must, by hypothesis, have no motive but their own 'natural' impulses. Only the Tao provides a common human law of action which can over-arch rulers and ruled alike. A dogmatic belief in objective value is necessary to the very idea of a rule which is not tyranny or an obedience which is not slavery.

It would be difficult to overstate the importance of this comment by Lewis regarding the political domain. One day we may possibly find ourselves in a situation portrayed by Orwell in his novel **1984** (1949/1984: 174):

> In Oceania there is no law. Thoughts and actions which, when detected, mean certain death are not formally forbidden, and the endless purges, arrests, tortures, imprisonments, and vaporizations are not inflicted as punishment for crimes which have actually been committed, but are merely the wiping-out of persons who **might** perhaps commit a crime at some time in the future.

Yes, "commit a crime", but how do you commit a crime when the concept of law is rejected? When postmodern religious elites attempt to recycle pre-modern morals in order to motivate the outcasts and marginalized by telling them to think about the "common good", the latter may easily retort: "As far as I'm concerned, society has never cared about me, so why should I care about society? The 'common good' is a convenient buzzword, but it's just one of the masks worn by the class interests of postmodern elites." This also appears in the (very postmodern) observations proposed by Spender, a main character in Ray Bradbury's science-fiction novel **Martian Chronicles** (1946/1982: 65):

> The simple-minded windbags. When I got up here I felt I was not only free of their so-called culture, I felt I was free of their ethics and their customs. I'm out of their frame of reference, I thought. All I have to do is kill you all off and live my own life.

And should anyone be surprised if the masses thumb their noses at the postmodern elite's attempts at guilt-mongering and moral manipulation? The masses may reply, as did Mao: Leave us alone, "Men's social existence determines their thought." Atheist and evolutionary biology professor at Cornell University, William B. Provine[391] made the following blunt observations on the cultural and ethical impact of a materialist cosmology (1990: 23):

> Let me summarize my views on what modern evolutionary biology tells us loud and clear — and these are basically Darwin's views. There are no gods, no purposes, and no goal-directed forces of any kind. There is no life after death. When I die, I am absolutely certain that I am going to be dead. That's the end of me. There is no ultimate foundation for ethics, no ultimate meaning in life, and no free will[392] for humans, either. What an unintelligible idea.

If one were to consider Provine's last statement about free will, it must be pointed out that this is far from an academic issue. In general, we believe ourselves free to think, choose and act according to our own will, but if in fact free will is actually an illusion and we are the puppets of our genes,[393] then all the individual's choices on which criminal law and the democratic system are based are also illusory. Both voting in a democratic election, as well as criminal behaviour, must then be explained by genetic factors. Civil and criminal responsibility then become little more than a cruel joke. It follows that it is impossible to have a truly free vote, because everything is determined either genetically, biochemically or by pheromones... Democracy becomes a ridiculous and expensive form of entertainment, an empty charade. And in this respect, the prison system, which is supposed to rehabilitate criminals, becomes a ludicrous waste of public money when in fact genetic or pharmacological manipulation would be more appropriate.

Does only pathetic postmodern "political correctness" prevent us from admitting that if human behaviour obeys a program written in one's genes, then all personal responsibility is removed? As a result, discrimination, castes, slavery and genocide can be justified once these things are portrayed as "genetically predetermined". The story line in the film **GATTACA**, where genes forever determine the individual's fate, could turn out to be prophetic. In the last lines of his essay **Chance and Necessity**, Jacques Monod, a renowned French biochemist made comments just as grim as Provine's (Monod 1971: 194-195):

> The old alliance is broken. At last, Man knows that he stands alone amidst the indifferent immensity of the Universe from which he emerged by chance. Neither his destiny nor his duty are inscribed anywhere. It is for him to choose between the Kingdom[394] and darkness.

According to the modern worldview, an absolute moral standard is viewed as an illusion resulting from baseless arbitrary social conventions or emotional reactions, nothing more. In any case, who would dare dictate to modern or postmodern man how to distinguish between light and darkness or between good and evil? That would be the height of arrogance and intolerance!

The next scene could take place in any Western country. Two criminals convicted of murder are brought into a courtroom. One walks in full of shame, his head bowed, not daring look anyone in the eyes. The other walks in smiling with his head up and avoids eye contact with no one. He displays no sense of shame, as shame is an irrelevant concept related to out-dated categories of good and evil. Why should he be ashamed? A huge cosmological and ethical chasm separates these two individuals. Which of them is the child of the postmodern worldview? It should be understood that individuals having adopted the worldview of the smiling criminal[395] now occupy key positions in government, in biotechnology labs, bioethics committees addressing the issue of euthanasia, in the media and they teach in medical schools... What will happen when they decide to go beyond the arbitrary conventions imposed by society up until now and get rid of the moral dead weight of millennia? Who will be there to stop them?[396] As philosopher Francis Schaeffer liked to say, "Ideas have consequences".[397] There's no safety net for this act...

S. J. Gould, who fought the influence of the Sociobiology school of thought as well as the more recent movement known as Evolutionary Psychology, recognized what was at stake when dealing with biological determinism and the repressed/larval consequences of modern religion. In his book **The Mismeasure of Man**, he raised the question: Why is biological determinism so pernicious, so persistent? Gould responded (1981: 26-28):

> ... because the errors of biological determinism are so deep and insidious, and because the argument appeals to the worst manifestations of our common nature.... Reductionism... reification... dichotomization... hierarchy... When we join our tendencies to commit these general errors with the sociopolitical reality of a xenophobia, that so often (and so sadly) regulates our attitude to "others" judged inferior, we grasp the potency of biological determinism as a social weapon — for "others" will be thereby demeaned, and their lower socioeconomic status validated as a scientific consequence of their innate ineptitude rather than society's unfair choices.
>
> The reasons for recurrence are sociopolitical and not far to seek: resurgences of biological determinism correlate with episodes of political retrenchment... or at times of fear among ruling elites, when disadvantaged groups sow serious social unrest or even threaten to usurp power. What argument against social change could be more chillingly effective than the claim that established orders, with some groups on top and others at the bottom, exist as an accurate reflection of the innate and unchangeable intellectual capacities of people so ranked?

Perhaps Gould is right about the role played by socio-political factors on the resurgence of biological determinism,[398] but he neglects, in our opinion the most important factor influencing its return, that is humans' desire for ideological and religious coherence. This desire to interpret human behaviour in a manner that is consistent with one's cosmological assumptions seems basic, almost instinctive. One must also ask how Gould would have responded if it turned out that biological determinism was not a matter of interpreting scientific data, but an irrefutable fact? Would Gould have blamed "nature" for human initiatives such as caste systems, slavery, genocide, paedophilia or racism? It would be rather vain to do so. But in a determined world, all phenomena are explicable in terms of material cause and effect. There is no reason to make humans an exception to this rule. A consistent interpretation of materialistic cosmological assumptions inevitably leads us to a deterministic view of man. Were this to take the form of a genetic, racial, hormonal or molecular determinism, it would be of little importance.

From a marketing perspective, it makes perfect sense to distance one's self from determinism and portray it as an "abuse" of materialistic cosmological assumptions. Religious taboos are not lightly violated. One convenient way to evade the horrific consequences of such determinism is by postulating that man escapes the determinism that rules over the rest of the animal world by means of culture and his language abilities. This is ironic as in some sense such a proposal turns man into a "spiritual being". To escape the full brunt of the consequences of determinism, it is sometimes stated that this is generally a "conservative ideology", used to justify the established order (religious or social), but this is too easy a way out as it ignores the fact that determinism has also taken revolutionary forms and been used to overthrow social order. Hitler, for example, used it to make war on the Jews and the so-called "racially inferior peoples". And for their part, Lenin and Stalin relied on social (class) determinism to overthrow and eliminate capitalists, make war on kulaks[399] and other groups deemed "counterrevolutionary".

In the postmodern scene, it must be grasped that progress in science has opened a huge ethical can of worms. If, for example, scientific progress enables us to clone human beings or make permanent changes to the human gene pool, why not do it? If it is technically possible and profitable in commercial[400] or military terms, why get hung up on out-dated scruples, why not move ahead? And since the sequencing of the human genome has been completed, what will we do with it? Why hesitate? Why waste precious time?[401] In an essay on the fashionable artistic elite, the New

York art critic Suzi Gablik makes comments on traditional societies (attached in one way or another to the Judeo-Christian worldview) with repercussions well beyond her primary concern, the current art scene. Her observations shed light on specific aspects of post-modern society (1984/1995: 77):

> Traditional societies have many disadvantages — which include con-siderable restraints on freedom — but as we find it harder and harder to resolve our own dilemmas, we may come to see the logic of traditional systems with new eyes. We may begin to perceive that it is wrongheaded — and perhaps even fatal — to have no proven standards of value, no constitutive rules that are inviolate. The extreme degree of freedom offered by our present-day pluralism has placed everyone under increased pressure to choose for themselves among unlimited alterna-tives. But with the breakdown of social consensus, it has become harder and harder to know how or what to choose, or how to defend or validate one's choice. The freedom from all determinants leads to an indetermi-nacy so total that, finally, one has no reason for choosing anything at all. Pluralism is the norm abolishing all norms. It means we no longer know where the truth lies. (The only truth pluralism allows is that it is abso-lutely true there is no such thing as absolute truth.).

As others have previously pointed out, pluralism's internal logic leads to conformism. If one were to dare defend an absolute of some sort, how would you go about it? In the past, Christian churches at times did not hesitate to claim that they possessed the truth. Many postmoderns view any assertion of an absolute as an open door to "intolerance" and oppression, the classic example typically cited being the Inquisition in the late Middle Ages. But generally, this fails to take into account that those who in the past opposed the most oppressive political or religious regimes have generally did so in the name of an absolute and that in many cases, those rejecting any absolutes submitted without hesitation to the powers that be.[402] One cannot claim that a reference to any absolute automatically opens a door to intolerance and oppression since this statement may be used as a mechanism ensuring the subjugation of the masses. In addition, this ignores a crucial point, in the Judeo-Christian worldview at least, a first point to consider is that Truth is a person, not an abstract philosophical statement (that one could claim "ownership" of) as with the Greeks. For example, Christ said: "I am the way and the truth[403] and the life. No one comes to the Father except through me." (John 14: 6). As a result, if a relationship of "ownership" exists, it is other than that which some Christian churches of the past may have imagined. Therefore, it is impossible for one to "possess" the Truth, but in varying degrees, one can belong to Truth... Of course the present generation would consider this is a bogus argument, because however the matter is presented, the basic issue remains the despised concept of Truth itself. Truth (the concept of an absolute, universal in scope) is unacceptable to the postmodern mind, regardless of how you justify it or package it. Like Louis XVI after the storming of the Bastille, there is no room for such a concept in the postmodern worldview. The irony is that even postmoderns, criticising the abuses done by Christians (evoking the Inquisition as a primary example), find themselves implicitly calling on an absolute morality in order to validate their critique. And if there is no absolute basis for their critique, then it can easily be written off as a trivial gut reaction, no more significant than saying, "I like (or don't like) your behaviour/attitudes..." To which others may legitimately retort: "So what?!"

Nietzsche was among the first to declare, "God is dead", but if one were to reflect seriously about the consequences of such a statement, then it should be understood that postmodern man is dead as well (or is at least laid low, with respect to the traditional concept). Few people living in the real world can accept all the logical implications of such a worldview. Going beyond what others would dare admit, Nietzsche in his essay **The Gay Science**, described the destiny of the "free spirit", pursuing his convictions to the very end (1882/1924: 287) and willing to experience:

> ... a freedom of will, whereby a spirit could bid farewell to every belief, to every wish for certainty, accustomed as it would be to support itself on slender cords and possibilities, and to dance even on the verge of abysses. Such a spirit would be a free spirit par excellence.

But following such a path to the end does involve certain risks. Nietzsche himself ended up insane, in the care of his sister.[404] The destruction of meaning, if all absolutes are rejected, certainly obsessed Nietzsche as well as many other eighteenth and nineteenth-century materialists. In an existential moment of silence, despite the rejection of the Absolute, Zarathustra's shadow eloquently expresses the human soul's hardwired need for stable reference points and the ultimate void where rejection of the Absolute leads (Nietzsche 1883/1999: ch. 69):

> On every surface have I already sat!... I become thin, I am almost equal to a shadow!" At last, in despair, such men do indeed cry out:

"Nothing is true; all is permitted," and then they become mere wreckage. "Too much hath become clear unto me: now nothing mattereth to me any more. Nothing liveth any longer that I love, — how should I still love myself! Have I still a goal? Where is MY home?" Zarathustra realises the danger threatening such a man. "Thy danger is not small, thou free spirit and wanderer," he says. "Thou hast had a bad day. See that a still worse evening doth not overtake thee!" The danger Zarathustra refers to is precisely this, that even a prison may seem a blessing to such a man. At least the bars keep him in a place of rest; a place of confinement, at its worst, is real. "Beware lest in the end a narrow faith capture thee," says Zarathustra, "for now everything that is narrow and fixed seduceth and tempteth thee."

Hitler, an admirer of Nietzschean[405] concepts such as the Übermensch/Superman and the "will to power", committed suicide in his bunker in Berlin, amidst the ruins of the Third Reich. There is an echo here of the bitter (and not at all politically correct) words of an ancient prophet.

Woe to those who draw sin along with cords of deceit, and wickedness as with cart ropes, to those who say, "Let God hurry; let him hasten his work so we may see it. The plan of the Holy One of Israel — let it approach, let it come into view, so we may know it." Woe to those who call evil good and good evil, who put darkness for light and light for darkness, who put bitter for sweet and sweet for bitter. Woe to those who are wise in their own eyes and clever in their own sight. Woe to those who are heroes at drinking wine and champions at mixing drinks, who acquit the guilty for a bribe, but deny justice to the innocent. Therefore, as tongues of fire lick up straw and as dry grass sinks down in the flames, so their roots will decay and their flowers blow away like dust; for they have rejected the law of the LORD Almighty and spurned the word of the Holy One of Israel. (Isaiah 5:18-24 NIV)

Postmodern Ghettos

> S. de B. - In general terms how would you define Good and Evil, at least what you call Good or Evil?
> J.-P. S. - Essentially Good is that which serves human freedom, allowing it to place the objects it has made, and Evil is that which obstructs human freedom, that which presents man as not free, creating the determinism that sociologists [promoted] some time ago.
> S. de B. - So your morality is based on man and has nothing much to do with God.
> J.-P. S. - None, now. But certainly concepts of absolute Good and Evil are derived from the catechism I was taught [when I was young].*
> (J.-P. Sartre in de Beauvoir 1981: 552)

In the previous chapter, we considered a quote from Mary Douglas examining the "polluter" concept. A "polluter" is someone who has gone beyond a limit that should not be crossed. He has left his place. He is one whose spoken word, or even the simple fact of his existence, calls into question central cosmological assumptions. Sometimes his transgression is conscious or deliberate, but often it is not. Given the danger posed by polluters, societies develop various mechanisms to keep them isolated or render them harmless.

In **History of Madness** for example, Michel Foucault examines the phenomenon of insanity in the West. Foucault argues that there is more than one way to view the insane and that the way we perceive them is largely determined by the prejudices and conceptions accepted by mainstream culture. Ultimately these prejudices and social concepts are rooted in turn in the dominant cosmology/worldview.

While the Middle Ages allowed the insane to speak and have a place in society, the Enlightenment rejected and excluded them. Because their speech was not 'reason'able it not only silenced the insane, it also excluded them physically, a presence that is also a form of discourse. In the seventeenth-century, the insane were put away with the poor, the lazy, vagrants and prostitutes. The insane were classified as individuals who must be corrected if not re-educated. Later the insane suffered even further isolation, being sent to asylums with others of their kind from then on under the parental responsibility of a physician. In actual fact, the psychologist's power has become a police power. This is a radical change, as it amounts to the power of the priest: the power of excommunication, exclusion from the community. Psychology becomes an ideologico-religious instrument[406] in fact. Though the insane were freed from their shackles, drugs eventually replaced these. Madness is now a mental illness and the insane, have become subordinates. If Reason is a path to salvation, madness must be excluded and is tolerable only if quarantined. We would rather not see their mocking grimaces or hear anything they might have to say.

In the postmodern context, who is the "polluter", the one who disturbs and transgresses taboos establishing the limits of that which can be thought or spoken? What discourse calls into question dominant conceptions and prejudices, central cosmological assumptions? Since the modern and postmodern religions are largely a reaction to the formerly dominant Judeo-Christian system, Christian discourse has become an object of loathing, to be excluded, ignored, forgotten. "Open-minded" Christians, content with the place given to religion (in private life) are of no interest to the postmodern ideologico-religious system. They pose no threat and bother no one. Coherent Christian discourse, on the other hand, is a problem, since at the heart of postmodern's irritation with Christianity, lies the Christian claim that there exists a truth before which all must submit. This is scandalous, it is in fact intolerable!

Since postmodern religion is "tolerant", it has, of course, a place for traditional religions, including Christianity. But as soon as the latter leave "their place" and dare question postmodern "truth",[407] they are immediately called to order. And if these reprimands are not enough, nothing prevents recourse to more convincing methods, that is to say forms of persecution. A priori, postmodern religion is "tolerant" and this of course excludes physical persecution.[408] Wherever possible, postmoderns attempt to ignore recalcitrants, but when the stakes are high enough they are not above attacks in the media, the destruction of the ideological adversary's credibility, exclusion from institutions and job loss.[409] The goal is always to reduce the real influence of religion[410] while permitting the physical existence of traditional religion[411] and maintaining the illusion of "tolerance".

The typical postmodern only has knowledge of (by way of the media) a subservient, flexible, marginalized Christianity. Postmoderns are typically "tolerant people" never daring to express an opinion on any religion and feel they are not entitled to do so. This attitude is clearly linked to the relativistic assumption that "Everyone has their own truth". But an encounter with a consistent

Christianity, daring to question this central assumption of postmodern religion,[412] produces a surprising shock. The postmodern finds himself in an embarrassing situation. He may say, more or less implicitly, "I have to change my perspective, I too have the right to judge you intolerant, immoral, proselytizing!" This exposes the fact that "tolerance" is not a right, but rather a privilege, granted to those who cooperate and submit to postmodern dogma. In fact, postmoderns only offer a limited form of freedom, freedom under probation so to speak, take it or leave it...

We have already noted that postmoderns, faced with a statement such as "behaviour X is a sin, a violation of divine law," find themselves in an embarrassing situation. The problem is that postmoderns reject such a claim (and, above all, its implicit assumption of an absolute law), but to criticize it they must leave their own domain, where "Everyone has their own truth,"[413] ending up in another, where absolute truth does exist... They are typically unaware of the fact that their criticism involves both hypocrisy and cheating, as it is based on presuppositions their cosmology does not support.

What exactly is this 'place' that postmoderns have assigned to religion and, in particular, to Christianity? A place, we are told, that for the "common good" religion should not leave? In the postmodern context, the Christian religion remains tolerable as a "private religion", as long as it accepts the dominance of postmodern religion in the public arena.[414] Frankly speaking, such a subservient religious discourse inevitably takes on the role of a Teddy Bear, a stuffed animal we hug at night when our nightmares and dark spectres terrorize us. It thus becomes little more than a psychological crutch, if not a discount tranquilizer, which individuals can take to manage stress and keep their place in the postmodern cosmos. As a result, religion still clings to its "place" at sad events such as death/funerals or at transitional life events such as marriage or the birth of a child.[415] Despite the decline in religious practice, churches still retain their architectural charm as desirable sites/settings for bridal fashion shows and the production of postmodern princess fantasies.

Religion also keeps its place in the aesthetic realm,[416] offering rich cultural symbolism that values and protects the intrinsic worth of humans. In this regard, it can serve as a crutch for a deficient materialist cosmology where the value of human life is reduced to dust. Christian discourse has been pushed into the domain of "private life". If it leaves this ghetto, or dares to question the truth of postmodern presuppositions, it loses its right to exist (within toler-ance). It then becomes designated as a legitimate target for any kind of verbal attack. Traditional "religious" speech will then be labelled with terms guaranteeing it will not be heard, labels such as "unbalanced", "intolerant", "reactionary", "extremist", "un-progres-sive", much the same reaction as that reserved for those said to promote "hate speech", etc. Anyone voicing such views should not be listened to. Though this process does not involve physically eliminating or isolating such individuals[417] one may eliminate their right to speak or their credibility, which amounts to the same... This explains the general lack of interest in what Christian leaders may have to say, but if they dare approach a subject at the heart of post-modern salvation, such as sexuality, the attitude of the postmodern elite becomes quite different. Hands off! Get lost!

Taking into account that postmodern Western culture is just as much a reaction to modernism as it is to Christianity, it should come as no surprise that it maintains an ambivalent, if not hostile relationship with the West's Judeo-Christian heritage. This con-trasts with postmodern discourse's generally more favourable atti-tude regarding Islam.[418] It demonstrates that postmodernism is primarily a reaction to Christianity or, put another way, the next logical step of a reaction to Christianity that the modern worldview left incomplete. This attitude manifests itself in different ways. Consider, for example, media attitudes about the persecution of Christian groups in the world[419] (which is a fact of life in Communist China and in many Islamic regimes, including Sudan and Indonesia). Persecution of Christians includes slavery, arrests, imprisonment, torture and death. Ignoring these realities is a con-stant of media behaviour. Such stories have little "news value" we are told, so they do not exist. Out of sight, out of mind. Attempting to bring such issues to the forefront, the American human rights activist Nina Shea wrote, "No one would call me biased if I decided to dedicate my life to the defence of Tibetan Buddhists. Among organizations involved in human rights, it is much more common to speak of Christians in terms of persecutors rather than perse-cuted." The ubiquity of stereotypes applied to Christians results in masking the phenomenon of Christian persecution in our time. Move along folks, nothing to see here...

As for the attitudes of moderns and postmoderns with respect to the individual, one can see that they are deeply influ-enced by concepts of freedom of conscience, which are primarily religious concepts, the legacy of dissidents from the Middle Ages, the Reformation and from the Evangelicals that followed in their footsteps. The philosopher of science Karl Popper pointed out some aspects of the Judeo-Christian contribution to the West (1945/1962, v.2: 271) "I do not deny that it is as justifiable to interpret history from a Christian point of view as it is to interpret it from any other point of view; and it should certainly be emphasized, for example, how much of our Western aims and ends, humanitarianism, freedom, equality, we owe to the influence of Christianity." René Girard notes that the concern for victims and rejection of scapegoating is a characteristic feature of Western culture, which is rooted in the Judeo-Christian heritage. He observes (1999/2001: 167-168):

> The essential thing in what goes now as human rights is an indirect acknowledgement that every individual or every group of individuals can become the "scapegoat" of their own community. Placing emphasis on human rights amounts to a formerly unthinkable effort to control uncontrollable processes of mimetic snowballing.
> (1999/2001: 168): The evolution I am rather haphazardly summarizing forms the basis of the effort of our societies to eliminate the permanent scapegoat structures that form their foundation, and this occurs to the extent we become aware of their existence. This transformation comes across as a timeless moral imperative. Societies that did not see the need for transforming themselves are nonetheless altered, always in the same direction, in response to the desire to make amends for past injustices and bring about more "humane" relations among their members. Each time a new frontier is crossed, those whose interests are damaged oppose this change intensely. But once the situation is altered, the results are never seriously contested. In the eighteenth and nineteenth centuries some people realized that this evolution was on the way to creating a group of nations whose uniqueness in terms of progress was further enhanced by their rapidly accelerating technological and economic progress.

When considering the flow of global immigration, where do refugees go? The West is often their chosen destination. Obviously economic and living standards play a role, but the rights and freedoms enjoyed in the West are also major attractions. According to data put forward by Marxist historian Henri Desroches, drawn from a study of early socialist movements in the nineteenth-century, distinguishing between political and religious movements is not an easy task. In the beginning of the socialist movement, these two social currents meet. The following quote sheds some light on the contribution of Christian dissident movements in the struggle for social justice in the West (Desroches 1974: 168):

> In the field of practical utopianism, it is certainly convenient to distinguish between that which comes from non-conformist religion and that which comes from secular socialism. However, as indicated by previously examined cases, we already see blurring in such classifications. In the views of Muenzer, that which is still religious dissent as well an anticipation of socialism and Engels noted — regarding the same Muenzer — that his theology of the Holy Spirit bordered on modern atheism, in the same way as his theology of the Kingdom of God bordered on the pattern of a future classless society. By contrast, in the thinking of Weitling, that which is already a preface to European socialism, is still a kind of postscript to a tradition of Christian dissidents. There is a similar ambiguity in the mental universe of Cabet, another nineteenth-century *religious* communist.*

Is it possible to believe, for example, in the sanctity of human life without referring to a divine endorsement? Perhaps, but religious discourse was the first to propose the concept of sacredness, leading eventually to that of the sacredness of humanity. In the West, concepts such as human nature, the law, justice, morality and equity, are, in fact, recycled religious concepts. But postmoderns have little interest in these matters. At times their attitude will be expressed in open hostility towards Christianity, but usually it takes the form of a constant effort to marginalize any residue of the Judeo-Christian worldview perceived to be in conflict with postmodern dogma. The anti-Western and anti-Christian prejudices of the modern ideologico-religious system, which dominated the twentieth-century, appear in various forms in the social sciences. In the postmodern context, it should come to no surprise that the Middle Ages in Western Europe, dominated by Christianity, were until recently regarded by historians as a period of great oppression and ignorance, the so-called "Dark Ages". French historian Jacques Le Goff observes (1999: 80):

> The men of what we call the Renaissance felt that the Middle Ages was a dark period between antiquity and the present, where the cultivation of literature, art, reappeared. The Middle Ages was in their minds a pejorative term. The devaluation of the Middle Ages was strengthened in the eighteenth-century, as leaders of the Enlightenment added to their grievances against this period the fact that religious and intellectual obscurantism ruled the time. Voltaire is the most virulent: "The whole of Europe languished in humiliation until the sixteenth-century."

Or, "This is the final stage of a brutal and absurd barbarity maintained, by means of informers and executioners, the religion of a god that executioners had put to death." And Voltaire concludes: "The comparison of these centuries with ours (the few perversities and misfortunes that we do find) should make us enjoy our happiness."*

Only recently has historical research begun to reconsider long-held views on the Middle Ages. To claim that this period has been rehabilitated would be overstating things, but nonetheless there is more appreciation of some of the contributions of that era. As for the contribution of the Middle Ages regarding gender relations, the general view is that this period was the undisputed reign of patriarchal oppression. Although aware of the shortcomings of this era, Le Goff has a different perspective and stresses that in aesthetic terms Christianity helped to promote and elevate women. Regarding marriage, for example, the Catholic Church had a positive influence in affirming the importance of the woman's consent. But how were things before the advent of Christianity? Le Goff notes (2000: 36):

> In Judaism, the wife is almost totally subordinated to her husband.[420] This case is somewhat more complex, and in some ways prefigures Roman Christianity since on the one hand a Roman woman was considered a minor, which meant she could not initiate a number of legal undertakings without her husband's consent, and on the other, the Romans developed an egalitarian conception of marriage, resulting in the famous formula *Ubi Gaius tu Gaia,* Where I am Gaius, you are Gaia.*

Discussing medieval Christianity's contribution to the advancement of women's status in the West, Le Goff concludes (2000: 38):

> In general, I think we should strike a balance between a dark view and an optimistic view of women's place in the Middle Ages. The tendency today is to belittle women's status both within Christianity and in the history of the West. For my part, I am especially impressed with the progress that women made in medieval Christian society. This obviously should not lead us to think they were equal with men,[421] but had come a long way[422]... and one will see worse later on. I firmly believe that the worst of times for women's status in Europe was the nineteenth-century.*[423]

This brings to mind the early twelfth-century writings and musical compositions by the Benedictine abbess Hildegard of Bingen. The marginalization and stigmatization of the contributions of Christianity to Western culture have also influenced several fields of study in the social sciences including psychology, as noted by Os Guinness (1992: 119):

> Modernity heavily favors psychology rather than religion as the best response to these crises of identity and faith. In the modern world, religion is perceived as part of the crisis while psychology is seen as part of the solution. In addition, religion is discounted as traditional, whereas psychology is prized as modern and scientific. But to cap it all, religion is virtually restricted to the private world, whereas psychology passes freely across the public/private divide. Industrial psychology, for example, has no counterpart in "industrial religion".

It must be acknowledged here that the practice of psychology is typically associated with presuppositions drawn from modern Darwinian cosmology. This cosmology then provides the basic outline of the conceptual framework within which psychological practice takes place. Other cosmologies are automatically excluded.[424]

In the West, traditional (Christian) religions have legitimacy only if they accept their marginality and the dominance of modern or postmodern discourse in the public arena. The same is true regarding intellectual, artistic or scientific matters.[425] For instance, in the opinion of many scholars, it is clear that the West owes the birth of science and democracy to the ancient Greeks. Western Christian civilization itself has nothing to do with it... And if the Greeks didn't give us science, perhaps the followers of Mohammed or the citizens of China taught us all we know? In an interview on the Edict of Nantes, French historian Jean Delumeau observes that changes in religious attitudes in sixteenth-century France had a major impact on politics. The proclamation of this edict meant, among other things, that it was possible to question the territorial concept of religion and the equation: one state = one religion (Hutin 1998):

> Is the Edict of Nantes just an odd, forgotten incident in the history of France?
> [JD] No, because it opened the way for the Declaration the Rights of Man. By recognizing Protestants freedom of conscience, their right to worship and banning forced conversions, the Edict of Nantes led minds to the Declaration of 1789 where it is stated that no one should be harassed or threatened because of their religious views.
> So it made secularism possible?
> [JD] Yes, for the first time political power found itself playing the role of referee over different religious groups. This was a significant advance

that, so many years ago, prepared the ground for today's secularism, that is to say respect for other peoples' beliefs, provided that others do not seek to impose theirs by force or deception. Secularism allows the State to take on the role of arbiter between believers and unbelievers and ensure public peace. Henri IV brought peace by imposing a new legislation on Catholics and Protestants who learned to live together.*

In the postmodern context, anti-Christian bias has not died off but has undergone metamorphosis, taking on new forms and influencing popular culture. For example, when French postmodern scholars point to the phenomenon of "le retour du religieux", the return of religion, one usually detects a note of dismay or irritation in their reaction, which they share with modern elites. After all, their ancient prophets had predicted that the twenty-first century would see religion[426] eliminated, becoming a thing of the past... a cultural artefact from a mythical, prescientific era. But that's not exactly what happened. In the syncretistic postmodern era, Christianity has a pariah status. Modern elites then view the "return of religion" as a deeply puzzling and troubling phenomenon[427]. In this regard, the Quebec lawyer and ethicist Guy Durand highlights the paradoxes of the postmodern attitude (2004: 32):

> In some quarters, speaking of Christianity in favourable terms is perceived as idiotic or may elicit accusations of indoctrination, whereas invoking Eastern or New Age doctrines will be perceived as cultured and elegant. Claiming that Jesus is the son of God will be greeted with a condescending smile, but if someone claims that God is a sacred mushroom, then typically this may draw a response that such teaching is part of the rich tapestry of human tradition!*

Of course moderns and postmoderns recognize the existence of the "religious phenomenon," and of Christianity in particular, but when the opportunity presents itself, they attempt to marginalize it in public life, to push it into its ghetto. In contrast to the United States, in Europe, such conflicts are less visible, for the simple reason that the marginalization process has largely done its work. It is, in fact, a *fait accompli*, where maintaining the status quo (sometimes using anti-cult laws) is all that remains to be done.[428]

One example of the postmodern attitude towards Christianity was the refusal in 2004 of several European countries, to consider or even recognize Christianity's cultural contribution in historical terms in the drafting of the proposed constitution for the European Community. Recognizing this contribution would appear to violate a taboo. In the U.S., the situation is different and Christians are still sufficiently numerous (and active) to the point where politicians feel obliged to court these voters (rather than ignoring them). Politicians on the Right know how to "speak to Christian concerns", but Christians are increasingly aware that their real influence in the system is negligible when measuring real progress on issues such as abortion, where in most cases nothing has changed in practical terms since 1973.[429] In the United States, Christians are active in social and political life. They do not accept "their place," and gaining greater influence on their part is certainly conceivable in the long-term (without leading to a fundamentalist hell where all the others are deprived of freedom).

Postmodern elites often oppose the missionary activities of various Christian churches in the Third World, arguing that this constitutes the exportation and illegitimate "imposition" of a Western religion, a new/old form of colonialism. This is a somewhat ironic claim as today, without exception, the West and its elites are no longer Christian, while the Third World is generally much more receptive to Christianity. In Europe, adherence to the Judeo-Christian worldview (and religious practices associated with it) is at its lowest point in over a millennium. Some may find it scandalous to note that a number of Christian groups would consider France, for example, a "mission field".

Although this is largely incomprehensible to our elites, the current appeal of Christianity in many parts of the Third World[430] may be explained in part by an examination of its initial influence in Europe. In his essay on the Irish contribution to the West (1995), professor Thomas Cahill examines the contrast between the Celtic (pre-Christian) worldview and the Christian worldview, shedding light on Christianity's appeal in the ancient world. In the pre-Christian world of ancient Europe, polytheistic religions dominated. These gods demanded various forms of worship and human sacrifice was a widespread practice. This is evidenced in the writings of contemporaries such as Julius Caesar and by archaeological discoveries such as Tollund Man.[431] In this regard, a note in Caesar's **Gallic Wars** describes some of the motivation for human sacrifice [De Bello gallico 1915: 6.16]

> The nation of all the Gauls is extremely devoted to superstitious rites; and on that account they who are troubled with unusually severe diseases and they who are engaged in battles and dangers, either sacrifice men as victims, or vow that they will sacrifice them, and employ the

Druids as the performers of those sacrifices; because they think that unless the life of a man be offered for the life of a man, the mind of the immortal gods cannot be rendered propitious, and they have sacrifices of that kind ordained for national purposes. Others have figures of vast size, the limbs of which formed of osiers [wicker] they fill with living men, which being set on fire, the men perish enveloped in the flames. They consider that the oblation of such as have been taken in theft, or in robbery, or any other offence, is more acceptable to the immortal gods; but when a supply of that class is wanting, they have recourse to the oblation of even the innocent.

Celtic deities had to be kept satisfied, fed, and this sometimes required human flesh. If one asked important favours of the gods, one had to be prepared to offer something significant in return. Business is business after all. Cahill explores the contrast between the Celtic and Christian religions through two archaeological artefacts produced by Celtic artisans, the Gundestrup cauldron[432] and the Ardagh chalice.[433] The Gundestrup cauldron was found in a bog in Denmark. It is made of silver and has several engraved panels portraying Celtic cosmology. One panel features a giant deity doing his cooking and tossing a writhing human in a pot. According to archaeologists, the Gundestrup cauldron was shattered into pieces and thrown into a swamp, as an offering to the gods. The Ardagh Chalice is also Celtic art and was designed for ritual purposes as well, but for a rather different ritual. Regarding the Ardagh Chalice, Cahill notes (1995: 143):

> Like the Cauldron, it was forged for ritual, but it makes a happier statement about sacrifice, for the God to whom it is dedicated no longer demands that we nourish him and thus become one with his godhead. The transaction has been reversed: he offers himself to us as heavenly nourishment. In this new "economy," we drink the Blood of God, and all become one by partaking of the one cup, the one destiny.

Durand examines the Western elites' anti-Christian prejudices and suggests a possible compromise. This compromise would allow for the recognition of Christianity's cultural and social contribution yet without leading to a totalitarian form of religious fundamentalism (that some fear) or, at the other extreme, avoiding a form of cultural or historical amnesia/lobotomy (Durand 2004: 35):

> During a panel discussion entitled "Religion in the Face of Obscurantism" moderated by Frank Olivier Giesbert on [the French television channel] TV5 in December 2003, philosopher André Comte-Sponville, a self-avowed atheist, asserted that our civilization faces two

dangers: that of nineteenth-century anti-religious clericalism and that of the current trend toward technicism [faith in technology] and nihilism. "Though I have no faith", he said, "I try to be a loyal atheist. What I call being 'loyal' is not a belief in any form of transcendence, but a sense of belonging and appreciation for the centuries that have made our civilization what it is. The real question before us," he continues, "is what is left of the Christian West after it has ceased to be Christian?" And then one of two things: if you answer, nothing is left of it, then you can no longer oppose anything, either fanaticism from the outside or nihilism from within, and, believe me the latter danger is much greater than the first. If you answer, something is left of it, it can't be a common faith since this no longer exists what is left can only be a common loyalty, that is to say, a shared commitment to very old values that we've received and have the responsibility to transmit. The only way to be faithful is to pass them on."[434] And the German philosopher Peter Sloterdijk added in the course of the same discussion: "Freedom from anti-religious obsession is a sign of mental health, even if dogmatic secularism is understandable given the fact that Christianity was for a long time closely linked [to the State]". Alain Finkielkraut observes "Today the debate is no longer between clericalism and secularism, but between two forms of secularism.*

5 / Cannibals

Le lendemain, je me réveille avec une envie de tuer... irrésistible ! Il fallait que je tue quelqu'un. Tout de suite ! Mais qui ?
Qui tuer ?... Qui tuer ?
Attention! Je ne me posais pas la question: «Qui tu es?» dans le sens: «Qui es-tu, toi qui cherches qui tuer? ou «Dis-moi qui tu es et je te dirai qui tuer.» Non !... Qui j'étais, je le savais !?
J'étais un tueur... et un tueur sans cible !
(Enfin... sans cible, pas dans le sens du mot sensible !) Je n'avais personne à ma portée. (Devos 1989: 34)

I'm going to ask the question
Answer if you can
Is there anybody's children can tell me
What is the soul of a man? (Blind Willie Johnson: 1930)

At the dawn of the modern era, a painting by Gauguin bore the title "Where Do We Come From? What Are We? Where Are We Going?"[435] Since the beginning of time humans have asked these questions: What is a human? What is our place in the cosmos? How did we get here? These questions arise in an individual's lifetime, but also form the backdrop for all cultural production. Assuming that the development of cosmologies and ideologico-religious systems is a characteristic of Homo sapiens, it should come as no surprise that presuppositions related to human identity are among the most basic issues that can be addressed. The twenty-first century West is in the throes of ideologico-religious turmoil and the definition of man is at the heart of presently contested cosmological issues. In this regard, Edward Rothstein, a New York Times journalist, made the following observations (2004):

> The human is the terrain over which the battles are being fought. The political problem with the manufacture of human embryos, however early in their development, is not just that it upsets opponents of abortion. It is that it shifts a barrier that might become porous, weakening the sacral quality of the human. And once that takes place, the slippery slope becomes far more slippery. Where are lines to be drawn? Will human life forms ultimately be harvested for the sake of other humans?

Enlightenment philosophers and their heirs have to a large extent abandoned the Judeo-Christian worldview in order to develop what they thought was a more rational system of thought, founded on a materialist cosmology, with marketing based on the prestige of science. It must be understood that the abandonment of the Judeo-Christian worldview did not occur overnight, but rather gradually, assumption by assumption. A first step was to push God back into a minor role, that of First Cause and then later on to call into question his existence as well as to challenge ecclesiastical authority, the cosmology proposed by the book of Genesis, the Bible's authority, Judeo-Christian sexual moral principles, etc. Obstacles to individual freedom were attacked and laid low. But in the background, a vast recycling operation was under way where concepts derived from the Judeo-Christian worldview were hijacked, repackaged and put to use for the modern worldview. Typically this was done unconsciously and initially in a clumsy, unsophisticated manner, as pointed out by Camus in connection with the French Revolution (1951/1978: 132):

> The revolutionary movement that was born in 1789 could not, however, stop there. God, for the Jacobins, is not completely dead, any more than He was dead for the romantics. They still preserve the Supreme Being. Reason, in a certain way, is still a mediator. It implies a pre-existent order. But God is at least dematerialized and reduced to the theoretical existence of a moral principle.[436]

Developing modern currents of thought generally relied on a number of concepts inherited from the Judeo-Christian culture, concepts considered useful. These concepts had been recognized for centuries in the West and over time came to be considered self-evident, obvious, taken for granted. One of the most important elements, recuperated by the humanists and their heirs, was the Judeo-Christian concept of man itself: a being created in the image of God and the summit of creation. Enlightenment philosophers obviously had to get rid of explicit links to Judeo-Christian cosmology, but man's privileged status, as the summit and steward of creation, was recycled and fully exploited. For instance, Denis Diderot argued (1755/1976: 213): "Man is the sole term from which one must begin and by which all must be judged."* In the modern context, this concept has undergone a makeover and another way of putting it is that man has become the pinnacle of the evolutionary process. A glorious title of course, but apparently all glory is fleeting. Of necessity, moderns attempted to remove all traces of theological language associated with this status, but nevertheless kept man's privileged position in nature (as the summit of evolution), making it the cornerstone of their worldview. In this new ideologico-religious context man is now the final goal, the culmination of evolution. In marketing such ideas, we are treated to high-sounding buzz-phrases such as: "We are the cosmos, made self-aware and self-conscious by evolution!" This retrieval and slip in meaning was invisible to most Westerners, as humans' special status had become so ingrained in the West, few noticed the sleigh of hand. Francis Fukuyama notes in this respect (2002: 156):

> The reasons for the persistence of the idea of the equality of human dignity are complex. Partly it is a matter of the force of habit and what Max Weber once called the *ghost of dead religious beliefs* that continue to haunt us. Partly it is the product of historical accident: the last important political movement to explicitly deny the premise of universal human dignity was Nazism, and the horrifying consequences of the Nazis' racial and eugenic policies were sufficient to inoculate those who experienced them for the next couple of generations.

But will this vaccine work much longer as memories of the Final Solution slowly fade away and the remaining generation of witnesses go to their final rest? One must insist on this rather paradoxical point, that the Judeo-Christian concept of human dignity finds itself preserved at the heart of the modern ideologico-religious system. If one considers man as the culmination of evolution, this status is nonetheless fragile. In the practice of psychiatry it should be noted that whether or not man's unique status is maintained has a dramatic impact both on society and the individual. A Nazi concentration camp survivor, the psychiatrist Viktor Frankl explains the cannibal logic inhabiting much postmodern thinking. He says (1959/1971: 212):

> An incurably psychotic individual may lose his usefulness, but yet retain the dignity of a human being. This is my psychiatric credo. Without it I would not think it worthwhile to be a psychiatrist. For whose sake? Just for the sake of a damaged brain machine that cannot be repaired? If the patient were not definitely more, euthanasia would be justified.

If one does call into question man's unique status (and the absolute value of each human life), consciously or not, one removes obstacles to the return of practices similar to those of the Nazis.[437] Of course such a statement may appear unnecessarily alarmist, if not inadmissible to some, but one should not ignore the fact that the first to be eliminated in the T4[438] euthanasia operation at the initial stage of the Final Solution were precisely the same people targeted by the current postmodern "compassion" rhetoric, that is to say, the physically and mentally disabled, those considered dependent, weak, marginal, unproductive or powerless. The majority of the deaths in the T4 programme were not drawn from the ranks of "inferior races", but were ordinary Germans. Administrative records indicate that the Nazi regime "offered compassion" to 70,000 individuals, but others believe that in all, 200,000 malformed, retarded or incurable German adults and children may have been eliminated.

Bioethics professor Ben Mitchell (1999) asserts that during Nazi rule, the German government produced several propaganda films advancing the cause of euthanasia, ensuring that it was more readily accepted by the public. Among these were **Was du erbst** (What You Inherit) and **Erb Krank** (The Hereditarily Ill). Under Hitler's orders, films such as **Opfer der Vergangenheit** (Victims of the past) as well as **Das Erbe** (The Inheritance) played in 5,300

German theatres. In 1939, **Dasein ohne Leben** (Existence without Life) was produced by the T4 euthanasia program reassuring those involved in this program that it was a humane and ethical procedure. Mitchell goes on to state (1999):

> Finally, the film with the highest production values was made in 1941. **Ich klage an!** (I Accuse) takes up a familiar story. Hanna Heyt, the heroine of the film, shows signs of physical deterioration due to multiple sclerosis. She makes it clear that she does not wish to spend her last days in a "vegetative state." Her husband, Thomas, in consultation with her physician, gives her an overdose, which kills her. A dramatic courtroom sequence follows. Thomas accuses the law of not helping in the case of his wife's suffering. The defense concludes that the law must be changed to allow mercy killing for humanitarian reasons. The film ends by putting the verdict in the hands of the audience.[439]

In the postmodern West, several factors presently contribute to the development of rationalizations, attitudes and practices comparable to those of the Nazis. It is likely that further investigation into the parallels in rhetoric and assumptions between Nazi pro-euthanasia propaganda and postmodern pro-euthanasia documentaries would be very instructive. Michell (1999) examines several aspects of the issue and there is reason to believe that a presentation of a subtitled Nazi film, followed immediately by a recent pro-euthanasia documentary, could also be rather eye-opening. Perhaps others will find the time to pursue these matters.

The Disposable Soul

> But for the last year or so — since he had been initiated — he had begun to taste as a fact what he had long held as theory. Increasingly, his actions had been without motive. He did this and that, he said thus and thus, and did not know why. His mind was a mere spectator. He could not understand why that spectator should exist at all. He resented its existence, even while assuring himself that resentment also was merely a chemical phenomenon. The nearest thing to a human passion which still existed in him was a sort of cold fury against all who believed in the mind. There was no tolerating such an illusion. There were not, and must not be, such things as men.
> (Lewis 1946/1965: 357)

> What is the Self?
> Suppose a man puts himself at a window to see those who pass by. If I pass by, can I say that he placed himself there to see me? No; for he does not think of me in particular. But does he who loves someone on account of beauty really love that person? No; for the smallpox, which will kill beauty without killing the person, will cause him to love her no more. And if one loves me for my judgement, memory, he does not love me, for I can lose these qualities without losing myself. Where, then, is this self, if it be neither in the body nor in the soul? And how love the body or the soul, except for these qualities which do not constitute me, since they are perishable? For it is impossible and would be unjust to love the soul of a person in the abstract and whatever qualities might be therein. We never, then, love a person, but only qualities.
> (Pascal 1670/1908, sect. V, 323)

Postmodernism contains within itself a strange contradiction. On the one hand, it celebrates to the highest degree the individual's aspirations, rights and self-fulfilment and, on the other, it propagates premises and assumptions that irrevocably undermine the concept of the individual as it has developed in the West to the present day. In the following pages, we will examine some of the consequences of postmodern core assumptions concerning humanity and the individual.

There is a growing trend among Western elites to call into question Homo sapiens' privileged and unique status in the natural order. Such questioning appears in fields of activity as well in social actors who a priori seem to have nothing in common. Man's special status, which has long occupied a central place in Western culture, now is the source of subliminal unease among our postmodern elites. Why should Homo sapiens be a species apart, something special? Why should humans be unique? What arrogance, what conceit! One source of postmodern irritation is the more or less conscious realization that the privileged status accorded to man in the West is the distant echo, a cultural residue, of the Judeo-Christian dogma which asserts that man was made in the image of God and for this reason has intrinsic value, a value setting him apart from all other living things in Creation. This concept of man is taught in Genesis of course, but is also found in the book of Psalms:

> What is mankind that you are mindful of them, human beings that you care for them? You have made them a little lower than the angels and crowned them with glory and honor. You made them rulers over the works of your hands; you put everything under their feet: all flocks and herds, and the animals of the wild, the birds in the sky, and the fish in the sea, all that swim the paths of the seas. LORD, our Lord, how majestic is your name in all the earth! (Ps 8: 4-9 NIV)

As Pascal was wont to do, these verses point out both the insignificance and the greatness of man, but more importantly, the source of his greatness. Man occupies an intermediate position between, on the one hand, God and the angels, and on the other, animals and the inanimate world. Made of flesh and spirit, matter and soul, he lives in both dimensions. Ancient cultures thus conceived man as a "rational animal", a being in whom opposed principles are united. In his essay **The Difference of Man**, American philosopher Mortimer Adler (1967: 286) lists four Christian cosmological presuppositions that formed the basis for the traditional Western perspective on man, considering him radically different from all other living beings.

1. The dogma of personality. Man alone is made in the image of God. He is distinguished from animals by possessing a soul.
2. The dogma of the special creation of man. Man cannot be explained solely in terms of natural causes.
3. The doctrine of individual immortality. It is postulated that after death the human soul is able to exist without the body and will be reunited with a recreated body at the resurrection.
4. The dogma of free will and moral responsibility. This implies that man must answer to divine law and is free in his choices, able to distinguish between good and evil.

Following the Enlightenment, the West has challenged and rejected these presuppositions one by one. This has not happened overnight, but by means of a long process of cultural erosion to which several generations of players and currents of thought have contributed. Moreover, here and there, in our social structures, forgotten residues of these assumptions still persist. There is good reason to believe that the social catastrophes of the twentieth-century have demonstrated their usefulness.

Occasionally social scientists with time on their hands compile lists of traits distinguishing humans from other animals. Amongst other things, one can consider the ability to appreciate beauty, or indeed the need to be surrounded by beautiful objects as a trait distinguishing man from animals. Man's superior capacity of language also comes to mind as well as music, awareness of his own existence (self-awareness), awareness of his future death (even when not imminent), his ability to develop and perceive his identity,[440] his ability to develop a belief system and build a culture/civilization on this basis. Man also produces an amazing diversity of cultures where ideologico-religious, linguistic, geographic and historical factors all play a role in their development. Another peculiar human trait is the moral sense, that is to say that, in their interaction, humans constantly evaluate the behaviour of others to determine whether it is consistent or not with the accepted standard.[441] In this regard the anthropologist Elvin Hatch notes (1983: 9):

> It is the content of moral principles, not their existence, that is variable among human beings. It seems that all societies have some form of moral system, for people everywhere evaluate the actions of kinsmen, neighbors, and acquaintances as virtuous, estimable, praiseworthy, and honorable, or as unworthy, shameful, and despicable. These evaluations take objective form as sanctions, such as open praise or rebuke; and in extreme cases, violence and execution. The ubiquity of the moral evaluation of behavior apparently is a feature which sets humanity apart from other organisms. It would be difficult to imagine squirrels, say, or lizards, exhibiting moral judgments of the kind that seem to be universal among human beings. Presumably non-humans evaluate one another only as threatening, useful,[442] and the like.

Though the most uncompromising Inquisitor of the Middle Ages and the most progressive postmodern differ in the cosmology to which they refer to justify their behaviour and attitudes, both still make and promote certain moral and ethical judgments. Reflecting on the influence of modern cosmological assumptions in the Soviet context, as related to individual rights, Russian historian Vadim Borisov offers an enlightening overview of the ferocious conflicts that took place on the battlefield of the concept of man in the twentieth-century[443] (1974/1981: 200-201):

> Deprived of divine authority, the concept of the human personality could now be defined conditionally, and, therefore, inevitably arbitrarily. The concrete person became a judicial metaphor, a contentless abstraction, the subject of legal freedoms and restrictions. And it is here, in the admission of the conditionality of the human personality, that we find the root of its calamitous ordeals in our barbarous world. If the human personality is conditional, then so are its rights. Conditional too is the recognition of its dignity, which comes into painful conflict with surrounding reality.... If the human personality is not absolute but conditional, the call to respect it is only a pious wish, which we may obey or disregard. Confronted with a force which demands disrespect for the personality, rationalist humanism has no logical arguments with which to refute it.
>
> In breaking the link between the human personality and the absolute source of its rights, and yet affirming them as something to be taken for granted, rationalist humanism has from the outset been inherently inconsistent, as Its more logical successors very quickly understood. Darwin, Marx, Nietzsche and Freud (and many others) resolved the inconsistency each in his own way, leaving not one stone upon another in the edifice of blind faith in man's dignity. They knocked the human personality off its phantom humanist pedestal, tore off and ridiculed its mantle of sanctity and inviolacy, and showed it its true station in life — as the cobblestone paving the road for "superman," or the drop of water destined with millions of others to irrigate the historical soil for the happiness of future generations, or the lump of flesh dragging itself painfully and uncomprehendingly to union with its fellows.[444] These men represented the theoretical, logical culmination of mankind's humanist rebellion against God. They declared "our innate moral consciousness" to be self-deception, noxious illusion, fiction — as demanded by a rationally ordered consciousness. This century's totalitarianism, trampling the human personality and all its rights, rhinocerouslike, underfoot, is only the application of this theory to life, or humanism put into practice.

Transposed in the modern cosmological context, the old concept of the person, endowed with rights and worthy of respect, cannot take root. In the twentieth-century it has served as a propaganda tool for ideologico-religious systems where individual humans, in actual fact, are viewed as insignificant epiphenomena. It is clear that the cosmological assumptions pertaining to man are not just toys that philosophers or theologians can play with, but these influence the whole spectrum of human reality. Borisov provides, a particularly penetrating analysis of the dilemma of the materialistic ideologies that dominated the twentieth-century attempting, despite the inconsistency of the initiative, to maintain the legitimacy of individual rights within a materialist cosmology that undermines the individual's value (1974/1981: 202):

> It has maintained its tradition of moral feeling unnaturally married to *atheism of the mind* (not of the heart!) while still believing in the inalienable rights of man as such. But this utopian humanism refuses to acknowledge its historical affinity with the "humanism" which has become a reality.[445] Furthermore, it even joins battle with it for these very rights. The clash is, by an irony of history, between two elements — the initial and the final — of *one and the same process*. It is an unequal struggle, with *utopian* humanism at a painful disadvantage. As we have already said, it cannot *logically* oppose[446] its brutal and consistent younger relative. The source of its courageous protest is irrational,[447] for it is that very moral light brought into the world by religion, but "rationalist humanism" cannot acknowledge this without ceasing to be itself. Its fate is tragic: it testifies both to the indestructibility of man's moral nature and to the hopeless dilemmas in which he is enmeshed when he overlooks the religious roots of that nature. It is precisely because of its atheism that humanism so often either slips into despair or, denying itself, adopts a belief in solutions through violence, when the human personality invariably becomes a tool. A humane attitude to life (a more precise term than the ambiguous "humanism"), if it ignores its origins, rests on flimsy, shifting foundations. As Dostoyevsky once observed, such unmindful "humaneness is only a habit, a product of civilization. It may completely disappear."

The materialist cosmology claims that everything that exists must be explicable in terms of natural laws. Because the materialist presupposition is considered absolute, any outside interference is excluded. Nothing can escape material determinism, not even man. When confronted with human reality, this attitude leads to a paradox: how will one explain humans and their behaviour? If talk about a human soul is forbidden, can we legitimately speak about the human mind?[448] What is the source of reason in man? Once the materialist presupposition is considered non-negotiable, it becomes entirely logical and consistent to consider human identity, personality and spirit as illusions, little more than a devious trick played by biochemical interactions or some other comparable material phenomenon. A consistent materialist perspective will therefore deny the concept of personality and consciousness or, at best, will attribute it to echoes of neural phenomena. This position is curiously similar to that of Buddhism, where in the final stage of the soul's journey, personality and the ego are annihilated. Thus, in a sense the coherent, enlightened materialist, has already reached Nirvana though perhaps he lacks only suicide or euthanasia to be rid of the last illusion, that of his bodily existence...

Psychology in the twentieth-century, which is bound up with the modern (materialist) cosmology, has participated in the erosion of the old concept of humanity, though at times it has rebelled against a pure and coherent materialism that would make man (as claimed by the behaviorists) a completely predetermined robot, and would horribly flatten human reality. As a result, psychology has been the scene of struggles for a form of self or ego concept. Taking into account materialistic presuppositions, nonmaterial entities cannot exist. Admitting that man is endowed with a soul or some other spiritual entity is then out of the question. Man is an animal. Nietzsche seems to have grasped this paradox when he commented in **Twilight of the Idols** (1895: chap 1, 35): "There are cases in which we are like horses, we psychologists, and become skittish: we see our own shadow looming up before us." Despite their materialistic presuppositions, psychologists found it difficult to resist the appeal of the concept of self. Psychologist Gordon Allport notes (1955: 37) that Freud played a major (though unintentional) role in the preservation of the ego concept. Allport adds that referring to the ego concept in a materialist framework is arbitrary; it is evoked a bit like a *deus ex machina*, to save both human dignity and the complexity of the data regarding human behaviour (Allport 1955: 37-38):

> The situation today seems to be that many psychologists who first fit personality to an external set of co-ordinates are dissatisfied with the result. They therefore re-invent the ego because they find no coherence among the measures yielded by positivistic analysis.[449] But unfortunately positivism and ego-theory do not go well together.

Despite the conceptual wasteland offered by the materialist cosmology, materialist presuppositions remain unquestioned, in principle, by the vast majority of Western elites. Noted multimedia artist and author of the essay **The Post-Human Condition**, Robert Pepperell asserted with little embarrassment or pointless subtlety (1997: 6):

The prevailing wisdom, variously expressed and argued for, is **materialism**: there is only one sort of stuff, namely matter — the physical stuff of chemistry, physics and physiology — and the mind is somehow nothing but a physical phenomenon. In short, the mind is the brain.

If one adopts a consistent attitude toward the modern cosmology, consciousness, ego, even reason, are reduced to mere illusion, the product of random neural patterns of varying complexity. Admitting the postulate of the soul, an entity conceived of as separate from the body in pre-Christian and Christian cosmologies, would challenge the very foundations of the materialist cosmology. Such a postulate is ruled out at the outset. Materialist cosmology is irrevocably one-dimensional. Steven Pinker is the author of several books on the brain and language and is also an MIT professor of cognitive sciences. In a public exchange with Richard Dawkins, he related the following anecdote (Pinker in Radford 1999):

> Yesterday I was on the radio with a professor of divinity who said it was crucial that we retain the idea of a unified self, a part of the brain where it all comes together — the ethical system of two billion people depends on it, he said. I replied there's considerable evidence that the unified self is a fiction — that the mind is a congeries of parts operating asynchronously, and that it's only an illusion that there's a president in the Oval Office of the brain who oversees the activity of everything.

Although few would have the courage to express themselves so brutally and so openly, no doubt such a claim would nonetheless enlist the support of the majority of our modern and postmodern elites. But physicist Sir Roger Penrose does not believe things are so simple. He notes (1994: 414-415) there are three mysteries that science has not solved concerning the interaction between the mind and the world around us. The first mystery is that mathematics can describe the physical world; the second is that physics can provide the basis for the mind and the third is that the mind can understand mathematical concepts.

Richard Dawkins, on the other hand, believes that living beings are, basically giant, hulking and awkward robots, controlled by their genes. In his view, determinism[450] is ultimately genetic. This being the case, the existence of the intellect and its capacities asks an unanswered question. The development of culture and, in particular, morality would be what some could call "the robots rebellion." Natural selection and our genes are only interested in survival. The paradox of the materialist point of view is that ethics often establishes objectives far beyond biological survival. Altruism can then be viewed as an inconsistent rebellion against the dictates of nature as well as the more complex cognitive processes such as moral reasoning or scientific induction. If we are purely natural creatures, made solely of matter and energy, what we view as our "self" is nothing more than brain functions producing the illusory perception of unity and coherence of a being in time. And such phenomena are nothing more than meaningless coincidence or, at best, capabilities that have favoured the survival of genes encoding such traits in their code/program. Then the following questions arise: Why struggle to maintain the illusion of morality, reason and individuality? Why fight against the ultimate value of survival? Survival is the sole value recognized by the material world.

The dominant materialist cosmology, it must be admitted, is dysfunctional. It finds it difficult to accomplish the task that society demands of it. The concept of man, in particular, finds itself forced into a mould that does not suit it, exposing ambiguities, paradoxes and contradictions. Because the object of study in the social sciences is precisely man himself, the disintegration of the concept of man, inherited from the Enlightenment, has had dramatic consequences. These sciences, which were built on this concept, find themselves in a *cul-de-sac* as shown by the Quebec sociologist Fernand Dumont (1981: 12):

> We are trapped. If we try to put the accumulated knowledge on human beings to use, we soon realize that anthropology does indeed talk about us, but from a place that does not seem to concern us. If we look to politics for something that could reconcile us in a common face of man, in a Community, we find ourselves lost in the contradictions of collective aspirations, in disparate ideologies that anthropology will encourage us to reject even more. Is there anything left beyond blind passion and anthropology in the absence of man?*

The collapse of the Enlightenment concept of man has been discussed by French anthropologist Marc Augé (1994: 116-117):

> One must begin with a general observation. After the death of God, it has been fashionable of late to celebrate the "death of man." Regarding the death of God, and regardless of one's personal feelings on the matter, the wider spectacle of our present circumstances seems to me to require some caution. What do we mean by the death of Man? Mainly the fact that [man as] the measure of all things (Descartes' *cogito*, extending Protagoras' aphorism) has itself become the object of science. Human reality has been divided and reconstituted, based on the

interests of each discipline. That the object [of study] of the humanities was also the subject did not change a thing, since epistemology, psychology and all the cognitive disciplines consider knowledge itself an object of knowledge. Existential pessimism flows from the observation that man is not God (or as a God he is dead), from the parallel observation that any object of study is artificial, a construct…*

The aforementioned impasse calls into question Social Anthropology itself… If man is dead, if the concept of man is nothing more than a Western artefact, what is left of anthropology? Social science research then becomes totally devoid of any universal content. All that is left is the perpetual accumulation of ethnological data, never being able to develop a perspective that would provide a framework giving an overall view. What is the point of studying the human condition, if you have no valid point of reference for it in cosmological terms, if we've lost what is human? One might as well collect postage stamps or beer bottle caps…⁴⁵¹ This is no longer a matter of "truth", but of interests. Everything is drowned in subjectivity. What is left then? Dumont's solution to this dilemma is rather pathetic (1981: 22):

> The issue of truth in question here [in the social sciences] is ultimately "truth" for me, "truth" for us. Experience in teaching is perhaps the best proof of this. In his task of introducing knowledge, the teacher constantly faces this primary obstacle, the student's insidious question: The knowledge that you are trying to teach me is probably [!] objectively true, but is it relevant, does it have meaning for me, to the point where I should dedicate my passion and my life to it? A teacher must both teach the knowledge of the true as well as awaken a sense of the pertinence of this knowledge. Nevertheless, and this is the paradox of the trade: a "truth" that is only "pertinent", that would immediately fill my need to give further meaning to my knowledge would ultimately only dress up, in a rational guise, my own passions.*

How then is one to distinguish between knowledge that is only a mask for passion and pure propaganda? Anthropology then becomes a malleable tool, ready to serve the interests of the day. If Social Anthropology is dead, one should not be stupid enough to breathe a word to granting organizations. Otherwise departments of anthropology might find themselves abolished or at best absorbed by biology departments.

It should be understood that in the West the process of challenging the concept of man is multifaceted. Attacks against the concept of man, as a distinct species, have come from different directions, and have occurred simultaneously. In the mid-twenti-eth-century, one of the attacks against the concept of humans took place in the legal domain and targeted humans at their point of origin, when they enter the world. Obviously this has to do with the debate on the legalization of abortion. In most Western countries, this battle has been won by the modern elites. Abortion is now legal and has been accepted since the 1960s, that is to say as a decrimi-nalized medical practice, and in most cases, supported and subsi-dized by the state.

At the other end of the human scenario, there are those pres-ently advocating euthanasia for the suffering, so that they can die "with dignity". It should be noted that the debate on euthanasia is mired in misunderstandings, between passive euthanasia, which involves abstaining from imposing extraordinary medical measures on a dying individual, and active euthanasia, where ordinary care is withdrawn from a suffering person, a person who could normally live much longer without any extraordinary medical measures. In common usage, the term "euthanasia" may thus include the con-duct of a physician injecting a lethal dose of a drug to a patient whose "quality of life" he questions, in some cases doing this with-out the express request of the targeted individual or that of his family. Such considerations must be placed in the wider context in the West where aging populations exert great pressure on health systems and where the financial "benefits" of active euthanasia among elderly and disabled people abandoned by society are increasingly felt by the administrators and providers of these sys-tems.[452] Examining our attitudes toward death, Meilaender high-lights a paradox in the modern worldview (2002: 26):

> More than thirty years ago Paul Ramsey wrote chapter three of his **Patient as Person**. That chapter, titled "On (Only) Caring for the Dying," remains one of the classic essays in bioethics. Thinking self–conscious-ly from within a Christian perspective, Ramsey noted how our desire to master death can turn in two, seemingly quite opposite, directions. We may strive to extend life as long as possible, or we may decide to aim at death when the game no longer seems worth the candle. Seemingly opposite, these two tendencies within our culture both have their root in that same fundamental desire to be master of death. We will hold it at bay as long as we can, and we will embrace it when that seems to be the only way left to assert our mastery. Neither way acknowledges the peculiarly "in–between" place that human beings occupy in the creation.

Meilaender notes that if we reject the concept of humans as beings cooperating with a greater power, we then assume the role of those giving life and therefore take upon ourselves the almost divine responsibility of judging the "quality of life" that we give/ permit to others. As part of this new role, sooner or later we will have to judge whether this or that particular life is meaningful or not. How will we respond? On what basis? In the current ideologico-religious context in the West, typically overvaluing individual liberty (against its responsibilities) and immediate gratification, such concepts are so important that the lives of others, if they are not perceived as "productive", contributing in some way to the common good, become perceived as discardable. As a result, what it means to be human (considered as a being in time) shrivels from its initial stage to its end. Man has become a hunted animal.

Beyond Self

It is the beginning of what is really a new species — the Chosen Heads who never die. They will call it the next step in evolution. And henceforeward, all the creatures that you and I call human are mere candidates for admission to the new species or else its slaves — perhaps its food.
(C. S. Lewis, That Hideous Strength 1946/1965 : 197)

It is comforting, however, and a source of profound relief to think that man is only a recent invention, a figure not yet two centuries old, a new wrinkle in our knowledge, and that he will disappear again as soon as that knowledge has discovered a new form.
(Foucault 1966/1994: xxii)

In recent years, one attack against man's special status has come from what is called the posthuman movement. Artificial Intelligence (AI) experts as well as artists and techno-visionaries are involved in this movement. That said, one must distinguish between the postmodern and the posthuman. Postmoderns[453] have questioned a large number of Enlightenment-derived cultural concepts expressed by humanism, concepts, which in many cases, were borrowed from the Judeo-Christian worldview. Among other things, postmoderns have rejected Western culture's special status, man as the summit of Creation/Nature, the objectivity of History,[454] the universality of various Western social and moral institutions including science, democracy. But since the individual is at the heart of this belief system, postmoderns typically observe a conceptual taboo[455] and avoid challenging the privileged and unique status of the Homo sapiens species. The posthuman movement, on the other hand, has quite unambiguously crossed that threshold. As far back as 1943, C. S. Lewis had foreseen this development[456] and wrote in **The Abolition of Man** (1943/1978: 45):

> Man's conquest of himself means simply the rule of the Conditioners over the conditioned human material, the world of *post-humanity* which, some knowingly and some unknowingly, nearly all men in all nations are at present labouring to produce.

Postmoderns sometimes argue that various artistic, ideological or social movements are "out-dated." Among posthumans, the Western concept of man itself is perceived as out-dated, defunct. These authors view human corporeality or bodily existence as an evolutionary accident, not a given that we must accept or an aspect of a divine gift. Ullman insists (2002: 63) that "Once you accept the definition of human life as artificial — designed, engineered — it is then an easy matter to say that the proper study of man is not man but some other engineered object, the machine." The concept of artificial life is usually the focal point of posthuman thinking. In addition, the postmodern and posthuman movements both question the scientific discourse asserting the existence of an objective, real world to which scientific theories must submit.[457] Posthuman writers such as Pepperell view the real world postulated by science as just another Western social construct, nothing more. As a result, one is left with little reason to contest the "reality" of the virtual world offered by computers. Everything (and nothing) is real. Materialism[458] remains one of the most important ideologico-religious posthuman assumptions, the quintessence of twentieth-century wisdom. This means that the ultimate form of determinism is material. The human mind, then, is reduced to a chemical epiphenomenon, an incidental side effect of neuronal interactions. In this view, the mind/brain distinction is an illusion. Everything is information, even personality.

Pursuing this logic, biologist Matt Ridley claims that, in the Darwinian framework, it is necessary to relativize the concept of human consciousness and identity. From that point on, such rela-tivization leads to an anti-humanism (Ridley in Morton 2000):

> Well I think the conceits that humans have tended to live with is that their own particular lives are very important, that, 'I'm an individual, the individual is what counts', and so on. And when you start to think of yourself as just another vehicle for a long line of genes that is trying to compete and survive into the next generation, it does slightly relegate you in one sense. One way of looking at it is that the human being is a disposable plaything of the genes, and I think people do find that threatening and humiliating, and perhaps that explains some of the antipathy to neo-Darwinian ideas. But I've always found it rather won-derful to think of myself as just this temporary aggregation of genes in a great long line of genes that go back to the primeval soup.

Perhaps there is some gratification to be had from fantasies about having been an ingredient in the primordial soup, but was it onion soup or bouillabaisse? This is certainly a subject worthy of deep meditation, of course… This view is "genetically" related to the materialist old guard, but the relationship with Eastern systems of thought (such as Buddhism[459]) is worthy of serious consideration as well in this context since, in its final stage, the posthuman belief system, like Buddhism, leads to the annihilation of personality. If one considers the posthuman attitude with regard to humans, proclaimed and nourished by science fiction, it is possible that in a more or less near future, the man - machine threshold will itself be dissolved. The posthuman school of thought argues that, tech-nically at least, infinite progress is possible. It is also assumed that human corporeality is a contemptible phenomenon, to be dis-carded or superseded as soon as technology allows. Some posthu-mans are the zealous promoters of the idea that all humans should be "improved" and equipped with computer chips, thus constitut-ing the next step in the evolution of the human species. In France, there are echoes of this ideology. For example, molecular biologist and author of **The Symbiotic Man** (1995/2000) Joël de Rosnay foresees the development of man as a hybrid life form, no longer truly human, but a synthesis of the biological, mechanical and electronic, a being which would be encompassed by[460] the emer-gence of a new global organism. This planetary macro-organism would be known as the Cybiont.[461]

In developing posthuman cosmology, despite his traditional (or sentimental) attachment to materialism, a posthuman author such as Pepperell admits that one should not rule out the concept of occult powers as an acceptable part of the cosmos.[462] Hard-core materialism is no longer cool. In the postmodern context, materialist assumptions no longer serve as a final limit or as truth. Among the proponents of the posthuman belief system, as with Gnostics and Neo-Platonists in the ancient world, the human body becomes an object of contempt; an obstacle to be superseded or discarded when possible in order to attain a higher 'spiritual' plane. Referring to evolutionary cosmology, posthuman authors[463] argue that man is no more than a step on the road of evolution, not its destination. If one accepts that man, in the course of the evolutionary process, is the result of a very large number of genetic manipulations, mutations occurring in random circumstances, then there can be no reason to object to pursuing this process (using human actors). Why should the Homo sapiens species be considered "untouchable" or "sacred"? Pepperell notes (1997: 101):

> What should be becoming clear is the divergence of this conception of human existence from the more traditional humanist one. If we can start to see how the most sacred of human functions, being and thought, operate in ways not dissected from other functions in the universe then we are moving away from the notion of humans as unique isolated entities and are moving towards a conception of existence in which the human is totally integrated with the environment in all its manifestations — nature, technology and other beings.

We clearly see here a process where cosmological assumptions regarding man are being eroded and replaced. The issue at stake here is critical for any civilization and, again, we must emphasize its profoundly ideologico-religious character.

The Ghost in the Machine

The experiment has not yet been brought to an end, but its principle is logical. If there is no human nature, then the malleability of man is, in fact, infinite. Political realism, on this level, is nothing but unbridled romanticism, a romanticism of expediency. (Camus 1951/1978: 237)

Man's special status is a theme explored in many venues of pop culture. In movies, for example, it underlies a number of science fiction films, including the legendary **Blade Runner** by director Ridley Scott. Can a machine become human? Are humans, as biological organisms, artificial, arbitrary constructs? None of these questions can be answered without reference (explicit or not) to cosmology. The whole debate on human cloning is intimately related to the question: What is man? How do you define man? On the other hand, as we shall see, research in artificial intelligence raises further questions: "Do computers[464] think?" The concept of Man, inherited from the Judeo-Christian worldview, and recycled by modern religion (through the humanist tradition), melts away like snow in the postmodern deconstruction furnace.

Science fiction literature involves recurring themes, with unavoidable cosmological implications. It raises questions such as: "Do machines or computers have a soul? Can they be creative? Can they learn/understand humour or make jokes? Can they have emotions or become human?" This brings to mind HAL the emotionally conflicted computer in the movie **2001: A Space Odyssey** (Kubrick, 1968), **Artificial Intelligence** (Spielberg, 2001) Isaac Asimov's sci-fi trilogy **Foundation** or, on a more popular level,[465] the film **Short-Circuit** (John Badham, 1986). Marvin Minsky, an expert on artificial intelligence, sees the human mind as no more than a computer made of meat. Man is a (biological) machine and nothing else, a concept entirely compatible with postmodern cosmology. Discussing the views of Philip K. Dick, author of **Do Androids Dream of Electric Sheep?** (the novel that inspired **Blade Runner**[466]), English professor Katherine Hayles examines this central cosmological concept of man (1999: 163-164):

> In a formulation strikingly reminiscent of Maturana and Varela, he [Dick] suggests that **the human is that which can create its own goal.** He goes on to develop other characteristics that, for him, set the human apart from the android: being unique, acting unpredictably, experiencing emotions, feeling vital and alive. The list reads like a compendium of qualities that the liberal humanist subject is supposed to have. Yet every item on the list is brought into question by the humans and androids of Dick's fiction. Human characters frequently feel dead inside and see the world around them as dead. Many are incapable of love or empathy for other humans. From the android side, the confusion of boundaries is equally striking. The androids and simulacra of Dick's fiction include characters who are empathic, rebellious, determined to define their own goals, and as strongly individuated as the humans whose world they share. What does this confusion signify?

Yes, the relevant question is in fact: What exactly does this confusion mean? In **Blade Runner**, replicants are introduced. These are humanoid clones, generally used for hard labour or dangerous tasks. They are implanted with a false, artificial memory.[467] The film leaves the viewer suspecting that the hero (Deckard) himself may also be a replicant. Such a question would certainly be troubling for the hero, but it is also for the viewer as it raises the question: What is a human if you take away his life history, his memories? Human awareness of being an individual, or of being unique, is this only an illusion? What is he then? Just an artificial, arbitrary construct? In the postmodern cosmology, the concept of man melts away like an ice cube on a hot summer day. All traditional reference points are irrelevant, illusory, of no use. In the postmodern framework, where everything is the product of arbitrary cultural constructs, this confusion is to be expected. It is the natural order of things.

In **Blade Runner**, Dick examines the android - human relationship, noting first of all that humans have a capacity for empathy[468] while androids do not. Empathy (or altruism) is the ability to care for others, to which one can add the ability to love. The movie's final scene[469] turns everything upside down. After a long chase between Deckard, the android hunter and Roy Batty, the Nexus-6 android, Deckard finds himself in trouble, clinging to the parapet of a building, on the verge of falling off. He finds himself totally at the mercy of his target, the blonde android Roy. When finally he lets go, the android saves Deckard by grabbing his hand and pulling him back up on the roof, before sharing the beauty of his life and then dying himself. This scene is critical, as at this point in the movie, according to Dick's definition, Roy the android has become human, even the saviour of humanity one could say. The initial situation is then reversed, the machine has become human, a conscious being demonstrating empathy, whereas Deckard, the killing machine, is cold, numbing his conscience with alcohol, to all intents and purposes appears to have lost that status.

One must be aware of the ethical and political consequences of such an arbitrary definition, as the definition suggested by Hayles and Dick here is only loosely based on Western tradition, but seems to have its ultimate basis in emotions and feelings. One must give long and hard thought to the consequences of adopting this definition of the human. If, for example, one uses this an approach, there is little doubt that the majority of the exhausted and starving Jews in Auschwitz would not have met the demands of such a definition of humanity (involving the capacity for empathy). One could say much the same of tired workers, caught in big city traffic on a Friday evening after a long week. "To be or not to be, that is the question!" In the postmodern context, the concept of humanity finds itself in a precarious situation, just like the character Deckard, barely holding on to the edge of the parapet, his fate uncertain.

Freeman Dyson,[470] one of the better known twentieth-century physicists, claims that one day men will find it necessary to abandon their usual bodily existence in order to meet the demands of space travel and fulfil their destiny, that of exploring the stars. The human soul would then be reincarnated in electronic form... "What kind of packaging for you miss? We offer economy class on a USB key, a designer CD case or luxury platinum disks (with optional military-grade back up)." Engineer Winfred Phillips (2000: chap 2) believes that such visions of the future are related to the assumption that the mind or human consciousness is very similar to software, that is to say, information and can thus be downloaded.[471] In her analysis of posthuman discourse, Mary Midgley stresses the promotion of concepts of this kind is linked to primordial needs, such as the thirst for power and the fear of death. But beyond these concepts, one finds that posthuman ideology has much in common with the great philosophical and religious traditions of the ancient world (Midgley 1992: 220-221):

1. They are in a very obvious sense *other-worldly*, pointing us away from the earth, the flesh and our familiar worldly pleasures.

2. In doing this they evidently posit a *soul* of some kind essentially separate from the body. Their position about this seems to be nearer to Plato and Descartes than to Christianity or Buddhism, because they conceive this soul as primarily intellectual. But that is surely a minor difference in comparison with the startling fact of putting it there at all.

3. They seem to think it appropriate for this soul to dismiss its present body with contempt as unimportant to it. In this contempt for the flesh and for other earthly things, they go, in fact, considerably beyond the religious positions just mentioned, all of which do something to balance this world-denying spirit by a recognition of the legitimate claims of the flesh and of our continuity with the rest of nature.

Midgley notes with some irony that the anti-body prejudices adopted by the posthuman movement lead to a strange paradox. If the purpose of abandoning our organic bodies here is to take on other (metallic or silica?) bodies elsewhere in the universe, why should matter be less vile there than it is here on Earth? Perhaps things will have to develop further, arriving at a final stage with completely disembodied intelligence as in **The Last Question**,[472] a short story by Isaac Asimov (1956). But among certain postmoderns the anti-body attitude is the source of some uneasiness. Such relativization calls into question a dominant idol on the postmodern altar, the individual's bodily existence.[473] In an interview with robotics researcher Rodney Brooks, Ellen Ullman,[474] a programmer and technology consultant, observes (2002: 69):

> ... I didn't much feel like a bunch of tricks. I didn't want to think of myself as *just molecules, positions, velocity, physics, properties — and nothing else*. He [Brooks] would say that this was my reluctance to give up my *specialness*; he would remind me that it was hard at first for humans to accept that they descended from apes. But I was aware of something else in me protesting this idea of the empty person. It was the same sensation I'd had while at the spiritual-robot symposium hosted by Douglas Hofstadter, an internal round-and-round hum that went, No, no, no, that's not it, you're missing something.

Though posthuman rhetoric takes on the aura of scientific prestige, in fact it establishes a new mythology/ideology with scientific jargon providing convenient packaging for its message. Posthumans ignore the fact that empirical science itself cannot provide presuppositions that can be used to situation or define what it is to be human. Katherine Hayles responds to Ullman's objection and highlights the ideological consequences of the posthuman movement, as seen by an external observer (1999: 286):

> What do these developments mean for the posthuman? When the self is envisioned as grounded in presence, identified with originary guarantees and teleological trajectories, associated with solid foundations and logical coherence, the posthuman is likely to be seen as anti-human because it envisions the conscious mind as a small subsystem running its program of self-construction and self-assurance while remaining ignorant of the actual dynamics of complex systems. But the posthuman does not really mean the end of humanity. **It signals instead the end of a certain conception of the human**, a conception that may have applied, at best, to that fraction of humanity who had the wealth, power, and leisure to conceptualize themselves as autonomous beings exercising their will through individual agency and choice.

Yes, of course, we get it, we get it... The old Western concept of the human is linked to the bourgeois, to the culture of the rich, the oppressors. That's all we need to know. Move along folks, nothing more to see here... In the last sentence, one notices Hayles exploiting language that, by means of negative associations, attempts to paste a pejorative label on the traditional

(Judeo-Christian) definition of the human and to silence, marginalize the opposition, ensuring its rejection. Marvin Minsky, another big AI promoter, asserts that the logic of posthuman thinking leads to a new moral system and a reassessment of the concept of human rights (1994: 113):

> Traditional systems of ethical thought are focused mainly on individuals, as though they were the only things of value. Obviously, we must also consider the rights and the roles of larger scale beings, such as the super-persons we call cultures, and the great, growing systems called sciences, that help us to understand other things. How many such entities do we want? Which are the kinds that we most need? We ought to be wary of ones that get locked into forms that resist all further growth. Some future options have never been seen: Imagine a scheme that could review both your and my mentalities, and then compile a new, merged mind based upon that shared experience.

So what does the "Gospel according to Marvin"[475] propose? What is the fate reserved for humans in his new utopia? Will we find ourselves in a caste society where robots, given their superior intellect, will gain power and humans will be tolerated only as slaves? What is to prevent such an outcome? Also, if Kurzweil's and other AI proponents' dreams come true, soon (properly programmed) robots may be entitled to vote and have the right to formulate utopias and recruit adherents to their religion.[476] At the same time, it would also be conceivable that these rights could be withdrawn from humans who fail to demonstrate the ability to exercise them "responsibly." Why not? What postmodern cosmological assumption would prevent such an outcome? In the heat of discussion, some posthuman authors (perhaps inadvertently) acknowledge the ideologico-religious character of their views. Hayles, for example, writes (1999: 239):

> To indicate the widespread reach of this refashioning of the human into the posthuman, in the following section I want to sketch with broad strokes some of the research contributing to this project. The sketch will necessarily be incomplete. Yet even this imperfect picture will be useful in indicating the scope of the posthuman. So pervasive is this refashioning that it amounts to a new worldview — one still in process, highly contested, and often speculative, yet with enough links between different sites to be edging toward a vision of what we might call the computational universe.

The Ultimate Test

> According to Rodney Brooks, director of MIT's artificial-intelligence lab, evolution spelled the end of our uniqueness in relation to other living creatures by defining us as evolved animals; and robotics, in its quest to create a sentient machine, looks forward to ending the idea of our uniqueness in relation to the inanimate world.
> *(Ullman 2002: 61)*

Twentieth-century pop culture has produced a multitude of novels and science fiction movies that examine, from various angles, the man/machine relationship as well as the human/computer relationship. Usually, this results in (implicitly) calling into question, in one form or another, man's unique status. Such questions do not just "appear", but follow abundant discussions in the field of Artificial Intelligence (AI) and revolve around the definition of humanity and its relationship to the machine or computer. Voices in the AI movement as well as in science fiction have explored at length this question of what it means to be human and claim that the computer can be (or may eventually be) as sentient as humans. Note that the relationship between man and the inanimate world is a profound question that has always interested (although in other forms) religion, philosophy, myths as well as cosmology.

Much pop culture thinking concerning the man/machine/computer relationship has its roots in discussions in the field of artificial intelligence, in particular with the Turing Test (TT), which serves as a benchmark. The Turing Test is actually a game, a game where a computer attempts to imitate the verbal behaviour of a human. This test has several objectives, but one of the more important ones is to assess whether it is possible for a computer to think. The test was first proposed by the British mathematician Alan Turing in his article **Computing Machinery and Intelligence** published in 1950. Turing was also a cryptanalyst, programmer and engineer. During World War II, he worked for British counter espionage and decryption, particularly on "Enigma", the code name for an encryption machine used by the German Navy to communicate with its submarine fleet. He later became a member of the Royal Society and professor of mathematics at Manchester University before his suicide in 1954. Turing's test consists of confronting a human judge with at least two opponents, one of whom is human and the other a computer attempting to imitate human verbal behaviour.[477] The judge must try to uncover which of the opponents is the computer. This is done blindly, asking each opponent questions by means of text messages, since demanding a verbal (audio) conversation would have increased the test's level of difficulty. The judge may question his opponents for five minutes and then make a decision. If the computer manages to deceive the judge in posing as a human, it may be considered as having passed the test. With such an outcome Turing considered that there would no reason to reject the notion that such a machine can "think" as long as it can properly mimic what we call human conversation.

It should be noted that at the time of publication Turing's article was primarily speculative as no computer was then capable of engaging in such a competition. On the other hand, since 1991 each year the Loebner competition (Saygin 2000: 511) has offered developers the opportunity to let their software/computer packages take on the TT. The first program (or "chatterbot") to win the unrestricted test[478] wins a gold medal and the $100,000 US prize. Although each year a prize is granted to the best software/computer package that best mimics human conversation,[479] the $100,000 prize assigned to the system that would pass the Turing test has never been awarded.[480]

Turing's approach is a bit odd, since with such a revolutionary claim one would expect it to be supported by clearly defined statements, but in the very first paragraph of his article, Turing dismisses such demands (1950: 433):

> I propose to consider the question, 'Can machines think?' This should begin with definitions of the meaning of the terms 'machine' and 'think'. The definitions might be framed so as to reflect so far as possible the normal use of the words, but this attitude is dangerous. If the meaning of the words 'machine' and 'think' are to be found by examining how they are commonly used, it is difficult to escape the conclusion that the meaning and the answer to the question, 'Can machines think?' is to be sought in a statistical survey such as a Gallup poll. But this is absurd. Instead of attempting such a definition I shall replace the question by another, which is closely related to it and is expressed in relatively unambiguous words. The new form of the problem can be described' in terms of a game which we call the 'imitation game'.

This is a rather strange way of putting things. Why avoid clear definitions when supposedly exploring a scientific hypothesis? Does offering one's hypothesis in the form of a game actually serve to evade the requirement of providing clear definitions or is this just a trick to divert our attention on this point? Though one can accept Turing's objection to the use of a common sense definition of the term 'thinking', why not propose a better, more precise definition? In effect, the test proposed by Turing raises several interesting questions. How can one **know** if a computer thinks? Is it possible to know? What exactly does the TT prove? Can this test prove that a computer thinks, without first of all defining what thinking is? In the rest of the article, Turing uses hypothetical situations to get us to accept (or at least believe) that machines think. However, one should not be coerced into accepting Turing's procedure, as he is like a participant in a shooting competition refusing to have a target set up for him, yet demanding we accept his "success" when he shoots anywhere he likes. Because Turing avoids specifying in advance what it is to 'think', all the steps involved in the TT are futile.[481]

In practical terms, though it is conceivable that a human judge might be tricked by a computer's imitation of human verbal behaviour, what exactly would this prove? When deconstructing Turing's rhetoric, one sees that it implies that were a software/computer package to deceive a human judge in a game where the objective is to mimic human conversation, this would be considered evidence of the computer's ability to "think". But is such a conclusion necessary? Does it follow? Are there any logical loopholes in the TT? For example, when it is claimed that water boils at 100°C, this can be proven by empirical observations. Can one proceed in the same manner with respect to Turing's assertions? How do you observe or measure "thinking"? Perhaps the matter might be settled just as well by stating that a computer that successfully passes the TT proves, not that the computer "thinks", but rather that the engineers and programmers behind the computer (a point which Turing never mentions) are intelligent and do think. If one critically examines the TT, it becomes obvious that Turing never clearly defines the link between the test's objective and the reasoning used to attain that objective. Is it possible that there is no obvious connection between the measuring device (the TT) and the object/process being measured (human thought)? If this were the case, then the TT would be comparable to attempts to "measure" the colours in a sunset using a wooden ruler.

Needless to say, accepting Turing's hypothesis (with or without the test) — that computers think — brings new support to the posthuman assertion that Homo sapiens are not unique. But beyond the technical challenge the TT poses for programmers or engineers, one must be aware that the Turing Test's primary objective is to enlist belief rather than to prove anything. Software designer and programmer Mark Halpern notes (1987: 83) that "The Test is, in short, not an experiment, but a trap. Its purpose is not to discover the truth, which Turing already knows, but simply to defeat the interrogator's prejudices and force him to bear witness to the truth as revealed to Turing."

There is a curious tendency in Turing's (1950) paper, that is to say, a propensity to anthropomorphize the computer, presenting it as an agent capable of thought and initiative. This is due to the fact that Turing refuses to discuss the programmer's contribution to the process of creating a computer (able to perform useful tasks). This is a rather paradoxical and significant observation, seeing that Turing himself did programming for and participated in the design of one of the very first electronic computers, the ACE (Automatic Computing Engine) as well as programming for the Manchester Mark I. Turing was thus well aware that without the involvement of engineers and programmers, a computer would be little more than a pile of useless matter, indeed just a clunky trinket.

But Turing's attitude is understandable. Assuming that the computer owes its capabilities to its programmer, logic forces us to recognize that living organisms (including us) also owe their existence, their genetic code and their capabilities to a Programmer/Designer.[482] Turing, as an orthodox representative of the modern religion, of course cannot abide such a concept, which would force him to ignore the critical role played by programmers and engineers in the development of computers, a highly-coordinated synthesis of hardware and software. If Turing and other Artificial Intelligence proponents took into account the essential role played by the programmer/engineer, this would force them to abandon any claim that the computer thinks, since the computer's faculties, even if endowed with the capacity to learn, are directly related to the intelligence, skill and time invested by its programmer.[483] The abstract approach taken here by Turing (i.e., "overlooking" the contribution of the programmer and other human agents) becomes ludicrous when one examines a concrete situation such as the Loebner competition. The competition itself is simply inconceivable without the contribution of real engineers responsible for the design of computers as well as programmers who may invest thousands of hours in the (perhaps vain) hope of winning a prize.[484] On the other hand, the computer's actual role is insignificant when one seriously considers all the contributions of the intelligent agents involved in the process? Although in his article Turing mentions computer software a few times, in the context of the TT he ignores the significance of this element. If a functional computer is the synthesis of various compatible hardware components, software itself is non material. It is not linked to, or determined by, any particular arrangement of matter, but consists of information that can be transmitted in various forms. Presumably Turing's materialist cosmology compelled him to ignore this side of things, especially since it calls to mind the dichotomous nature of the human body/ soul postulated by almost all pre-modern civilizations.

In competitions such as the encounter between Deep Blue, a computer designed by IBM, and Gary Kasparov, a world chess champion,[485] one can assume, for example, that the Deep Blue support team hired a competent (intelligent) network manager to ensure the proper operation of the computer for the duration of the encounter rather than a chimpanzee more interested in his next banana or a teenager more interested in the video game that he just bought.[486] The involvement of intelligent agents is then not a small matter, as Turing seems to suggest. Regarding the significance of these encounters, the philosopher John Searle offers a rather caustic perspective (in Weber 1996):

> "From a purely mathematical point of view," Professor Searle said, "chess is a trivial game because there's perfect information about it. For any given position there's an optimal move; it's solvable. It's not like football or war. It's a great game for us because our minds can't see the solution, but the fact that we will build machines that can do it better than we can is no more important than the fact that we can build pocket calculators that can add and subtract better than we can.

In practice one must be aware that a range of contextual factors may influence the outcome of the TT. If, for example, the judge/interviewer has a list of criteria (guiding his questions) and these criteria are known to the programmer, then the software's chances of winning the TT will increase. However, if the interviewer has a long list of criteria that are unknown to the programmer, the software's chances of winning will necessarily decrease proportionally. In addition, if the interrogator has a sudden inspiration to ask a novel and difficult question, the chances are that the software will be unable to respond adequately.[487] Arguably, in general, the more the programmer knows about the judges;[488] the better the chances are that his software will pass the test. There is another matter to consider. If one does not take for granted that competitors will adhere to high ethical standards,[489] one must factor in the possibility that a programmer could bribe a judge. And of course, objectively this also could influence the test results. On the other hand, if the software is programmed with the ability to learn from its exchanges, then this could also affect the outcome. But it must be stressed that such learning ability cannot be achieved without an additional programming effort and creativity at the programmer's expense.[490] In other words, a software/computer entity demonstrating a capacity to learn is a higher level of embodied intelligence than is the ordinary software/computer entity. It represents, in concrete terms, the programmer's intelligence in its basic functions just as much as in its more advanced capabilities. Mark Halpern observes (1987: 91):

> AI programs will achieve great usefulness, even (in some fields) indispensability, but they will not be hailed as their fond authors wish them to be; that prize will forever elude them. For as they come to play better chess than Capablanca, and prove theorems that would have defeated Gauss, and put human chemists out of work, it will become equally well understood that they are not doing any of these things in "interesting" ways — ways that deepen human insight into the problems being dealt with. The computer will not really be playing chess, proving theorems, or doing chemistry, but merely executing the appropriate algorithm quickly enough to seem miraculous to humans. The results may be invaluable; the means will be dismissed as just another example of how man spins off specialized machinery to deal with problems he has (in principle) solved, in order to free himself for the mental play he calls 'thinking'.

Regarding contextual constraints that influence the outcome of the TT, the more the judges know about programming (and also about the particular software programmers involved in the competition and the strategies they may rely on), the greater the difficulties for competing software. It is clear that the quantity and quality of information available to both judges and programmers is critical in determining the test's final results. A priori, the software (of which the computer is merely the physical embodiment)[491] is directly and totally at the mercy of the quality of its programming as well as the programmer's in-depth knowledge of the objective of the test[492], that is to say, simulating human conversation. No doubt that in this context the contributions of an experienced linguist, a playwright or even a radio talk show host[493] could prove to be useful.

But beyond these practical considerations, there is evidence that the TT may be better understood as a packaging method for certain cosmological assumptions. This issue is sometimes flushed out in discussions on the TT. For instance, Saygin evokes objections to the TT as well as Turing's response (Saygin 2000: 470):

> Perhaps the most important objection is the argument from consciousness. Some people believe that machines should be conscious (e.g., aware of their accomplishments, feel pleasure at success, get upset at failure, etc.) in order to have minds. At the extreme of this view, we find solipsism. The only way to really know whether a machine is thinking or not is to be that machine. However, according to this view, the only way to know another human being is thinking (or is conscious, happy, etc.) is to be that human being. This is usually called the other minds problem and will show up several times in the discussions of the TT. 'Instead of arguing continually over this point it is usual to have the polite convention that everyone thinks'[494] (Turing, 1950, p. 446). Turing's response to the argument from consciousness is simple, but powerful: The alternative to the IG (or similar behavioral assessments) would be solipsism and we do not practice this against other humans. It is only *fair* that in dealing with machine thought, we abandon the consciousness argument rather than concede to solipsism.

Is the argument from consciousness in fact an extreme form of intellectual narcissism, comparable to solipsism?[495] If Turing had already provided convincing evidence that computers think, his response would be entirely acceptable, but this is not the case. Instead Turing avoids the issue and attempts to marginalize the argument from consciousness by insinuating that on "moral grounds" this is a flawed perspective. But why bring up moral considerations in this context? If we deconstruct the argument here, Turing is suggesting that it would be better to be perceived as "generous", showing a bit of "openness", allowing for intelligence and thinking in machines, and this, in a context where it is argued that it would be "chauvinistic" and "narrow-minded" not to accept that machines think. Turing proves nothing, but is manipulating us, basically demanding an act of faith on our part, as again no empirical evidence is offered to back up his claim that machines think or are self-aware. In fact, his argument presupposes we have already admitted that they are human (or at least like humans). Note that Turing's argument could only develop in a conceptual framework where human's unique status has already been badly shaken. Consequently questions of this sort can gain entry. To minds like

Turing's, the task is then to revise, to redefine what it means to think, what it means to be human...

To presuppose that human thought is characterized by understanding the content of an exchange raises an additional question for the TT. The philosopher John Searle has formulated an objection to the TT that has been much debated since. This is known as the **Chinese room argument** (Searle 1980), a thought experiment. Imagine Searle confined to a room with a slot through which one can introduce and receive messages written in Chinese. Though Searle does not understand the Chinese language, he has access to a (huge) reference book providing the answers to all imaginable messages. Searle then uses this book to write his answers. From the outside it appears that the room's inhabitant understands Chinese, but this is an illusion. Searle claims the situation is much the same for a software/computer successfully passing the TT. The computer can of course give an outside observer the impression of being able to hold a conversation, but in fact it understands nothing of its content and, like Searle, it has no awareness of the subject of these exchanges.[496] Hayles' previously mentioned essay, drops a critical admission regarding the TT (1999: xiv):

> Think of the Turing test as a magic trick. Like all good magic tricks, the test relies on getting you to accept, at an early stage, assumptions that will determine how you interpret what you see later.

Though the point made by Hayles rarely gets the attention it deserves, its importance can hardly be overstated. This raises the obvious question: What exactly are the presuppositions that the TT attempts to convince us of? Is it possible that the ultimate objective of the TT is to get us to believe[497] certain cosmological assumptions? Robin Gandy, a mathematician and former student of Turing, had discussions with Turing concerning his 1950 article and notes (Gandy 1996: 125):

> In fact Turing believed, or at least saw no reason not to believe, much more than this; that there would, eventually, turn out to be no essential difference between what could be achieved by a human intellect in, say, mathematics, and what could be achieved by a machine. The 1950 paper was intended not so much as a penetrating contribution to philosophy but as propaganda.[498] Turing thought the time had come for philosophers and mathematicians and scientists to take seriously the fact that computers were not merely calculating engines but were capable of behaviour which must be accounted for as intelligent; he sought to persuade people that this was so. He wrote this paper — unlike his

mathematical papers — quickly and with enjoyment. I can remember him reading aloud to me some of the passages — always with a smile, sometimes with a giggle.

Is it possible to determine the ideologico-religious perspective providing the basis for the assumptions referred to by Turing in his article? One section in Turing's article analyzes various arguments that could be raised against his theses. Among other things, he mentions what he calls the "theological argument"[499] (1950: 443), which of course refers to cosmological concepts shared by most monotheistic religions. This argument claims that man is distinct from the animal kingdom by the fact that he has an immortal soul. In a note of irony, Turing observes that if machines or animals have no soul perhaps this should be taken as an indication of a deficiency or disability in God.[500] With respect to the Judeo-Christian perspective, Turing's position is unambiguous (1950: 443) "I am unable to accept any part of this [argument]..." If one accepts modern cosmology, as does Turing, which considers man the product of a long evolution, there is no reason to grant man special status. Who knows? Perhaps evolution's ultimate purpose may be to make insects the dominant species on Earth rather than humans. Turing's argument is, in short, a product consistent with the more orthodox assumptions of the modern materialist cosmology.[501] And if the TT offers, in fact, an origins myth, it should be noted that just as Charles Darwin's **Origin of Species** challenged the old cosmological human/animal distinction, the TT, for its part, attacks another critical cosmological dichotomy, that which distinguishes man from the inanimate world. Another side to this issue is that the anthropology of religion shows us quite often that origins myths are expressed by means of theatrical techniques, eventually taking the form of ritual. In the case of the Loebner prize, this is precisely what happens. This award is, in a sense, a ritual celebration of our "oneness" with, and assimilation by, nature.

Another argument raised against the TT is Gödel's incompleteness theorem. Turing called this the "mathematical objection" (1950: 444-445). Gödel's theorem asserts that even in elementary parts of arithmetic, there are assumptions that can neither be proved nor disproved within this system. Many critics of Turing's position consider that Gödel's theorem implies that the computer, which can be compared to a powerful calculator, and does not have a mind, cannot get out of its own system, become introspective or develop self-awareness. Turing admits that machines are limited, but considers this of little importance seeing that the human intellect is often limited and often makes mistakes too. Turing believes that if a particular machine cannot answer a specific question, there is reason to believe that another, more advanced machine, will know how. But not everyone believes that this question is so easily resolved. J. R. Lucas, University of Oxford professor of philosophy, observed (1961):

> Gödel's theorem seems to me to prove that Mechanism is false, that is, that minds cannot be explained as machines. So also has it seemed to many other people: almost every mathematical logician I have put the matter to has confessed to similar thoughts, but has felt reluctant[502] to commit himself definitely until he could see the whole argument set out, with all objections fully stated and properly met.

Other authors assure us that there is a misunderstanding and that it is somehow "illegitimate" to apply Gödel's theorem outside the field of mathematics.[503] Is it possible that a prohibition against "exporting" Gödel's theorem may be primarily related to territorial instincts among mathematicians? Perhaps it would be best to let others come to a decision on the issue, but while we wait for a verdict, it should be noted that often human thinking makes progress by making use of analogies, that is to say by applying a principle outside a field where it was originally designed or used.

In the twenty-first century, ideas proposed by Turing as well as his views regarding the man/machine relationship, have deeply penetrated Western culture. The posthuman and artificial intelligence movements have pursued issues raised by Turing. It is sometimes argued, "If it were possible to build machines smarter than us, why shouldn't they take our place at the top of the evolutionary process?" We are getting to a point where some recognize that man, as a distinct organism, may be dissolved in a posthuman conceptual acid, with man as he has been known through the centuries on one side and, on the other the machine, and in between, an infinite series of variations which could be designated (without being too fussy about distinctions) cyborgs, machines comprising supplementary organic elements derived from living humans, from clones, if not from human corpses.[504] In the posthuman context, no concept should be excluded if there is reason to think it might have some benefit. After all, aren't humans just clay, to be shaped at will?

Posthuman authors, whose views find their basis in the logic of the Darwinian cosmology, address the human as an arbitrary cultural construct with no independent existence and to which no one can guarantee the future (in its traditional form). In the opinion of these authors, there is no such thing as a threshold where one might pass from the human to the nonhuman state. The following is a good example of this logic at work (Hayles 1999: 84):

> Of all the implications that first-wave cybernetics conveyed, perhaps none was more disturbing and potentially revolutionary than the idea that the boundaries of the human subject are constructed rather than given. Conceptualizing control, communication, a system, cybernetics radically changed how boundaries were conceived. Gregory Bateson brought the point home when he puzzled his graduate students with a question koanlike in its simplicity, asking if a blind man's cane is part of the man?

Of course, since the blind man finds the cane useful and one cannot "prove" that the cane is not part of the blind man, this would seem to prove that Bateson is right. But this is not an empirical matter as it is impossible to prove that the cane is part of the blind man and one can just as easily adopt the opposite view, holding that any added artefact (even if useful) will not become part of man. It is possible to treat the cane as just a tool, a useful tool no doubt, but nevertheless distinct from man. That an artefact or mechanism is considered "useful" does not change its identity. All this is linked to the presuppositions one holds and has nothing to do with empirical evidence. On the other hand, if one accepts Bateson's argument and exploits this kind of logic, it could lead to a situation where a paraplegic with artificial limbs, a pacemaker and corneal implants could be stripped of his/her civil rights as he/she would be no longer considered "quite human".

The important point to remember here is that the posthuman movement is primarily an ideologico-religious belief system, which may be accepted or rejected as such. Of course its proponents will never accept this label, but beyond the cool new jargon[505] used by posthuman proponents, that it is a belief system is evident when one carefully examines statements like the following one. Pepperell explains the "cognitive medium" concept, which involves the idea that intelligence, the mind (and creativity) can be attached to any object (Pepperell 1997: 21):

As I shall explain, I will use this term [cognitive medium] as a short-hand reference to the combined sensory and conscious media. I will also try to remind the reader that the cognitive medium is, in fact, continuous with environmental and organic media. If this seems a little awkward now, it will become clearer with familiarity. **Remember, we are trying to overcome two thousand years of accumulated beliefs.** (emphasis added)

But why "two thousand" years? Why "beliefs"...? What could Pepperell possibly be referring to here? Is it a coincidence that Christianity happens to be 2,000 years old? Yeah, must be... Since the objective is to change/replace core beliefs, beyond the gratification found in using high-sounding pseudoscientific jargon, the goal here is inevitably ideologico-religious.[506] The Posthuman movement echoes statements made by Filostrato, a character in **That Hideous Strength**, a science fiction novel by C. S. Lewis (1946/1965: 173):

That is the point. In us organic life has produced Mind. It has done its work. After that we want no more of it. We do not want the world any longer furred over with organic life, like what you call the blue mould — sprouting and budding and breeding and decaying. We must get rid of it. By little and little, of course. Slowly we learn how. Learn to make our brains live with less and less body: learn to build our bodies directly with chemicals, no longer have to stuff them full of dead brutes and weeds. Learn how to reproduce ourselves without copulation.

The ancient view of man, which considered him a unique rational animal, has been abolished, eliminated. This cosmological shift, linked to the question: What is man?, can have real conse-quences when it comes time to address the man/machine relation-ship. In the final analysis, the game is played on the basis of implicit cosmological assumptions. From a posthuman perspec-tive, it is conceivable that human consciousness could be down-loaded to a computer or to a cyborg and continues to "live" after the death of its owner's physical body. At a time when multina-tional corporations are energetically engaging in biotech research where the profit motive[507] is typically dominant, their instruments of terror[508] (or creation, from their point of view) will be genetics, bionics and computer science. As demonstrated by Hume and Wittgenstein, science can only tell us what is technically possible; to know what is desirable or good, one must look elsewhere. According to Hume and Wittgenstein, science has nothing to say on such matters. When scientists go to work, free of any moral restriction, held back only by what technology can do and can find funding for, one must accept that there no longer is any obstacle to the resumption of Joseph Mengele's vivisection experiments on humans if this were ever found useful for some reason (and a brilliant marketing guru could of course eradicate any inconvenient connection with the emotional reaction caused in the mind of the general public by the word "Nazi").

It must be remembered that if the redefinition of the human species, in terms of "superior" and "inferior" races, carried out by the Nazis, had grave social consequences that will forever mark the history of the West, we must not delude ourselves about the possible danger, in our time where technology has acquired great power, of a much more radical redefinition of the human than even the Nazis could ever dreamed of. While this danger[509] may not take the same form in sociological terms, it would be irresponsible to ignore its existence. In a context where the concept of man is disintegrating, why would one even bother promoting "human rights"?[510] If man is nothing, why defend man, why make a fuss? And if nonetheless there are those who would still defend man, perhaps it is because they still believe man is something more than an arbitrary biological assemblage? In his essay **The Empty Universe**, C. S. Lewis observed evolving attitudes towards man and the cosmos in the West which can be traced back to the influence of neo-positivist and behaviorist philosophy, and pondered on the consequences of posthuman attitudes (1986: 81-82):

> The process whereby man has come to know the universe is from one point of view extremely complicated; from another it is alarmingly simple. We can observe a single one-way progression. At the outset the universe appears packed with will, intelligence, life and positive qualities; every tree is a nymph and every planet a god. Man himself is akin to the gods. The advance of knowledge gradually empties this rich and genial universe: first of its gods, then of its colours, smells, sounds and tastes, finally of solidity itself as solidity was originally imagined. As these items are taken from the world, they are transferred to the subjective side of the account: classified as our sensations, thoughts, images or emotions. The Subject becomes gorged, inflated, at the expense of the Object. But the matter does not rest there. The same method, which has emptied the world, now proceeds to empty ourselves. The masters of the method soon announce that we were just as mistaken (and mistaken in much the same way) when we attributed "souls", or "selves" or "minds" to human organisms, as when we attributed Dryads to the trees. Animism, apparently, begins at home. We, who have personified all other things, turn out to be ourselves mere personifications.

In the posthuman perspective, the real question is not: Can/will a computer think?, but rather does man think or is he a robot determined by his genes, his pheromones or his relationship with his parents?[511] In the view of historian of science Stanley L. Jaki, man's particular claim is that of being an agent, someone who intervenes and, in many ways, directs (1969/1989: 308):

> Man is man only as long as he is interested in keeping in mind that a stone is not a flower, a stick is not a bird, and that an abacus, however sophisticated, is not thinking. Man is man only as long as he refuses to be flotsam and jetsam in the endless sea of things and events, but instead grabs the rudder available to him. More important, man also has to make a careful estimate of the proper use of that rudder. Most directly, that rudder is man's computing, calculating ability, but ultimately it implies man's whole being, his entire uniqueness. For by his very nature man is a steersman, a *kybernetes*, a cybernetician, and in order to live up to his very nature he should not shy away from the duties and responsibilities deriving from his peculiar condition.

Managing the Human Herd

All flesh is not the same flesh: but there is one kind of flesh of men, another flesh of beasts, another of fishes, and another of birds. There are also celestial bodies, and bodies terrestrial: but the glory of the celestial is one, and the glory of the terrestrial is another. There is one glory of the sun, and another glory of the moon, and another glory of the stars: for one star differeth from another star in glory. So also is the resurrection of the dead. It is sown in corruption; it is raised in incorruption: It is sown in dishonour; it is raised in glory: it is sown in weakness; it is raised in power: It is sown a natural body; it is raised a spiritual body. There is a natural body, and there is a spiritual body. And so it is written, The first man Adam was made a living soul; the last Adam was made a quickening spirit. Howbeit that was not first which is spiritual, but that which is natural; and afterward that which is spiritual. The first man is of the earth, earthy: the second man is the Lord from heaven. As is the earthy, such are they also that are earthy: and as is the heavenly, such are they also that are heavenly. And as we have borne the image of the earthy, we shall also bear the image of the heavenly. (1Cor 15: 39-49)

How is an individual's value to be determined? What relative value does one individual have compared to an animal or a computer? How can this value be justified? If the individual is made in the image of the Judeo-Christian God his/her value is fixed, invariable, infinite,[512] but in the present context, dominated by Enlightenment or postmodern cosmology, how are such matters resolved? How can granting a special status to man be justified? And if man's special status is rejected, then man must accept getting no more attention than any other animal. The Austrian psychiatrist Viktor Frankl made the following observations (1959/1971: 176-177):

More specifically, this usefulness is usually defined in terms of functioning for the benefit of society. But today's society is characterized by achievement orientation, and consequently it adores people who are successful and happy and, in particular, it adores the young. It virtually ignores the value of all those who are otherwise, and in so doing blurs the decisive difference between being valuable in the sense of dignity and being valuable in the sense of usefulness. If one is not cognizant of this difference and holds that an individual's value stems only from his present usefulness, then, believe me, one owes it only to personal inconsistency not to plead for euthanasia along the lines of Hitler's program, that is to say, "mercy" killing of all those who have lost their social usefulness, be it because of old age, incurable illness, mental deterioration, or whatever handicap they may suffer. Confounding the dignity of man with mere usefulness arises from a conceptual confusion that in turn may be traced back to the contemporary nihilism transmitted on many an academic campus and many an analytical couch.[513]

Shortly after World War II, Nazi concentration camp atrocities became known to the general public. This generation also remembered lively previous debates on animal vivisection, a debate similar to that currently regarding GMOs.[514] Vivisection was practiced as part of experiments involving the dissection of live animals for medical or scientific research. It was in this context that the Oxford scholar C. S. Lewis made the following remarks, which are still relevant today (1947/2002: 227):

> Once the old Christian idea of a total difference in kind between man and beast has been abandoned, then no argument for experiments on animals can be found which is not also an argument for experiments in inferior men. If we cut up beasts simply because they cannot prevent us and because we are backing our own side in the struggle for existence, it is only logical to cut up imbeciles, criminals, enemies, or capitalists for the same reasons. Indeed, experiments on men have already begun. We all hear that Nazi scientists have done them. We all suspect that our own scientists may begin to do so, in secret, at any moment.

When a cosmology does not demand universal dignity for all people, this leads to very real consequences. Under the Nazi regime, concentration camp physicians initiated various scientific experiments on prisoners. Since the cosmology referred to by the Nazis ranked men in "superior" and "inferior" races, all this in the context of the struggle for survival, there was nothing to prevent the exploitation of human beings for scientific experimental purposes. These humans were considered to belong to so-called "inferior races". In scientific terms, Nazi concentration camp experiments had demanding protocols, involving hypothesis testing and gathering detailed empirical observations. Prisoners were subjected to various experiments[515] such as air decompression simulating a drop in altitude of 20,000 metres, injections of malaria and typhus, tolerance to poison gas and conditions of extreme cold, infections initiated to verify the effectiveness of sulphanilamides, bone and muscle tissue transplants, sterilization, poison injections and experiments with burns due to incendiary bombs. Joseph Mengele, nicknamed the "Angel of Death", was the chief physician at Auschwitz. Twins were Mengele's favourite guinea pigs on which he studied blood transfusions and organ transplants. Part of his research consisted of practicing vivisection on children, at times removing their genitals.

There is a malaise in the West. A subliminal malaise, occurring here and there in attacks on and in the disintegration of Judeo-Christian cosmological concepts (though hypocritically recycled by nineteenth and twentieth-century ideologies) among moderns and, in more advanced form, among postmoderns. The question is: Why should Homo sapiens enjoy a unique status? If man truly is a product of the evolutionary process, basically such a status is an aberration. Isn't man just an organic entity, a site enabling diverse biochemical reactions, and no more? The ancients believed man to be the fusion of body and soul, a rational animal. However, this dichotomous view can no longer be held as valid now that a mature and coherent materialist cosmology has become widely accepted.

In the West, when it serves its interests, materialism is content to live comfortably in the shade of the Judeo-Christian heritage, but the modern religion cannot provide any reason for granting special rights to humans. We are told of course, that man has "an innate sense of morality" and that this capability was produced by evolution. Modern and postmodern belief systems also assert that morality can exist spontaneously, with no particular basis and mouth rhetoric to the effect that man has a "moral nature", but when attempting to establish the consistency of such claims by examining twentieth-century geopolitical history unfortunately these appear pathetically naive.

It must be noted that building a civilization on the basis of a materialist cosmology has been attempted, the experiment has been carried out. The Nazis, having adopted materialistic presuppositions, beginning in 1941[516] developed a program to improve the genetic makeup of the Aryan race. From their redefinition of man, ranking them in "superior" and "inferior races"[517], arose the Final Solution whose goal was the elimination of the genetically defective in populations living in territories administered by the Third Reich. The objective was to produce, through a process of selection, a race of supermen. This is the same logic used by a breeder to select cows giving more milk or to obtain faster horses. As everyone knows, the Final Solution led to the extermination of six million Jews during World War II.[518] But to implement their program it was necessary to anaesthetize the conscience of the individuals called to carry it out. One must wonder whether words such as those of Nietzsche were not found in the mouths of Nazi concentration camp managers in order to stifle the voices of their conscience as well as those of their subordinates (Nietzsche 1882/1924: sect. 325):

> What Belongs to Greatness. Who can attain to anything great if he does not feel in himself the force and will to inflict great pain? The ability to suffer is a small matter: in that line, weak women and even slaves often attain masterliness. But not to perish from internal distress and doubt when one inflicts great suffering and hears the cry of it, that is great, that belongs to greatness.

The path to consistency is on-going and finds expression in the postmodern cosmology. In this context, it is claimed that all animals are created equal. Ernst Haeckel, one of the nineteenth-century's most prominent Darwinian proponents, made explicit the cosmological logic redefining man's place in the cosmos (1899/1934: 289-290):

> Christianity has no place for that well-known love of animals, that sympathy with the nearly related and friendly mammals (dogs, horses, cattle, etc.), which is urged in the ethical teaching of many of the older religions, especially Buddhism. Whoever has spent much time in the south of Europe must have often witnessed those frightful sufferings of animals which fill us friends of animals with the deepest sympathy and indignation.[519]... Darwinism teaches us that we have descended immediately from the primates, and, in a secondary degree, from a long series of earlier mammals, and that, therefore, they are "our brothers"; physiology informs us that they have the same nerves and sense organs as we, and the same feelings of pleasure and pain. No sympathetic monistic scientist would ever be guilty of that brutal treatment of animals which comes so lightly to the Christian in his anthropistic illusion to the "child of the God of love."

Repackaging this logic in the twentieth-century, an ethologist like Jane Goodall claims one must consider chimps as part of "our family" (in Wise 2000: X). By the same logic, if one opposes the death penalty for humans, it goes without saying that one must also oppose similar acts to animals. Thereafter, the behaviour of the more extreme animal rights activists becomes understandable. These activities range from defaming zoos as "inhumane", attempting to assassinate the president of a medical research company, causing fires in fur boutiques, to spray painting women wearing fur coats or beating up zoo employees. One of the best-known movements is the Animal Liberation Front (ALF), which is active in Britain and the United States. Since 1982, it has been placed on the FBI list of terrorist organizations in connection with several fires and bombings.[520]

A CSIS report (1992)[521] points out that since 1980 in the United States alone, animal rights groups have carried out raids against more than 29 research institutions resulting in more than 2,000 animals stolen, property damage over $7 million and the destruction of years of scientific research. Activist animal defence groups are engaged in similar activities in Britain, Western Europe, Canada and Australia. In these countries, many of these groups have claimed responsibility for bomb attacks against cars, institutions, shops and the residences of research personal. These activists defend their behaviour alleging it is politically motivated, in the same way as battles in a war of liberation fought on behalf of an oppressed people. In short, this is animal "Holy War"...

These activists claim their activities are motivated by the animals' quality of life. But would one of them dare to come between a cougar taking down a deer or a grizzly devouring the salmon it just caught? If we examine the actions of these organizations, there is no evidence that predatory activities of this kind (that is to say initiated by other animals) interest them at all because such phenomena do not bring man's status into play. Beyond the rhetoric, it appears that it is rather man's dominant status that they cannot tolerate and seek to challenge. The preamble of the **Universal Declaration of Animal Rights**[522] clearly sets out the cosmological foundations advocated by animal rights activists.

> Considering that Life is one, all living beings having a common origin and having diversified in the course of the evolution of the species, - Considering that all living beings possess natural rights, and that any animal with a nervous system has specific rights, Considering that the contempt for, and even the simple ignorance of, these natural rights, cause serious damage to Nature and lead men to commit crimes against animals,
> Considering that the coexistence of species implies a recognition by the human species of the right of other animal species to live
> Considering that the respect of animals by humans is inseparable from the respect of men for each other, It is hereby proclaimed that...

It should be understood that the legitimacy of all the claims made above depend on the acceptance of the first sentence, which postulates the Darwinian cosmology. If this first claim is rejected, then of course the rest falls apart.[523] The notorious antispecist[524] Peter Singer, professor of bioethics at Princeton University, is a committed and coherent believer in the materialist cosmology and considers productivity (in either economic or intellectual terms) as central to his definition of the human. The antispecist school of thought denies and explicitly rejects man's privileged status in nature as proposed by the Judeo-Christian cosmology. This privileged status has gained such authority in the West that it profoundly influenced the moral and legal culture and even Enlightenment devotees subsequently recycled it for their own purposes. In the past, evolutionists have made gratuitous claims about man as "the summit of evolution", but Singer is one of the few to coherently pursue the evolutionary perspective in human-animal relations to its logical end. In Singer's view, if one is to show any concern for the principle of equality, there is no reason, after rejecting the concept of "inferior races", to arbitrarily stop there and limit this principle to the human species alone. For Singer, claiming that the human species has a higher value than other animals is in effect a form of racism. Singer notes, for example (1979/2011: 101):

> Hence, we should reject the doctrine that killing a member of our species is always more significant than killing a member of another species. Some members of other species are persons, some members of our own species are not.... So it seems that killing a chimpanzee is, other things being equal, worse than the killing of a human being who, because of a profound intellectual disability, is not and never can be a person.

In ethical terms Singer proposes a consequentialist or utilitarian perspective, which involves evacuating morality to focus only on the practical outcome of a position. That which is defined as useful is then considered moral. Singer offers the following presupposition: among humans it is the ability (and awareness) of suffering which allows someone to have interests and be considered a person. Thus, it is absurd to believe a stone or a tree may have an interest. If we accept this cosmological principle, and as Singer's perspective continues to develop, it demands a distinction between the individual's biological existence, his belonging to the species Homo sapiens and true human consciousness. The Swiss philosopher François-Xavier Putallaz[525] raises an important issue with Singer's argument (2003):

> If I deliberately use the terms *body* and *soul*, it is to immediately expose the tradition to which Singer belongs to without admitting as much. His analysis presupposes a dualistic philosophical conception of the human individual, where the fact of being biologically and genetically a member of the human species is considered distinct from gaining the status of a self-conscious and rational being. Because one's

biological properties are disconnected from one's psychic (and spiritual) properties, Singer can place a chimpanzee and a disabled child on his shopkeeper's scales, claiming that the difference between the interests of these two individuals weighs in favour of the primate.*

Singer believes that only in the presence of consciousness can one claim that an individual biologically belonging to the Homo sapiens species, is actually considered a real person. As a result, in biological terms, belonging to the species Homo sapiens is no longer enough. Many ethical and legal repercussions follow from such principles. The most controversial is Singer's justification of infanticide. The argument is simple: if equitable consideration of interests demands going beyond the species threshold to take into account an individual animal's capacity for suffering, and thus its degree of consciousness, then it becomes necessary to coldly evaluate these relative capabilities in both the human foetus and in an individual adult animal of another species. This is how humans must be viewed when one accepts the dictates of materialist cosmology (Singer 1979/2011: 135-136):

> On any fair comparison of morally relevant characteristics, like rationality, self-consciousness, awareness, autonomy, pleasure and pain and so on, the calf, the pig and the much derided chicken come out well ahead of the fetus at any stage of pregnancy — whereas if we make the comparison with an embryo, or a fetus of less than three months, a fish shows much more awareness.

When Singer establishes consciousness as a criterion for the detection of humanity, such a cosmological presupposition has dramatic consequences. Singer notes that consciousness increases the capacity to suffer. He observes that experiments on animals are typically justified by the fact that their consciousness is not as developed as that of humans, which implies a lower capacity to suffer. But Singer responds by telling us that the logic of this criterion implies that, in the case of a human whose consciousness is not developed, there is no reason, then, why we should not treat such a person as an animal, that is to say, as a potential subject for scientific experiments (Singer 1979/2011: 52):

> This does not mean, of course, that it would be *right* to perform the experiment on animals, but only that there is a reason, and one that is not specisist, for preferring to use animals rather than normal adult humans, if the experiment is to be done at all. Note, however, that this same argument gives us a reason for preferring to use human infants

— orphans perhaps — or severely intellectually disabled humans for experiments rather than adults, because infants and severely intellectually disabled humans would also have no idea of what was going to happen to them. So far as this argument is concerned, nonhuman animals and infants and severely intellectually disabled humans are in the same category; and if we use this argument to justify experiments on nonhuman animals, we have to ask ourselves whether we are also prepared to allow experiments on human infants and severely intellectually disabled adults. If we make a distinction between animals and these humans, how can we do it, other than on the basis of a morally indefensible preference for members of our own species? [italics original]

If one takes into account the grave implications of postmodern cosmology, it is especially important to develop a critical perspective that deconstructs its rhetoric and exposes its implicit presuppositions. If this is not done, when the day comes when things go off the rails, one will be left with little more than pointless emotional objections against views such as those of Singer, and no understanding of their cause or source.

In the twentieth-century, the traditional concept of humanity has come under attack from various quarters. The door is now open to the acceptance of attitudes toward humans, which once would have been considered barbaric. If man is now regarded as just one animal among others[526] — a product of evolution — what barrier may still hinder the development of a consensus among our elites, from viewing humans as a population of biological organisms with no special status, to be "managed" like any other animal population? And if over time it is determined that the human population has grown too much, why not establish management rules as is the case for deer in Canadian forests or rabbits in Australia; when "surplus" population growth threatens the environment or the interests of farmers, the hunting season is extended in order to remove a quota of individuals? Should we forbid asking such questions? Why should such questions be deemed "improper"? On the basis of which cosmological presuppositions? In the postmodern context, there is no obstacle to the implementation of such logic.

We have been propelled into a new era where the capabilities of biological and genetic technologies are growing exponentially. One must then ask who will use these tools and what will be the limits of their power? How will such limits be justified? To which cosmology will our elites refer to in justifying the difficult decisions that sooner or later must be made? As Francis Fukuyama points out the dangers we face will not be the same with which previous generations have had to deal (2002: 53):

> The term *social control*, of course, conjures up right-wing fantasies of governments using mind-altering drugs to produce compliant subjects. That particular fear would seem to be misplaced for the foreseeable future. But social control is something that can be exercised by social players other than the state — by parents, teachers, school systems, and others with vested interests in how people behave. Democracies, as Alexis de Tocqueville pointed out, are subject to a "tyranny of the majority", in which popular opinions crowd out genuine diversity and difference. In our day this has come to be known as political correctness, and it is worthwhile worrying about whether modern biotechnology will not soon be in the business of providing powerful new biological shortcuts to the reaching of politically correct ends.

In the Western materialistic cosmological context, long before reaching biological determinism's dead end, unbeknownst to the general public[527] our elites from time to time go back to the West's cosmological closet to dig out comforting old Judeo-Christian concepts, cherry-picked according to the needs of marketing opportunism and passing ethical fads. With determinism, the landscape seen at the edge of the abyss is not very reassuring... It's a bottomless pit. Although few are aware of it, the residual legacy of the Judeo-Christian worldview (and its resulting values) serves as our civilisation's crash barrier.[528] Of course, many will have difficulty conceiving that the West could slip into barbarism on a large scale, but one should stop and think for a moment: How is it, for example, that a country as advanced in cultural and scientific terms as Germany, producing artistic geniuses like Dürer, Bach, Brahms and Handel, also produced individuals like Hitler, Himmler, Mengele and Goebbels, who were put into power at the head of this nation? In general, one may hope that Western populations will be safe as long as their elites avoid putting into practice all the implications of the postmodern cosmology. As long as they are content with spouting rhetoric and scholarly essays, read only by other scholars, we (as a civilization) may get away with it, up to a certain point. But it must be realized that often universities and intellectuals are the incubators and midwives of ideas, which later on find zealots with the nerve to widely apply them in a society's dominant institutions. Hitler was not crazy, a "deranged" individual, but was rather the logical progeny of a dysfunctional civilization developed on the basis of a flawed cosmology. Hitler was thus a coherent man. Concerning Hitler, Pichot states (2009: 207-208):

> Hitler did not invent very much; in most cases he was content to take up ideas that were in the air and to pursue them to their logical conclusions. Euthanasia and profound meditation on 'lives not worth living' were commonplaces of the time — and not only in Germany, even if the Nazis made great use of them and conducted propaganda around this theme. More or less all countries, in Europe and the United States, saw organizations campaigning for the legalization of euthanasia. This was inspired by a kind of symmetry; eugenics (good birth) and euthanasia (good death) were the conditions for a good life — more important than social and economic reforms.

Dysfunctional Complementarities

A woman needs a man, like a fish needs a bicycle.[529]

In postmodern times, another area where the concept of the human has been attacked is that of sexual identity. Since the Industrial Revolution, the West has witnessed a revolution in gender relations: voting rights for women, increased access to education and the labour market, and improved conditions for divorce for women. Technology has also offered us the power to control our reproductive capabilities, upsetting behaviour patterns and roles between the sexes. In addition, proponents of homosexual and radical feminist ideologies have attempted to blur or erase, if possible, the male-female distinction. In the West, traditional concepts of sexuality have been deconstructed and, by exploiting fertility technologies, it may be conceivable to abrogate sexual complementarity even in matters of reproduction. If nature puts up barriers to our self-fulfilment, why not just step over them? A lesbian couple may therefore obtain a child via insemination (artificial or not) and a male gay couple can, if needed, obtain the services of a "rental uterus"... What may be the long-term consequences of such attitudes on a growing child in such a context, one day realizing that he or she is a "product" made to fill a need,[530] rather than a gift? Exploring the traditional concept of the child, Meilaender observes (2002: 25):

In the passion of sexual love a man and woman step out of themselves and give themselves to each other. Hence, we speak of sexual ecstasy — a word that means precisely standing outside oneself, outside one's own will and purpose. No matter how much they may desire a child as the fruit of their love, in the act of love itself they must set aside all such projects and desires. They are not any longer making a baby of their own. They are giving themselves in love. And the child, if a child is conceived, is not then the product of their willed creation. The child is a gift and a mystery, springing from their embrace, a blessing love gives into their arms.

This makes a difference in how we understand the meaning of children. A product that we make to satisfy our own aims and projects is one whom we control — and, indeed, over whom we increasingly exercise "quality" control. A gift that springs from our embrace is one whom we can only welcome as our equal. We are not divine makers, but human begetters. And the child is not the product of our will, of any quasi–divine fiat, but, simply, one of us, who takes his or her place in the community of human generations.

Self-defined sexuality in the twenty-first century, like the quest for the Holy Grail in the High Middle Ages, appears to be another manifestation of the postmodern quest for complete autonomy in all spheres of life. Francis Schaeffer remarked on this matter (1982/1994: vol.1, 37):

Some forms of homosexuality today are of a similar nature, in that they are not just homosexuality but a philosophic expression. One must have understanding for the real homophile's problem.[531] But much modern homosexuality is an expression of the current denial of antithesis. It has led in this case to an obliteration of the distinction between man and woman. So the male and the female as complementary partners are finished. This is a form of homosexuality which is a part of the movement below the line of despair.[532] In much of modern thinking, all antithesis and all the order of God's creation is to be fought against — including the male-female distinctions. The pressure toward unisex is largely rooted here. But this is not an isolated problem; it is a part of the world-spirit of the generation which surrounds us. It is imperative that Christians realize the conclusions which are being drawn as a result of the death of absolutes.

Sexual complementarity and interdependence are dead... In Dostoyevsky's words, regarding sexuality, everything is possible... All constraints (as well as what was formerly called "human nature") must be abolished. In the United States, a new sexual liberation movement, known as polyamory, has begun. This movement claims that monogamy is "unnatural" and that nothing should prevent involvement in simultaneous emotional/sexual relationships. In New York, several polyamorist organizations have emerged and a Poly Pride Day is held annually in Central Park by the Polyamorous NYC organization. A propaganda documentary **Three of Hearts: A Postmodern Family**[533] hyping the normality of such relationships by portraying a polyamorous relationship of 13 years, which produced two children. In the Netherlands, a triple marriage between two women and one man made headlines[534] in 2005. In legal terms though, the cohabitation contract (or *samenlevingscontract* in Dutch) does not carry all the advantages of a normal marriage. But seeing that historically the gay marriage cause has advanced step by small step, it should not be unexpected that this sort of cohabitation agreement be a temporary arrangement, until multiple partner marriages are fully recognized by society. In the grand scheme of things, these contracts would be then not anomalies, but precedents rather, until that day when all prejudices have been toppled and minds 'broadened' by popular culture.

In postmodern religion, being of the male or female sex is considered an "out-dated" concept and an insignificant limitation. Propaganda tells us that nothing should thwart an individual's aspirations, impulses or desires, not even one's sexual identity. As a result, human sexuality is abolished. Open the door to the unisex hermaphrodite! Today, if we look in the mirror, there is no reflection. Complementarity must be abolished since, in the postmodern perspective, it entails 'coercion', 'subjugation' and 'dependence'. However, if one accepts complementarity, this implies that to be fully interdependent one must not only accept, but also value the Other. But, in the postmodern view, this is unacceptable[535] because individual autonomy is a supreme principle. There is a striking contrast then between postmodern and traditional views, the traditional view considered marriage sacred, merging concepts of fertility, interdependence and symmetry, ensuring a community's continuity in time. This involved not only the marriage of individuals, but also of lineages, values and meaning.

In the view of our elites, man must be redefined, rebuilt from the ground up and this includes his sexuality. The concept of man is then both full and empty. Beyond the abolition of complementarity, the quest for total autonomy remains absolute. The cosmology's logic is thus expressed in the redefinition of gender relations. Of course the debate over gay marriage fits perfectly in this context.

In psychological terms, Francis Fukuyama makes a rather sobering observation, noting that in the postmodern West the use of psychotropic drugs as a means of social control also helps further dissolve any "disturbing" residues of sexual complementarity (2002: 51-52):

> There is a disconcerting symmetry between Prozac and Ritalin. The former is prescribed heavily for depressed women lacking in self-esteem; it gives them more of the alpha-male feeling that comes with high serotonin levels. Ritalin, on the other hand, is prescribed largely for young boys who do not want to sit still in class because nature never designed them to behave that way. Together, the two sexes are gently nudged toward that androgynous median personality, self-satisfied and socially compliant, that is the current politically correct outcome in American society.

The twentieth-century saw the rehabilitation/promotion of abortion, homosexuality and much more. What does the postmodern twenty-first century hold in store for us? Is there any reason to believe that the logic of postmodern cosmology will stop there? What might be the presently socially rejected phenomena which are destined to be widely accepted in the near future? What is to stop, for example, the rehabilitation of polygamy, paedophilia, necrophilia or bestiality? On a more basic level, this amounts to asking a critical underlying question: What are the limits (if any) to the marketing power of postmodern religion as well as to the postmodern elites' class interests?

Biotech Man

> *Science today treats man as less than man, and nature as less than nature. And the reason for this is that modern science has the wrong sense of origin; and having the wrong sense of origin, it has no category sufficient to treat nature as nature any more than it has to treat man as man. (Schaeffer 1982/1994: vol. V, 50)*

> *At the same time, the fable of degeneration has been revived, not in its old form, too hollowed out to be of use, but in a modern one. Geneticists have announced with trumpet calls in the media that humanity is threatened by several thousand genetic diseases. All the same, as the new eugenics longer bears on a population but on the individual, this threat is not accompanied by a discourse about degeneration, but rather on the way in which future parents can avoid, thanks to prenatal detection, having a child affected by one or other of these diseases — while awaiting the possibility of curing them in an indefinite future. (Pichot 2009: 221)*

The biotechnology revolution has gained tremendous momentum in the last decades of the twentieth-century and opens up on a practical level, a potential challenge to what it means to be human like no other generation has ever seen. Various technologies can now be used to modify the genetic structure of living creatures, from single-celled organisms to plants and animals. Pronuclear injection of DNA, gene targeting in stem cells and cloning (nuclear transfer[536]) are among some of the genetic tools now available. When creating transgenic plants, gene transfer is typically done by means of an intermediary, often a bacterium or a virus. Since the 1970s, these technologies have seen tremendous growth and are being used in medicine,[537] agriculture, food production and environment management. Substances such as insulin, erythropoietin (EPO) and growth hormones are being produced by biotechnology. These new genetic technologies can be exploited not only to produce proteins, but also vaccines for hepatitis B and MMR (measles - mumps - rubella). In 1997, the Roslin Institute in Scotland announced encouraging trials with the alpha-1-antitrypsin (AAT) protein, produced in the milk of "Tracy", a transgenic sheep. Once marketed, the final product appears in the form of a nasal spray, used in combating cystic fibrosis.

Although they are the product of serious scientific work, biotechnology is still subject to marketplace fads. A company in Taiwan has developed a zebra fish marketed under the name Night Pearl[538] which has a gene inserted from a fluorescent coral. As a result, transgenic zebra fish now glow in the dark. Other specimens of the Night Pearl fish have a red or green glow derived from genes from jellyfish and other types of corals. In other areas, multinational firms finance ambitious projects in the hope of profits that could be gained by obtaining patents on organisms (plants or animals) resulting from these processes. This is of course a subject of bitter debate. Can you patent an organism in which a gene or two has been modified as you would a machine that someone invented? The organism, in its natural state, already contains a large number of mechanisms that are not the subject of any patent. What is actually added to the organism is insignificant compared to its existing structures and biological mechanisms (to the extent that they are even known). It should be noted that patents have been granted for modified animals, but at present commercial interests mainly focus on agriculture (and plants in particular).

That patents can be granted for genetically modified living organisms raises some fundamental questions. Since the dawn of time, living organisms (animals and plants in particular) have been part of the human heritage. Anyone can buy and sell them, but the right of use remains limited to individual organisms. In fact, they belong to everyone. On the other hand, in the field of agriculture, more extensive rights are demanded to the point where genetically modified organisms may be considered "inventions", that is to say, as if they had been created *ex nihilo*.[539] Now suppose I buy a new car that comes with a blue paint job. I then drive home, put it in my garage, sand off all the original paint and give it a coat of red paint. To do a good job, I must work methodologically and use all my car painting expertise. Suppose also that once this is done I have a magic wand (which I did not make myself[540]) allowing me to produce, with no effort at all, as many red cars as I like. The next day, I drive one of my cars down to the patent office for a patent application, expecting that my work and painting expertise be recognized (and rewarded) by a patent for all the copies of my red cars. Notwithstanding my expectation, should the patent office then feel under any obligation to grant this patent? Perhaps it would be useful to make a detailed assessment, comparing my contribution with that represented, in terms of expertise, by the pre-existing mechanisms in blue car I bought (and copied)? Everyone would agree that one can be recognized as the owner of a particular organism/animal/plant, but until recently no one would have thought of demanding a copyright for this organism (and all of its progeny). This is a right of an entirely different order. There is a related joke circulating on the Internet, which goes as follows:

> A group of scientists designated a representative to meet with God and give Him notice that science had progressed sufficiently that He had become obsolete.
> The delegate was received in God's office and said, "God, we no longer need you. We have gotten to the point where we can now clone human beings and do miraculous things so we don't need you anymore. "
> God patiently listened to these statements and said, "Well, to resolve this disagreement what would you say to a little contest? The objective would be to create a human being. If you win, I'll retire."
> The scientist responded to this challenge, "You're on!"
> But God added one condition: "We'll do this the same way as when I created Adam." The scientist replied, "Sure, why not" and bent to the ground to pick up a handful of dirt.
> God looked at him sadly and said, "No, no, no! Get your own dirt..."

That researchers should seek compensation for their work is entirely understandable, but is issuing patents on these organisms the appropriate way to do so? Biotechnology raises many serious issues. In this section, our attention will focus almost exclusively on a narrow range of biotech processes, namely the development of transgenic organisms. As time goes by, all organisms are likely to become either a resource for or the target of genetic engineering. For example, in May 2001 Nexia Biotechnologies, a Canadian firm, announced the commercialization of BioSteelT fibre based on spider silk produced in goat's milk. This product results from the introduction of a spider gene in transgenic female dwarf goats. The spider silk molecules are secreted in the goat's milk, then harvested and processed to recover the desired molecules. The resulting fibre can be used for the production of high tech bulletproof vests. In agriculture, in 1996-1997 Monsanto began marketing its first transgenic plants[541] in the U.S. with Roundup Ready® (herbicide tolerant) and Bollgard® (insect resistant) cotton plants.

In 2003, Dr. Huizhen Sheng led a team of scientists at the Shanghai Second Medical University using transgenic techniques for the production of stem cells. Their procedure involved the fusion of human cells with rabbit embryos.[542] These embryos are allowed to develop for a few days before being destroyed in order to harvest the desired stem cells. Stem cells can be found in some adult tissues, in umbilical cord blood, aborted foetuses and in human embryos developed in test tubes. Since the use of human embryos is subject to controversy,[543] Dr. Sheng said that this technique would allow the use of stem cells without using or destroying human embryos.

This leads to an entirely novel situation. Previously, we only had power over individual organisms,[544] but now we are gaining access to technology with the potential to affect all future generations. All species are at risk of having their genetic material modified or damaged. Biotechnology raises many new questions. How is one to decide in these matters? On one side there are those who say that the progress of science should never be impeded, and, on the other, those who argue that we should never change nature. When examining the literature on biotechnology, even among researchers there is still some reluctance to wielding so much power. Fear of public opinion influences this reaction of course, but after Auschwitz, it seems a lesson has been learned in granting unlimited power to scientists. It is now accepted that no scientific or technological advance can be done in the absence of ethical oversight. Some may also claim that if a new technology exists, this does not necessarily mean that it must be used and that in a civilized and healthy society science cannot be conducted in an ethical vacuum. But this raises an additional question: Is there any agreement now on what constitutes a "healthy and civilized society"? In the postmodern, pluralistic West, one must admit that no such consensus exists. Therefore, unless one is dishonest, ethics and all the grand principles on which civilized society rests cannot be considered as "given" or beyond question. One must come clean and make clear which cosmology provides the basis for the proposed ethical system. This cosmology must then be justified rather than portrayed as a "truth" that has already been agreed upon, an implicit consensus. But in the postmodern era, such openness is the exception... More often than not, the primary goal of ethical discussions in the biotech industry literature seems to be to reassure the public about the fact that experts have already given thought about the issues and have established a "consensus" that all must accept which, in turn, ensures the unimpeded flow of research grants and market access.

When confronted with the far-reaching power of transgenic technology,[545] the question: "What does it mean to be human?"

takes on critical importance. Developments in the biotech industry are creating strong economic pressures that, in biological terms, may come to dissolve the specific nature of the Homo sapiens species. Seeing that the commercial opportunities may be too good to be passed up, exploiting the genomes of various species or their organs or tissues has become commonplace. In most Western countries, there remain some residual taboos against human cloning. Since one possible application of this type of technology would be the "production" of super geniuses or super soldiers, cloned from Nobel Prize winners or Olympic athletes, these taboos may possibly be related to the emotional shock caused by genetic programs initiated by the Nazis for the improvement of the Aryan race[546] in the first half of the twentieth-century. This remains a sensitive issue in the West. On the other hand, it may be that cloning creates an existential malaise as it, more or less explicitly, calls into question the idea that each person is a unique entity, belonging to no one, and whose biological blueprint answers to no human controller. Cloning indirectly raises questions about one's unique value as an individual. If we can make as many copies of an individual as we want, what is one particular copy worth? Unlike the so-called "normal person", a clone (notwithstanding all its/his/her desirable qualities) would likely be considered a "product" or just "a copy". Another technology, stem cell research, raises great hopes for the treatment of various diseases and the development of organ tissues, which could be used for organ transplants. But obtaining human stem cells typically demands destroying a human embryo,[547] which in the postmodern cosmological framework may be a perfectly acceptable solution, but is unacceptable in others.

Technology already allows for the creation of hybrid organisms, non-human organisms to which human genes are introduced in order to develop tissues and organs that later on could be introduced in humans. For example, one can raise pigs into which human genes are injected enabling them to develop human organs (a liver, for example) that could then be transplanted into humans in need of a new organ. In this regard, the French virologist Claude Chastel notes (1998):

> Since the early 1990s, the xenotransplantation problem, that is to say, the grafting of organs, tissues or cells from animals into humans, has, for a variety of reasons, shaken as well as caused much excitement in the transplantation community. While human donors tend to become harder to find, waiting lists of potential recipients gets longer: about

43,000 patients per year in the United States. This is not new, but it tends to worsen, partly because the public has lost its natural generosity, in reaction to cases of criminal abuse (some organ trafficking) or stories that got wide media coverage: tainted blood, pituitary hormone extraction and bovine spongiform encephalopathy (BSE) transmission to humans. A recent upsurge of interest has come, in addition, from advances in the immunology of hyperacute rejection of xenografts and prospects to avoid such problems through the use of transgenic pigs, one could say "humanized", and thus better tolerated.*

But xenotransplantation techniques are not without their critics, as Chastel points out that this type of practice involves certain risks (1998):

> Pigs, despite being "humanized" by transgenesis (which does nothing to eliminate their endogenous or latent viruses), are barely safer than baboons or chimpanzees from a virological point of view. Many virologists, including Robin Weiss in London, Glasgow and David Onions Jonathan Allan in San Antonio, Texas, rightly feel that the risks of xenozoonosis, if one were to engage in large-scale clinical trials in humans, are too great (a risk in any case certainly greater than zero). Unfortunately, we see some forging ahead anyway: xenografts from pigs or baboons have already been done in some countries and, setting aside any reservations, surgeons are preparing to proceed with human experiments which are dangerous in health terms, if not ethically reprehensible.*

But of course there is a market for such technologies. Chastel (1998) estimates the potential market, in the next ten years, to be six billion dollars! It goes without saying that market pressures will demand that a supply be created to meet this demand. And man is not the only organism targeted by transgenic methods. As more and more species have their genomes sequenced, more and more organisms are likely to be plundered for their genetic traits or become targets of engineering.

Driven by astonishing advances in technology, the biotech industry inevitably raises the issue of the definition of man. Should human genes or organs be transplanted into pigs in order to answer the demand for transplant organs? But before addressing these technical questions, one must first determine the ethical/religious context in which our response will be formulated. To which cosmology/worldview shall one refer to answer such questions? Underscoring the difficulty of taking a position in the debate on biotechnology between the technophiles and the technophobes, the anthropologist Mikhael Elbaz notes the emotional side of this debate which both parties face (2002: 27) "If it is difficult to decide between technophiles and technophobes, one must take into account the literally religious zeal with which this debate is conducted, a debate from which the majority is excluded."* Seeing this debate cannot be satisfactorily resolved without preferring one cosmological perspective over the rest, one should not be surprised at the high emotions that this debate elicits given the medical, agricultural, economic and religious stakes on the table. It is essential, first of all, to force out into the open the cosmologies underlying the various positions, then examine their credibility as well as their long-term effects.

Biotechnology involves various levels of risk. Some dangers are simply the lot of any new technology, that is to say, carrying the potential to be exploited by a malicious user. With nuclear technology, it is possible, for example, both to supply electricity to a city and simply wipe it off the map. This is obviously the case of any technological innovation. Even at a far more limited level of complexity, a sharp kitchen knife can just as well serve to prepare a delicious meal or be used to accomplish a vicious murder. No technology can escape this kind of risk, which is, after all, linked, not to technology per se, but to the human condition. That said, some forms of biotechnology involve an additional level of risk, an inherent risk, which is not related in any particular way to the evil intentions of its users, but is due to the very existence of the technology. This is related to the long-term impact of this technology on the biosphere, the environment shared by all living organisms on planet Earth. Of course in the confusion surrounding biotechnology, some dangers are imaginary,[548] such as having one's genes modified after eating food containing an ingredient made from a transgenic organism.

Over the course of the twentieth-century, politicians and scientists have faced the challenge of controlling nuclear power without provoking world destruction. And despite a few blunders, one can say that overall our worst fears have been avoided. But there is good reason to believe that the challenge raised by the development of biotechnology is of a different order and in the long term the issues posed by nuclear technology may seem small in comparison. Though atomic bombs have the power to destroy entire cities and affect the generation of survivors exposed to radioactivity for the rest of their lives, nonetheless this remains fairly limited in scope. On the other hand, the tools provided by the biotechnology revolution are generally less expensive and more mobile than nuclear technology and have the capability to irreversibly affect all the following generations as well as the vast ecosystems to which we belong and on which we depend. This is not a small matter.

These technologies raise a question fraught with many risks: Do we fully understand what the implications are for the development and exploitation of biotechnology? For example, Escherichia coli is a bacterium well known to microbiologists. It was among the first organisms to have its genetic code studied. This is one reason why it has been a subject of choice for much transgenic engineering. For example, in 1978, a human gene encoding insulin was introduced into this bacterium to get it to produce human insulin.[549] Many transgenic manipulations target E. coli. But there is one important detail to keep in mind; E. coli is also present in the human digestive system. What would happen if a genetically engineered E. coli was released into the environment or accidentally dumped into a hospital sewer? Once in the environment, is it even conceivable to reset things to the way they were before? It is easy for those promoting these technologies to argue that there is no danger, but is it so easy to answer the question: How do we **know** that there is no danger? What are the reference points against which such claims can be evaluated? Some people, attempting to reassure us state:

> Plants have been the subjects of genetic improvement since ancient times. The earliest farmers were the ancient Sumerians in the valley of the Euphrates. They selected the best plants, carefully preserving seeds for the next season. This gave rise to wheat, as we know it today. In the nineteenth-century, breeding techniques developed in agriculture. Most of the plants we eat today are hybrids resulting from many years of breeding and selection for the best offspring. Corn, for example, is a domestic species derived from a cross whose performance is one hundred times higher than its ancestor teosinte. Current transgenic techniques only pursue the same effort to improve the genetic makeup of living organisms.

Implicitly then, opposing GM technology amounts to opposing progress. But such an argument is dishonest. An important point has been swept under the carpet, namely that in the past all breeding methods were practiced within the framework offered by the natural gene pool, that is to say the set of genetic traits available to a particular species. It is essential to understand that transgenic technology completely disregards the limitations imposed by the species gene pool.[550] Not all of the involved researchers will admit the existence of this threshold, but it must be remembered that in 1974, after developing the first transgenic organism, geneticists set up, without the involvement of any government agency, a self-imposed one year moratorium[551] on research in order to consider the standards that were to be adopted for the use of such technologies and to protect the public from any potential danger. Clearly, the researchers involved were aware of crossing an important threshold; otherwise they would have simply gone ahead with their scientific work using the same procedures that had served so well in the past. In the postmodern context, which denies the existence of any absolute law, very few barriers hinder the development of technology in any form. Here are a few of those barriers:

- technical constraints (do we have the technology to do it?)
- economic constraints (can it be funded, marketed and make a profit?)
- social constraints (can it be made acceptable to the public?)
- legal restrictions (is it allowed in the country where the laboratory is located?)

One should be aware that in the postmodern context, these barriers are only temporary and are typically surmountable. This is especially true of public opinion as well as legal constraints, which should be considered flexible in the long-term.[552] Overall, the dominant logic comes down to the mantra: "If there's money to be made with a product/technology, it will get to market." Today, when the legal framework does not allow the use of certain technologies, one can simply open a new laboratory in another country where laws are more flexible and the leaders more understanding, or at least amenable to certain financial incentives.

One attitude that could be of use at this time is humility. In the last 30 years genetics has made huge advances. The output, in terms of scientific articles and research projects, has increased exponentially. Among the more prestigious accomplishments is the sequencing of the human genome in 2000.[553] The genomes of many other species are being targeted, but having said that we do not know what most of the information already collected means. We have little understanding of many possible implications of our interventions. Perhaps humility is not a great selling point when it comes time to apply for research grants or market products, but there is reason to believe that this virtue is needed more than ever. Would it be overstating things to say that our situation could be compared to that of two teenagers finding a turbocharged race boat tied to a dock, unattended? They jump in, cast off and put the pedal to the metal. These kids have no idea where they're going, but they will certainly get there at top speed.

There is no doubt that biotech research institutes, companies and industry associations are concerned with ethical issues. They have put together bioethics committees producing voluminous reports, but in many instances, their primary function is marketing, as they are paid to promote the latest product the industry has decided should constitute a response to a market need. The fundamental question is: "Can we make this thing into a product that will sell?" (which means, first of all, will the consumer accept it as a legitimate product?). For the industry, these committees may play a useful role by examining procedures used in the development of their products. Externally, the literature put out by these bioethics committees (for a general audience) is full of reassuring language. Buzz-words such as: "worry", "dialogue", "dignity", "information", "security", "consensus", "caution", "concerns", "human rights", "respect", "sensitivity", "understanding", "responsibility" and "conservation" are abundantly used, massaging away the sceptical consumer's concerns.

A UNESCO report states (2005: 3): "bioethics is a systematic, pluralistic and interdisciplinary field of study involving the theoretical and practical moral issues raised by medicine and life sciences as applied to human beings and humanity's relationship with the biosphere." This, of course, does not put the cards on the table and make clear which cosmology is referred to when resolving issues raised by biotechnology. Further down the same page of the report, it is explained that bioethics finds its basis in various social sciences, amongst them anthropology, psychology, political science and sociology. Obviously these fields of research are largely dominated by the modern cosmology (with some incursions by postmodernism). This observation is essential to understanding the context in which cosmological bioethical reflections are developed as well as the direction taken by decision makers.

In the ancient world, ethics was usually expressed in the form of divinely sanctioned tables of laws or an oath (such as the Hippocratic oath) to which concerned individuals had to subscribe. These societies founded their ethical discourse on the recognition of absolute laws, to which one could recognize some variations in interpretation from one culture to another. In the postmodern cosmological context, the idea that man should be held accountable to any entity other than himself is rejected. The law, when administered by the postmodern State, is a vestige of the distant past. It's no accident that the most common expression of postmodern ethics is the Charter of Rights. Postmoderns would not consider it inconceivable to reduce the issue of individual responsibility to a matter of marketing, to what the public can view as "acceptable". Since there is no absolute law, individuals are answerable only to those writing their pay cheque or the consumer (if they manage to get their voices heard). From this perspective, bioethics is understood as an attempt to make sense of the relationship between humans and the biosphere that surrounds them, based on assumptions provided by the dominant cosmology. This does not exclude the (usually friendly) coexistence of modern and postmodern elements or assumptions when such arrangements suit the parties involved. But avoiding any explicit reference to a cosmology has in fact been found to be an incredibly effective approach to avoid serious criticism (or comparisons). One needs only to refer to apparently neutral fields of knowledge in social sciences, which are subservient to modern or postmodern cosmology.

One of the objections occasionally put forward by critics of transgenic technologies is that these technologies violate the natural order by crossing the species barrier.[554] Defenders of these techniques reply that in biology there is no unanimously accepted definition of a species. In their view then, the species barrier is no more than an arbitrary human construct. What are we to think of all this? Is a species just an accident in the evolutionary process or is it the reverse in fact, a trait related to the basic order of creation, something worthy of our respect? Whether or not it is explicitly referred to, cosmology always defines relationships between humans and other living organisms as well as providing limits to these relations. One's choice of cosmology dramatically changes one's perception and behaviour towards the living world around us. How do we go about defining our relationship with the biological environment, in particular our view of gene pools from different species? Do we consider them simply as a resource, to be freely exploited with no restriction of any sort, or are species gene pools something worthy of respect, to which we will eventually be held accountable before our Creator?[555]

Postmodern man, regarding his relation with the terrestrial ecosystem and his concept of man, is faced with issues whose importance can hardly be overstated. In the decision-making process, the transition from one cosmology to another[556] has far-reaching consequences. In the evolutionary cosmological context, for example, the species concept is rather plastic. It is, in short, a freak outcome. For example, in **The Origin**, Darwin asserted, (1859/1958: 67):

> From these remarks it will be seen that I look at the term species, as one arbitrarily given for the sake of convenience to a set of individuals closely resembling each other, and that it does not essentially differ from the term variety, which is given to less distinct and more fluctuating forms. The term variety, again, in comparison with mere individual differences, is also applied arbitrarily, and for mere convenience sake.

Indeed, within the framework proposed by evolutionary cosmology the existence of distinct species is somewhat an unexpected phenomenon, an aberration in effect, as species set up a 'useless' barrier to the transmission of potentially useful genetic traits generated by mutations. If too many obstacles to transmission appear, traits may be lost. And without the transmission of useful genetic traits from one individual to another and from one generation to the next, evolution will not take place. Evolution comes to a grinding halt and one ends up in a situation with total species stability, an outcome which would have pleased pre-Darwinian biologists, who considered that species were unchanged since the dawn of Creation. The rejection of the fixity of species has then been at the heart of the Darwinian proposal from the start.[557] If Darwinism was absolutely true, one should not expect the species barrier to exist. If one accepts Darwinian cosmology, the species barrier is therefore an arbitrary, unpredicted occurrence. This is a point that Darwin comes back to several times in **The Origin** (1859/1958: 63):

> Many years ago, when comparing, and seeing others compare, the birds from the separate islands of the Galapagos Archipelago, both one with another, and with those from the American mainland, I was much struck how entirely vague and arbitrary is the distinction between species and varieties. On the islets of the little Madeira group there are many insects which are characterized as varieties in Mr. Wollaston's admirable work, but which it cannot be doubted would be ranked as distinct species by many entomologists. Even Ireland has a few animals, now generally regarded as varieties, but which have been ranked as species by some zoologists.

It should come as no surprise that Neo-Darwinism has no interest in the existence of species and offers a world dominated by a biological continuum, interrupted by minor genetic variations. Variety is all that counts. It is true that a minority of evolutionists claim that species is also an important evolutionary development, but this seems due, not to a coherent theoretical perspective, but rather a concession to the real biological world, which has its own rules. Based on Darwinian cosmological assumptions, no one has any reason to worry about transferring genes beyond the species barrier. On moral grounds, accountability is a non-issue except to those who pay for the research or buy the end products. The palaeontologist Stephen Jay Gould had to face the species problem, as in geology there clearly are well-documented distinct species, appearing suddenly and remaining stable thereafter for long geological periods. Gould remarked (1991):

> Under this model, "the species problem in paleontology" — I put the phrase in quotes because it then resounded through our literature as a catechism — centered upon the difficulty of stating where ancestral species A ended and descendant species B began in such a continuously graded transition (the problem, so formulated, has no objective answer, only an arbitrary one). And yet, while thus stating the issue in general writings, all paleontologists knew that the practical world of fossil collecting rarely imposed such a dilemma. The oldest truth of paleontology proclaimed that the vast majority of species appear fully formed in the fossil record and do not change substantially during the long period of their later existence[558] (average durations for marine invertebrate species may be as high as 5 to 10 million years). In other words, geologically abrupt appearance followed by subsequent stability.

Another factor tending to blur the vacuous evolutionary species concept is the fact that such a species concept was exploited by the Nazis and eugenicists to argue that some varieties/breeds in humans had become (or were becoming) new races (and eventually distinct species). Based on concerns specific to his field of study, palaeontology, Gould, in the development of his thought, had issues with the traditional evolutionary view of species as only an arbitrary construct (1991):

> Species are real units, arising by branching in the first moments of a long and stable existence. A trend arises by the differential success of certain kinds of species. (if large-bodied horses either arise more frequently or live longer than small-bodied horses, then a trend to increased size will permeate the equine bush.) Speciation is

the real cause of change, not an arbitrary consequence of artificial division of a continuum.

Admittedly, only the paleontological data demands such admissions, not Darwinian logic itself. Indeed in recent years, Gould's school of thought (known as Punctuated Equilibrium or "Punk-Eek") has made little progress in biological circles. In actual fact, this school of thought, though it is consistent with paleontological data, in biological terms demands "miracles"[559] with the appearance of each new biological family or genus. Furthermore, if one assumes that species are the product of millions of years of evolution, could this then be the basis for granting any dignity to species? Before responding to this question, it should be understood that evolution itself has in the past, with no qualms at all, eliminated thousands of species along with their gene pools. If one is being consistent, one must recognize that in this context, use of the term "respect" for species is just empty words.

On the other hand, if one looks at the ancient cosmological perspective proposed in Genesis, it is immediately apparent that the biological class "kinds" (the Hebrew term is "mîyn") are created by God and that this concept is associated with reproduction.[560] As a result, biological "kinds" are worthy of respect. It should be noted that Darwin was reacting to a species concept widely accepted in Europe which considered species, as known and understood by Europeans of the time, as entities fixed since the dawn of time. This concept of the absolute fixity of species is not found in Genesis and actually has its roots in the Greek species concept first promoted by Aristotle and later spreading to the West through the writings of Thomas Aquinas, the Scholastics, Renaissance thinkers and many others. Pichot notes (2009: 244) that Carl Linnæus, who founded the scientific system for the classification of plants and animals, for a moment considered that only the kind was fixed and that species were subject to some variation. In any case, the increase in biological knowledge would have made the abandonment of the concept of the absolute fixity of species inevitable, as scientists' understanding of species was then in its infancy. Darwin only slightly hastened this process. The origins model proposed by Genesis implies, among other things, an initially high level of complexity followed by a subsequent decline[561] via a process of mutational change and other entropic processes affecting the gene pools of various kinds as well as interspecies interactions manifested by degradation of symbiotic relationships, becoming over time, parasitic. The Hebrew "mîyn" concept does not exclude variations outside of human observation, as this simply constitutes a redistribution of the original gene pool. One may encounter reshuffling and loss of information, but no true gains in information. Therefore, the emergence of new varieties does not constitute new kinds, but only results in the reshuffling of the original gene pool.

There is evidence that the morphological species definition, which has long dominated biology, has been the source of many problems. The morphological approach to the species definition is in fact superficial and bases its classification on the observable behaviour of organisms tending to maintain their external physical characteristics over time. When we have in-depth knowledge of the organisms in question, as is the case with domestic animals, this approach is typically valid, but it is a different matter with wild animals. Biologists indeed observe many organisms, apparently from different species, to be still inter-fertile after the second generation. Such observations challenge the morphological definition, which has long been dominant in this area. In such cases it is useful to refer to reproduction as a criterion, as does Genesis, but it is interesting to note that the approach proposed by the biologist Ernst Mayr, in his biological species concept or BSC,[562] also demands that members of a same species remain inter-fertile to the second generation. Mayr's concept also has its problems and does not apply well to microorganisms such as bacteria where reproduction is asexual and genetic exchanges occur at times other than reproduction. It is probably no coincidence that biologists will assert that although the BSC is considered the best hypothesis to date, nevertheless it should never be forgotten that the species concept remains a purely human invention, conceived in order to explain and define the world in which we live. This is an inevitable outcome imposed by Darwinian cosmology.

In the Middle Ages, the personal hygiene practices of the Jews protected them, to some extent, from the worst effects of epidemics such as the plague. A microbiology manual, notes (Black 2005: 8):

> One group that escaped the plague's devastation was the Jewish population. Ancient Hebrew laws regarding sanitation offered some protection to those who practiced them. The relatively clean Jewish ghettos harbored fewer rats to spread the disease. When Jews did fall ill, they were carefully nursed and treated with herbal remedies rather than

by strenuous purging or excessive bleedings with dirty instruments. As a result, a smaller proportion of Jews than gentiles died of the disease. Ironically, some gentiles regarded the Jews' higher survival rates as proof that Jews were the source of the epidemic.

Is it possible that principles derived from a religious cosmology thousands of years old could prove their worth regarding the dangers of biotechnology? Elbaz remarks (2002: 29):

> Judaism, this ancient civilization, has kept up, despite the passage of time, dietary laws which are characterized by the fact that they intersect the main categories of any normative culture: placing in opposition, selecting to differentiate, distinguishing to expose the outline. It is ironic that the most repeated ethical demands regarding GMOs are precisely those the kashrut symbolic system pays much attention to: a) strict regulations b) traceability with experts, c) an information channel for consumers and/or believers.*

In the postmodern context, it is not inconceivable that the Homo sapiens specie's biological and genetic uniqueness be abolished through a series of gradual, imperceptible steps. Raymond Kurzweil,[563] a posthuman thinker, has predicted the advent of machines — computers capable of surpassing man's intellectual capabilities. He shrewdly notes the fundamental cosmological problem underlying many debates in the West today (1999: 2):

> Before the next century is over, human beings will no longer be the most intelligent or capable type of entity on the planet. Actually, let me take that back. The truth of that last statement depends on how we define human. And here we see one profound difference between these two centuries: The primary political and philosophical issue of the next century will be the definition of who we are.

Kurzweil's point is critical and its importance can hardly be overstated. Looking at the biotechnology revolution in this light, it is important to understand that such issues are inevitably cosmological and religious. The redefinition of what it means to be human, in relation to the inanimate world, is at the heart of the artificial intelligence ideology, but also has profound consequences on the development of various biotechnologies. The attitude one takes towards man is determined by one's prior choice of a cosmology. This is consistent with one of the mantras favoured by twentieth-century left-wing intellectuals: The infrastructure is determinant in the final instance. If one then exchanges or abandons one cosmology for another, this inevitably changes how one views man and his relationship to the environment. And once this stage is reached, then all the rules of social and environmental interaction will be subject to this influence. The American historian Richard Weikart notes, for example (2004: 75) that in late nineteenth- and early twentieth-century Europe almost all Christian churches and even most anti-clerical seculars supported the concept of human life's sacred value (though they did not use theological terms to address the issue). This attitude was reflected in European law, which explicitly prohibited assisted suicide, infanticide and abortion. According to historian Udo Benzenhöfer, during the Middle Ages and up to modern times, no European would have even thought of defending assisted suicide before the second half of the nineteenth-century. In Germany, from the late nineteenth- and early twentieth-century, Weikart notes (2004: 75-76):

> Only in the late nineteenth and especially the early twentieth-century did significant debate erupt over issues relating to the sanctity of human life, especially infanticide, euthanasia, abortion, and suicide. It was no mere coincidence that these contentious issues emerged at the same time that Darwinism was gaining in influence. Darwinism played an important role in this debate, for it altered many people's conceptions of the importance and value of human life, as well as the significance of death....
>
> What aspects of Darwinism brought about this transformation in thinking about the value of human life? First, Darwinism altered some people's conceptions of the human position in the cosmos and in the organic world. T. H. Huxley had dubbed this the question of *Man's Place in Nature*, and many German Darwinists, including Ernst Haeckel, considered this one of the most important aspects of Darwinism. The traditional Christian view of the value of human life was one idea Haeckel wanted to revise in the light of evolution. In his 1904 book, *The Wonders of Life*, he remarked that "the value of our human life appears to us today, on the firm foundation of evolutionary theory, in an entirely different light, than it did fifty years ago." How did Haeckel think it had changed? Stated succinctly, Haeckel did not think that human life was particularly valuable, nor did he think that all people had the same value.

The value granted to a being produced by forces of chance and natural selection and that given to another, a being created in the image of a Creator before whom one day all will appear to give account of themselves, are obviously not the same. The transition from a monotheistic cosmology to a materialist or postmodern cosmology significantly changes one's perception of issues such as the value of individual life. It must therefore be understood that the outworking of all the consequences of a cosmology and the development of a coherent ethical system is a lengthy and complex process, demanding the accumulated wisdom of generations. It is our hope here that examining the cosmological presuppositions in this process may help avoid a few pitfalls along the road.

Concluding this section, the current challenge of biotechnology (beyond the technical issues involved) is to develop a perspective that is consistent with one's cosmology. The problem in the postmodern context is that in general postmoderns prefer to avoid any discussion of the link between their ethical positions and their cosmology. Many would consider these matters to be too painful, as the task of identifying and making their cosmology explicit would be too "distasteful" for most. Ignoring the link between ethical positions and cosmology has the advantage of maintaining the postmodern ideological-religious system out of the public's view and also allows one to use ethical language, while the real issues are often product marketing or maintaining the flow of research grants.

Homo Sapiens and Its Ecological Niches

> *Listen and hear my voice; pay attention and hear what I say. When a farmer plows for planting, does he plow continually? Does he keep on breaking up and working the soil? When he has leveled the surface, does he not sow caraway and scatter cumin? Does he not plant wheat in its place, barley in its plot, and spelt in its field? His God instructs him and teaches him the right way. Caraway is not threshed with a sledge, nor is the wheel of a cart rolled over cumin; caraway is beaten out with a rod, and cumin with a stick. Grain must be ground to make bread; so one does not go on threshing it forever. The wheels of a threshing cart may be rolled over it, but one does not use horses to grind grain. All this also comes from the Lord Almighty, whose plan is wonderful, whose wisdom is magnificent. (Isaiah 28: 23-29 NIV)*

When looking at debates about our relationship with the environment, one realizes that the question of what it means to be human is at the heart the various adopted positions. Are humans special or are they just one organism amongst many others and nothing more? Is man's status arbitrary or absolute? What is his relationship with nature? In the West, two opposing positions vie for attention. On the one hand, we see the modern position, expressed via savage capitalism or brutal communism, which both see the environment as a resource to be exploited at will and for which man has no accountability. In reaction to the modern position, the postmodern perspective rejects this attitude towards the environment, but instead sets up the environment (explicitly or not) as a supreme value, even a deity to be worshipped, in effect replacing modern man, now dethroned as an object of worship. Some postmodern environmentalists deliberately reject the special status of humans, which leads to the principle that the environment must be protected **from** man and not **for** man. As a result, nature has absolute precedence over man. The traditional human/animal relationship is then turned upside down. Here as elsewhere, the answers to our questions will vary depending on the cosmology adopted. Steven Wise, an activist lawyer defending animal rights, believes that the current legal situation (in relation to the human/animal distinction) is based on an *out-dated* cosmology (2000: 4):

> For four thousand years, a thick and impenetrable legal wall has separated all human from all nonhuman animals. On one side, even the most trivial interests of a single species — ours — are jealously guarded.

We have assigned ourselves, alone among the million animal species, the status of "legal persons." On the other side of that wall lies the legal refuse of an entire kingdom, not just chimpanzees and bonobos but also gorillas, orang-utans, and monkeys, dogs, elephants, and dolphins. They are "legal things." Their most basic and fundamental interests — their pains, their lives, their freedoms — are intentionally ignored, often maliciously trampled, and routinely abused. Ancient philosophers claimed that all nonhuman animals had been designed and placed on this earth just for human beings. Ancient jurists declared that law had been created just for human beings. Although philosophy and science have long since recanted, the law has not.

This demonstrates the fact that one's attitude towards the human/animal distinction entirely depends on prior cosmological choices. Wise (implicitly) refers to this when he alludes to "principles" that philosophy and science have rejected. If philosophy or science have rejected some principles, it remains unclear which philosophy and which science are concerned by his claim, but one can be sure at least that Wise himself rejects these principles. The illusion of neutrality is maintained here largely by taking care to avoid any mention of the words "religion" or "belief" when discussing one's own views. That said, no question concerning the relationship between man and the environment can be resolved without referring (implicitly or explicitly) to cosmology, an origins myth or religion. Whether one is a hunter-gatherer, medieval, modern or postmodern, one's degree of technological and cultural development changes nothing. Religion is inescapable.

Regarding his relationship with the environment, a question arises for postmodern man. With technological power unprecedented in human history, he considers himself the bearer of great responsibility for the environment. On the other hand, he considers himself a product of evolution, itself a process devoid of design or purpose. This process has, on many occasions in the past, initiated the ruthless elimination of many organisms. In past geological epochs many organisms have gone extinct:[564] trilobites, ammonites, Orthoceras, Velociraptors, mammoths, pterodactyls, the woolly rhinoceros and Allosaurus. Moreover, many species of mammals, invertebrates and plants no longer exist. If this is the case, the question must then be asked: Why should man be at all concerned about the disappearance of a few species while (for a brief moment) he finds himself in the place of the dominant species? Aren't these extinctions simply part of the natural order of things and part and parcel of the evolutionary process? If we too are part of the great evolutionary chain of life, and nothing more, why should our predatory activities be viewed differently from those of a dinosaur taking down its favourite meal or from a geological event, like a volcanic eruption, killing off the last mammoth? Why should we feel "guilt" or "responsibility" about such matters?

Why must the Homo sapiens species assume any particular responsibility toward other living things, a responsibility that no other species before man has bothered to take on? Why go on such an ego-trip, assuming the role of manager[565] and claiming responsibility for the direction of evolution and life on Earth? Who do we think we are? Western postmoderns would be hard put to acknowledge that this constitutes a subliminal admission of man's stewardship, a role proclaimed long ago in Genesis? How is it that a Judeo-Christian fetish finds itself an object of veneration on the postmodern altar? And if one refuses to acknowledge this link, where did postmoderns get this concept?

The erosion of man's privileged status has consequences in the field of medical research where animals are subjected to experiments for medical or pharmaceutical research. Some animal rights activists claim that any medical research involving experiments on animals should be stopped, even when it can be shown that these may aide the discovery of cures or treatments for human diseases. That humans may suffer from diseases, suffering that could have been avoided if research on animals had been allowed to continue, is considered of secondary importance. On the other hand, defenders of animal rights condemn Harp seal hunters on the northeast coast of North America by claiming that the hunters use "inhumane" methods to dispatch the seals. But in a context where the "human" concept no longer has any specific content, does a statement of this nature makes any sense at all? Is this anything more than empty words, the expression of mere emotion?

Things are much the same when animal activists call for more "humane" treatment of farm or laboratory animals. In the postmodern cosmological context, how do we know what "humane" treatment of animals is? Where do we get the principles/doctrines that should guide our attitudes and behaviour? Another question is: How does anyone know what animals want or need in the first place? Should we be forced to accept that animal rights activists have discovered a truth, a secret knowledge of human/animal relationships, and that everyone else has to convert to this view or force (through legislation if necessary) farmers or laboratory managers to adopt the activists' ideological presuppositions? Why is it that the farmers' and lab managers' truths are not good enough for them? On what basis do we "know" the environmentalists' truths and sacred knowledge to be transcendent, absolute, to be imposed on others? These views must be justified and discussed. Or does this boil down to power plays and access to circles of influence in media, politics and the judiciary? But again apparently these are questions one is not supposed to ask...

The Darwinian worldview cannot tolerate a qualitative difference between man and animals. From this perspective, the difference can only be quantitative,[566] that is to say that man differs by the fact of possessing more neurons, more highly developed language skills, greater capacity for innovation, a more refined ethical system, etc. This conclusion stands in stark contrast with the Judeo-Christian tradition,[567] which considers every human to be made in God's image and, therefore, unique, irreplaceable, regardless of how others may value his potential or abilities.

Regarding man's linguistic abilities, the postmodern perspective tells us there is only a quantitative difference between humans and apes. Man merely uses more complex vocabulary and grammar than those of monkeys. There is no qualitative difference. American mathematician William Dembski (2004: 8) rejects this view however and argues that human language, with its infinite capacity to adapt to different contexts and to create novel concepts and metaphors, has no analogue in the animal world. The famous linguist, Noam Chomsky, further develops this argument adding (1972: 100):

> When we study human language, we are approaching what some might call the "human essence," the distinctive qualities of mind that are, so far as we know, unique to man and that are inseparable from any critical phase of human existence, personal or social.... Having mastered a language, one is able to understand an indefinite number of expressions that are new to one's experience, that bear no simple physical resemblance and are in no simple way analogous to the expressions that constitute one's linguistic experience; and one is able, with greater or less facility, to produce such expressions on an appropriate occasion, despite their novelty and independently of detectable stimulus configurations, and to be understood by others who share this still mysterious ability. The normal use of language is, in this sense, a creative activity. This creative aspect of normal language use is one fundamental factor that distinguishes human language from any known system of animal communication.[568]

The postmodern view leads to intractable contradictions. The Social Sciences present us with man, a being practicing agriculture, composing cantatas, exploring the mysteries of genetics, believing himself responsible for the environment, conceiving a saga, telling a joke, writing a philosophical essay, walking on the Moon, giving his dog a name and searching for the meaning of life. These abilities reflect man's unique status, but they are also cause for gnashing of teeth among postmoderns since on a subliminal level, they point to the One who gave these gifts. It should come as no surprise then that postmoderns ignore these unique attributes and reject man's special status, since this concept contradicts the evolutionary origins myth which claims that man is part of nature and that there is no reason to grant him special status of any sort. The American philosopher Mortimer Adler, argues that if the difference between humans and animals is only quantitative, this leads to the conclusion that there is no reason to treat humans differently from animals (Adler 1967: 8-9):

> If a difference in degree suffices to justify a difference in treatment, why would not superior men be justified in treating inferior men in whatever way men think they are justified in treating non-human animals because the latter are inferior in degree.... Think instead of killing animals for the enjoyment of the sport; or, in another context, of killing them for the purposes of vivisection in the course of medical research. Now, if these actions can be justified by nothing more than a difference in degree between human and non-human animals, why is not the same justification available for the actions of Nazis or other racists?

If we are to adopt the evolutionary cosmology in a completely consistent manner, then why worry if baby seals, dolphins or peregrine falcons go extinct as a result of man's economic or recreational activities? Isn't this simply the way things work? While some may not resist the urge to take action to stop these activities, they do so at odds with the evolutionary processes that gave them life. Does the lion care about the survival of the antelope species he's devouring? Does a mosquito care if it transmits malaria to its host or does the chicken, when pecking its weaker companion to death? If the dinosaurs of Jurassic and the large mammals of the Quaternary have become extinct, should the other surviving species feel "guilty" or "responsible"? Of course not. And if one claims, to avoid this pitfall, that man is "different" because he is "aware" of his actions (and consequences) and that this fact imposes added responsibility, then despite all protests, we find ourselves back at square one, i.e., man's unique status. This is in fact hypocrisy, a dishonest recycling of Judeo-Christian concepts. Camus refers to such schemes in **The Rebel** when he observed (1951: 78): "Nietzsche saw clearly that humanitarianism[569] was only a form of Christianity deprived of superior justification, which preserved final causes while rejecting the first cause."

Peter Schwartz, director of the Ayn Rand Institute, observes that (2000: 1) environmentalist rhetoric typically frames the relationship between man and the rest of nature (including pets, farm animals and wild animals) in terms of conflict. Men's rights are expressed as being in competition with animal rights, even with those of an ecosystem. Some environmental fundamentalists claim that nature has its own right to exist and that this right supersedes any human interest. On the other hand, if one starts from the opposite premise, that is to say that human life is the standard by which we judge all else, such "conflicts" disappear. Whether these conflicts are real or not depends on one's prior choice of cosmological assumptions, on one's starting point. If one accepts that human life is in fact the standard by which we judge all things, then only man and his needs can be considered as an end in itself[570] or an ultimate end. Whether man has precedence over nature or vice versa, it is important to understand that regardless of one's choice of presuppositions, in either case, the choice will be anchored in and linked, on the logical level, to a cosmology, a belief system, a worldview, a religion. Everyone is out to market their worldview and make converts, even if this process is barely discernable or never admitted. Usually the trick is to do this one presupposition at a time rather than making a dramatic conversion appeal. Of course anyone can assert that man has a responsibility to the environment and to other living beings, but unless these assertions are justified in a consistent manner within one's cosmology they are no more than empty words.

Accepting the premise that human life is the standard by which we judge all else, leads us to make choices based on whether they make us (humans) healthier, smarter and happier. For example, when a craftsman decides he will use a piece of wood to make furniture or a beam, he does not consider the interests of the tree. When a beer manufacturer decides to produce ale rather than a lager must he beforehand consider the yeast's interests? And why not push the logic a little further? Who can really consider themselves competent to represent the interests of calves, baby seals or lab rats if he has never been a calf, baby seal or lab rat himself? What is the basis for some people's claim to speak for "oppressed animals"? Of course, the modern position, arguing that we are the pinnacle of evolution and as a result we bear the responsibility for this planet's biosphere, is still widespread. In marketing terms, this gives man a certain self-serving prestige. In an interview, Ernst Mayr [EM], world-renowned biologist and modern high priest, shared his thoughts on the matter (in Campbell 1993: 419):

> You've also written that we humans have extraordinary responsibility because of our uniqueness as a species.
> [**EM**] Yes, humans are basically responsible for all the bad things that at the present time happen to our planet, and we are the only ones who can see all these things and do something about them. If we would stop the human population explosion, we would have already won two-thirds of the battle. That we live here just as exploiters of this planet is an ethic that does not appeal to me. Having become the dominant species on our planet, we have the responsibility to preserve the well-being of this planet. I feel that it should be a part of our ethical system that we should preserve and maintain and protect this planet that gave origin to us.

How extraordinarily arrogant! How can we know that we are in fact the only ones to "see all these things".[571] And where does this responsibility for managing the planet come from? How can the assertion of a link between biological dominance and global responsibility be justified? From which origins myth is this presupposition drawn? In any case, aren't insects more dominant in terms of numbers? How can we know if they don't already have their own environmental agenda, based on their own interests? In the final analysis, isn't Mayr's claim a form of interspecies neo-colonialism? Why such a moralizing tone? Why all this guilt-mongering on those whose ethics happens not to include concepts of the planet's protection and conservation (as understood by Mayr)? There is every reason to believe that this "responsibility for the planet" that Mayr talks about is nothing but an implicit rip-off (one of many) of the old Judeo-Christian stewardship concept, a responsibility given by God to men.[572] Regarding the paradoxes of the materialist cosmology, a door opened by Darwin, Paul Dernavich made the following scathing remarks (2001):

> Why do we consider compassion for the sick to be a good thing when it can only give us a disadvantage in our vicious eat-or-be-eaten world? Why would these traits emerge so late in the game, when one

would think evolution would be turning us into refined, high-tech battle machines? We cannot acquire a transcendent or "higher" purpose through evolution, any more than a sine wave can develop separation anxiety. And yet many who swear by the powers of Darwin and empiricism also cling, hypocritically, to a quite unproven assumption that the human race is somehow set apart, created for a glorious destiny. Just as determinists argue undeterministically, scientists believe unscientifically. The most serious offenders in this category have to be the various minds behind the Humanist Manifesto,[573] who roundly reject the metaphysical even as they affirm it, by assumption, in their grand prescriptions for humanity.

From an evolutionary point of view, if an organism is incapable of adapting to changes in its environment, who are we to intervene? And if this organism does not adapt, shouldn't we conclude that its extinction is no more than a natural occurrence, if not actually a desirable outcome according to the cosmology proposed by the theory of evolution? After all isn't the struggle for survival supposed to lead us on to bigger and better things? And if we do in fact intervene to save a species that is failing to adapt, isn't this a form of arbitrary, incoherent behaviour? Doesn't this constitute a violation of the natural balance of things where normally only natural selection decides the fate of a species? We need to be reminded that the evolutionary process isn't compassionate, rational or premeditated. The disappearance, in the past, of species such as the dinosaurs, mammoths or trilobites does not answer to any rule of reason, compassion or to any benevolent plan.

In postmodernism, where the Homo sapiens species' unique status is being challenged from all sides, it is no great leap that some should want to grant personal rights to apes. The Great Ape Project[574] proposed this in 2003. This project was founded in New Zealand by Peter Singer and Paola Cavalieri in 1993 and would call upon the United Nations to amend the Bill of Rights so as to include the great apes.[575] Many people would consider this idea to be rather silly, but it should be understood that these proposals are quite consistent with the principles of Darwinian cosmology.

This is not a small matter. But if the proposal were actually to go ahead and be implemented, new questions would arise. If all were to agree to view apes as "persons", should they then be held legally responsible for their actions? Will they be able to go about as they please, free from any supervision? Will they be required to attend school, to wear clothes, to pay their subway ticket, to respect the Highway Code if they drive a car and pay their taxes? Could apes engaging in a legal agreement be taken to court if they do not keep their promises? Could they be required to do military service or be charged with rape?[576] If not, would it be possible then to take those who have granted such rights to court? In this context of upheaval, a thought taken from Darwin's own personal correspondence[577] sounds a note of Victorian irony regarding the human/animal relationship (Darwin 1888, vol. I):

> But then with me the horrid doubt always arises whether the convictions of man's mind, which has been developed from the mind of the lower animals, are of any value or at all trustworthy. Would any one trust in the convictions of a monkey's mind, if there are any convictions in such a mind?

Beyond primates, what about other large mammals? If a bear, cougar, lion or tiger were to kill a human being, could it be held criminally responsible? If convicted, would it be sentenced to imprisonment?[578] The fact is, all these rights and responsibilities are derived from human's special status. If such questions are rejected as "out of order", one must ask why? The nineteenth-century had not yet gauged the full impact of the adoption of a materialistic cosmos. Cultural inertia, for a brief while, made man's unique status seem beyond question. But for Darwin's grandchildren, the situation is quite different. Author and scholar C. S. Lewis explored the same contradiction that gave pause to Darwin between modern/ materialist presuppositions and reason, and argued (1962: 162):

> Long before I believed Theology to be true I had already decided that the popular scientific picture at any rate was false. One absolutely central inconsistency ruins it;.... The whole picture professes to depend on inferences from observed facts. Unless inference is valid, the whole picture disappears. Unless we can be sure that reality in the remotest nebula or the remotest part obeys the thought-laws of the human scientist here and now in his laboratory — in other words, unless Reason is an absolute — all is in ruins. Yet those who ask me to believe this world picture also ask me to believe that Reason is simply the unforeseen and unintended by-product of mindless matter at one stage of its endless and aimless becoming. Here is flat contradiction. They ask me at the same moment to accept a conclusion and to discredit the only testimony on which that conclusion can be based.[579] The difficulty is to me a fatal one; and the fact that when you put it to many scientists, far from having an answer, they seem not even to understand what the difficulty is, assures me that I have not found a mare's

nest but detected a radical disease in their whole mode of thought from the very beginning. The man who has once understood the situation is compelled henceforth to regard the scientific cosmology as being, in principle, a myth; though no doubt a great many true particulars have been worked into it.

The ancient Judeo-Christian cosmology gave basis and support for human reason. The historical narrative begins with an intelligent Agent, endowed with personality and reason, initiating his actions through the spoken word. This Being is conscious. He has thoughts and feelings and acts to meet specific goals. The narrative tells us that this Agent created man in His image, endowed with reason, like his Creator. Since Creation results from the intervention of this intelligent Agent, it represents a divine order, and it follows that its principles can be understood by human reason.[580] Although the origin of human reason is not an issue in the context of this cosmology, it is subject to obvious limitations and constraints[581] and remains useful nonetheless. The Enlightenment[582] thinker René Descartes addressed this matter in his **Discourse on Method** and explored the basis for reason in the Judeo-Christian cosmological context (1637: pt. iv):

> For how do we know that the thoughts which occur in dreaming are false rather than those other which we experience when awake, since the former are often not less vivid and distinct than the latter? And though men of the highest genius study this question as long as they please, I do not believe that they will be able to give any reason which can be sufficient to remove this doubt, unless they presuppose the existence of God. For, in the first place even the principle which I have already taken as a rule, viz., that all the things which we clearly and distinctly conceive are true, is certain only because God is or exists and because he is a Perfect Being, and because all that we possess is derived from him: whence it follows that our ideas or notions, which to the extent of their clearness and distinctness are real, and proceed from God, must to that extent be true. Accordingly, whereas we not infrequently have ideas or notions in which some falsity is contained, this can only be the case with such as are to some extent confused and obscure, and in this proceed from nothing (participate of negation), that is, exist in us thus confused because we are not wholly perfect. And it is evident that it is not less repugnant that falsity or imperfection, in so far as it is imperfection, should proceed from God, than that truth or perfection should proceed from nothing. But if we did not know that all which we possess of real and true proceeds from a Perfect and Infinite Being, however clear and distinct our ideas might be, we should have

no ground on that account for the assurance that they possessed the perfection of being true.[583]

And if Descartes' thinking put too much emphasis on a Supreme Being, our modern elites may prefer the views of another Frenchman, Pierre Simon de Laplace,[584] who stated "We have no need of that hypothesis," but to do without "that hypothesis", it is perhaps best to avoid thinking too much about the consequences of one's presuppositions. This kind of activity may, on occasion, trouble one's sleep.

Sometimes conflicting postmodern expectations regarding nature take a tragicomic turn when humans assume the right to speak for animals (and against other humans they have identified as "oppressors"), claiming that they know what is best for them. How do they come by such illumination? A remarkable gift of inter-species telepathy, perhaps? This brings to mind a story from British Columbia, that of the male killer whale Luna, who was separated from his pod of killer whales in 2001 in Puget Sound. Luna has been getting along since then. He eats and is active, but will not join his *family* and seeks the attention of humans. He sometimes rubs up against ships and is reported to have damaged a few small boats. It is feared that one day he may injure himself or a human. During the summer of 2004, attempts were made to capture him and reunite him with his family, as pro-whale activists had determined that it was better that Luna return to his original pod. Canadian Wildlife Services found themselves charged with this task. The funny thing is that a local First Nation group, for their part, resolved that Luna was the reincarnation of a recently deceased chief and decided to oppose Luna's capture by drawing him out of the reach of government vessels sent to capture him... And what is Luna's take on the matter? Who knows? Maybe he just has had enough of killer whale cultural conformism and wants to become a Hollywood star or just needed to get away from his overbearing and domineering killer whale mom? Further episodes can be expected in this postmodern soap opera...[585]

Hunger

> *Wouldn't it be dreadful if some day in our own world, at home, men started going wild inside, like the animals here, and still looked like men, so that you'd never know which were which.*
> *(Lewis 1951/1970: 117)*

> *Try all of Soylent's delicious flavors: Soylent red, Soylent yellow, and new, delicious, Soylent green. Made from the finest undersea growth.*
> *(Richard Fleischer, 1973, 97 min)*

The fact that the concept of man as a unique creature has long been part of Western culture doesn't mean that everyone can invoke this concept in a coherent and legitimate manner. Postmodern environmentalist discourse enjoys spouting moral rhetoric about our "duties" towards other species and the semi-deified environment even if the concept of "duty" has no logical basis in materialist or postmodern cosmology. Here's a typical sample of this sort of rhetoric:

> Today, life on this planet faces the most critical moment of its 3.5-billion-year existence. Never before, even when the dinosaurs disappeared at the end of the Cretaceous sixty-five million years ago, have we seen such a drastic reduction in biodiversity on the planet. Our brothers and sisters of the forest [the trees] are in danger. This is a desperate time for our Mother Earth, because when a species dies, part of her dies as well. It's time to put our lives on the line for our Mother, to defend her. The forest is part of us. When loggers kill the living forest, they kill us all. Man gets his rights from the same source as the tadpole. Man's rights are no more sacred than the rights of its other children, any more than the ladybug singing at the pond's edge. Man has the greatest power for good and evil. For this reason his responsibilities to Mother Earth are also greater.

The incoherence of such rhetoric must be pointed out as, on the one hand we find man's special status rejected, but on the other, the responsibilities derived from this special status are claimed to be binding... Writing at an earlier time when the concept of Man still seemed secure, Julian Huxley wrote in his introduction to one of the many editions of **The Origin of the Species** (in Darwin 1859/1958: xv):

Thus in the light of the science of evolutionary biology which Darwin founded, man is seen as not just part of nature, but as a very peculiar and indeed unique part. In his person the evolutionary process has become conscious of itself, and he alone is capable of leading it on to realizations of possibility. A century after Darwin's modest statement that light will be thrown on the origin of man, we can truly say that, as a result of Darwin's work in general and of *The Origin of Species* in particular, light has been thrown on his destiny.

But why *man alone*? Even the most fervent Darwinist should recognize here that there is an implicit plagiarizing of man's special status, a concept bequeathed by the Judeo-Christian worldview. If claims are made by modern or postmodern discourse, that man is responsible for nature,[586] other questions arise: Who entrusted him with this responsibility? Who wrote his job description? If some ignore or neglect their "duty" to nature, what penalties will they incur? In postmodernism, man's privileged status is now rejected. But of course, Huxley is right that as a result of Darwin's work "light has been thrown" on man's destiny and the materialist/Darwinian origins myth has played a pivotal role in the erosion and rejection of the old Judeo-Christian concept of man. Some postmodern evolutionists like Richard Dawkins categorically reject (when it suits their interests) the claim of a distinct status for humans. Dawkins then arrives at a position that is diametrically opposed to (and more consistent than) that of Huxley's (Dawkins 2001):

> People who cheerfully eat cows object violently to abortion. Not even the most vehement "pro-lifer" would claim that a human foetus feels pain, or distress, or fear, more than an adult cow.[587] The double standard, therefore, stems from an absolutist regard for the humanity of the foetus. Even if we don't eat chimpanzees (and they are eaten in Africa, as bushmeat) we do treat them in otherwise inhuman ways. We incarcerate them for life without trial (in zoos). If they become surplus to requirements, or grow old and miserable, we call the vet to put them down. I am not objecting to these practices, simply calling attention to the double standard. Much as I'd like the vet to put me down when I'm past it, he'd be tried for murder because I'm human.
>
> Human means special, unique, sacred, of infinite worth, to be venerated as the possessor of "human dignity." Animal means to be treated kindly, but put to human use, painlessly destroyed when usefulness is past, killed for sport, or as a pest. A rogue lion that kills people will be shot, not in revenge, not as a punishment, not as a deterrent to other lions, not to satisfy the relatives of the victim, but simply to get it out of the way: not punishment, but pest control. A rogue human who kills

people will be given a fair trial, and if sentenced will probably not be killed. If he is killed, it will be with grisly ceremony, after appeals, and in the face of massive, principled objection. Of all the justifications offered for capital punishment, one that will never be heard is pest control. It has no place in penal theory. Humans, to the absolutist mind, are forever divided from animals.

Of course coming from a university professor, statements of this sort are certainly provocative, but if the administrator of a senior's nursing home were to offer such thoughts in public, this could be cause for some concern... What does it mean to be human? This is an existential question if there ever was one... If in fact human life is no longer a sacred value and if we are just part of nature and if other organisms such as the black widow or the polar bear[588] practice cannibalism,[589] why get excited if one human being kills and eats another? Why cling to out-dated taboos?

Now if Dawkins's logic were to be followed here, one might speculate that grocery stores, which already maintain counter space for selling meat from various mammals such as pork, mutton, beef and horsemeat,[590] might open up space where they could legitimately sell human meat.[591] In an effort to improve marketing, well-placed booths could be installed where people would have the opportunity to taste free samples and be handed interesting new recipes. No doubt Hannibal Lecter[592] would be sold on such a concept. And then perhaps some poor families would be able to bring in some desperately needed cash by selling the body of their grandfather, recently deceased in a nursing home, to the local butcher shop, as could a street gang, bringing in the bullet-ridden body of a rival gang member knocked off in urban guerrilla warfare.

For the capitalist, all this raises the prospect of new markets and further driving the economy. Why ignore all these potential market opportunities? Isn't the prohibition against cannibalism just an arbitrary cultural construct, just one more unnecessary taboo waiting to be deconstructed? After all, protein is protein, regardless of its source. And later, if this market were to grow, expansion into facilities raising human babies could be considered, "unwanted" human babies let's say, that would be slaughtered like cows or pigs, then selling the meat of these children or young adults on the market. And there would be the added bonus that their organs could supply the growing market for transplants.[593] "Inconceivable!" you say? Ah, but in our time, one must never let this word slip out, since many forms of behaviour or attitudes which are widely accepted now, were utterly "inconceivable" only a generation or two ago...

Though the preceding lines were offered on a note of black humour, our purpose is very serious, that is to say, illustrating the power of cosmological presuppositions/beliefs. If man is a being set apart from others, it is quite logical and consistent to treat his body with special regard, but if this presupposition is rejected, then there is nothing to oppose eliminating the traditional respect shown to the human body (funerals, coffins, tombs, prayers, etc.). Everything is connected. If postmodern cosmology becomes socially dominant (and consistently applied), it will not be without consequences.

According to the dominant perspective, man is no more than a product, a product to be improved to meet customer demand. But if further improvement is impossible, why not consider "discontinuing" the product? In the syncretistic context prevailing in the West, dominated by the postmodern ideologico-religious system, we should not be surprised to find our elites "reengineering" at will a concept as fundamental as Man. But take into consideration that, up until now, they have been able to do so without having to account for their underlying cosmology, as a result the work of spreading the postmodern faith has been made much more easy. We sail on unknown seas and one should not ignore the enormous consequences of these changes in perspective. The fact that it is impossible to offer any answer to the question of man to man, man to animal, man to computer, human to the environment relationships, without referring to cosmology, to an origins myth can hardly overemphasized.

6 / Postface

Listen, I've summed them all up: the teacher who laughs with children at their God and at their cradle is ours already. The barrister who defends an educated murderer by pleading he is more mentally developed than his victims and could not help murdering them for money is already one of us. Schoolboys who murder a peasant for the sake of a thrill are ours. The juries who acquit all criminals are ours. A public prosecutor who trembles in court because he is not sufficiently progressive is ours, ours. Administrators, authors — oh there are lots and lots of us, and they don't know it themselves. (Dostoyevsky, The Possessed 1872/1971:421)

The king is surrounded by persons whose only thought is to divert the king and to prevent his thinking of self. For he is unhappy, king though he be, if he thinks of himself.
(Pascal 1670/1908: sect. II, 139)

Social anthropologists typically study non-Western cultures in an attempt to develop a comprehensive understanding of a particular society. Amongst other things, this involves understanding their ideologico-religious system and examining its influence on social structures. This is a classic perspective in Social Anthropology, but anthropologists rarely apply it to the West (their own culture) to any depth. The present work attempts to fill this gap. Once this perspective is adopted, logic demands we should consider every social structure as religious or, at very least, as having a religious dimension. The legal system, for example, which manages the behaviour of members of a society, always refers, more or less implicitly to a cosmology allowing it to sort out human behaviour, that which is permitted or forbidden. Of course real societies are rarely under the influence of only one cosmology. To get a clear picture it is then necessary to delve into a nation's history and take into account ideologico-religious systems that were dominant in the past. It is much the same when individuals participating in the economic system attempt to establish whether a tank, a chocolate bar or a condom is "useful". Answering the question: "If there is demand for product X, does this mean that it must be produced and put on the market?" is a religious act, since to answer the question cosmological presuppositions must be identified (usually unconsciously) and their relative importance determined. To claim that only market forces apply in such matters is also, in the last analysis, a religious statement.

A point where the postmodern religion finds itself diametrically opposed to the great monotheistic traditions, including Christianity, is the question of whether cosmological presuppositions should be explicit or not. The great monotheistic traditions have always made these explicit in the form of sacred writings, catechisms or creeds. The postmodern religion, on the other hand given its invisibility and the denial of its religious character, is forced to reject their existence and also compelled to disseminate its presuppositions in an implicit manner, by means of an almost infinite variety of conceptual vehicles, be they scientific, artistic or cultural.[594] The postmodern religion is a special case in that it does not openly offer its presuppositions for discussion or comparison. Rather, it typically frames the discussion, more or less explicitly, by suggesting that its concepts are in fact the starting point of any "reasonable" exchange and that any deviation from or criticism of its presuppositions is in fact a sign of ignorance if not "perverse" thought.[595] Once such a perspective is adopted, it is difficult to engage a serious discussion with a person or institution that believes its outlook on law, politics, sexuality or any other matter is cannot be the subject of debate or analysis, but should be considered a matter of "decency". Postmoderns consider it "indecent" to find themselves forced to come clean and acknowledge that their presuppositions are beliefs, demanding faith too. A demand of this nature would force postmoderns to make explicit the cosmology that shapes (more or less consciously) the values and presuppositions they impose on the general public. Such a revelation would inevitably call into question postmodern neutrality and also force an accounting for inconsistencies between the postmodern cosmology and postmodern moralizing.

Postmoderns tend to frame any discussion regarding religion within a dichotomy that resembles the proverbial Procrustean bed. Here is the choice we are offered: *enlightened pluralism* ("everybody has their own truth") or fanaticism, madness and death. This implies that those who do not "understand" pluralism are either unbalanced or dangerous lunatics. But framing any possible discussion in this way is simple enough to understand: it is a reaction to anything perceived as a potential threat with respect to a central postmodern belief, that is the individual as judge of all, the standard and absolute epistemological norm. When confronting those who dare question presuppositions drawn from the official line, a strategy used in recent years by "institutional rhetoric" is: "The game is over, accept defeat. Now you have to play the game by our rules." This is spin-doctoring public discourse, basically. It is one component of the general anaesthesia being administered to the West. If the dominant postmodern discourse claims that all have their own truth, once deconstructed, this amounts to the assertion that "no one has any truth" or, more bluntly, "truth does not exist." Yes, once you abolish all truth, the individual is the last absolute…

Postmodern institutional discourse is rather fearful of spin coming from opposing camps. Postmoderns know well the power of spin on public opinion. Spin from critics will naturally be condemned as "disinformation", even though postmoderns themselves use it on a daily basis. But the characteristic of spin, when it works like it's supposed to, is that it allows one to virtually lay hold of an outcome that is not yet within grasp. German, Russian, American and Japanese propaganda in World War II are good examples. However, historically, when all the cards are on the table, spin (whether capitalist, Nazi, Zionist, communist or Islamic) is not an infallible tool. In time, the phenomenon of entropy also seems to apply to the influence of ideologico-religious discourse.[596]

Although in one sense, the postmodern is no more than the logical outcome of existing trends in the modern belief system, in others it makes a radical break with the modern. While moderns proclaimed truth in science, postmoderns, with varying degrees of consistency, have claimed that all have their own truth and science should no longer be considered transculturally valid, but rather a meta-narrative produced by Western civilization. If, in modern discourse, man is viewed as the summit of evolution, in postmodern discourse (especially the posthuman movement) man sees himself reduced to the status of an insignificant species, a transient stage in the evolutionary process. While modern ideologies invested great energy in collective projects (i.e., communist or socialist vs. capitalist perspectives on society), postmodern discourse, for its part, targets the individual. Postmodern interest in community is then expressed through interest groups, since, a priori, nothing can be greater than the individual. It should be noted that capitalist ideology, given its interest in the individual as a consumer, has fed this line of thought.

This essay will probably be condemned for being "biased", "promoting an agenda" and so on. Some may be surprised that I freely admit that such an accusation has a basis. But it must understood that "bias" is absolutely unavoidable in any case as it is rather unreasonable and naïve to expect a serious deconstruction/challenge to the postmodern ideologico-religious system to be developed from within, by its own followers. An external perspective (with all its faults) is essential and is the only thing that makes counteracting and seeing through the subjectivity and biases of mainstream thinking possible. The real question then is: Must the perspective presented here be rejected because it is perceived as "marginal" or, on the contrary, should it get more attention since it is in effect a novel perspective on the current situation? No doubt that the ideologico-religious commitments of the various parties will play a crucial role in the process of answering this question.

In volume II of this work we will pursue our thinking on postmodern religion and examine more closely what the development of ethical thinking in the context of the postmodern belief system involves. The following chapters will be devoted to analyzing the postmodern cosmology and identifying methods used to establish/justify/market it.

7 / Bibliography

Note: Given the volatile nature of the Internet, no guarantees can be offered regarding the long-term validity of web addresses provided below. In many cases, if an article is no available at the indicated URL, a few appropriate keywords typed into the usual search engines will often locate it..

(1769/2009) The Bible [King James Version] Online Bible (Macintosh version 4.1.1)

(1973, 1978, 1984, 2011) The Bible: New International Version (NIV). www.biblegateway.com/versions/New-International-Version-NIV-Bible/

Adler, Mortimer (1967) The Difference of Man and the Difference It Makes. Holt, Rinehart and Winston, Inc. New York

Allport, Gordon (1955) Becoming: Basic Conditions for a Psychology of Personality. Yale University Press New Haven CN 106 p.

Anonymous (1940) German Martyrs. pp. 38-41 Time magazine 23 Dec., vol. 36 no. 26

Anonymous (1879) Pensées de Bacon, Kepler, Newton et Euler sur la religion et la morale. A. Mame Tours [France] 384 p.

Asimov, Isaac (1959) Nine Tomorrows. Doubleday & Company Garden City

Augé, Marc (1974a) La construction du monde. Maspero Paris 142 p.

Augé, Marc (1974b) Dieux et rituels ou rituels sans dieux. pp .9-36 in Anthropologie Religieuse: textes fondamentaux. John Middleton (ed.) Larousse Paris 251 p.

Augé, Marc (1982) Génie du Paganisme. Ed. Gallimard Paris 336 p.

Augé, Marc (1994) Le sens des autres: Actualité de l'anthropologie. Fayard [Paris] 199 p.

Baars, Donald L. (1972/1983) The Colorado Plateau: A Geologic History. Univ. of New Mexico Press

Balassoupramaniane, Indragandhi (2003) La nouvelle mission des tribunaux. Le Journal du Barreau [du Québec] 15 octobre vol. 35 no. 17 www.barreau.qc.ca/journal/frameset.asp?article=/journal/vol35/no17/barreaude-montreal.html

Barabanov, Evgeny (1974/1981) The Schism Between the Church and the World. pp. 172-193 in Solzhenitsyn et al. From Under the Rubble. Regnery Gateway Chicago IL 308 p.

Barham, James (2004) in Why I am Not a Darwinist. pp. 177-19 Uncommon Dissent. (William Dembski, ed.) ISI Books Wilmington Delaware 366 p.

Barker, Eileen (1979) Thus Spake the Scientist: A Comparative Account of the New Priesthood and its Organisational Bases. pp. 79-103 Annual Review of the Social Sciences of Religion, vol. 3 Mouton Netherlands 236 p.

Barlow, Nora (1958/1993) The Autobiography of Charles Darwin 1809-1882. Harcourt Brace Jovanovich New York www.uiowa.edu/~c016003a/Charles%20Darwin%20Religious%20belief.htm

Basen, Gwynne (1992) On The Eighth Day: Making Perfect Babies. National Film Board of Canada and Cinefort 102 min.

Bateson, Gregory) Steps to an Ecology of Mind Ballatine Books New York 1977 749 p.

Begley, Sharon (2001) The Roots of Evil. pp. 30-35 NewsWeek May 21

Bennett, Paul (2005) How to Sail accross the Atlantic (or the World) in 25 Easy Lessons. pp. 44-50; 83-86 National Geographic Adventure vol. 7 no. 1 Feb.

Bergman, Jerry (1999) Darwinism and the Nazi Race Holocaust. pp. 101-111 Creation Ex Nihilo Tech Journal vol. 13 no. 2) www.trueorigin.org/holocaust.asp

Bergman, Jerry (2001) Influential Darwinists Supported the Nazi Holocaust. CRS Quarterly vol. 38 no. 1 pp. 31-39 http://creationresearch.org/

Bergman, Jerry (2003) The Galileo Myth and the Facts of History. pp. 226-235 Creation Research Society Quarterly Volume 39, Number 4 March. www.creationresearch.org/crsq/abstracts/Abstracts39-4.htm

Bergman, Jerry (2008) Slaughter of the Dissidents : The Shocking Truth About Killing the Careers of Darwin Doubters. Leaf Cutter Press Southworth WA xvi - 478 p.

Berkowitz, Peter (1996) Science Fiction; postmodernism exposed. p. 15 The New Republic, July 1, peterberkowitz.wordpress.com/1996/07/01/science-fiction-post-modernism-exposed/

Berman, Paul (1997) The Philosopher-King is Mortal. The New York Times Magazine (May 11; Late Edition - Final , Section 6), pp. 32-36 http://query.nytimes.com/gst/abstract.html?res=FA0713FF35550C728DDDAC0894DF494D81&incamp=archive:search

Black, Jacquelyn G. (2005) Microbiology: Pinciples and Explorations. (6th edition) John Wiley & Sons Hoboken, NJ 920 p.

Boisvert, Yves (1999) Postmodernité et religion: L'éthique est-elle une nouvelle «religio» civile au service de la démocratie postmoderne? Religiologiques, no. 19 printemps www.unites.uqam.ca/religiologiques/19/19texte/19boisvert.html

Bonnette, Dennis (2003) Origin of the Human Species. Sapientia Press Naples, FL www.ewtn.com/library/humanity/fr93207.txt

Borduas, Paul-Émile (et al.) (1948) Le Refus global. http://page.infinit.net/histoire/refus-gl.html

Borisov, Vadim (1975/1981) Personality and National Awareness. pp. 194-228 in Voices From Under the Rubble. Alexander Solzhenitsyn (ed.) Regnery Gateway Chicago IL 308 p.

Bouveresse, Jacques (1998) Qu'appellent-ils penser? Quelques remarques à propos de l'affaire Sokal et de ses suites. Conférence du 17 juin 1998 à l'Université de Genève. Société romande de philosophie, groupe genevois. Cahiers Rationalistes, octobre et novembre http://hypo.ge-dip.etat-ge.ch/athena/bouveresse/bou_pens.html

Bracher, Karl Dietrich (1969/1995) Hitler et la dictature allemande.

Éditions Complexe [Paris] 681 p.

Bracher, Karl Dietrich (1970) The German Dictatorship: The Origins, Structure, and Effects of National Socialism. Praeger New York xv – 553 p.

Bradbury, Ray (1946/1982) The martian chronicles. Bantom Books New York 181 p.

Breton, André (1924) Manifesto of Surrealism. www.tcf.ua.edu/Classes/Jbutler/T340/SurManifesto/ ManifestoOfSurrealism.htm

Burridge, Kenelm O. L. (1979) Someone, No one: An Essay on Individuality. Princeton U. Press Princeton NJ 270 p.

Cahill, Thomas (1995) How the Irish Saved Civilisation. Nana Talese/Random House New York 245 p.

Cameron, Nigel M de S. (1992) Life and Death After Hippocrates: The New Medecine. Crossway Wheaton IL 187 p.

Campbell, Neil (1993) Biology. (3rd edition) Benjamin-Cummings Pub Co. San Francisco CA 1280 p.

Camus, Albert (1942/1991) The Myth of Sisyphus: And Other Essays. Vintage New York 224 p.

Camus, Albert (1947/1991) The Plague. (Stuart Gilbert translator) Vintage International New York 308 p.

Camus, Albert (1951/1978) The Rebel: An Essay on Man in Revolt. (trans. Anthony Bower). Knopf New York, NY. xii - 306 p.

Carrel, Alexis (1922) Eugénique et sélection. Alcan Paris

Carter, Stephen L. (1989) The Religiously Devout Judge. Notre Dame Law Revue 64 /932 www.puaf.umd.edu/courses/puaf650/materials-Religion-Carter.htm

Cayley, David (1992) Ivan Illich in Conversation. Harper Collins Scarborough ON 299 p.

Cecil, Robert (1972) The Myth of the Master Race: Alfred Rosenberg and Nazi Ideology. B.T. Batsford London 266 p.

Cesar, Jules (58 - 52 BC/1915) Caesar's Commentaries. Everyman's Library no. 702. (Edited by Ernest Rhys, Translated by W. A. Macdevitt), [De Bello Gallico]. www.gutenberg.org/ebooks/10657

Chastel, Claude E. (1998) Xénotransplantation et risque viral. Virologie vol. 2, no. 5, sept.-oct. www.john-libbey-eurotext.fr/fr/revues/bio_rech/vir/ sommaire. md?cle_parution=631&type=text.html

Cherki, Eliezer (2005) Les conceptions politiques de l'islam. Jerusalem Post (French edition) no. 900547 4 au 10 juillet www.harissa.com/D_forum/Israel/lesconceptions.htm

Chomsky, Noam (1972) Form and Meaning in Natural Languages. in Language and Mind, enlarged edition. Harcourt, Brace, Jovanovich New York

Chomsky, Noam & Herman, Edward S. (1988) Manufacturing Consent:

The political economy of the mass-media. Pantheon New York xvi - 412 p.
http://www.advocacyagainstcensorship.com/quotes/qtchomsky.html
Chomsky, Noam & Herman, Edward S. (1988/2003) La fabrique de l'opinion publique: la politique économique des médias américains: essai. (traduit de l'anglais par Guy Ducornet) Serpent à plumes Paris 331 p.
Clarke, Arthur C. (1986/1987) Songs of Distant Earth. Del Rey/Ballantine New York 319 p.
Collins, Warwick (1994) The Fatal Flaw of a Great Theory: Now that the environmental theories of Marxism have collapsed so spectacularly, perhaps the same fate will befall Darwinism. pp. 7-10
The Spectator (31 Dec.) vol. 273 no. 8686
Colson, Charles W. (1996) Kingdoms in Conflict. pp. 34-38 First Things 67 Nov.
www.firstthings.com/ftissues/ft9611/articles/colson.html
Cornwell, John (2003) Hitler's Scientists: Science, War, and the Devil's Pact. Penguin Books London
Cusset François (2005) La French theory, métisse transatlantique. pp. 10-13 Sciences Humaines (mai-juin, HS spécial no. 3)
Darwin, Charles (1859/1958) The Origin of Species: By Means of Natural Selection or the Preservation of Favoured Races in the Struggle for Life. New York, Mentor Books 479 p.
Etext: www.gutenberg.org/ebooks/2009
Darwin, Charles (1871) The Descent of Man and Selection in Relation to Sex. Vol. 1 [1st ed.] John Murray London 424 p.
http://darwin-online.org.uk/content/frameset?itemID=F937.1&viewtype=text&pageseq=1
Darwin, Charles (1888) The Life and Letters of Charles Darwin Including An Autobiographical Chapter: edited by his son Francis Darwin. Volumes I & II.
www.gutenberg.org/ebooks/2087
Darwin, Charles (1887) Life and Letters of Charles Darwin, Including an Autobiographical Chapter (vols. I & II) [published by his son Francis Darwin] C. Reinwald Paris
Dawkins, Richard (1986) The Blind Watchmaker. Norton New York xiii - 332 p.
Dawkins, Richard (1989), Book Review. (of Donald Johanson and Maitland Edey's Blueprint). The New York Times, section 7, April 9.
Dawkins, Richard (2000) The Descent of Man (Episode 1: The Moral Animal) (a series of radio shows presented in January and February 2000 by the Australian Broadcasting Corporation, produced by Tom Morton) www.abc.net.au/science/descent/trans1.htm
Dawkins, Richard (2001) The word made flesh: Today we can read human and ape genetic legacies. In 50 years, we could resurrect the past, says Richard Dawkins. The Guardian Thursday December 27,

www.guardian.co.uk/Archive/Article/0,4273,4326031,00.html
Dawkins, Richard. (2003) A Devil's Chaplain: Reflections on Hope, Lies, Science, and Love. Houghton Mifflin Boston, MA 266 p.
Dawkins, Richard. (2004) Dawkins interviewed by Bill Moyers [Evolution]. PBS website 03 December 2004 http://richarddawkins.net/videos/64-interview-at-pbs-with-bill-moyers
De Beauvoir, Simone (1981) La cérémonie des adieux; suivi de Entretiens avec Jean-Paul Sartre, août-septembre 1974. [Paris]: Gallimard, 559 p.
De Beauvoir, Simone (1984) A Conversation About Death and God. Harper's magazine, February pp. 38-39 http://www.harpers.org/archive/1984/02/0073254
De Fontenay, Elisabeth (2004) L'altruisme au sens extra-moral. pp. 68-74 Sciences & Avenir (hors série) no. 139 juin/juil.
De Vries, Hent & Weber, Samuel eds. (2001) Religion and Media. Stanford U. Press Stanford CA 649 p.
Debray, Régis (1981) Critique de la raison politique. Gallimard Paris (coll. Bibliothèque des idées) 473 p.
Debray, Régis (1983) Critique of political reason. Verso London 384 p.
Debray, Régis (2002a) L'enseignement du fait religieux dans l'école laïc. Ed. Odile Jacob [Paris]
Debray, Régis (2002b) L'institution républicaine et laïque doit s'emparer de l'étude du fait religieux comme la clé d'un enseignement ouvert à la complexité et à la tolérance. www.ac-versailles.fr/pedagogi/ses/ecjs/sequences/seconde/ecole-et-religion.html
Debray, Régis (2004) Du surnaturel à la télévision.[597] http://adperso.phpnet.org/content.php?pgid=phiart
Deichmann, Ute (1996) Biologists under Hitler. (trans. Thomas Dunlap) Harvard University Press Cambridge, MA & London 468 p.
Dembski, William ed. (2004) Reflections on Human Origins. pp. 3-15 Professorenforum-Journal, vol. 5, no. 3 www.campusfürchristus.de/proforum/volumes/v05n03/Artikel1/dembski.pdf
Deringil, Selim (2000) "There Is No Compulsion in Religion": On Conversion and Apostasy in the Late Ottoman Empire: 1839–1856. pp. 547-575 Society for Comparative Study of Society and History vol. 42 no. 3 www.journals.cambridge.org/action/displayAbstract?fromPage=online&aid=54957
Dernavich, Paul A. (2001) Darwinian Dissonance? www.infidels.org/library/modern/features/2001/dernavich1.html
Derr, Thomas S. (1992) Animal Rights, Human Rights. pp. 23-30 First Things 20 February www.firstthings.com/ftissues/ft9202/articles/derr.html
Descartes, René (1637) A Discourse on Method. (etext) www.gutenberg.org/ebooks/59

Descartes, René (1641/1907) Meditations on First Philosophy. (trans. John Veitch) W. Blackwood and Sons, Edinburgh - London clxxxi - 292 p. www.filepedia.org/meditations-on-first-philosophy

Desroches, Henri (1974) Les Religions de Contrebande: essais sur les phénomènes religieux en époques critiques. Maison MAME France 230 p.

Devos, Raymond (1989) À plus d'un titre: Sketches inédits. Olivier Orban (Presse Pocket) Paris 178 p.

Dick, Philip K. (1968/1982) Blade Runner/Do Androids Dreams of Electric Sheep? Del Ray/Ballantine New York 216 p.

Dick, Philip K. (1978/1985) How to Build a Universe That Doesn't Fall Apart Two Days Later. in I Hope I Shall Arrive Soon, Mark Hurst ed., Paul Williams St. Martin's, NY www.geocities.com/pkdlw/howtobuild.html

Diderot, Denis, (1755/1976) Œuvres complètes, vol. VII: Encyclopédie III. Hermann Paris

Diderot, Denis (1769/1963) Correspondance. (janv. 1769 – déc. 1769) vol. IX [Georges Roth ed.] Éditions de Minuit Paris 1963 261p.

Dostoyevsky, Fyodor (1872/1971) The Devils: The Possessed. (Trans. David Magarshack) Penguin Books London 669 p.

Dostoyevsky, Fyodor (1879/1933) The Brothers Karamazov. (Constance Garnett trans.) Modern Library New York 822 p.

Douglas, Mary (1966/1979) Purity and Danger: An analysis of the concepts of pollution and taboo. Routledge & Kegan Paul London 188 p.

Dreesens, Richard, (1994) Entrevue avec Enki Bilal, extraite de « Canal-BD ». http://bilal.enki.free.fr/afficher_interview.php3?fichier_de_l_interview=interview3

Dumont, Fernand (1981) L'anthropologie en l'absence de l'homme. PUF Paris 369 p.

Durand, Guy (2004) Le Québec et la laïcité: Avancées et dérives. Éditions Varia Montréal 124 p.

Durant, John (1981) The Myth of Human Evolution. pp. 425-438 New Universities Quarterly vol. 35 Autumn

Eagleton, Terry (1987) Awakening from modernity. [Review of two books by J.-F. Lyotard] Times Literary Supplement no. 4377 p. 194. 20 Feb.

Eckstein, Cheryl M. (1996) One of Our Children is Dead. Ability Network Magazine vol. 5 no. 2 – Winter www.chninternational.com/v5n2p37.html

Eisenburg, Léon (1974) Ethique et science de l'homme. pp. 324-340 in Morin et Piattelli-Palmarini (eds.) L'unité de l'homme (Vol.3) Seuil Paris 390 p.

Einstein, Albert (1939) Science and Religion I, Address: Princeton Theological Seminary, May 19, www.sacred-texts.com/aor/einstein/einsci.htm

Elbaz, Mikhaël (2002) Cuisine de Dieu – aliments profanes. Prohibitions alimentaires du judaïsme, organismes génétiquement modifiés et

Bibliographie

enjeux éthiques. Avis: Pour une gestion éthique des OGM, Commission de l'éthique de la science et de la technologie (gouv. du Québec) 45 p.

Ellison, Michael (2000) The Men Can't Help it. The Guardian - Tuesday January 25 www.guardian.co.uk/g2/story/0,3604,240812,00.html

Eliot, T. S. (1954/1982) Selected Pœms. Faber and Faber Bungay Suffolk 127 p.

Ellul, Jacques (1954/1964) The Technological Society. Vintage Books New York 449 p.

Ellul, Jacques (1962) Propagandes. A. Colin Paris 335 p.

Ellul, Jacques (1966) Propaganda: The Formation of Men's Attitudes. (Konrad Kellen and Jean Lerner Trans.) Knopf New York

Ellul, Jacques (1973) Propaganda: The Formation of Men's Attitudes. Vintage Books New York 352 p.

Engel, Pascal (2004) La bête humaine. pp. 12-13 Sciences et Avenir, HS no. 139 Juin/Juillet

Fast, Howard (1963/67) The First Men. pp. 9-38 The Worlds of Science Fiction. Robert P. Mills (ed.) Paperback Library New York

Feyerabend, Paul K. (1975/1979) Against Method: Outline of an anarchistic theory of knowledge. Verso London 339 p.

Firth, Raymond (1981) Spiritual Aroma: Religion and Politics. pp. 582-601 American Anthropologist Vol. 83 no.3 Sept.

Fleischer, Richard (1973) Solyent Green. (97 min.) Producer; Walter Seltzer, Russel Thacher, script: Harry Harrison and Charlton Heston; Metro-Goldwyn-Mayer distributor

Foucault, Michel (1961/2006) History of Madness. ed. Jean Khalfa, trans. Jonathan Murphy and Jean Khalfa Routledge London

Foucault, Michel (1966/1994) The Order of Things: An Archaeology of the Human Sciences. Vintage Books New York 416 p.

Foucault, Michel (1966) Les mots et les choses: Une archéologie des sciences sociales. Gallimard Paris 400 p.

Frankl, Viktor E. (1959/1971) Man's Search for Meaning: An introduction to Logotherapy. Simon & Schuster/Pocket Books New York 220 p. www.4shared.com/document/FX9PlnGl/_psiho__-_frankl_viktor_e_-_ma.htm

Fukuyama, Francis (2002) Our Posthuman Future: Consequences of the Biotechnology Revolution. Picador New York 272 p.

Gablik, Suzi (1984/1995) Has Modernism Failed? Thames & Hudson New York 133 p.

Galileo (1615) Letter to the Grand Duchess Christina. www.fordham.edu/halsall/mod/galileo-tuscany.html

Galileo (1632/1953) Dialogue Concerning the two Chief World Systems - Ptolemaic and Copernican. University of California Press Berkeley

Gandy, R. (1996). Human versus mechanical intelligence. pp. 125-136 in

Peter Millican, & A. Clark (eds.), Machines and thought. Oxford University Press Oxford

Gariépy, Stéphane (1999) Le protestantisme et ses valeurs. www.samizdat.qc.ca/vc/theol/protest.htm

Garvey, John (1981) Beyond Proof & Disproof: The Religions of Pro-Choice and Pro-Life. pp. 360-361 Commonweal 19 June

Gauvin, Jean-François (2000) L'histoire des sciences au service de la culture scientifique. Bulletin du GIS en muséologie scientifique et technique. Le MuST, no. 3 www.smq.qc.ca/publicsspec/smq/gis/must/bulletin/archives/200004/indexp4.phtml

Geertz, Clifford (1973) The Interpretation of Cultures. Basic Books New York 470 p.

Gellner, Ernest (1992/1999) Postmodernism, Reason and Religion. Routledge London/New York 108 p.

Giesen, Rolf (2003) Nazi Propaganda Films: A History and Filmography. McFarland & Company, Inc. North Carolina

Girard, René (1999/2001) I See Satan Fall Like Lightning. Gracewing Leominster UK 199 p.

Glassman, Jim (1997) TechnoPolitics Program No. 734, 15 Nov., The Blackwell Corporation [producteur: Neal B. Freeman] ARN Library Files www.arn.org/docs/techno/techno1197.htm

Glen, William (1994) The Mass-Extinction Debates: How Science Works in a Crisis. [On the mass-extinction debates: an interview with Stephen Jay Gould] Stanford University Press Stanford, California

Godawa, Brian (2002) Hollywood Worldviews. IVP Downers Grove IL 208 p.

Goodstein, David Cal (2002) Conduct and Misconduct in Science. www.physics.ohio-state.edu/~wilkins/onepage/conduct.html

Gosselin, Paul (1979) Myths of Origin and the Theory of Evolution. www.samizdat.qc.ca/cosmos/origines/myth.htm

Gosselin, Paul (1986) Des catégories de religion et de science: essai d'épistémologie anthropologique. (thèse Univ. Laval) www.samizdat.qc.ca/cosmos/sc_soc/tm_pg/tdm.htm

Gould, Stephen Jay (1980) The Panda's Thumb. Penguin London

Gould, Stephen Jay (1981) The Mismeasure of Man: Revised and Expanded edition. WW Norton New York London 417 p.

Gould, Stephen Jay (1991) Opus 200. pp. 12-18 Natural History, August vol. 100 no. 8 www.stephenjaygould.org/library/gould_opus200.html

Gould, Stephen Jay (1997a) Nonoverlapping Magisteria. (This view of life column) pp. 16, 18-22, 60-62 Natural History vol. 106, no. 2, www.stephenjaygould.org/library/gould_noma.html

Gould, Stephen Jay (1997b) Darwinian Fundamentalism. The New York Review of Books vol. 44, no. 10 · June 12, www.nybooks.com/articles/1151

Gould, Stephen Jay (2000) The First Day of the Rest of Our Life. (the arrival of the new millenium). Natural History April,
http://findarticles.com/p/articles/mi_m1134/is_3_109/ai_61524419/

Grassé, Pierre-Paul (1980) L'Homme en accusation: De la biologie à la politique. Albin Michel Paris 354 p.

Greeley, Andrew M. (1972) Unsecular Man: The Persistence of Religion. Shocken Books New York 280 p.

Green, R. L. & Hooper, Walter (1979) C. S. Lewis: A Biography. Collins Fount London

Griffiths, Paul J. & Jean Bethke Elshtain (2002) Proselytizing for Tolerance. pp. 30-36. First Things no. 127 November
www.firstthings.com/ftissues/ft0211/articles/exchange.html

Guibet Lafaye, Caroline (2000) Esthétiques de la postmodernité: Etude réalisée dans le cadre d'une coopération entre l'Université Masaryk de Brno (République tchèque) et l'Université Paris 1 Panthéon-Sorbonne. http://nosophi.univ-paris1.fr/docs/cgl_art.pdf

Guiness, Os (1973) The Dust of Death: a critique of the counter-culture. Inter-Varsity Press Downers Grove IL 419 p.

Guiness, Os & Seel, John (1992) No God but God. Moody Press Chicago IL 224 p.

Guiness, Os (2001) Time For Truth. Baker Grand Rapids MI 128 p.

Haeckel, Ernst (1899/1934) The Riddle of The Universe. (Translated by Joseph McCabe) Watts & Co./The Rationalist Press London 824 p.
www.archive.org/details/riddleoftheunive034957mbp

Halpern, Catherine (2005) Jacques Derrida (1930-2004) Le subversif. pp. 52-53 Sciences humaines (mai-juin, HS spécial no. 3)

Halpern, Mark (1987) Turing's Test and the Ideology of Artificial Intelligence. pp. 79–93 Artificial Intelligence Review vol. 1 no. 2

Halvorson, Richard (2002) Questioning the Orthodoxy: Intelligent Design theory is breaking the scientific monopoly of Darwinism. Harvard Political Review 14 May
http://richh.blogs.com/rhonline/files/20020514orthodoxy.pdf

Harvey David (1989) The Condition of Postmodernity: An Enquiry in the Origins of Cultural Change. Basil Blackwell Oxford ix - 378 p.
www.scribd.com/doc/47806639/The-Condition-of-Postmodernity

Hatch, Elvin (1983) Culture and Morality: Relativity of Values in Anthropology. Columbia University Press New York 163 p.

Hawking, Jane (2004) Music to Move the Stars: A life with Stephen. McMillan New York 480p.

Hawkins, Michael (1997) Hunting Down the Universe: the missing mass, primordial black holes and other dark matters. Little, Brown 278 p.

Hayles, N, Katherine (1999) How We Became Posthuman: Virtual Bodies in Cybernetics, Literature, and Informatics. U. of Chicago Press Chicago & London 350 p.

Hegar, Alfred (1911) Die Wiederkehr des Gleichen und die Vervolkommung des Menshengeschlectes. pp. 72-85 Arhiv für Rassen und Gesellshaftsbiologie 8

Hendln, Herbert (1997) Seduced by Death: Doctors, Patients and the Dutch Care. W.W. Norton New York 256 p.

Herdt, Gilbert; Stoller, Robert J. (1990) Intimate communications. Columbia U. Press New York 467 p.

Himmelfarb, Gertrude (1959/1968) Darwin and the Darwinian Revolution. W. W. Norton & Co. New York

Hitler, Adolf (1925/1941) Mein Kampf. Raynald C. Hitchcock New York 1003 p. www.archive.org/stream/meinkampf035176mbp/ meinkampf035176mbp_djvu.txt

Hitler, Adolf (1944/1973) Hitler's Table Talks 1941-44: His Private Conversations. Translated by Norman Cameron and R.H. Stevens Weidenfeld and Nicolson London xxxix - 746 p.

Hobbes, Thomas (1651/1974) Leviathan. (Edited with an introduction by C.B. Macpherson) Penguin London (Penguin Classics) 728 p.

Horgan, John (1995) Profile: Fred Hoyle: The Return of the Maverick. pp. 46-47 Scientific American March vol. 272 no. 3

Hsu, Feng-Hsiung, Thomas Anantharaman, Murray Campbell et Andreas Nowatzyk (1990) A Grandmaster Chess Machine. pp. 44-50 Scientific American Oct. vol. 263, no. 4 www.disi.unige.it/person/DelzannoG/AI2/hsu.html

Hugo, Victor (1987) Œuvres complètes. Robert Laffont Choses vues / Histoire – Bouquins

Hume, David (1740) A Treatise of Human Nature. Project Gutenberg Etext www.gutenberg.org/ebooks/4705

Hume, David (1748/1910) An Enquiry Concerning Human Understanding. P.F. Collier & Son (Harvard Classics Volume 37) : New York 445 p. www.gutenberg.org/ebooks/9662

Hutin, Jeanne-Emmanuelle (1998) Henri IV voulait vraiment la paix du royaume: Les explications de l'historien Jean Delumeau. Dimanche Ouest-France - 15 février www.ouest-france.fr/dossiershtm/editnantes/delumeau.htm

Huxley, Aldous (1958/2007) Brave New World Revisited. Vintage Canada xvi - 407 p. www.huxley.net/bnw-revisited/

Huxley, Julian (1927/1957) Religion without Revelation. Harper New York 252 p.

Huxley, Julian (1958) Introduction. pp. ix-xv (in The Origin of the Species). Mentor New York 479 p.

Jaki, Stanley L. (1969/1989) Brain, Mind and Computers. Regnery Gateway Washington DC 316 p.

Jaki, Stanley L. (1974/1986) Science and Creation. Academic Press New

York 367 p.

Johnson, Blind Willie (1930) Soul of A Man. Columbia Records 14582-D

Johnson, Phillip (1995) What (If Anything) Hath God Wrought? Academic Freedom and the Religious Professor. Academe Sept.

Johnson, Phillip (2002) The Right Questions: Truth, Meaning & Public Debate. InterVarsity Press

Jones, D. Gareth (1984) Brave New People: Ethical Issues at the commencement of life. InterVarsity Press Downers Grove IL 221 p.

Jorion, Paul (2000) Turing, ou la tentation de comprendre. l'Homme no. 153 pp. 251-268

Journet, Nicolas (2005) L'Affaire Sokal: pourquoi la France? pp. 14-16 Sciences humaines (mai-juin, HS spécial no. 3)

Karlekar, Karin Deutsch (2003) Freedom of The Press 2003: A Global Survey of Media Independence. Freedom House Rowman & Littlefield Publishers, Inc. New York http://freedomhouse.org

Karsz, Saul (1974) Théorie et Politique: Louis Althusser. Fayard Paris 340 p.

Kass, Leon (2004) Entretien: La posthumanité ou le piège des désirs sans fin. (propos recueillis par A. Robitaille). pp. 80-90 Argument vol. 7 no. 1 www.revueargument.ca

Kepler, Johannes (1601/1979) Concerning the More Certain Fundamentals of Astrology. Proceedings of the American Philosophical Society vol. 123 no. 2 pp. 85-116 April www.jstor.org/pss/986232

Kreeft, Peter (1994) C. S. Lewis for the Third Millenium. Ignatius Press San Francisco CA 193 p.

Kreeft, Peter (1996) The Journey: A Spiritual Roadmap for Modern Pilgrims. InterVarsity Press Downers Grove IL 128 p.

Kreeft, Peter (1999) A Refutation of Moral Relativism: Interviews with an Absolutist. Ignatius Press San Francisco CA 177 p.

Kuhn, Thomas S. (1970) The Structure of Scientific Revolutions. University of Chicago Press [Chicago] xii - 210 p.

Kurzweil, Raymond (1999) The Age of Spiritual Machines: When Computers Exceed Human Intelligence. Viking Press New York xii - 388 p. www.penguinputnam.com/kurzweil/excerpts/chap6/chap6.htm

Lallemand, Suzanne (1974) Cosmologie, Cosmogonie. pp. 20-32 in Marc Augé (ed.) 1974a

Landau, Paul (2004) La légalité des attentats-suicides au regard du droit musulman. http://forum.subversiv.com/index.php?id=8680

Larson, Edward J. & Larry Witham (1999) Scientists and Religion in America. Scientific American vol. 281 no. 3 Sept.

Laudan, Larry (1988) The Demise of the Demarcation Problem. pp. 337-366 in But is it Science? The philosophical question in the Creation/Evolution controversy. M. Ruse (ed.)

Prometheus Buffalo NY 406 p.

Le Goff, Jacques (1999) Le Moyen Âge de Jacques Le Goff (Entretien). pp. 80-86 L'Histoire no. 236

Le Goff, Jacques (2000) Le christianisme a libéré les femmes. pp. 34-38 L'Histoire no. 245

Leithart, Peter J. (1996) The Politics of Baptism. pp. 5-6 First Things no. 68 Dec.
www.firstthings.com/article/2007/11/002-the-politics-of-baptism-25

Lévi-Strauss, Claude (1962) La Pensée Sauvage. Plon Paris 389 p.

Lévi-Strauss, Claude (1966) The Savage Mind. University of Chicago Press [Chicago]

Lévy-Leblond, J.-M. & Jaubert, Alain (1972/75) (Auto)critique de la science. Seuil Paris (coll. Points. Sciences; S53) 310 p.

Lewis, C. S. (1940) The Problem of Pain. Geoffrey Bles The Centenary Press London ix - 148 p.

Lewis, C. S. (1943/1977) Mere Christianity. MacMillan New York 190 p.

Lewis, C. S. (1943/1978) The Abolition of Man: Reflections on education with special reference to the teaching of English in the upper forms of schools. Collins Glasgow 63 p.
Etext: www.columbia.edu/cu/augustine/arch/lewis/abolition1.htm

Lewis, C. S. (1946/1965) That Hideous Strength. Collier/MacMillan New York 382 p.

Lewis, C. S. (1947/2002) God in the Dock. (Walter Hooper ed.). Eerdmans Grand Rapids MI 347 p.

Lewis, C. S. (1951/1970) Prince Caspian. MacMillan New York 216 p.

Lewis, C. S. (1955) Surprised by Joy. Harcourt Brace Jovanovich New York 238 p.

Lewis, C. S. (1955/1970) The Magician's Nephew. MacMillan New York 186 p.

Lewis, C. S. (1961/2001) A Grief Observed. HarperOne [New York] 76 p.

Lewis, C. S. (1962) They Asked for a Paper. Geoffrey Bles London 211 p.

Lewis, C. S. (1986) Present Concerns. Harvest/Harcourt Brace & Co. London/New York 108 p.

Lewontin, Richard (1997) A review of Carl Sagan's book Billions and Billions of Demons. pp. 28-32 New York Review of Books, Jan. 9, vol. 44 no.1
www.nybooks.com/articles/article-preview?article_id=1297

Linnaeus, Carl von (1744/1972) L'équilibre de la nature. Librairie philosophique VRIN Paris

Lucas, John Randolph (1961) Minds, Machines and Goedel. pp. 112-127 Philosophy 36
http://users.ox.ac.uk/~jrlucas/Godel/mmg.html

Luckmann, Thomas (1970) The Invisible Religion. MacMillan New York 128 p.

Lunney, James (2003) Private Members' Business: Appointment of Judges, 37th Parliament, 2nd Session, Edited Hansard, number 096,

Tuesday, May 6, 2003, section 19:30
www2.parl.gc.ca/HousePublications/Publication.aspx?Language=E&M
ode=1&Parl=37&Ses=2&DocId=874791

Lyden, John C. (2003) Film as Religion: Myths, Morals and Rituals. New York University Press 287 p.

Lyotard, Jean François (1979/1984) The Postmodern Condition: A Report on Knowledge. (Foreword by Fredric Jameson) University of Minnesota Press Minneapolis MN xxv-110 p.

Lyotard, Jean-François (1996) Musique et postmodernité. pp. 3-16 Surfaces vol. 6. 203 (27/11)
http://pum12.pum.umontreal.ca/revues/surfaces/vol6/lyotard.html

MacCormac, Earl R. (1976) Metaphor and Myth in Science and Religion. Duke U. Press Durham NC 167 p.

Mao Tse-Toung (1957) Speech at the Chinese Communist Party's National Conference On Propaganda Work. March 12, 1957
www.marxists.org/reference/archive/mao/selected-works/volume-5/mswv5_59.htm

Mao Tse-Toung (1963) Where do Correct Ideas Come From?
www.marxists.org/reference/archive/mao/selected-works/

Marceau, Richard (2003) Excerpt from the proceedings of the House of Commons [Canada] during the second and final hour of debate considering motion M-288 (Process for appointing judges). Proposed by the MP for Charlesbourg/Jacques-Cartier, Richard Marceau, edited Hansard; 37th Parliament, 2nd session, number 128, Friday, September 26, 2003, section 1325
www2.parl.gc.ca/HousePublications/Publication.aspx?DocId=1067009&Mode=1&Parl=37&Ses=2&Language=E#T1325

Marx, Karl (1859/1977) A Contribution to the Critique of Political Economy. Progress Publishers Moscow
www.marxists.org/archive/marx/works/1859/critique-pol-economy/

Mauriac, François (1958/2006) Foreword. pp. xvii-xxi in Night by Elie Wiesel, Hill and Wang New York xxi - 120 p.

Mayr, Ernst (1942) Systematics and The Origin of Species. Columbia University Press, New York

Mayr, Ernst (1997) Interview. pp. 8-11 Natural History; May; vol. 106 no. 4

Mchugh, Josh (2003) Google Sells Its Soul. pp. 130-135 Wired vol. 11 no. 1 January
www.wired.com/wired/archive/11.01/google.html

Meilaender, Gilbert (2002) Between Beasts and God. pp. 23-29 First Things no. 119 January
http://print.firstthings.com/ftissues/ft0201/articles/meilaender.html

Mely, Benoît (2002) Est-ce à l'école laïque de valoriser «le religieux»? Observations critiques sur le rapport Debray. les Cahiers Rationalistes, (sept.-oct.) - no. 560
http://perso.wanadoo.fr/union.rationaliste44/Cadres%20Dossiers%20

en%20Ligne/Dossiers_en_ligne/Laicite/Dossier%20Mely/
mely%20rapport%20debray.htm

Mendum, Mary Lou (2001) Defending the Teaching of Evolution in the Public Schools: Ten Tips For Letter Hacking. NCSE Reports 1996; March 19 16(4): 19-20
www.ncseweb.org/resources/articles/
4633_ten_tips_for_letter_hacking_3_19_2001.asp

Messall, Rebecca (2004) The Long Road of Eugenics: From Rockefeller to Roe v. Wade. pp. 33-74 Human Life Review, Fall
www.nla.org/Documents/eugenics.pdf

Midgley, Mary (1985) Evolution As a Religion: Strange Hopes and Stranger Fears. Methuen London/New York

Midgley, Mary (1992) Science as Salvation: A modern myth and its meaning. Routledge London & NY 239 p.

Miller, Kristin J. (1996) Human Rights of Women In Iran: The Universalist Approach And The Relativist Response. Emory International Law Review, vol. 10 no. 2 Fall
www.law.emory.edu/EILR/volumes/win96/miller.html

Minsky, Marvin (1994) Will Robots Inherit the Earth? Scientific American, October pp. 108-113
www.ai.mit.edu/people/minsky/papers/sciam.inherit.txt

Mitchell C. Ben (1999) Of Euphemisms and Euthanasia: The Language Games of the Nazi Doctors and Some Implications for the Modern Euthanasia Movement. pp. 255 – 265 Omega: The Journal of Death and Dying vol. 40, no. 1
www.ncbi.nlm.nih.gov/pubmed/12580198

Mohammad (≈650ap. JC/1876) The Koran: translated from the Arabic, the suras arranged in chronological order. (with notes and index. By J. M. Rodwell) xxviii - 562 p.
www.gutenberg.org/ebooks/3434

Monod, Jacques (1971) Le hasard et la nécessité: essai sur la philosophie naturelle de la biologie moderne. Seuil Paris 197 p.

Monod, Jacques (1971) Chance and Necessity. Alfred A. Knopf New York

Morton, Peter (1984) The Vital Science: Biology and the Literary Imagination, 1860-1900. George Allen & Unwin London

Morton, Tom (2000) The Descent of Man Episode 1: The Moral Animal Broadcast on The Science Show on ABC Radio National Presented and produced by Tom Morton
www.abc.net.au/science/descent/trans1.htm

Muggeridge, Malcolm (1978) Christ and the Media. Eerdmanns Grand Rapids MI (London Lectures in Contemporary Christianity) 127 p.

Muggeridge, Malcolm (1979) The Great Liberal Death Wish. Imprimis, the monthly journal of Hillsdale College. May, vol 8, no. 5
www.orthodoxytoday.org/articles/MuggeridgeLiberal.shtm

Muggeridge, Malcolm (1988) Confessions of a Twentieth-century Pilgrim. Harper San Francisco 144 p.

Murguía, Guillermo Agudelo; Agudelo, Juan Sebastián (2002) The sentient universe. In search of the theory of cosmic evolution. Research Institute on Human Evolution. www.humanevol.com/doc/doc200302100400.html

Nadeau, Robert (2004) Démocratisation ou chasse aux sorcières. Journal du Barreau du Québec vol. 36 no. 4 - 1er mars www.barreau.qc.ca/journal/frameset.asp?article=/journal/vol36/no4/justiceetsociete.html

Nietzsche, Friedrich (1882/1924) The Joyful Wisdom [The Gay Science]. (trans. Thomas Common, P. V. Cohn & M. D. Petre) MacMillan New York (Volume X: Complete works of Friedrich Nietzsche, Oscar Levy ed.) 370 p. http://ebooks.adelaide.edu.au/n/nietzsche/friedrich/n67j/

Nietzsche, Friedrich (1883/1999) Thus Spake Zarathustra: A Book For All and None. (Thomas Common, trans.) Project Gutenberg Etext #1998

Nietzsche, Friedrich (1895) Die Götzen-Dämmerung - Twilight of the Idols. (Translation by Walter Kaufmann and R.J. Hollingdale) www.handprint.com/SC/NIE/GotDamer.html

Nietzsche, Friedrich (1901/1967) The Will to Power. Vintage Books New York

Novak, Michael (2006) The Truth About Religious Freedom. pp. 17-20 First Things Vol. 161 March www.firstthings.com/article/2007/01/the-truth-about-religious-freedom-3

Orwell, George (1949/1984) Nineteen Eighty-Four. (Signet Classic, with an afterword by Erich Fromm) Penguin Putnam New York 267 p.

Pascal, Blaise (1670/1908) Pensées. JM Dent & sons London (William Finlayson Trotter, trans. Everyman's library. Theology and philosophy [no. 874]) xix-297 p. http://oregonstate.edu/instruct/phl302/texts/pascal/pensees-contents.html

Pearcey, Nancey (2004) Total Truth. Crossway Wheaton IL 479 p.

Penrose, Roger (1994) Shadows of the Mind: A Search for the Missing Science of Consciousness. Oxford UP, Oxford xvi - 457 p.

Pepperell, Robert (1997) The Post-Human Condition. Intellect Exeter UK xi – 206 p.

Pfeiffer, John E. (1972) The Emergence of Man. Harper & Row New York 550 p.

Phillips, Winfred (2000) The Extraordinary Future. www.mind.ilstu.edu/published/Phillips/PhillipsTOC.html

Pichot, André (2000) La société pure: De Darwin à Hitler. Flammarion Paris 453 p.

Pichot, André (2009) The Pure Society: From Darwin to Hitler. Verso [London] 360 p.

Popper, Karl R. (1945/1962) The Open Society and its Enemies. Routledge & Kegan Paul London 2 volumes

Porush, David (1992) Transcendence at the Interface: The Architecture of Cyborg Utopia — or — Cyberspace Utopoids as Postmodern Cargo Cult.
www.cni.org/pub/LITA/Think/Porush.html

Porush, David (1994) Hacking the Brainstem: Postmodern Metaphysics and Stephenson's Snow Crash. pp. 537-571 Configurations 2.3

Pournin, Kim (2004) Jacques Lacan: Un héritage au compte-gouttes. Le Figaro [le 2 septembre]
www.lefigaro.fr/litteraire/20040902.LIT0016.html

Proctor, Robert (1988) Racial Hygiene: Medicine under the Nazis. Harvard University Press Cambridge, Massachusetts

Propp, Vladimir (1928/1968) Morphology of the Folktale. Translated by Laurence Scott, introduction by Svatava Pirkova-Jakobson. University of Texas Press Austin & London xxi - 158 p.

Provine, William B. (1990) Response to Phillip Johnson. (Letter) pp. 23-24 First Things no. 6 Oct.
www.arn.org/docs/johnson/pjdogma2.htm

Provine, William B. (1994) Darwinism: Science or Naturalistic Philosophy? A debate between William B. Provine and Phillip E. Johnson at Stanford University, April 30, 1994
www.arn.org/arn/orpages/or161/161main.htm

Purtill, R. L. (1971) Beating the Imitation Game. pp. 290-294 Mind vol. 80 no. 318

Putallaz, François-Xavier (2003) La mode de l'antispécisme: un défi pour l'anthropologie? in Quelle conception de l'homme aujourd'hui? (Actes du 5ᵉ Colloque International de la Fondation Guilé, Domaine de Guilé Boncourt 18 et 19 octobre 2002) Guilé Foundation Press Suisse
www.guile.net/fr/ies/livres/conception_homme_aujourdhui.pdf?PHPS ESSID=fe034d0aef145c93d5e2f5424e5b64b8

Radford, Tim (1999) Is Science Killing The Soul? A public exchange at Westminster Central Hall in London with Steven Pinker and Richard Dawkins (Feb. 10)
www.edge.org/3rd_culture/dawkins_pinker/dawkins_pinker_index.html

Raymo, Chet (2000) A New Paradigm for Thomas Kuhn: Steve Fuller argues that Kuhn's ideas were anything but revolutionary. pp. 104-105 Scientific American vol. 283 no. 3 Sept.
www.sciam.com/article.cfm?articleID=000C138A-D70A-1C73-9B81809EC588EF21

Reszler, André (1981) Mythes politiques modernes. PUF Paris 230 p.

Richards, Robert J. (1992) The Meaning of Evolution: The Morphological Construction and Ideological Reconstruction of Darwin's Theory. University of Chicago Press [Chicago] (coll. Science and Its Conceptual

Foundations) 206 p.

Riess, Curt (1956) Goebbels, Joseph: 1897-1945. Fayard Paris 669 p.

Robert, Michel (2003) Allocution prononcée au Banquet-bénéfice de l'institut Canadien d'Administration de la Justice en hommage à l'honorable Charles D. Gonthier, Juge de la cour suprême du Canada au Ritz Carlton de Montréal 1er Mai 2003 www.tribunaux.qc.ca/c-appel/propos/Allocution_JJ_Michel%20 Robert_Charles_D_Gonthier%2001-05-03/Allocution%20banquet%20 b%E9n%E9fice%20Charles%20Gonthier.pdf

Rose H.& S. Rose eds. (2000) Alas Poor Darwin: Arguments Against Evolutionary Psychology. Harmony Books New York

Rosnay, Joël de (1995/2000) The Symbiotic Man: A New Understanding of the Organization of Life and a Vision of the Future. McGraw-Hill [New York] 299 p.

Rothstein, Edward (2004) The Meaning of 'Human' in Embryonic Research. The New York Times (Arts) March 13 www2.kenyon.edu/Depts/Religion/Fac/Adler/Misc/Human.htm

Rousseau, Jean-Jacques (1755/1985) Discours sur l'origine et les fondements de l'inégalité parmi les hommes. Gallimard [Paris] (Folio- Essais) 185 p.

Rowe, Dorothy (1982) The Construction of Life and Death. John Wiley & Sons Chichester (UK) 218 p.

Ruse, Michael (2004) L'altruisme animale. pp. 62-66 Sciences & Avenir (hors série) no. 139 juin/juil.

Ruse, Michael (2005) The Evolution-Creation Struggle. Harvard University Press 336 p.

Russell, Bertrand (1935/1997) Religion and Science. Oxford Univeristy Press Osford 255 p.

Russell, Bertrand (1957) Why I Am Not a Christian and Other Essays. Simon & Schuster New York ix-266 p.

Sade, Marquis de (1795/1965) Marquis de Sade: Justine, Philosophy in the Bedroom & Other Writings. (Translated by Richard Seaver and Austryn Wainhouse) Grove Press New York 755 p.

Sartre, Jean-Paul (1938/2007) Nausea. New Directions New York 178 p.

Sartre, Jean-Paul (1980) Jean-Paul Sartre (avec Benny Levy): L'espoir, maintenant. pp. 19, 56-60 in Le nouvel observateur 10 March no. 800

Saygin, Ayse Pinar; Ilyas Cicekli & Varol Akman (2000) Turing Test: 50 Years Later. pp. 463–518 Minds and Machines vol. 10

Sayous, Pierre André (1881/1970) Études littéraires sur les écrivains français de la Réformation. (2 t. en 1 v.) Slatkine Genève

Schaeffer; Francis (1976/1995) How Should We Then Live?: The Rise and Decline of Western Thought and Culture. Crossway Wheaton, IL 288 p.

Schaeffer; Francis (1982/1994) The Complete Works of Francis Schaeffer: A Christian Worldview. Crossway Books Wheaton IL vols. I-V

Searle, John (1980) Minds, brains, and programs. pp. 353-373 in D.

Hofstadter & D. Dennett (eds.), The Mind's I: Fantasies and Reflections on Self and Soul. Basic Books New York

Schmitz, Christin (2004) Quebec's chief justice sees a need to change traditional legal training. pp. 1, 7 The Lawyers Weekly May 7 vol. 24 no. 1

Scholte, Bob (1980) Anthropological Traditions: their definition pp. 53-87 in Anthropology: Ancestors and Heirs. Stanley Diamond (ed.) Mouton The Hague 462 p.

Scholte, Bob (1983) Cultural Anthropology and the Paradigm-Concept. pp. 229-278 in Functions and Uses of Disciplinary Histories. Graham, Wolf et Weingart (eds.) Reidel Dordrecht 307 p.

Schwartz, Peter (2000) Man and Nature: the Real Conflict. www.intellectualcapital.com/issues/issue381/item9641.asp

Shaffer, Butler (2005) Extremism In Defense of the Status Quo. www.lewrockwell.com/shaffer/shaffer95.html

Sheldon, Tony (2005) Killing or caring? BMJ (British Medical Journal); vol. 330: 560 (12 March), NEWS http://bmj.bmjjournals.com/cgi/content/extract/330/7491/560

Singer, Peter (1979/2011) Practical Ethics. Cambridge University Press Cambridge 352 p.

Singham, Mano (2000) Teaching and Propaganda. Physics Today June, [Opinion] www.aip.org/pt/opin600.htm

Smith, Pierre (1974) La nature des mythes pp. 248-263 in Morin et Piattelli-Palmarini (eds.) L'unité de l'homme (Vol.3) Seuil Paris 390 p.

Sokal, Alan D. (1996a) Transgressing The Boundaries: Towards a Transformative Hermeneutics of Quantum Gravity. pp. 217-252 Social Text no. 46/47, spring/summer www.physics.nyu.edu/faculty/sokal/transgress_v2/transgress_v2_singlefile.html

Sokal, Alan D. (1996b) A Physicist Experiments with Cultural Studies. pp. 62-64 Lingua Franca, May/June www.physics.nyu.edu/faculty/sokal/lingua_franca_v4/lingua_franca_v4.html

Solzhenitsyn, Alexander I. (1978) A World Split Apart. Commencement Address Delivered at Harvard University. June 8, 1978 www.forerunner.com/forerunner/X0113_Solzhenitsyns_Harvar.html

Speer, Albert (1970) Inside The Third Riech: Memoirs. Macmillan New York 596 p.

Supertramp (1987) The Logical Song (album: Breakfast in America) Rick Davies / Roger Hodgson

Stark, Rodney (1999) Atheism, Faith, and the Social Scientific Study of Religion. pp. 41–62 Journal of Contemporary Religion 14 (1)

Stark, Rodney (2003) For The Glory of God: How Monotheism Led to Reformations, Science, Witch-Hunts, and the End of Slavery. Princeton University Press Princeton

Steiner, George (1974) Nostalgia for the Absolute.

C.B.C. Publications Toronto 61 p.

Steiner, George (2001) Grammars of Creation. Yale University Press New Haven 347p.

Straughan, Roger (1999) Ethics, morality and animal biotechnology. Biotechnology and Biological Sciences Research Council, Swindon UK 28 p.

Strobel, Lee (2004) The Case for a Creator. Zondervan Grand Rapids MI 340 p.

Tertullian, (≈200 ap JC) Traité du baptême [*De Baptismo*]. 18, 5. Sources chrétiennes 35. 92-93

Thompson, Gary (1997) Rhetoric Through Media. Allyn & Bacon London 658 p.

Thornhill, Randy & Palmer, Craig T. (2000) A Natural History of Rape: Biological Bases of Sexual Coercion. MIT Press 272 p.

Thuiller, Pierre (1972) Jeux et enjeux de la science: Essai d'épistémologie critique. Laffont Paris 332 p.

Tipler, Frank J. (2003) Refereed Journals: Do They Insure Quality or Enforce Orthodoxy? ISCID - June 30, www.iscid.org/papers/Tipler_PeerReview_070103.pdf

Tocqueville, Alexis de (1835/1838) Democracy In America. vol. I (trans. Henry Reeve) Adlard and Saunders New York xxx - 464 p. www.gutenberg.org/ebooks/815

Tocqueville, Alexis de (1840/1847) Democracy In America. vol. II (trans. Henry Reeve) Edward Walker New York www.gutenberg.org/ebooks/816

Toulmin, Stephen (1957) Contemporary Scientific Mythology. pp. 13-81 in Metaphysical Beliefs. Alasdair MacIntyre (ed.) SCM Press London 216 p.

Turing, Alan (1950) Computing Machinery and Intelligence. pp. 433–460 Mind vol. 59 no. 236 www.abelard.org/turpap/turpap.htm

Ullman, Ellen (2002) Programming the Post-Human. pp. 60-70 Harpers Magazine October

UNESCO (2005) First Intergovernmental Meeting of Experts Aimed at Finalizing a Draft Declaration on Universal Norms on Bioethics UNESCO Headquarters, 4-6 April 2005 (Room XI, Fontenoy building) SHS/EST/05/CONF.203/4 http://unesdoc.unesco.org/images/0013/001390/139024e.pdf

Universalis (2003) Encylopaedia CD-Universalis. Mac version 8

Veith, Gene Edward jr. (1994) Postmodern Times. Crossway Books Wheaton IL 256 p.

Verhagen, Eduard & Sauer, Pieter J.J (2005a) The Groningen Protocol — Euthanasia in Severely III Newborns. pp. 959- 962 N Engl J Med vol 352 no. 10 March 10 http://content.nejm.org/cgi/content/full/352/10/959

Verhagen, Eduard & Sauer, Pieter J.J (2005b) Correspondance. p. 2355
New Engl J Med. vol. 352 no. 22 June 2

Voltaire (1761) L'education des filles.
Etext: http://un2sg4.unige.ch/athena/

Vonnegut, Kurt Jr. (1961) Mother Night. Dell Publishing New York

Vonnegut, Kurt Jr. (1969/1975) Slaughterhouse Five: or the Children's
Crusade, a Duty-Dance with Death. Dell Publishing Co. Inc, New York,
225 p.

Weber, Bruce (1996) A Mean Chess-Playing Computer Tears at the
Meaning of Thought. New York Times, February 19

Weikart, Richard (2004) From Darwin to Hitler: Evolutionary Ethics,
Eugenics, and Racism in Germany. Palgrave Macmillan New York

Weil, Simone (1949/1979) The Need for Roots. (Arthur Wills trans., preface
by T. S. Eliot) Octogon Books New York xv - 302 p.

Weinberg, Steven (1977) The First Three Minutes: A Modern View of the
Origin of the Universe. Basic Books New York 224 p.

Wells, H. G. (1893) Text-Book of Biology.[598] [with an introduction by G. B.
Howes], 2 vols London: [Clive]

Wells, H. G. (1902) Anticipations of the Reactions of Mechanical and
Scientific Progress Upon Human Life and Thought. Bernhard
Tauchnitz, Leipzig

Wells, H. G. (1905) A Modern Utopia.
www.marxists.org/reference/archive/hgwells/1905/modern-utopia/

Werth, Paul W. (2000) From "Pagan" Muslims to "Baptized" Communists:
Religious Conversion and Ethnic particularity in Russia's Eastern
Provinces. pp. 497-523 Society for Comparative Study of Society and
History vol. 42 no. 3

White, Lynn (1978) Medieval Religion and Technology. U. of California
Press Berkeley 360 p.

Whitehead, Alfred N. (1929/1958) The Function of Reason. Beacon Press
Boston 90 p.

Wilberforce, William (1822) Lettre à l'empereur Alexandre sur la traite des
Noirs. G. Schulze London
www.gutenberg.net/1/0/6/8/10683/

Wise, Steven M. (2000) Rattling the cage: Toward Legal Rights for
Animals. Perseus Cambridge MS 362 p.

Wittgenstein, Ludwig (1921/1922) Tractatus logico-philosophicus. Ogden
bilingual edition Routledge 209 p.
German and English Etext: www.kfs.org/~jonathan/witt/tlph.html

8 / Notes

1 - We will occasionally use here the somewhat unwieldy expression "ide-ologico-religious system". In general, it should be noted that in the follow-ing pages, the terms religion, belief system, ideology and even philosophy, will be deliberately used in an interchangeable fashion. We thus reject the significance of the sacred/profane dichotomy that typically distinguishes these concepts.

2 - A materialist cosmology thus affirms that all that exists in the universe results from material causes and in which effects are linked to natural laws.

3 - Eschatology is the part of an ideology or religion that deals with the future or the end times.

4 - The French Universalis 2003 encyclopaedia (in an entry on Hindu con-cepts of Heaven and Hell) observes:

> In ascending order, one encounters Indra's paradise, full of danc-ers and musicians, Shiva's paradise, where the god and his family reign, Vishnu's paradise, made of gold and strewn with lotus-covered ponds, Krishna's paradise, with his dancers and devotees and finally Brahma's paradise, where souls enjoy the company of celestial nymphs.*

5 - On this subject, see Porush (1992).

6 - The term myth is acceptable in this context as it is commonly employed in the social sciences in a wider sense (for example, by P. Smith (1974), E. MacCormac (1976), A. Reszler (1981), and others), that is not inevitably an account of past events involving supernatural beings or forces, but simply a form of cultural packaging permitting the transmis-sion of cosmological beliefs, beliefs on origins in particular.

7 - Due to cultural inertia, to a certain extent, but also because they were deemed "of use", at least for the time being.

8 - French intellectual Régis Debray writing on this subject, notes (1981: 413):

> The Christian Incarnation is the initial source of our political faith. While agreeing to be born and die to redeem us, the Christian God sacralized profane history, giving it one meaning, and only one. From that point on the understandable world of meaning was rigor-ously superimposed on the world of irreversible events. To believe in this God-process, is to believe that history does not proceed in vain, coming from nowhere, going nowhere, step by step. To believe in History-process, is to believe that transcendence works through immanence, thus access to transcendence proceeds solely through immanence. This is the first condition setting up politics as the supreme art or salvation as political masterpiece. Since the rational Logos took on the Flesh, we too can redeem the totality of reality by

making its hidden rationality ours.*

9 - It is a little known fact that early IBM computers were used by the Nazis to administer their concentration camps. On this subject, see Edwin Black's book, **IBM and the Holocaust**. 2001.

10 - Though typically not very orthodox in their beliefs.

11 - The concept of unilinear history is engraved into the collective memory of the Western World by works such as Bossuet's **The Discourse on Universal History** (1681). Bossuet began his study of history with the Genesis account and ended with the kings of France... Opening the door for postmodernism, French anthropologist Claude Lévi-Strauss stated (1962: 341) "History is thus never History in an absolute sense, but history-for. It is biased even if considered objective, it remains inevitably partial, which is still a kind of bias." On this subject philosopher J. - F. Lyotard notes (1996: 3-4):

> The West is that part of the human world that invented the Idea of emancipation, of the self-development of communities and has attempted to carry out this idea. The implementation of this idea finds support in the principle according to which history is viewed as the record of the progress of freedom in human space and time. The first expression of this principle is Christian, the last Marxist.*

12 - Albert Camus provides one example, among others, of Judeo-Christian influence on the concept of history (1956: 189):

> In contrast to the ancient world, the unity of the Christian and Marxist world is astonishing. The two doctrines have in common a vision of the world which completely separates them from the Greek attitude. Jaspers defines this very well: "It is a Christian way of thinking to consider that the history of man is strictly unique." The Christians were the first to consider human life and the course of events as a history that is unfolding from a fixed beginning toward a definite end, in the course of which man achieves his salvation or earns his punishment. The philosophy of history springs from a Christian representation, which is surprising to a Greek mind. The Greek idea of evolution has nothing in common with our idea of historical evolution. The difference between the two is the difference between a circle and a straight line. The Greeks imagined the history of the world as cyclical.

13 - Michael Novak provides an interesting nutshell view of the modern perspective on religion, noting differences between moderns in Europe and in the United States (2006: 17):

> Atheists in Europe have their own approach to religious liberty. In personal life, they do not take religion seriously, naturally, but they do recognize it as a social reality that needs to be dealt with. Politically, however, their aim since the French Revolution of 1789 has been to expel religion from public life and confine it to the private sphere. They have attempted to place the state firmly over religion so

the state dominates all spheres of public life. By such "secularization" and "laicization," the secularists hope to speed the inexorable decline of religion, for they are certain that the future will be less religious than the past — and that this will be a good thing.

14 - The German historian Karl Dietrich Bracher explored this question by noting the religious character of the phenomenon (1970/1995: 30-31):

> In fact, modern dictatorship is distinguished from the historical absolutism in that it requires the annihilation of the individual. It forcibly integrates him into gigantic mass organizations and to profess a high political ideology now elevated to the rank of religion (or a substitute for religion). This sanctification of the political field is based on a supreme political myth — in the case of Fascism, that of an imperial past; in that of Communism, a social Utopia to come; in that of national-socialism, finally, the doctrine of racial superiority.*

15 - If it ever did is another matter. Further discussion of the concept of the "Christian West" is found in an exchange with atheist Paul Baird which includes a discussion of the West's "multiple-personality disorder" (note dated December 24, 2010).

Moral Absolutes: An Exchange With Atheist Paul Baird
http://samizdat.qc.ca/cosmos/philo/morals_Paul_Baird.htm

16 - In North America at least.

17 - Some may consider this unthinkable. Camus, for example, notes (1951/1978: 19): "If our time readily admits that murder has its justifications, it is because of this indifference to life which is nihilism's trademark." (Camus 1951/1978: 146) "Cynicism, the deification of history and of matter, individual terror and State crime, these are the inordinate consequences that will now spring, armed to the teeth, from the equivocal conception of a world that entrusts to history alone the task of producing both values and truth." Anthropologist Ernest Gellner has explored the legacy of the Enlightenment borrowed by the Nazis (1999: 88).

18 - In Quebec, the signers of the **Refus global** manifesto, forerunners of the Quiet Revolution (influenced by Enlightenment ideas as well as by modern twentieth-century thinkers), in 1948, said (Borduas 1948):

> Scientific instruments have provided us extraordinary means of investigation and control over things too small, too fast, too pulsating, too slow or too big for us. Reason thus allows deep penetration into the world, but a world where we have lost our unity.*

19 - Efficiently wasting time on game consoles, cell-phones and other gadgets...

20 - Which states that man will eventually be outcompeted by other life forms in the Darwinian struggle for survival. These new life forms may include bioinformatic syntheses or cyborgs. The term 'transhumanism' also appears as a synonym.

21 - Lyotard wouldn't be thinking of the fall of the Berlin Wall or the Iron Curtain by any chance?

22 - Gellner writes, perhaps in jest, regarding postmodernism (1999: 29): "In anthropology, it means in effect the abandonment of any serious attempt to give a reasonably precise, documented and testable account of anything."

23 - Or "The world is stoned/crazy".

24 - French anthropologist Suzanne Lallemand, outlines major elements involved in the cosmology concept, along with the more restricted cosmogony concept (Lallemand 1974: 20-21):

> The cosmology and cosmogony concepts are semantic fields of unequal magnitude, the former term tending to encompass the latter. Indeed, anthropology can define cosmology as a set of beliefs and wisdom, composite knowledge, framing the natural and human world. As to cosmogony (the part of a cosmology focusing on the creation of the world) it depicts, in the form of myths, the origins of the cosmos and the birth of society. Thus, cosmology — which we consider of primary interest — appears to be a prerequisite for synthesis and the search for a total worldview. It is reductive, since it identifies and gives priority to certain elements perceived to be the founding principles of the universe. It is also explanatory, as it directs and brings together the natural and cultural traits of the group that produced it.*

25 - Steiner notes that some attribute this state of affairs to a confrontation with Enlightenment thinking and others, to the development of the theory of evolution. Steiner himself takes no stand on this matter.

26 - Christian theology, of course.

27 - Or, for those with poor navigational skills, a statue of St. Christopher…

28 - A well-known socialist for much of his life, while serving in Moscow as a correspondent for the Manchester Guardian, Muggeridge was one of the first Western journalists to break the story about the famine in Ukraine under Stalin in the 1930s. This famine was initiated by the Soviet state with the intent of eliminating the Ukrainian peasant masses, considered to be counter-revolutionary. Millions died as a result.

29 - At present this perspective is accepted and explored by a number of anthropologists. French anthropologist Marc Augé notes, for example (1982: 320):

> We do not define religion as a cultural system rather than we view culture, apprehended in its most contrasted manifestations, as a virtually and implicitly religious system.*

30 - Augé, for example, discusses football (soccer for North Americans) games in terms of religious rituals. He adds (1982: 318):

> But ritualistic logic is related not only to material and ideological domination between communities. It is the source of all collective behaviour that may transmit to communities, irrespective of the principle of their constitution, a consciousness, perhaps ephemeral, of their identity and in Durkheimian terms, their sacredness. In mod-

ern societies, social gatherings are neither exclusively, nor primarily religious in the narrow sense. Economic life, trade unions, political and, more importantly, sporting events give rise to the largest mass events. One could also mention large gatherings around performers of modern forms of pop music (rock, reggae).*

31 - We see here a forerunner of anthropological works by Carlos Castaneda in the 1960-1970s in which he conveyed his experiences with the Indian sorcerer Don Juan.

32 - In the East, where belonging to a community is very important, the collision with the postmodern perspective may be rather brutal.

33 - Camus adds (1951: 93):

> What, in fact, does this apology for murder signify if not that, in a world without meaning and without honor, only the desire for existence, in all its forms, is legitimate? The instinctive joy of being alive, the stimulus of the unconscious, the cry of the irrational, are the only pure truths that must be professed. Everything that stands in the way of desire — principally society — must therefore be mercilessly destroyed.

34 - If in Soviet times, the joke was "They pretend to pay us and we pretend to work", today ordinary people may say much the same of postmodern elites "They pretend to give us values, meaning of life, and we pretend to believe…"

35 - And with another Frenchman, structuralist anthropologist Claude Levi-Strauss, binary oppositions abound too.

36 - Though of Jewish origin, Einstein did not have a very orthodox conception of God. At most, he could be considered a deist.

37 - In a comment on the Heisenberg uncertainty principle.

38 - Readers with some understanding of French can check out the first chapter of my thesis **Des catégories de religion et de science: essai d'épistémologie anthropologique.** (1986)
www.samizdat.qc.ca/cosmos/sc_soc/tm_pg/tdm.htm

39 - See also Benson Saler (1977) **Supernatural as a Western Category.** pp. 31-53 Ethnos, vol. 5 no 1, Spring

40 - This subject is briefly discussed in an article in French on Quebec Montagnais: Gosselin, Paul (1989) **Épistémologies culturelles et projection de catégories de pensée.** pp. 45-62 Cahiers Ethnologiques N. S. vol. 17, no 10
www.samizdat.qc.ca/cosmos/sc_soc/surnat.html

41 - In the final analysis, such politicians are basically content not to rock the boat and to mouth words put in their mouths by media and legal elites. Despite the apparent sincerity and fervour of their personal beliefs, inevitably such politicians do nothing to challenge abortion or any other postmodern 'rights'.

42 - While public expression of religious views is common (as long as no State funding is involved), typically this changes almost nothing in regards

to actual public policy. Even Christian festivals such as Christmas have been reshaped to politically correct standards and public figures and institutions typically avoid direct reference to Christ.

43 - This primarily focuses on adherents of the Judeo-Christian worldview.

44 - Even if they are unaware of the process, adherents of the Judeo-Christian worldview may also be affected by the marginalization of their beliefs. In attending Sunday morning services, they can express their beliefs, but the rest of the week they live in other world, a world saturated with modern and postmodern presuppositions and where chance is deemed the source of all that exists (no personal judging God). This is an indifferent world, where, beyond mere subjectivity, meaning is evacuated. When faced with stresses that will not go away or tragic events, suicidal thoughts may emerge along with the lie of death's escape. In such circumstances, Christians compromised in their cosmology may find the weight of life's real issues bringing them to question the credibility of their hope.

45 - J.-F. Lyotard offers the following observations on the postmodern worldview (1996: 6):

A superficial reading of the postmodern is to view it as a modern 'revolution'. The very idea of revolution belongs to the modern representation of a sudden leap in progress in the march toward freedom. This has no meaning outside the framework that postulates men's emancipation as history's ultimate goal. If the term "postmodern" has any meaning, it must avoid this philosophy of history, as it is supposed to augur the downfall of all grand narratives.*

46 - Syncretism involves the belief that no religion is absolutely true. This logically entails that individuals are free to choose their own gods and their own "truth". The pop-culture saying: "Everyone has their own truth" is one expression of this concept.

47 - Such societies will likely feel less need to explicitly codify doctrines and rites since doctrines and rituals are not believed to be absolute, hence change, modification or addition to these will not be considered a serious threat, … As long as a few core beliefs remain untouched of course. Marc Augé notes (1974b: 35):

In the same way, sudden mutations are rare in history and social organizations are rarely upset at once and entirely, due to internal revolution or external intervention. It is not surprising that ideological coherence may persist even though the social order is disrupted and damaged. That this is the case is observed by the fact that so-called syncretistic cults generally seem less to substitute themselves to traditional religions rather than to add themselves to the mix (disregarding what they explicitly borrow from them).*

48 - Concerning Theravada Buddhism, the French encyclopaedia Universalis observes (2003):

We should restrict ourselves to the Founder's core message: awareness of the misery of existence, the belief that the source of this misery is desire, belief in salvation understood as the extinction of all desire (deliverance). In addition, life must be lived frugally, becoming a "saint" (*Arhats*), an unattached being, that is to say, finally, become a begging monk (in Pali: *bhikkhu*). But, since not all will feel called to this state, lay faithful are then encouraged to retreat from time to time in monasteries which thus benefit from substantial donations.*

49 - And the answer to the question "Who am I?" is always connected, in terms of logic, to the implicit question "Where do we come?".

50 - Which leads to an underlying question: "How do you justify these rules?" And this leads in turn to the basic concepts of good and evil and their origin.

51 - Expressed in terms of Christian theology, one would frame this with the question: "Where is salvation found?" Obviously each salvation concept must be consistent with the principles established by the cosmology of the specific belief system of which it is a part. In attempting to understand a religion within its own logic, expectations that a salvation concept 'should be' expressed in Christian or Marxist terms are irrelevant.

52 - Even to their own members.

53 - See also John C. Lyden, **Film as Religion: Myths, Morals and Rituals** (2003).

54 - A phenomenon explored by a number of French social scientists:

Marc Augé, Football, de l'histoire sociale à l'anthropologie religieuse. Le Débat, n° 19, février 1982, p. 59-67

Manuel Vazquez Montalban, Le football, religion laïque en quête d'un nouveau Dieu, Le Monde diplomatique, août 1997.
www.monde-diplomatique.fr/1997/08/VAZQUEZ_MONTALBAN/8972

Jean-Marie Brohm, La religion sportive. Éléments d'analyse des faits religieux dans La pratique sportive. p. 101-117 Actions et Recherches Sociales, n° 3, 1983

Denis Müller, Le football comme religion populaire et comme culture mondialisée: brèves notations en vue d'une interprétation critique d'une quasi-religion contemporaine. p. 299-314. in Marc Dumas, François Nault & Lucien Pelletier dir., Théologie et Culture. Presses de l'Université Laval, Québec, 2004
http://www.contrepointphilosophique.ch/Ethique/Pages/DenisMuller/Football.doc

For the most part, articles in English are more light-hearted and less a matter of serious scholarly investigation.

Illya McLellan, The Cult Of Football: A Religion for the Twentieth-century and Beyond. Bleacher Report September 20, 2008
http://bleacherreport.com/users/4352-illya-mclellan

Stephen Tomkins, Matches made in heaven. BBC Tuesday, 22 June, 2004
http://news.bbc.co.uk/2/hi/3828767.stm

S. Crawford, American football as religion: some theoretical perspectives. pp. 12-20 International Review for the Sociology of Sport 1989 vol. 24 no. 1

www.cabdirect.org/abstracts/19891870121.html;jsessionid=D13664CE5B
04BDBEE602C5D015BE5468
Note that "football" = soccer outside North America. It should be observed
that studying popular sports is a safe area of investigation for most scholars, far from their own beliefs...

55 - The posthuman movement states that man, Homo sapiens, is actually
a rather miniscule step in the evolutionary process and that in the near
future, he will be replaced by more efficient digital or cyborg sentient
beings.

56 - In the postmodern religion, of course.

57 - Media owners are not necessarily the ones with the greatest influence,
as opposed to the gatekeepers in these organisations who on a day-to-day
basis actually control the flow of information and determine which items
are significant and worthy of interest and those that aren't.

58 - About this institution, cf. Larson and Witham (1999).

59 - To which one could add a handful of prestigious scientific journals,
where, if a scientists succeeds in getting an article accepted, such a publication may influence his career.

60 - Regarding education, the system in the United States is exceptionally
decentralized when compared to those in many other Western nations. It
should come as no surprise that battles over content control are hotter
there...

61 - If non-postmodern views were consistently and ruthlessly eliminated
in the educational system, such censorship would become far too obvious.

62 - Such arbitrariness became stark reality both under communism with
Stalin as well as in Hitler's Nazi Germany. Discussing Nazi legal reality,
German historian K. D. Bracher states (1970: 363):

> But in every basic respect, the principles of a society governed
> by law had been destroyed by the Third Reich in the very first weeks
> of its rule. The principle of "no penalty without law" had already been
> violated by the law of March 29, 1933, authorizing prosecution (of
> the Reichstag arsonists) on the basis of ex post facto penal regula-
> tions. And conservative lawyers helped to pave the way by writing
> expert opinions and cooperating. These early encroachments
> became general practice two years later when it was officially stated
> that anything that violated the "healthy national spirit" (gesundes
> Volksempfinden) was punishable even if no specific provisions existed
> that dealt with such violations. The arbitrariness of the leadership
> thereby was made a principle of law, and the leadership alone deter-
> mined what this "national spirit" was supposed to be. The "people"
> could not and were not supposed to express their feelings, for that
> would have violated the. tenet of the leader state.

The arbitrary character of the Law, once divorced from divine sanction, was
a thought that had occurred many years ago to the early Enlightenment
thinker Thomas Hobbes (1651/1974: 316)

That Law can never be against Reason, our Lawyers are agreed; and that not the Letter, (that is, every construction of it,) but that which is according to the Intention of the Legislator, is the Law. And it is true: **but the doubt is, of whose Reason it is, that shall be received for Law?**

This is of course a very serious question, but as far as I know, it appears Hobbes had "better" things to think about and did not come back to this critical issue.

63 - Or, conversely, abolish the very concept of crime.

64 - Though such matters may be arranged from time to time when necessary. One of the best-known cases is the 1925 Scopes Trial. Wikipedia mentions about the main protagonist of this trial, John T. Scopes that:

Scopes' involvement in the so-called Monkey Trial came about after the American Civil Liberties Union (ACLU) announced that it would finance a test case challenging the constitutionality of the Butler Act if they could find a Tennessee teacher willing to act as a defendant. A band of businessmen in Dayton, Tennessee, led by engineer and geologist George Rappleyea, saw this as an opportunity to get publicity for their town and approached Scopes. Rappleyea pointed out that while the Butler Act prohibited the teaching of human evolution, the state required teachers to use the assigned textbook, **Hunter's Civic Biology** (1914), which included a chapter on evolution. Rappleyea argued that teachers were essentially required to break the law. When asked about the test case, Scopes was initially reluctant to get involved, but after some discussion he told the group gathered in Robinson's Drugstore, "If you can prove that I've taught evolution and that I can qualify as a defendant, then I'll be willing to stand trial."

http://en.wikipedia.org/wiki/John_Scopes (19/4/2011)

65 - There is little reason to believe that a legal system, fully consistent with the Judeo-Christian worldview, has ever existed even in the West. Christian influence on the legal system has always been partial and fragmented. For example, it took almost two millennia to eliminate slavery as a social institution.

66 - Although the manner in which Islam is expressed may vary from one country to another and one era to another.

67 - This brings to mind the Christian convictions of one of the most radical nineteenth-century abolitionists, the American John Brown.

68 - A contact observed that Revolutionary France had abolished slavery earlier, in 1794. This apparently contradicted the objective of Wilberforce's 1822 letter to the emperor of France. Further research helped sort things out. Apparently Napoleon later reinstated slavery in France in 1802. Slavery was only permanently abolished in France in 1848. In Pennsylvania, Quakers were the driving force in getting the slave trade abolished as early as 1769 and eventually emancipation began in 1780. One cynical observer

noted that abolition took place in Revolutionary France only due to the fact that the leaders of the revolution needed allies against England. Another issue is that proponents of the Enlightenment have always been quick to rip off desirable/fashionable Judeo-Christian concepts. While Voltaire (for example, in his **Lettres Philosophiques**, published in 1734) prized and could see a future for the Quaker's egalitarian ideals, he condescendingly mocked the source of their ideals, that is the New Testament. In France, for example, the Free-Mason Victor Schoelcher initially supported slavery, but when abolitionist thinking became fashionable he switched and became an ardent abolitionist and as an elected member of the Assemblée nationale introduced the decree abolishing slavery in France in 1848. Though in Islam freeing slaves is considered as good penance for sins, Muslim countries have been generally more reluctant to abolish slavery than Western states. The last nations in the world to ratify the abolition of slavery were Saudi Arabia in 1962 and Mauritania in 1981, but with still no implementing decree yet adopted in 2000! See also: http://en.wikipedia.org/wiki/Islam_and_slavery

69 - In Western countries other than Canada and the US, the political system may be ideologically efficient enough on it's own to dispense with judicial activism. Whether power is highly centralised or not is a big factor in such considerations.

70 - Or, to be less ambiguous, one can be sure at least that CG's opinions are not drawn from the Judeo-Christian religious belief system. From which religious belief system CG's opinions are drawn is then an open question.

71 - Or perhaps the distinction is of no importance...

72 - In the traditional sense of the term.

73 - This occurred, for example, with the nominations of Justices Robert Bork (1987) and Clarence Thomas (1991).

74 - Which, in fact, is a clear indication of partiality and bias.

75 - Such a response is rather peculiar. It raises other questions. Why should the democratization of appointments to the Supreme Court be something to be feared, who exactly are these 'witches' and why should they fear the result of such a process? What is it with these 'witches'? What might such a process reveal about them?

76 - Marceau cynically observes (2003: M288, 1325):

> We have turned our judges into the new high priests. They have a mystical set of texts; they make pronouncements from on high, literally a raised dais; there is an initiation period; they speak a language not easily understood by those without legal backgrounds; they even wear priestly robes. All they need now is a little incense. And based upon yesterday's experience in front of our buildings, possibly with the change in marijuana laws we will even accomplish that.

77 - Implicitly reminding others of their truth and universality.

78 - Note that in the West, when the State has dramatically moved away

from the Judeo-Christian heritage, slavery again becomes possible. Not nineteenth-century capitalist slavery perhaps, but a slave State, that is to say that religious and political prisoners working without pay in forced labour camps. This state of affairs existed in Nazi concentration camps, in the Soviet Gulag and still exists in the Chinese Laogai. On this subject see: http://www.theepochtimes.com/news/4-3-24/20545.html
For another study on the role played by Christianity in the elimination of slavery, see Rodney Stark (2003) **For The Glory of God: How Monotheism Led to Reformations, Science, Witch-Hunts, and the End of Slavery**. Princeton NJ Princeton University Press

79 - This concept is borrowed from Judeo-Christian culture, which asserts that history has meaning because of the fact that the Creator himself has intervened in history and has taken part in it in human form (the Incarnation). This worldview also asserts that history is significant, it has purpose, a goal towards which it leads.

80 - As opposed to the ancient Greek philosophers, Christians would obviously add that truth is not an abstract, ruthless concept, but a person.

81 - The **Humanist Manifesto** comes to mind.

82 - French philosopher Jacques Ellul has provided an interesting analysis of this issue. Discussing what he calls "sociological propaganda", Ellul notes (1966: 63):

> Such propaganda is essentially diffuse. It is rarely conveyed by catchwords or expressed intentions. Instead it is based on a general climate, an atmosphere that influences people imperceptibly without having the appearance of propaganda; it gets to man through his customs, through his most unconscious habits. It creates new habits in him; it is a sort of persuasion from within. As a result, man adopts new criteria of judgment and choice, adopts them spontaneously, as if he had chosen them himself. But all these criteria are in conformity with the environment and are essentially of a collective nature. Sociological propaganda produces a progressive adaptation to a certain order of things, a certain concept of human relations, which unconsciously moulds individuals and makes them conform to society. ... But sociological propaganda is inadequate in a moment of crisis. Nor is it able to move the masses to action in exceptional circumstances. Therefore, it must sometimes be strengthened by the classic kind of propaganda, which leads to action. At such times sociological propaganda will appear to be the medium that has prepared the ground for direct propaganda; it becomes identified with sub-propaganda.

83 - Syncretism is a principle that accepts the juxtaposition of religious dogma from very disparate and even incompatible sources. Syncretism denies the concept of absolute and universal truth. The Bahà'i Faith is a somewhat exotic example of Western syncretism.

84 - Sometimes non-Christians clearly see what many Christians will not...

Anthropologist Ernst Gellner notes (1992: 4):

> For instance, 'modernist' believers are untroubled by the incompatibility between the Book of Genesis and either Darwinism or modern astro-physics. They assume that the pronouncements, though seemingly about the same events the creation of the world and the origins of man - are really on quite different levels, or even, as some would have it, in altogether different languages, within distinct or separate kinds of 'discourse'. Generally speaking, the doctrines and moral demands of the faith are then turned into something which, properly interpreted, is in astonishingly little conflict with the secular wisdom of the age, or indeed with anything. This way lies peace - and doctrinal vacuity.

85 - History shows that court jesters have always been found entertaining, though on occasion they may wear out their welcome if they persist in voicing dangerous or unpleasant truths.

86 - The Nonoverlapping Magisteria concept assigns non-conflicting domains of authority and responsibility to both science and religion. Religion, rules over the domain of morality and science has authority over the observable physical world. Gould provides this overview (2000):

> We will surely need the benefits of science, if only to feed and keep healthy all the people that science has permitted us to rear to adulthood. We will also need, and with equal force, the moral guidance and ennobling capacities of religion, the humanities, and the arts, for otherwise the dark side of our personalities will win, and humanity may perish in war and recrimination on a blighted planet.

87 - Gould was a tenor, I believe.

88 - Of course, as long as long as the central concept of evolution itself is left unchallenged.

89 - Dawkins, rejecting postmodern presuppositions, therefore believes (as do Christians) in Truth, before which all must submit. So should religion then be allowed to go on with business as usual in a 'cute' walled ghetto? Dawkins does **not** like this idea at all.

90 - Critique inevitably implies a standard to which the thing criticized is compared. If you do away with this standard, then all you have left is emotional manipulation and bullying. In this context, critique is reduced to pathetic ranting along the lines of "I don't like your ideas or behaviour (and I don't think others should either)!"

91 - Articles, interviews, books etc. on the Sokal affair (both pro and con) can be found on Alan Sokal's web page. www.physics.nyu.edu/faculty/sokal/

92 - Sokal wrote (1996a):

> Rather, they cling to the dogma imposed by the long post-Enlightenment hegemony over the Western intellectual outlook, which can be summarized briefly as follows: that there exists an external world, whose properties are independent of any individual

human being and indeed of humanity as a whole; that these properties are encoded in *eternal* physical laws; and that human beings can
obtain reliable, albeit imperfect and tentative, knowledge of these
laws by hewing to the *objective* procedures and epistemological
strictures prescribed by the (so-called) scientific method.

93 - It should be noted that in this quote Raymo takes care to confuse the
empirical data with the presuppositions required by materialistic ideologies.

94 - Perhaps a few ironic observations by philosopher David Hume may be
appropriate in this context (1748, Section VIII, part 2):

> There is no method of reasoning more common, and yet none
> more blameable, than, in philosophical disputes, to endeavour the
> refutation of any hypothesis, by a pretence of its dangerous conse-
> quences to religion and morality. When any opinion leads to absurd-
> ities, it is certainly false; but it is not certain that an opinion is false,
> because it is of dangerous consequence. Such topics, therefore,
> ought entirely to be forborne; as serving nothing to the discovery of
> truth, but only to make the person of an antagonist odious.

No doubt some will not grasp the implicit irony of Hume's comments
(taken out of context here admittedly), but there are times when a lack of
imagination can be a great defence mechanism.

95 - This may bring to mind an encomium by Thomas Huxley published in
the **Life and Letters of Charles Darwin**. Huxley notes (in Darwin 1888: v.
I ch. XIV):

> ... the name of Charles Darwin stands alongside of those of
> Isaac Newton and Michael Faraday; and, like them, calls up the grand
> ideal of a searcher after truth and interpreter of Nature. They think of
> him who bore it as a rare combination of genius, industry, and
> unswerving veracity, who earned his place among the most famous
> men of the age by sheer native power, in the teeth of a gale of popu-
> lar prejudice, and uncheered by a sign of favour or appreciation from
> the official fountains of honour; as one who in spite of an acute sen-
> sitiveness to praise and blame, and notwithstanding provocations
> which might have excused any outbreak, kept himself clear of all
> envy, hatred, and malice, nor dealt otherwise than fairly and justly
> with the unfairness and injustice which was showered upon him;
> while, to the end of his days, he was ready to listen with patience and
> respect to the most insignificant of reasonable objectors.

Some, in their enthusiasm, have actually proposed a modern religious feast
day in honour of Charles D. See www.darwinday.org

96 - Such individuals may be perceived as martyrs for the cause of sexual
freedom, those daring to push the limits of individual self-fulfilment and
go beyond arbitrary traditional restrictions.

97 - Which brings to mind trash TV talk shows like the Jerry Springer Show.

98 - That is to say, the Judeo-Christian worldview. This issue will be
explored in volume II of this study, but those with no access to this volume

may consult **The Judeo-Christian Cosmology and the Origins of Science** (Gosselin 1987)
www.samizdat.qc.ca/cosmos/sc_soc/cosmoeng.html
One may also consult works by Stanley L. Jaki, in particular **Creation and Science** (1974).

99 - One might be tempted here to accuse Gould of ripping off the old Judeo-Christian concept of Man's uniqueness, made in God's image.

100 - To which S. J. Gould was also opposed. One of his contributions to this debate is found in More things in heaven and earth, pp. 101-126 published in a collection of essays edited by H. Rose and S. Rose entitled: **Alas Poor Darwin: Arguments Against Evolutionary Psychology**. Harmony Books New York

101 - This expression may seem "abused" here, but S. J. Gould (1997b) uses precisely the same terms when dealing with evolutionists in the UK. This concept is quite justified, as Sociobiology is a deliberate attempt to explain human behaviour, as a whole, in a coherent or "fundamentalist" fashion, by referring exclusively to the fundamental assumptions of Darwinian evolution.

102 - Original unpublished quote supplied by Ruse (2011).

103 - Cf. Strobel (2004:140).

104 - Which amounts to the same thing for most of these authors.

105 - When convenient, this remains true in postmodern societies as well.

106 - This applies even more to civilizations.

107 - Unless the fish escapes its fish bowl…

108 - It should be remembered that modern as well as postmodern mythology presents itself as liberating individuals from so-called "religious prejudices". Admitting one's own ideologico-religious role in this context can be rather difficult.

109 - Here Gablik addresses the issue in terms of artistic creativity, but one may obviously transpose her comments in ideological and religious terms. If this is contemplated, conformism appears to be rather widespread.

110 - Also attributed to Sophie Volland.

111 - Such documents are directly derived from Christian creeds. Though in terms of content they express doctrines **very** different from the Christian creeds, in terms of ideological packaging (form), they are directly derived from the creeds.

112 - Quite possibly Steiner is echoing here thoughts expressed years before by French novelist François Mauriac in the foreword to Elie Wiesel's novel **Night** (1958/2006: xvii-xviii)

… nothing I had witnessed during that dark period had marked me as deeply as the image of cattle cars filled with Jewish children at the Austerlitz train station. … At that time we knew nothing about the Nazis' extermination methods. And who could have imagined such things! But these lambs torn from their mothers, that was an outrage far beyond anything we would have thought possible. I believe that on that day, I first became aware of the mystery of the iniquity whose exposure marked the end of an era and the beginning of another. The dream conceived by Western man in the Eighteenth-century, whose dawn he thought he had glimpsed in 1789, and which until August 2, 1914, had become stronger with the advent of the Enlightenment and scientific discoveries — that dream finally vanished for me before those trainloads of small children.

So what then is the source of this "mystery of iniquity"? Why should its source or cause be "veiled"? Perhaps if certain taboos are discarded a rational explanation may be contemplated. What if one goes back in time and reassesses the ideologico-religious roots of European civilization? What if when the Enlightenment severed its link to the Judeo-Christian cosmology it did not just get rid of the troublesome meddler (God), but, as a result, also got rid of the basis for man's special value, individual beings created in God's image, the *imago dei*? What if, once this link was broken, (previously) "unthinkable" horrors and nightmares then became possible, appearing as actual reality? Perhaps on such matters, Dostoyevsky (or Solzhenitsyn) would have bluntly responded: Enough nonsense about "mysteries"! Open your eyes! If God is dead, then **anything** is permitted, **anything** is possible! Try to get that into your thick and arrogant skulls!

113 - A friend once remarked: "What exactly is civilization? What is the criterion or yardstick by which we should measure what exists and compare it to what should exist? Is civilization defined by the amount of libraries, the number of years spent in university, the number of languages spoken, the number of pixels of resolution on the average computer screen, the number of scholars admitted to the French Academy, one's cell phone bandwidth or the number of Big Macs sold? How does one mesure civilization?"

114 - Of course this needs to be qualified. There is no single modern ideology, but rather a wide range of ideologies and movements marking the modern era, ideologies that accept in whole or in part the modern materialist cosmology. Among these one can number: Dadaism, Nihilism, Trotskyism, determinism, relativism, fascism (despite exploiting religious symbols), Maoism, robber baron capitalism, biological racism, sadism, scientism, existentialism, psychoanalysis, humanism, Sociobiology, Behaviourism, some forms of environmentalism, positivism, surrealism (which overlaps, in fact, modern and postmodern worldviews) and various nationalist ideologies.

115 - But such accountings are serious matters and are typically avoided by Enlightenment devotees. Disciples of the Enlightenment, unsurprisingly, much prefer to portray themselves and their theological predecessors (which include the botched attempts of Renaissance thinkers to develop an alternative worldview), as purveyors of light and dispellers of prejudice and intolerance. One must also consider that concepts such as self-examination and repentance are not intrinsic parts of the Enlightenment ideologico-religious belief system. C. S. Lewis provides a

less naïve view here of the Renaissance (which is transferable to the Enlightenment of course) that may help dispel some illusions (1955: 71):

> I do not much believe in the Renaissance as generally described by historians. The more I look into the evidence, the less trace I find of that vernal rapture which is supposed to have swept Europe in the fifteenth-century. I half suspect that the glow in the historians' pages has a different source, that each is remembering, and projecting, his own personal Renaissance; that wonderful reawakening which comes to most of us when puberty is complete.

116 - The objective of a séance is to attempt to communicate with the dead through a medium.

117 - No doubt some may find the term "pagan" offensive or derogatory, but it is used here only to denote cultures of ancient times that did not identify with Jewish or Christian presuppositions.

118 - Others before Gould have also discussed this ethical vacuum. Leon Eisenburg found that science has disappointed many people who had come to it seeking all-encompassing MEANING (including ethics). Eisenburg noted (1974: 324):

> Scientists come to accept that there is a crisis of ethics in science. Many people naively believed that the canons of the scientific method would automatically produce researchers with an ethical commitment to truth, justice and the betterment of man. We have only to read the history of our time to discover that scientists can serve the interests of evil powers and even act as executioners.*

Eisenburg does not discuss **why** people should expect science to supply ethics in the first place (despite David Hume's observations on the is/ought problem made long ago).

119 - Of course some will reject such a solution and persist in writing serious, weighty books on the ethics of materialism. But typically such works are of interest only to scholars and other ivory tower drones and end their days dismally collecting dust on the shelves of university libraries. Is there any chance any of these might become bestsellers, changing the course of history? Seriously...? In any case, all too often such works are parasitic on Judeo-Christian concepts of morality, concepts that cannot coherently be justified in the context of a materialist cosmology. The flip side of this situation (ironically, since the NOMA concept was proposed by a Jew), is that Gould's position could be viewed as a form of intellectual apartheid. On the one hand we are told that only science can claim to explain the wide world around us, the material cosmos and, on the other, science cedes to religion the administration of a miniscule psychological ghetto in which it can take refuge, that is morality and the far reaches of the human soul. Such generosity... If a twenty-first century man with traditional religious convictions hopes to escape this ghetto and have a voice in social affairs, then good acting skills, allowing him to pass as a materialist (or postmodern), may come in handy. But if, for example, he dares to utter, in the public

arena, comments on current issues expressing a perspective explicitly referring to the Judeo-Christian worldview then people (such as Judge Reinhardt whom we met in chapter 1) will quickly advise him to go back to his ghetto and leave good people alone.

120 - Gould implicitly recognizes this and also notes that some of his (atheist) colleagues reject his NOMA concept (1997: 62) as they view it as legitimatizing religion, albeit in a limited fashion.

121 - That is, the Australian Broadcasting Corporation.

122 - Such high-sounding assertions are much too easily dropped, but one may well wonder where exactly Dawkins gets his concept of "immorality" from and what its basis might be...

123 - Where genetic determinism plays a central role. As a critic, S. J. Gould played an important role in this debate.

124 - These events took place between 1994 and 1997. A number of members of the Ordre du Temple Solaire cult committed suicide in this time period, both in Europe and in Québec. A similar crisis erupted in the United States in March 1997. Thirty-nine members of the Heaven's Gate cult (some of whom were website developers) committed suicide in San Diego, California. They believed they had to leave their earthly bodies to board an alien spaceship, travelling behind the Hale-Bopp comet, in order to reach a higher plane of existence.

125 - Though the most zealous and devoted still go on pilgrimages to TalkOrigins and do battle with the heretics...

126 - Debray's criticisms also targeted Marxism. At the time, this demanded some courage in France, despite the fact that communism's prestige was on the wane. Other French thinkers had also made the same link. Saul Karsz, a Marxist writer questioning the supposed dichotomy between political ideology and religion, noted (1974: 197):

> For example, when he [Marx] considered religious ideology as a illusory representation (opium of the people) hiding reality (social inequalities) and that had to be replaced *in situ* by a true representation, that is a political representation. But this political representation may function as an upside down religion, as the true religion. Instead of analysing religion and taking it over, politics takes its place to tell men, with earthly language, that which religion tells them using the language of heaven.*

127 - That is, not reframed in Enlightenment terms.

128 - See also an article by Mely 2002,

129 - See Dawkins' article **The future looks Bright** (The Guardian, June 21, 2003)
http://books.guardian.co.uk/review/story/0,12084,981412,00.html
In marketing terms, Wired magazine has examined this very issue: **Religion Be Damned**, vol. 11, n° 10, October 2003.
www.wired.com/wired/archive/11.10/view.html?pg=2

130 - As a matter of doing some justice to those billions and billions of

years of evolution…

131 - Oddly enough, this is precisely the solution seized upon by the atheist and signer of the Humanist Manifesto Isaac Asimov in his short story **The Last Question** (1956). Old myths die hard…
www.multivax.com/last_question.html

132 - About this character, a contact offered the following observations:

> As a character, Tintin appears as the champion of "pure reason", humanistic altruism and enlightened globalization. He was born in a strongly Catholic environment, under the watchful eye of the Church and kept many Catholic concepts such as themes of hell for the wicked, mercy and forgiveness toward the adversary, non-violence when possible, interventions of Providence, etc. The Tintin series ends up discussing totalitarian regimes and keeping a watchful eye on a "sound and legitimate monarchy", in keeping with the Catholic Church's perspective in the 1930s in Europe and in Belgium in particular.

133 - Those capable of reading French may usefully consult chap. 3 (**La nouvelle église universelle**) in (Auto)critique de la science. Seuil Paris 1975 Lévy-Leblond, J.M. & Jaubert, A. (eds.) 310 p.

134 - From the **Cream Complete** album. See also:
www.lyricsdomain.com/3/cream/anyone_for_tennis.html

135 - Cf: Crick: **Directed Panspermia** (1973) Icarus July p. 341; **Life Itself**. (1981) Simon & Schuster New York

136 - Cf. Hoyle: **Evolution from Space** The Omni Lecture (1982)

137 - That is the concept claiming that life can, somehow, spring up from non-life, contradicting Pasteur's empirical findings that spontaneous generation is impossible.

138 - In his writings, Lewis uses an equivalent term, "naturalistic".

139 - Even those that for the moment escape the reach of our scientific instruments and are said to be due to "chance". This is actually little more than an admission of our ignorance of the real causes involved. Statistical models are only tools providing a rough grasp of phenomena that may be encountered at the molecular level, for example.

140 - That determinism may be genetic, hormonal or due to some other factor doesn't really matter in the long run. Some, in the modern cosmological context, attempt to save human freedom of choice from absolute determinism by invoking quantum indeterminacy, but this is rather futile as ultimately, material causes remain the ultimate cause of all human behaviour and cultural or intellectual production. That random or unpredictable motions of molecules may be involved in these processes does not change the fact that the material causes determine everything. Modern cosmology still excludes, in absolute terms, the assumption that humans might be polar entities, composed of body and soul. Materialism excludes the possibility that humans may have a dimension other than empirical.

141 - A coherent Christian would never accept that reason be considered infallible. Taking into account the doctrine of the Fall, he would believe rather that reason, like everything else about humans, is fallen and also prone to error. But since man is made in God's image, he may nonetheless use reason to discover useful things. Reason then is valuable, but limited.

142 - Paedophile's freedom of (sexual) expression perhaps?

143 - Which is probably a good fit with his ingrained anti-Semitism.

144 - This would be particularly true in academic, scientific and educational circles.

145 - Excluding perhaps a brief comment made at the Nobel awards ceremonies.

146 - And in some cases, if for some reason he has been involved in some scandal (for example, being an out-of-the-closet creationist), a laboratory may not provide much refuge, as thereafter he may even have difficulty finding funds for his research work.

147 - Typically linked either to scientific, artistic or literary elites.

148 - Some aspects of this mythology are explored by Berkeley law professor, Phillip Johnson, in his essay **Gideon's Uncertain Trumpet** (1998: 127-143).

149 - We see here another (thinly veiled) postmodern reaction (one of many) to Christianity. Of course this is a carryover from the modern worldview. Though moderns and postmoderns disagree on many points of doctrine, regarding the Judeo-Christian worldview, the kneejerk reaction is the same and dark rhetoric about witch-hunts, the "oppressive Dark Ages" or "patriarchal monotheistic despotism" quickly come to the fore.

150 - We have a rather sharp contrast here with modern ideologies where explicit discourse is dominant. Regarding Nazism, K. D. Bracher notes (1970: 250):

> The theory of the totalitarian state demanded a militant ideological mobilization on behalf of an internally closed ruling system of maximal efficiency. Beyond that, however, the function of this theory lay in the conscious preparation for the goals of domination spelled out in the ideology.

151 - The founders of the United States had their greenbacks engraved with the motto "In God We Trust". If tradition were to be erased, today they might more truthfully write "In Government We Trust".

152 - And eventually sets up its own (materialistic) ecclesiastical hierarchy. See Barker (1979).

153 - One might think that our politically correct elites are incapable of humour, but it appears that even goodthinkers can crack a good joke from time to time.

154 - There is some irony in the fact that another science fiction author, Ray Bradbury in **Fahrenheit 451**, opposed this view of censorship.

155 - It seems one can hardly overestimate the emotional, ethical and moral impact caused by the double disasters of the Holocaust and the

Soviet gulag among modern elites in the twentieth-century. Dreams of progress through science and the rational State were exposed as cruel and sadistic nightmares. The postmodern concept of tolerance seems more a reaction, a direct consequence of this half-awakening. But such a reaction is emotional rather than logical, as postmoderns have little basis with which to justify their disapproval. How can one claim that such and such conduct is "inhumane" when the concept of the "human" has so disintegrated and amounts to little more than an empty shell?

156 - This phenomenon is not without precursors. André Breton, in the **Manifesto of Surrealism** (1924), notes "Surrealism is based on the belief in the superior reality of certain forms of previously neglected associations, in the omnipotence of dreams, in the disinterested play of thought."

157 - In simple terms, syncretism is an (explicit or implicit) attitude postulating that all religions are equivalent and can be taken apart and randomly put back together with no significant conflict. This attitude opens the door to innovative carpet-baggers offering new religious systems, that is to say belief systems assembled from disparate religious elements, even elements drawn from clearly incompatible belief systems. The end result is a form of packrat religion. Syncretism is then a perfect fit with global capitalism as it too says, "the customer is always right!" Icons and symbols are typically the first items filched.

158 - In my opinion this trait must be linked to the fact that postmodern religion is, to a large extent, a reaction to a very explicit religion, Christianity, which was once dominant in the West.

159 - At present, the dominant cosmology assumes that "the world we know finds its origin only in natural and certainly impersonal processes." Obviously this presupposition is borrowed from the modern religion. Although widely accepted, it is conceivable that this cosmology be dropped at some point. This could occur, not necessarily on scientific grounds, but because from a postmodern perspective this cosmology implies an implicit belief in the superiority of Western science. But on the flip side, another factor works to prop up the status quo. Seeing an origins myth involving a Creator could lead to a shift to absolute law, postmoderns thus have a vested interest in keeping the materialist origins myth in place despite the contradictions this involves.

160 - In this respect, Nietzsche foreshadows many postmodern thinkers when he says (1882/1924: 285):

> How much faith a person requires in order to flourish, how much "fixed opinion" he requires which he does not wish to have shaken, because he holds himself thereby is a measure of his power (or more plainly speaking, of his weakness). Most people in old Europe, as it seems to me, still need Christianity at present, and on that account it still finds belief. For such is man: a theological dogma might be refuted to him a thousand times, provided, however, that he had need of it, he would again and again accept it as "true"

according to the famous "proof of strength" of which the Bible speaks. Some have still need of metaphysics; but also the impatient longing for certainty which at present discharges itself in scientific, positivist fashion among large numbers of the people, the longing by all means to get at something stable (while on account of the warmth of the longing the establishing of the certainty is more leisurely and negligently undertaken): even this is still the longing for a hold, a support; in short, the instinct of weakness, which, while not actually creating religions, metaphysics, and convictions of all kinds, nevertheless preserves them.

Such observations are also relevant when considering the gut reactions of modern elites when facing serious criticism of their origins myth, the theory of evolution.

161 - Of course this opens the door to the occult, shamans, UFOs and who know what else. As a result, fetishes, symbols or rituals of all sorts may legitimately be "borrowed" from any religious system.

162 - That is to say that History has meaning and that this meaning implies an improvement of the human condition. The concept of unilinear history (with a beginning, middle and end of time), which for a long time dominated the West, is then eroded or even discarded. It can no longer be universal. Postmoderns have abandoned the grand narratives, there are no more heroes. Symbolism and ritual have no fixed meaning.

163 - This is typically defined in emotional terms, that is to say measured in terms of "feelings of happiness".

164 - And when individual self-fulfilment (or potential self-fulfilment) is not a realistic outcome, when all other options have been exhausted, postmodern logic leads inevitably to suicide and euthanasia.

165 - This implies the rejection of the collective ideologies that so dominated the twentieth-century.

166 - Certain forms of aesthetic enjoyment or artistic creativity may complement this presupposition. Postmodern soteriology is multi-faceted. Inasmuch as religion can be perceived as a path to self-fulfilment (and does not conflict with other postmodern core beliefs), it may also be integrated.

167 - Though expressed in different terms, Hinduism shares this assumption (Maya).

168 - If this assumption is translated in popular language, it could be put the following way: "It is forbidden to forbid!" (recalling student slogans in the May 1968 uprisings in France). Postmodern thought exudes paradoxes and contradictions.

169 - And making the individual the centre inevitably subtracts power and influence from grassroots power structures such as the family and gives the State greater access to (and power over) the individual.

170 - This brings to mind an ironic comment by C. S. Lewis in **The Problem of Pain** "What we want in fact is not so much a father in Heaven as a grandfather in heaven — a senile benevolence who, as they say, 'liked to see

young people enjoying themselves."

171 - Generally, elite scientists keep such assumptions implicit and assumed in their statements and writings, but some authors, less concerned with social etiquette, such as renowned palaeontologist Richard Lewontin, approach the matter with rather unusual frankness (1997: 28):

We take the side of science in spite of the patent absurdity of some of its constructs, in spite of its failure to fulfill many of its extravagant promises of health and life, in spite of the tolerance of the scientific community for unsubstantiated just-so stories, because we have a prior commitment, a commitment to materialism. It is not that the methods and institutions of science somehow compel us to accept a material explanation of the phenomenal world, but, on the contrary, that we are forced by our a priori adherence to material causes to create an apparatus of investigation and a set of concepts that produce material explanations, no matter how counterintuitive, no matter how mystifying to the uninitiated. Moreover, that materialism is absolute, for we cannot allow a Divine Foot in the door.

172 - Or in theological terms, this is the matter of salvation, finding freedom from life's alienation.

173 - Although of course their relative importance may remain the subject of heated discussion and controversy.

174 - The first three groups in this list.

175 - From the Arab word "sunna" (custom or tradition).

176 - Dominant in Saudi Arabia.

177 - Considered by many Muslims as a racist sect (defending black supremacy). It is somewhat closer to the Sunni branch of Islam.

178 - Many environmentalists argue that the environment must be protected **from** man and not **for** man.

179 - Often lawyers.

180 - It would appear that the poet T. S. Eliot had put his finger on this ideological influence (1945/1982: 111):

In this street
There is no beginning, no movement, no peace and no end
but noise without speech, food without taste.
Without delay, without haste
We would build the beginning and the end of this street.
We build the meaning:
A Church for all
And a job for each
Each man to his work.

181 - This analysis rings true in the author's opinion. The 1974 Watergate scandal, which ended with the resignation of U.S. President Nixon, demonstrated media's political power. But could a reverse-case scenario even be conceivable in a Wesetern democratic system? That is to say a journalist or media company owner losing his job (or influence) solely due to political

pressure? It goes without saying that the incidence of governmental control over the press and media is commonplace in the Islamic world and in Communist China.

182 - Especially if one considers the number of media mergers that have taken place worldwide since the 1970s. On the issue of media mergers, see Robert W. McChesney (1999) **Rich Media, Poor Democracy: Communication Politics in Dubious Times**. U. of Illinois Press 448 p.

183 - Although primarily concerned with political and ideological issues, Noam Chomsky has observed a similar phenomenon (1988/2003: xvii):

> After twelve years of increased competition for advertisers and for the abolition of boundaries between editorial and commercial departments, newsrooms have become small multinational empires and have reduced their budgets along with their enthusiasm for investigative journalism that might potentially challenge power structures. This period saw the creation of new sources of information and the artillery barrage against dissidents and critics has intensified, reinforcing the influence of the ruling elite.*

184 - Unless, God forbid, such individuals find themselves involved in a scandal of some sort. Needless to say, the media typically finds a "good scandal" much too hard to resist.

185 - Or, "Weltanschauung", to use the term coined by the nineteenth-century German philosopher Alexander von Humboldt.

186 - In linguistics, though the Sapir-Whorf hypothesis is not unanimously accepted, it appears to have limited application on a technical level. But in postmodern discourse, language manipulation is a clear indication of intent to channel and shape thinking.

187 - This is especially true when attempting to translate poetry, puns and jokes...

188 - The French expression (in the original text): "je t'aime", is more ambiguous as the French verb "aimer" does not distinguish between "liking" someone and "loving" someone.

189 - When dealing with such statements, the context of one's relationship with the speaker provides important clues with which one can decode such messages.

190 - Of course Popper's statement should be read in context. Popper was discussing the (democratic) takeover of the German state by the Nazis in the 1930s and not postmodern elites (non-violently) marginalizing their critics.

191 - In the immediate aftermath of the (2010) Terry Jones Koran-burning scandal, I was in my car listening to a CBC radio broadcast featuring interviews with Canadians giving their reactions to Pastor Jones proposal to burn copies of the Koran. One of the interviewees was an atheist, expressing views consistent with the Enlightenment/Modern tradition. He voiced concerns about biased media attitudes, which was ignoring the violent reactions of Muslims and though disagreeing with Jones' views, defended

his freedom of expression. Another interviewee was a high profile Canadian journalist, closer to the postmodern worldview. In his opinion, the sooner Jones was put in handcuffs, the better, regardless of the charges that could be brought against him! This suggests an attitude of serious concern, as postmodern elites seem quite prepared to arbitrarily revoke human rights when they see fit and launch a new Inquisition against any daring to propagate beliefs deemed "heretical", uh, that is, "intolerant"...

192 - Without all the physical consequences, of course.

193 - In the postmodern context, the danger would be primarily ideological (contamination with non-pomo concepts).

194 - Of course the consequences of such ostracism are **not** the same.

195 - For some very strange reason this quote was not translated into the English version of Bracher's book, but was in French. Was this lost (or added) in translation? Hard to tell...

196 - In German this comes out as *Gemeinnuetzige Kranken-Transport gmbh* or under the acronym GEKRAT.

197 - Typically a Protestant, rarely a Catholic.

198 - Or is attempting to become one.

199 - More or less successfully.

200 - That is, principles or presuppositions considered incompatible with the postmodern worldview.

201 - And the stronger the reaction, the stronger the indication that this participant's core beliefs were challenged by the said web site.

202 - That is to say a gentle (unhastened) death, death without unnecessary suffering in a context where physicians actually regarded the Hippocratic oath as a binding commitment rather than an antiquated piece of literature.

203 - Such as food, clothing, hygiene and shelter.

204 - On this subject cf. Mitchell (1999).

205 - Of course using such a term in this context will be considered "offensive". Unfortunately the author has neglected to use the available less jarring anaesthetized expressions, but it remains a fact that pulling a trigger is not the only way to end a life. In this world, despite postmodern lobotomizing rhetoric, cause and effect still must be taken into account.

206 - In his essay **Madness and Civilization: A History of Insanity in the Age of Reason** (1961).

207 - Of course in this perspective, the ancient Christian distinction between sinner and sin (love the sinner, but not the sin) must be forcibly removed as it has the unfortunate consequence of making the homosexual accountable for his behaviour.

208 - Orwell notes, speaking of Big Brother and his party, (1949/1984: 178): "It systematically undermines the solidarity of the family, and it call its leader by a name which is a direct appeal to the sentiments of family loyalty."

209 - Darwin's letter is dated 21, 22, 24 October 1873.

210 - Or networks...

211 - Considered from an ideologico-religious perspective, this claim is

highly significant. In theological terms, it answers the question: Where is Truth?

212 - Though censorship is a thorny problem (not just from a technical perspective, but also from a marketing perspective), in the long term one may expect more and more pressure to bring the Internet "under control" in the West. Countries such as Communist China have already shown the way. It can be done, though in the future central governments may not always be the initiators of such measures.

213 - While avoiding to do so in the case of "friendly" participants in the exchange. This tactic helps maintain the illusion of postmodern "neutrality".

214 - Since all the material in an interview can rarely be used in the final product, this form of censorship becomes rather invisible (except in the case of a live interview), as eliminating material is unavoidable for technical reasons (time or space constraints).

215 - Local media are sometimes more receptive to critical perspectives.

216 - Of course lesser-known individuals can be ignored with impunity.

217 - Foucault makes an important point on this matter (1966/1994: 242):

> Ideology does not question the foundation, the limits, or the root of representation; it scans the domain of representations in general; it determines the necessary sequences that appear there; it defines the links that provide the connections; it expresses the laws of composition and decomposition that may rule it. It situates all knowledge in the space of representations, and by scanning that space it formulates the knowledge of the laws that provide its organization. It is in a sense a knowledge of all knowledge.

218 - Regarding the "successful religion" concept, cf. Gosselin 1986, chap. 2. www.samizdat.qc.ca/cosmos/sc_soc/tm_pg/ch2_eng.htm

219 - Excluding for the moment the natural sciences, where the modern materialist rear-guard still maintains its power-base. Admittedly, postmodern influence varies from one country to another in the West. For the foreseeable future, major social institutions in Europe still appear to be a safe haven for modern elites.

220 - But there are no guarantees, as all courtiers crave an audience.

221 - Now on a slow news day, a "good scandal" may be much too hard for the media to resist. In the first chapter, The law of human nature, of **Mere Christianity**, C. S. Lewis examines the primal, interpersonal basis of scandals.

222 - A live interview offers fewer options for filtration/editing, but an experienced interviewer can manage. He is the one, after all, asking the questions. It must be said that if the person interviewed is very prestigious, this will limit things somewhat. One approach would be to ask questions that, more or less discreetly, bring attention to the interviewee's marginal (out-dated, unprogressive) status and lack of credibility.

223 - Although this goes back quite some time, Aldous Huxley explored various aspects of this process (1958/2007: 296):

In their propaganda, today's dictators rely for the most part on repetition, suppression and rationalization — the repetition of catchwords which they wish to be accepted as true, the suppression of facts which they wish to be ignored, the arousal and rationalization of passions which may be used in the interests of the Party or the State.

224 - Jacques Ellul adds (1973: 17):

Propaganda must be continuous and lasting — continuous in that it must not leave any gaps, but must fill the citizen's whole day and all his days; lasting in that it must function over a very long period of time. Propaganda tends to make the individual live in a separate world; he must not have outside points of reference. He must not be allowed a moment of meditation or reflection in which to see himself vis-à-vis the propagandist, as happens when the propaganda is not continuous. At that moment the individual emerges from the grip of propaganda.

If one finds a coherent reference point outside the dominant system of thought, then it becomes possible for a thinker like Noam Chomsky to make a substantive criticism of a political system to which the majority is nonetheless subject.

225 - In this dialogue **Libby** defends the relativistic perspective while **'Isa** favours the concept of absolute moral law.

226 - That would attempt to go beyond empty emotional statements, such as: "I like this, I don't like that."

227 - Camus adds (1951: 280):

Must we therefore renounce every kind of rebellion, whether we accept, with all its injustices, a society that outlives its usefulness, or whether we decide, cynically, to serve, against the interest of man, the inexorable advance of history? After all, if the logic of our reflection should lead to a cowardly conformism it would have to be accepted as certain families sometimes accept inevitable dishonor. If it must also justify all the varieties of attempts against man, and even his systematic destruction, it would be necessary to consent to this suicide.

228 - An exception to this rule would be the rare case where the individual actually voicing such criticisms is himself part of the elite and has media access, (Malcom Muggeridge, for example).

229 - During the 1973 Watergate scandal, the public witnessed the disgrace and fall from power of an American president following investigations by the press. But in the democratic West has the reverse ever been seen, that is to say, a major journalistic figure finding himself losing his job (or influence) due to direct political initiative? Regarding Watergate, Chomsky believes that this event is not an instance where the media have gone too far, but rather that the media bears part of the responsibility for such a situation (1988: 300):

In short, the very examples offered in praise of the media for their independence, or criticism of their excessive zeal, illustrate exactly the opposite. Contrary to the usual image of an "adversary press" boldly attacking a pitiful executive giant, the media's lack of interest, investigative zeal, and basic news reporting on the accumulating illegalities of the executive branch have regularly permitted and even encouraged ever larger violations of law, whose ultimate exposure when elite interests were threatened is offered as a demonstration of media service "on behalf of polity." These observations reinforce the conclusions that we have documented throughout.

Obviously, when the interests of the State and the media converge, situations, such as that described by Chomsky, should come as no surprise.

230 - Of course it does help if there is some material to work with in the first place.

231 - Note the implicit hypocrisy in such a statement as it disregards the fact that **everyone** attempts to influence others. Such statements imply the speaker is above such behaviour.

232 - This leads to paradoxical situations in postmodern societies. In France, the Muslim community's growth has exposed the contradictions of the ideology of tolerance (and the concept that all religions are "the same"). In 2005 in Canada, the province of Ontario seriously considered establishing Islamic courts to settle family law matters (divorce cases) among Muslims. Rejecting the demands (rights?) of Muslims opens the door to charges of "intolerance" and yet if Muslims were demarginalized, then other religions could make similar demands. This could lead to social conflicts between Islamic and postmodern assumptions and expose postmodern religious dogma. The stakes are high.

233 - The National Center for Science Education is an organization whose main function is to maintain and defend the ideological monopoly of the theory of evolution in American schools, that is to say, from primary school to university (though of course it is likely they would not phrase their objectives exactly in such a manner).

234 - This statement will get the attention it deserves in volume 2 of **Flight From the Absolute.** That said, one could get a glimpse of the author's views on this matter by checking out an old article (Gosselin 1979).

235 - That is in a context where other methods of persuasion are available. Needless to say, this non-violent policy was not consistently followed by Mao.

236 - Though of course traditional religious discourse may be expressed in one's "private life". Like a vestigial organ, traditional religious discourse may impotently persist in the virtual reality of one's thought life.

237 - Of course some individuals may "weather" such aggression much easier than others if it happens that their livelihood is based in institutions that postmoderns have little control over.

238 - Or even heresies. That the postmodern is also a reaction to modern postmodern explains its attitude towards Western science and in particular to Western science's epistemological status. J-.F. Gauvin warns the rem-

nants of the modern elite (2000: 4):

> Before the Sokal hoax, one of the first salvos launched by scientists came from Paul Gross and Norman Levitt in a book entitled **Higher Superstition: The Academic Left and Its Quarrels with Science** (Baltimore, Johns Hopkins University Press, 1994). Denouncing the writings of environmentalists, feminists, multiculturalists (that is American Afrocentrics) and radical postmodernists, who have made science-bashing their new pastime and religion, the authors warn the scientific community that this could result in short and medium term harm to the population. Anti-science resentment comes, in their opinion, from the romantic tradition and has always been dissatisfied with Enlightenment rationalism.*

239 - To which J.-F. Lyotard vaguely alludes (1979: 30):

> It is therefore not at all surprising that the representatives of the new process of legitimation by "the people" should be at the same time actively involved in destroying the traditional knowledge of peoples, perceived from that point forward as minorities or potential separatist movements destined only to spread obscurantism.

Of course Lyotard is discussing the behaviour of modern elites here, but there is good reason to believe that postmodern elites also pursue this tradition in their own deconstructed way.

240 - Like the postmodern elites find use for a ProLife activist planting bombs at an abortion clinic: if such individuals did not exist, they would have to invent them. The West's demonized past, of course, recalls real historical events. But these events are useful particularly in ideological terms, as they are quite efficient bridge-burning mechanisms. Turning back then becomes impossible, unthinkable.

241 - Or any modern ideologies derived from this worldview.

242 - The concentration camp system in Communist China where prisoners find themselves enslaved and exploited for their labour. Manufactured products are sold for the benefit of those managing the camps.
Cf : Wu, Harry (1992) **Laogai - the Chinese Gulag**. Westview Press 247 p.

243 - When it comes to geopolitical analysis of twentieth-century movements, the orthodox post-modern perspective on this issue takes it for granted that racism is typical of "conservative", "extreme right" thinking. But such views ignore relevant historical data. In the early twentieth-century, most social scientists, under the influence of Darwinism, were racist and extensively published articles and books on so-called "inferior races". This concept had been popularized to such an extent that even a left-leaning activist such as English author H. G. Wells, despite some reservations regarding the "inferior race" concept, nonetheless grimly asserted (1905: ch. 10):

> The true objection to slavery is not that it is unjust to the inferior but that it corrupts the superior. **There is only one sane and logical thing to be done with a really inferior race, and that is to exterminate it.**

348

Such issues were also discussed in **Anticipations** (1902), another book by Wells.

244 - In this particular case, there is reason to believe that Gould is thinking of the dominant variant of Darwinian theory holding that evolution is a slow accumulation of mutations, in contrast to Gould's theory of evolution [punctuated equilibrium] postulating that evolution takes place very quickly in relatively short periods of time (where a large number of mutations can radically transform a species). According to Gould, geological time is mostly static in terms of evolution. Nothing happens.

245 - Also referred to as "continental drift".

246 - When one looks at this issue in the context of the Enlightenment, one finds this worldview has enthroned Science as the ultimate form of human reason, in fact, as the ultimate epistemological reference point or to employ less ambiguous language, as Truth. One ground-breaking postmodern reaction to the sacred, 'untouchable' status claimed for science by modern thinkers was voiced in the book **Against Method** by Paul K. Feyerabend. Feyerabend notes how hard it is even for very original Westerner thinkers to question this role (1975/1979: 302):

> Even bold and revolutionary thinkers bow to the judgement of science. Kropotkin wants to break up all existing institutions — but he does not touch science. Ibsen goes very far in unmasking the conditions of contemporary humanity — but he still retains science as a measure of the truth. Evans-Pritchard, Lévi-Strauss and others have recognised that 'Western Thought', far from being a lonely peak of human development, is troubled by problems not found in other ideologies — but they exclude science from their relativisation of all forms of thought. Even for them science is a neutral structure containing positive knowledge that is independent of culture, ideology, prejudice.

Of course Feyerabend's disgraceful and "heretical" claims (coming from a philosopher of science to boot) were the object of much scandal and consternation when first uttered in the 1970s.

247 - Another major modern saint would be Charles Darwin. A saint perhaps but certainly not a martyr, as Darwin never suffered any real persecution to speak of, unless one were to stoop so low as to count snide caricatures in daily newspapers. Typically martyrs or heretics do not get a saint's burial either.

248 - Regarding the historical situation between Galileo and the Catholic Church, cf: Jerry Bergman (2003) **The Galileo Myth and the Facts of History**.

249 - Of course one finds this concept in various places in the Bible, that is that all of nature is subject to laws established by God. It is implicit in Genesis 1-2, but is also found in the Psalms, for example:

> Praise ye the LORD. Praise ye the LORD from the heavens: praise him in the heights. Praise ye him, all his angels: praise ye him, all his

hosts. Praise ye him, sun and moon: praise him, all ye stars of light. Praise him, ye heavens of heavens, and ye waters that be above the heavens. Let them praise the name of the LORD: for he commanded, and they were created. He hath also stablished them for ever and ever: he hath made a decree which shall not pass. (Psalm 148: 1-6)

250 - This, of course, is a translation from a French text, not the original Latin.

251 - This parallels the preceding case of Judge Bork whose nomination to the Supreme Court failed.

252 - Such stressful procedures can largely be avoided if the system is set up more efficiently, that is by consistently filtering out non-postmodern candidates for positions at lower levels influence and responsibility.

253 - Of course some of my readers will find that grouping such issues in a list immediately raises a red flag and identifies Muggeridge as... But the flip side of that coin is that this conditioned response also labels the reader, but as??

254 - There is no reason to expect that this observation should not apply to editors (print media) and to program directors (TV) as well.

255 - The dilemma of attaining complete ideological control and uniform in media is not new. In the Nazi context, historian K. D. Bracher observed (1970: 255):

> The regime continued to tolerate non-Nazi papers because it thought to turn their prestige to advantage at home and abroad. Not until August 1943, was that last great paper of this kind, the *Frankfurter Zeitung*, abolished. But the expression of independent opinion, let alone criticism, called for the art of writing and reading between the lines. What set these papers apart from the party press was their individual style rather than additional information. Goebbels, through his system of internal press conferences and stream of "directives," succeeded in imposing a uniformity of news and interpretation soon after the creation of the Propaganda Ministry (March 1933). He was a skilled enough journalist to appreciate the necessity of tolerating some variation to avoid the danger of boring the reader to death and consequently diminishing the propaganda value of the press.

256 - The French translation of Chomsky's book seems to have an expanded introduction not appearing in the 1988 version of **Manufacturing Consent.** As a result it was necesary to translate this excerpt rather than quote Chomsky directly. PG

257 - It should be noted that the usual arrangement in the West, where the press, as an institution, serves to limit or offset state power, is the result of a long social history. Western societies, once dominated by Judeo-Christian influence, slowly come to the view that no individual or social institution should enjoy absolute power. British historian Lord Acton (1834-1902) famously stated that "power corrupts and absolute power corrupts abso-

lutely." Such a perspective is compatible with the Christian assumption that man is a fallen being, incapable of living a totally just life. To prevent abuse, the powers of various social institutions must then be in equilibrium. This principle appears in Scripture when one of the greatest apostles saw his statements subject to review (by non-Christians) in the episode of the disciples from Berea (Acts 17: 10-11). No man, no human authority, is then above scrutiny from God's word. We encounter this principle again in a somewhat more implicit form in the First Epistle to Corinthians, where the relative importance of the various parts of the community are discussed in terms of an analogy: the body.

> For by one Spirit are we all baptized into one body, whether we be Jews or Gentiles, whether we be bond or free; and have been all made to drink into one Spirit. For the body is not one member, but many. If the foot shall say, Because I am not the hand, I am not of the body; is it therefore not of the body? And if the ear shall say, Because I am not the eye, I am not of the body; is it therefore not of the body? If the whole body were an eye, where were the hearing? If the whole were hearing, where were the smelling? But now hath God set the members every one of them in the body, as it hath pleased him. And if they were all one member, where were the body? But now are they many members, yet but one body. And the eye cannot say unto the hand, I have no need of thee: nor again the head to the feet, I have no need of you. Nay, much more those members of the body, which seem to be more feeble, are necessary: (1Co 12: 13-22)

Elsewhere in the Old Testament, one finds opposition to absolute power in the book of Esther where Mordecai, a Jewish bureaucrat, refuses to bow down to Haman (as before a deity), the right-hand man of King Ahasuerus/ Xerxes (see chap. 3 particular). In the Old Testament, this theme also appears a few times in the book of Daniel. The prophets, on numerous occasions serve to limit the absolute power of Israelite kings (by criticizing them). In historical terms, moreover, in Israel it should be noted that the role of prophet actually precedes that of king. In addition, when the kingdom of Israel was established, it is stated that the king must be subject to God's law no less than his people (1Sam. chap. 12) as is the case with Solomon's advice to his son in 1Kings chapter 2.

258 - The reaction to the publication of Hawkins' book in scientific media provides us valuable information on defence mechanisms exploited by the scientific establishment. Murguía and Agudelo observe (2002: chap. 5):

> Hawkins' book is part theory and part exposé and when it came out reviewers everywhere remarked, not on the need for such a critique of the establishment, but on the bitterness with which Hawkins dealt with the community. The reviews were unfortunate since they did not pay attention to Hawkins' criticisms. In fact, most reviewers reverted to the thwarted logic of blaming Hawkins' past, psychological make-up, etc. to explain the reasons for the book, as if Hawkins

had had the audacity to point a finger at some completely innocent stranger.

Yes, of course, what a repulsive individual, daring to accuse scientists, so chaste and so pure, of such things. It goes without saying that Hawkins is neurotic, base and suspect. Otherwise, how could he dare make such statements? Egad! Such criticisms are sufficient proof of his guilt…

259 - Knee-jerk reactions in biology are the same of course when it comes to any serious criticism of the theory of evolution.

260 - Larson is a historian, Witham, a journalist.

261 - That is to say that involving adherence to a materialist cosmology. At present, there are few proponents of postmodern religion in the natural sciences. Jane Hawking's biography (2004), wife of astrophysicist Stephen Hawking, provides interesting revelations of the materialist dogmas held by modern scientific elites.

262 - The author views such labels as bogus. While the term "irreligious" defines what these people do **not** believe in, it is hypocritically silent about what these particular people **do** believe. The implication is of course that these people have gone "beyond religion" or "have no need of religion", which is patent nonsense.

263 - This amounts to cultural determinism. Such determinism inevitably implies that if the same individual (looking at this matter from a statistical perspective), were born in India, would be a Buddhist, in France, a materialist, in Africa, an animist or Moslem and in Germany, a Protestant or Catholic. The matter of the truth of one's beliefs is of course ignored here. Fate or destiny then would be geographic (or temporal).

264 - When marketing issues are set aside, this is something well understood by most coherent (and honest) moderns. William B. Provine, professor of biology at Cornell University, for example, states (1990: 23):

> … when he [Darwin] deduced the theory of natural selection to explain the adaptations in which he had previously seen the handiwork of God, Darwin knew that he was committing cultural murder. He understood immediately that if natural selection explained adaptations, and evolution by descent were true, then the argument from design was dead and all that went with it, namely the existence of a personal god, free will, life after death, immutable moral laws, and ultimate meaning in life. The immediate reactions to Darwin's On the Origin of Species exhibit, in addition to favorable and admiring responses from a relatively few scientists, an understandable fear and disgust that has never disappeared from Western culture.

265 - These figures have in common the fact that they accept without question the dominance of the materialist (so-called "scientific") cosmology as well as the marginalization of (monotheistic) religions into the ghetto of "moral" and "spiritual" issues.

266 - Irshad Manji, is a Canadian Muslim, but also a lesbian. A media favourite in the West (with interviews on Oprah), she has written a number of

books including **The Trouble With Islam: A Wake-up Call For Honesty and Change** (2003).

267 - For a few concrete examples of discrimination in regards to criticisms of the theory of evolution, read the following telling comments by British novelist Warwick Collins (1994: 7):

> My own introduction to the practice of Darwinism occurred when I was a biology undergraduate at Sussex University. My tutor was the brilliant theorist Professor John Maynard Smith, a disciple of JBS Haldane and — like Haldane — a Marxist. I liked Maynard Smith, but when I raised certain objections to Darwinian theory I was told that I would not be permitted to air them publicly, and that he would personally block publication of a paper which I had written on the subject. If I continued, my status as one of his inner group of researchers and students would be withdrawn. I persevered with my interest in the problems of Darwin's theory but found, as time went on, that I could not function in the pervading university atmosphere, and left my studies for a wider world.

But if by chance the individual daring to criticize the theory of evolution has religious beliefs, Christian beliefs in particular, this makes things much worse. Cf: Bergman, Jerry, **The Criterion** (Richfield, MN: Onesimus Publishing, 1984) and **Slaughter of the Dissidents** Leaf Cutter Press (2008). See also Bergman, **Intolerance in America: The Case History of a Creationist**. www.rae.org/intolerance.html

268 - There is little reason to believe that the situation should be much different among other elite groups mentioned above.

269 - One could look at the case of Forrest Mims, science journalist about to be hired by Scientific American magazine, but dropped when his rejection of evolution came to the attention of the editor. Here is a detailed biography (as well as the establishment perspective on the Scientific American vs. Mims case):

http://en.wikipedia.org/wiki/Forrest_Mims
www.talkorigins.org/indexcc/CA/CA320_1.html
And Mims' (and other more critical) perspectives on this case:
www.forrestmims.org/scientificamerican.html
http://creation.com/scientific-american-refuses-to-hire-creationist
Other cases of discrimination in universities related to views on origins are documented by the movie **Expelled** (2008) with Ben Stein.

270 - A priest or priestess is, by definition, an intermediary between men and God (or the gods). Cf : Barker (1979).

271 - When modern elites were at the height of their power.

272 - That is excluding modern ideologies such as Nazism and Communism, which establish classes of humans (either inferior races or counter-revolutionary social classes) who are unworthy of salvation.

273 - This involves seeking the observable causes of observable phenomena/processes.

274 - A particular myth no doubt, one distinguished by claiming the sacred aura of science. But Darwin was not the first to attempt to meet this need. One can also recall Jean-Baptiste de Lamarck and his concept of evolution through the inheritance of acquired characteristics.

275 - But in a Darwinian context this might be more coherently (though less elegantly) stated as "but he will still have the solid satisfaction of knowing that he has followed his own desires or urges, rather than those imposed by others".

276 - Hitler was not immoral or amoral. The reverse is actually true. Hitler had his own morality. In his opinion the highest moral value was that of the superior race, the Aryan race, which he framed in Darwinian terms of the survival of the fittest. Thus Hitler attacked Communists and the labour movement as immoral because in promoting internationalism they called into question the Nazi principle of the primacy of race. In his view, such internationalism would inevitably contaminate the purity of the Aryan race. Hitler developed his moral perspective in his book **Mein Kampf**. He claimed the philosophy of the [Nazi] people (1925/1941: 420-421):

> ... by no means believes in the equality of races, but recognizes along with their differences their higher or lower value, and through this knowledge feels obliged, according to the eternal will that rules this universe, to promote the victory of the better, the stronger, and to demand the submission of the worse and weaker. It embraces thereby in principle the aristocratic law of nature and believes in the validity of this law down to the last individual being. It recognizes not only the different value of races, but also the different value of individuals.... But by no means can it approve of the right of an ethical idea existing, if this idea is a danger for the racial life of the bearer of a higher ethic.

277 - All this is fine until **your** number comes up and it is your turn to be eliminated by the process of natural selection.

278 - That is if you happen **not** to be the one in power, the alpha male or female or whatever.

279 - Russell adds this comment (1935/1997: 237-238):

> The theory which I have been advocating is a form of the doctrine which is called the "subjectivity" of values. This doctrine consists in maintaining that, if two men differ about values, there is not a disagreement as to any kind of truth, but a difference of taste. If one man says "oysters are good" and another says "I think they are bad," we recognize that there is nothing to argue about. The theory in question holds that all differences as to values are of this sort, although we do not naturally think them so when we are dealing with matters that seem to us more exalted than oysters.

280 - Here again, Wittgenstein is in agreement with Russell, who believes that moral judgments are a matter of taste. This should come to no surprise, as Wittgenstein was both a student and friend of Bertrand Russell.

281 - But this perspective is not unrelated to the fact that the materialist worldview, claiming the prestige of empirical science, should be constituted in this way, as science was originally developed in a symbiotic/dependant relationship with the Judeo-Christian worldview (on this subject, see **Flight from the Absolute**, vol. II). At the time, there was no need for science to provide a moral discourse, as this was taken care of by the Christian religion to everyone's satisfaction. Note that Albert Einstein, who was also concerned with an ethical issue of great importance (the atomic bomb), arrived at a position quite different from Russell's, resulting from serious reflection on Hume's is/ought paradox and recognizing the limitations of science (Einstein 1939):

> The aspiration toward such objective knowledge belongs to the highest of which man is capable, and you will certainly not suspect me of wishing to belittle the achievements and the heroic efforts of man in this sphere. Yet it is equally clear that knowledge of what is does not open the door directly to what should be. One can have the clearest and most complete knowledge of what is, and yet not be able to deduct from that what should be the goal of our human aspirations. Objective knowledge provides us with powerful instruments for the achievements of certain ends, but the ultimate goal itself and the longing to reach it must come from another source. And it is hardly necessary to argue for the view that our existence and our activity acquire meaning only by the setting up of such a goal and of corresponding values. The knowledge of truth as such is wonderful, but it is so little capable of acting as a guide that it cannot prove even the justification and the value of the aspiration toward that very knowledge of truth. Here we face, therefore, the limits of the purely rational conception of our existence.

282 - In the twenty-first century Sade would find himself in good company with the fierce logic of bioethicist Peter Singer who claims that it is legitimate to consider using children with mental disabilities as guinea pigs for scientific or medical experiments since, based on Singer's criteria for humanity, they are not really self-aware.

283 - Sade was certainly not a guilt-ridden creature; he had absolutely no interest in such hang-ups. His concept of moral conscience is much more straightforward and coherent than that of Darwin (1795/1965: 332):

> Let us deign for a moment to illumine our spirit by philosophy's sacred flame; what other than Nature's voice suggests to us personal hatreds, revenges, wars, in a word, all those causes of perpetual murder? Now, if she incites us to murderous acts, she has need of them; that once grasped, how may we suppose ourselves guilty in her regard when we do nothing more than obey her intentions?

Compare Sade's position on murder to that of J.-P. Sartre's, which we will discuss later on in this chapter. Which is most logically consistent?

284 - And when the time comes, evolution will eventually eliminate too.

285 - This is an excerpt from a letter to W. Graham, dated July 3, 1881, which is also available online.
http://www.darwinproject.ac.uk/entry-13230
286 - Though in practice postmodern elites will limit, via mechanisms of manipulative political correctness, that which may be expressed or "tolerated".
287 - No admirer of Hitler, Simone Weil added this observation on Hitler's view of inconsistencies in Enlightenment thought (1949/1979: 241):

> Hitler has clearly perceived the absurdity of the eighteenth-century conception, still in favor today, and which already had its roots in Descartes. For the last two or three centuries, people have believed that force rules supreme over all natural phenomena, and at the same time that men can and should base their mutual relations upon justice, recognized as such through the application of reason. This is a flagrant absurdity. It is inconceivable that everything in the universe should be entirely subjected to the rule of force and that Man should be able to escape the effects of this, seeing that he is made of flesh and blood and that his mind wanders here and there at the mercy of sensory perceptions. There is only one possible choice to be made. Either we must perceive at work in the universe, alongside force, a principle of a different kind, or else we must recognize force as being the unique and sovereign ruler over human relations also. In the first case, one places oneself in radical opposition to modern science as founded by Galileo, Descartes, and several others, pursued through the eighteenth-century, notably by Newton, then in the nineteenth, and now in the twentieth. In the second case, one places oneself in radical opposition to the humanism which arose at the time of the Renaissance, triumphed in 1789, and which, in a considerably degenerated form, served as the inspiration for the whole of the Third Republic.

288 - Of course then research done, or books written, by sociobiologists must also be genetically determined…
289 - Such as the "enlightened" statements of French eugenicist Charles Richet, winner of the 1913 Nobel Prize for medicine (in Carrel, 1922: 34, 54):

> What! Should we strive to produce improved breeds of horses, dogs, pigs or plums and beets and yet make no effort to create less defective human races …? What astonishing carelessness. … Methods of selection will serve to create less defective human races, give muscle more strength, silhouettes more beauty, intelligence more penetration, … character more energy, increase longevity and robustness. What amazing progress! … One need not punish [the degenerate], but rather separate them from us. Their tainted blood must not corrupt the generous blood of a strong race.*

290 - That said, it must be pointed out that at no time in its history was the West totally dominated by the Christian worldview. This worldview always

had competition either from pre-Christian religions, Greek paganism, Greek philosophers, Islam and later on the Enlightenment and its many derivative ideologies.

291 - But never with perfect consistency, as it took centuries to eliminate the institution of slavery in the West. And this is just one example among many others, such as Luther's reformed Germany, which persecuted the Jews, the Inquisition, pogroms, religious wars, etc...

292 - Historian Richard Weikart notes (2004: 10):

Another reason that the Darwinian devaluing of human life should not be treated as proto-Nazi is because similar ideas circulated in the United States, Britain, and other democratic countries. Ian Dowbiggin and Nick Kemp in their fine studies of the history of the euthanasia movement in United States and Britain, respectively, both emphasize the crucial role played by Darwinism in initiating and ideologically underpinning the euthanasia movement. Dowbiggin states, "The most pivotal turning point in the early history of the euthanasia movement was the coming of Darwinism to America." Kemp strongly supports this point, claiming, "While we should be wary of depicting Darwin as the man responsible for ushering in a secular age we should be similarly cautious of underestimating the importance of evolutionary thought in relation to the questioning of the sanctity of human life." Many studies on the eugenics movement in the United States, Europe, and elsewhere likewise show the importance of Darwinism in mediating a shift toward eugenics and other related ideas, including biological determinism, inegalitarianism, scientific racism, and the devaluing of human life. The ideas expressed by Madison Grant, president of the New York Zoological Society, in **The Passing of the Great Race** (1916), sound ominously close to Nazi ways of thinking (and Hitler owned the German translation of Grant's book). Therein Grant wrote, "Mistaken regard for what are believed to be divine laws and a sentimental belief in the sanctity of human life tend to prevent both the elimination of defective infants and the sterilization of such adults as are themselves of no value to the community. The laws of nature require the obliteration of the unfit, and human life is valuable only when it is of use to the community or race." Stefan Kühl has even explicitly shown the many links between the American eugenics movement and the Nazi eugenics program. Thus, the Darwinian devaluing of human life was not just a German phenomenon and it led to many human tragedies outside of Germany, such as the compulsory sterilization campaigns in the United States and Scandinavia. Nowhere did it reach the catastrophic level of Germany, however, since only in Germany did a dictator rule with the power to pursue his radical agenda under the cover of war.

Taking into consideration the basic materialistic worldview shared by Nazi elite as well as by elites in the West generally, the question of the events in Nazi Germany becomes less: How did such a shocking outcome occur? But rather why did worse outrage not occur in the rest of the West? That is a much more serious question…

293 - Which blithely ignores Hume's conclusion regarding the is/ought paradox.

294 - Outside the context of the administration of justice, of course… It might even be amusing to replace the terms "police officer" by that of "terrorist", "Mafia hit-man" or "pissed-off teenager".

295 - This is especially true if they are well educated and have successfully submitted to a university brainwashing…

296 - Who, to some extent, become the lepers, the untouchables, of postmodern civilization.

297 - But where does this concept of "normality" come from? Which cosmology provides its basis?

298 - What about the Hippocratic Oath, for example, that all physicians, until recently, had to take before beginning to practice? This oath demands, among other things, the renunciation of any behaviour that could harm the patient. It explicitly mentions never offering poison to a patient or suggesting its use. Cf. also Hendin (1997).

299 - Its marketing strategies are undeniably superior to that of any twentieth-century eugenic propaganda.

300 - Professor of philosophy of art at the Philosophical Institute of the Madrid Centre for Scientific Research (CSIC).

301 - That is a transcendent authority, standing above the individual or even society.

302 - Fieldwork is the classical research method in Social Anthropology. Also called "participant observation", it requires that anthropologists live in a non-Western society, studying the culture for a period lasting from a few months to over a year. Ideally, they live like the people they are studying, learn the language, eating the same food, living in the same houses and in general being involved in everyday life.

303 - When such ethical emotions are not shared and widespread.

304 - Similar reactions were commonly encountered among administrators of Nazi concentration camps and the Soviet Gulag.

305 - British sociologist Os Guinness notes that many of the contradictions of the postmodern religion are exposed in the course of an encounter with Evil (2001: 103):

> (…) have you ever heard an atheist exclaim "Goddammit!" and mean it? We can all be taught not to judge; we can all be told that there are no moral absolutes. But when we come face to face with raw, naked evil, then relativism, nonjudgmentalism, and atheism count for nothing. Absolute evil calls for absolute judgment. Instinctively and intuitively, we cry out for the unconditional to condemn evil unconditionally. The atheist who lets fly "Goddammit!" in

the face of evil is right, not wrong. It is a signal of transcendence, a pointer toward a better possibility — and unwittingly a prayer.

306 - René Girard notes, for example (1999: 212-213): "In France, indeed, humanism developed as a reaction against the Christianity of the Ancien Regime which was accused of complicity with the power of the State, and for good reason of course."*

307 - Translator's note: This does not translate well, but could be rendered "Crush the despicable!" Voltaire was alluding to abuses by royalty and clergy and to particular superstitions and intolerance promoted by clergy among the common people.

308 - There is even reason to believe that the postmodern West has developed a self-loathing trait. The West despises itself, particularly its Judeo-Christian legacy.

309 - And of a particular religious context...

310 - This may vary from one country to another. Some Islamic nations may be more "contaminated" or infiltrated by Western ideas than others.

311 - This paragraph draws material from:

Hermann, Peggy (1999) L'existence d'une conception des droits de l'homme propre aux états musulmans. DEA de droit international. Faculté de droit de Montpellier I. Directeur de mémoire: M. Michel Levinet

http://www.memoireonline.com/12/05/42/m_conception-droits-de-l-homme-etats-musulmans.html

312 - Where the encounter between the native French, typically secular (in the Enlightenment tradition), and immigrants from Africa (typically from an Islamic culture) has resulted in various frictions and both social and ideological divergences. In Canada, on the other hand, the situation is quite different. In Ontario and Quebec, in 2005, the introduction of religious courts governed by Sharia law to handle divorce cases among Muslims has even been considered. In Quebec, the establishment of Islamic courts was rejected. At the time of writing, the situation is not settled in Ontario.

313 - Concerning Saudi Arabia, for example, the Ministry of External Affairs of Canada offered in its "Travel Report" document, some information for Canadian travellers (07/09/2005):

> The importation, use, or possession of any item that is held to be contrary to the tenets of Islam is also prohibited. The observance and practice of other religions is forbidden, as well as the import and use of associated religious books and materials.... Imported and domestic audiovisual media and reading materials are censored.
>
> http://www.voyage.gc.ca/dest/report-en.asp?country=258000

314 - A law student, at the time.

315 - At least in terms of logical consistency.

316 - In one of his orations Zarathustra observes that this quest for a home, for an Absolute, is a temptation even for the most hardened atheist or relativist (Nietzsche 1883/1999: LXIX. The Shadow):

To such unsettled ones as thou, seemeth at last even a prisoner blessed. Didst thou ever see how captured criminals sleep? They sleep quietly, they enjoy their new security. Beware lest in the end a narrow faith capture thee, a hard, rigorous delusion! For now everything that is narrow and fixed seduceth and tempteth thee.

317 - In terms of morality, existentialism prefigured and opened the door to postmodernism.

318 - That is transcending the individual or culture.

319 - Voltaire, the prototype of the intellectual activist, seems to have been one of the first to make use of the term. As such, this brings to mind his **Treatise on Tolerance** (1763).

320 - But why not tolerate intolerance? Wouldn't this be just as logical, just as coherent? But in such a case, the postmodern ideologico-religious system would not necessarily dominate the public arena.

321 - Since the term "superior" is of course taboo, the actual terms used would probably be synonyms such as "more open", "more tolerant", "pluralistic" and similar nonsense.

322 - One wonders if Dostoyevsky may have read Hume on this matter?

323 - The sociopath may also add: "There is no reason I should be constrained to treat anyone in a 'humane' fashion or grant them any status whatsoever. I can establish my own definition of humanity. If I find myself in a subordinate position in a power relationship (and a potential victim), my only hope is that my potential oppressor (whether modern or postmodern) is not very coherent in his beliefs and still adheres to a less ruthless code of ethics that has no basis in his worldview. But if he adopts values consistent with his worldview, I will have no recourse as long as he is dominant, unless by chance I can eliminate him and take his place." In the abortion debate in developed countries, this logic follows its inevitable course. Good thing unborn infants can't talk, who would listen anyway?

324 - It follows that if I can escape the power of the State, then there is no reason why I should not express all my instincts, even the most violent, and the most perverse.

325 - Defined, of course, in relation to my own interests. Why not?

326 - Which brings us inevitably back to Sociobiology or to other comparable deterministic theories...

327 - That is to say these moral systems no longer have anything in common, no common ground that could provide a basis for discussion or compromise.

328 - It is unlikely there has ever been a situation where one religion ruled absolutely over a society. Logically this would be a religion that had eliminated all rival contemporary religions as well as all traces of rival religions in the past.

329 - Defined of course in the context of concepts compatible with the religion or ideology in question and not necessarily in terms that would be consistent with Christian theology.

330 - Evangelical groups are movements derived from the Reformation, regarding Scripture as the sole authority in matters of doctrine and behaviour. Among these Protestants, conversion is considered legitimate only after the age of reason. Infant baptism is thus rejected.

331 - This is confirmed by the Apostle Paul in the New Testament:

> Brothers and sisters, think of what you were when you were called. Not many of you were wise by human standards; not many were influential; not many were of noble birth. But God chose the foolish things of the world to shame the wise; God chose the weak things of the world to shame the strong. God chose the lowly things of this world and the despised things — and the things that are not — to nullify the things that are, so that no one may boast before him. (1Cor. 1: 26-29 NIV)

332 - One might refer also to John 6: 14-15 where (after being offered free lunch) the Jews wanted to proclaim Jesus their King. Jesus declined this offer (in strong contrast to the attitude of the Prophet Mohamed who seized political power at the first opportunity). In this regard, we may note also that a significant part of the New Testament epistles were written while their authors were in prison.

333 - This relationship is also designated by the term "caesaropapism".

334 - Russian art historian Eugeny Barabanov describes this phenomenon as follows (1974/1981: 178-179):

> Of course the "union" of the Church and state under Constantine, and the Church-state "symphony", whose ideologist and legislator was Justinian, differ sharply from the contemporary state of affairs. The Byzantine state considered itself a Christian state, and the emperors, when they subordinated the Church to their needs, nevertheless regarded themselves as instruments of God's will. The organism of the Church did not so much suffer from the external force of the state as secretly go along with it, from inside, in a process of identifying the Church with the empire, of erasing the borders between Church and state, of affirming their close (too close!) unity. It was in this false perspective of an ostensibly self-evident "symphony" that the historical fate of the Russian Orthodox Church developed until the 1917 revolution. And when tsarism fell, the Church suddenly found itself face to face with a hostile, atheistic state which applied rather different methods from those of the Christian Emperors.

There is evidence that sometimes the postmodern context also mirrors such a symphony, not between church and State, but between the State and mass media. Of course such a relationship, like other Church-State relationships in the past, is not always harmonious, but nevertheless it involves basically a symbiotic relationship where everyone gets a piece of the pie.

335 - Apparently attitudes have not changed much, as since the fall of the

Iron Curtain, the Russian Orthodox Church has sought the establishment of laws limiting or prohibiting non-Russian religions in this territory.

336 - From 411 AD, Donatists were hunted by imperial police. Death was the punishment required by law for those holding prohibited meetings.

337 - These massacres of French Protestants (or Huguenots) began on August 23rd 1572 and initially targeted the Protestant elite in Paris and in other large cities. Cf: en.wikipedia.org/wiki/St._Bartholomew%27s_Day_massacre

338 - Beginning in the second and third centuries, the issue was debated among Christians. Tertullian (≈160-220AD) on one hand, in his treatise **On Baptism/De Baptismo**, noted:

> Of course, the Lord said: Let the children come to me [Mt 19: 14]. Yes, let them come, but when they are older. Let them come when they are old enough to be educated, when they have come to know He to whom they come. Let them become Christians when they are able to know Christ.

339 - That is to say, the right of all believers to read and interpret Scriptures for themselves. And this principle has eventually led to access to education among Evangelicals as in order to understand and make informed choices, one must be able to read. See also Francis Schaeffer (1982/1994, vol. V p. 124).

340 - These are lay leaders, taking on responsibilities in the local church (1 Tim 5: 17).

341 - But there was a precedent in Ireland as early as the fourth-century due to the influence of St. Patrick. See Cahill (1995: 114, 148).

342 - What is in fact the doctrine of papal infallibility if not the naked assertion of hierarchical power before which all must submit?

343 - Such a critical attitude is linked to the fact that each culture or state, even if it applies the term "Christian" to itself, should be considered as a relative, imperfect and partial expression of the divine order, in relation to the absolute reference point found in the Bible. Discussing the social/political contribution of Christianity, particularly community-focused Christian groups such as the Quakers or Shakers, the French Marxist sociologist Henri Desroches observed (1974: 35):

> These were basically the three major phases of the old Left-Wingers, like so many lesser-known forms of Western religious consciousness. If one were to summarize them using limited and crude imagery, it was as if, after a first age of Christianity had been shaped by Catholicism in the feudal era [glaringly omitting the contribution of the underground Christianity of the preceding period, prior to the conversion of Constantine in 321 AD], then appeared a second age of Christianity shaped by the dominant Protestantism of the bourgeois era, followed by generations of seekers stubbornly wrestling to resurrect a Christianity of a third era, that of a time located beyond class divisions.*

Discussing the origin of democratic values in the West, the anthropologist Kenelm Burridge underscores Christianity's contribution (1979: 188):

> It should be remembered that Christianity as a political force started as a democratic and egalitarian movement and found acceptance, as it does today, among slaves, outcasts, and the disfranchised over against established hierarchies. Moreover, Christianity itself is subject to the same dialectic. If, over the years, established denominations have frequently had to come to terms with and surrender to restrictive and hierarchical political forms, European and Western democratic forms, we may remind ourselves, are not derived from Athens, which depended on forms of slavery, but from the modes developed by the Church and its religious orders. Millenarian and similar movements as well as reformist movements within the Church itself have always started by emphasizing egalitarian and democratic forms. Their later corruption and betrayal is as endemic and necessary to the process as is Judas to the Last Supper.

Our High school or university textbooks typically tell us that democracy was born in ancient Greece. In politically correct circles it is sometimes too quickly forgotten that in Greece, only individuals born to the noble classes could vote and participate in political life. Slaves had no part in the major democratic institutions, despite the fact that at times they made up 75% of the population. Schaeffer, meanwhile, reports (1976/1995: 87, 108, 113) that in the churches of the Reformed tradition, the concept of man, made in God's image, had important repercussions in terms of the life of the Church and opened the door to the concept of the priesthood of believers and a beginning of democracy with the admission of church elders. In other areas, the concept of the law of God, standing above the laws of men, served as a defence against the encroachments of the absolute power of kings. In countries where the Reformation sunk deep roots, the absolute power of kings was opposed and limited. In following this logic, countries affected by the Reformation generally established decentralized political systems, with power divided between various functions. A quick look at geopolitics reveals a convergence between countries most deeply affected by the Reformation and countries where democratic traditions are the deepest. This is no coincidence. Regarding restrictions affecting the power of kings (and the spark that gave birth to democracy in the West) Pierre Sayous, a nineteenth-century author, compared Catholic and Protestant attitudes (1881: 335):

> Where did these two great minds part? For if Calvin demands as much of this subject as did the prelate, Bossuet demands nothing less of the prince than the reformer. If both carefully note that obedience is due first of all to God against whom we should not obey men, but among them this observation has a quite different implication. Who will decide that the leader has gone against God? — The Church, according to Bossuet, the individual, says Calvin who thought

only of religious doctrines when he recommended resistance. So that which was the exception under Louis XIV, in the sixteenth-century became a general fact. Religious persecution was the cause, as it accustomed people's minds to rebellion by placing them between obedience to man, royal ordinances and "the edict of the heavenly herald St. Peter: It is better to obey God than men."* [Acts 5; 29]

344 - One might also look into the renewed symbiotic relationship between the Orthodox Church and Russian state since the fall of the Iron Curtain. Other aspects of such issues are explored by Leithart (1996).

345 - Or the reign of Terror. Following the French Revolution, from 1793 to 1794 an estimated 16,000 to 40,000 people (viewed as anti-revolutionary) were killed. Many went under the guillotine.

346 - Cf also http://wikiislam.net/wiki/Dar_al-Harb

347 - The ENAP is the National School of Public Administration, a college offering Master's and PhD programmes in administration in the province of Quebec.

348 - The Christian religion needless to say, and moreover a Christianity greatly influenced by the Reformation and the Evangelical movement.

349 - Which led to absurdities such as the imprisonment of 16th century composer Louis Bourgeois for changes made to a church songbook.

350 - This provides another dimension to the continuous attacks experienced by the new political regime in Iraq since the fall of Saddam Hussein. Beyond the political and nationalist considerations, it should be noted that there is evidence that many neighbouring countries may view this potentially democratic system, where a greater freedom of thought and expression could exist, as an "infection" that should be stopped at all costs. These disturbances then are not only political, as we understand this concept in the West, but also religious.

351 - Paul Landau, an expert on Islamic movements, makes the following comments on jihad as a military practice (2004):

"Jihad", Bat Ye'or observes, "is basically the extension of a sacred sanction to Bedouin raiding practices" [3]. This sacred sanction, coupled with the institutionalization of the raid, is subject to detailed conditions and modalities of jihad, in other words, the development of Islamic war legislation. The law of war was codified by Muslim theologians of various schools of jurisprudence (Hanafi, Maliki, Hanbali, Chafi'ite ...). Specific rules have been enacted (and applied depending on time and place) to combatants and non-combatants, prisoners, plunder, etc.*

352 - As well as political submission to the Islamic armies facing them.

353 - Sometimes translated as "idolaters" or "polytheists."

354 - The only thing that really counts is the final result, that is, that men submit to the Prophet's law.

355 - Here is some information provided to travellers by the Canadian Department of External Affairs, in its "Travel Report" document, giving

some idea of the day-to-day reality in this country (07/09/2005):

Canadians working as teachers in Saudi Arabia should not discuss political or religious issues with students or school employees.... Women are not allowed to drive cars or to ride bicycles. Dancing, music, and movies are prohibited. Women and men are not allowed to mingle in public unless accompanied by other family members. A woman can be charged with prostitution if she is found associating with a man who is not a relative. Restaurants have two sections, one for men only and the family section where families, accompanied females and unaccompanied females are served. Women and children need the permission of a male relative to depart Saudi Arabia.... The importation, use, or possession of any item that is held to be contrary to the tenets of Islam is also prohibited. The observance and practice of other religions is forbidden, as well as the import and use of associated religious books and materials, the importation of pornographic materials, and the possession of weapons. Imported and domestic audiovisual media and reading materials are censored. Saudi Arabia is a traditional, conservative monarchy. Islam is the official religion and its precepts regulate all areas of daily life. Islamic practices and beliefs are closely adhered to in the country's customs, laws, and regulations. Respect religious and social traditions to avoid offending local sensitivities. Women should observe the strict Saudi dress code and wear conservative and loose-fitting clothes, including a full-length cloak (abbaya) and a head scarf. It is illegal for women to drive. Men should not wear shorts in public or go without a shirt. In order to avoid the Mutawa's attention upon arrival, visitors should seek guidance concerning acceptable clothing.... Homosexuality is a criminal offence. Those convicted may be sentenced to lashing, a prison sentence, and/or death. Canadians who are involved in incidents involving the Mutawa should report them to the Canadian Embassy in Riyadh.

356 - Also translated "false deities".

357 - Available at: freedomhouse.org

358 - And these prohibitions are typically accompanied by an implicit obligation, to criticize Israel. Since it is impossible to voice serious criticisms of the political regimes in power, a pressure valve is useful, even essential to channel social tensions away from "sensitive matters".

359 - The author is well aware that some of the above statements regarding Islam may offend some readers. Some will no doubt be inclined to say that the author does not "understand" Islam as he is not a scholar or specialist on this subject. If one actually takes the time to provide specific historical or cultural refutation or qualification of one statement or another, the author will then immediately plead guilty as charged. But if, on the other hand, it is claimed that the author did not understand Islam by suggesting, a priori, that anyone daring criticize Islam does not "understand"

it, then, regarding the purpose of the present discussion, such an objection will be regarded as empty and meaningless. The objective here is not "enlightenment", but as far as possible, to determine the accuracy of the offered data and observations.

360 - One must of course include true Christianity in this category.

361 - Parts of this paragraph are drawn from discussions with L. Robitaille.

362 - Denys Arcand, a Quebec filmmaker, who directed the film **Le Confort et l'Indifférence** [Comfort and Indifference] (1981), knows something about such matters. His movie describes the erosion of nationalistic ideals in Quebec during the May 1980 independence referendum. The view advanced by Arcand in this movie is that Quebecers are much more attached to their material comfort than to their political ideals. Since Glasnost, directors of Russian films have also explored this theme. The film **Little Vera** (Vassili Pitchoul - 1988) comes to mind. French graphic novel creator Enki Bilal notes in this regard (Dreesens 1994):

> Ideological systems are no more. This is clear with the failure of two totally imperfect systems: capitalism and communism. The most spectacular failure of course being that of communism. We all know the tragedies this entailed. But capitalism has also failed, and liberalism attempts to restructure itself without any real ideology. If Europe struggles so much to get itself together, it is because there is no common project. There is fear and anxiety, that's all. Politicians govern with anxiety in their guts because they lack the ability to see beyond the next election. This leads to huge paradoxes.*

363 - An attitude that has its dangers, as pointed out by K. D. Bracher in his study of Nazi ideology (1970: 18):

> Leonard Krieger's **The German Idea of Freedom** (1957) analyzes acutely how, even among the majority of [German] liberals, the idea of freedom was overwhelmed by the idea of the state as a force above society assuring unity and efficiency, power and protection, and standing above the parties. In the age of Romanticism, this concept of the state, which originally sought to insure the rights of the citizen in society but which ultimately benefited defensive, conservative forces, came to dominate the legal and political thinking of the people. By accepting the primacy of external unity over internal freedom, the democratic, constitutional, and reform movements once again became subjugated to the power of the nobility, the military, and the bureaucracy.

364 - Unless all reject his status as a victim and he finds no other way out.

365 - Unless, perhaps, we were so endowed by nature's Author?

366 - Marx for example, noted in the Preface to his **Contribution to the Critique of Political Economy** (1859/1977):

> The totality of these relations of production constitutes the economic structure of society, the real foundation, on which arises a legal and political superstructure and to which correspond definite

forms of social consciousness.... It is not the consciousness of men that determines their existence, but their social existence that determines their consciousness.

Of course Marx would have excluded his own thoughts and works from such a statement... Mao, for his part, echoed Marx, saying (1963) "It is man's social being that determines his thinking."

367 - In his essay **History of Madness**, Foucault (1961/2006) noted a parallel in the Age of Enlightenment where Reason was established as the means of salvation. Following this logic, the insane were marginalized and excluded. Others, they educated. The entry on insanity in the **Universalis Encyclopaedia** observes (2003):

> The age of rationalism emphasizes this break both intellectually and socially. Descartes devoted at least one famous text to madness. But his objective was to exclude madness from the order of reason. The insane cannot think, and thinking cannot be unreasonable. The certainty of thought, which relies entirely on its immediate presence to itself — *verum est index sui*, Spinoza would say — cannot be subject to doubt. At best, the insane can only pretend to think and has nothing to teach anyone who truly thinks, except to warn against the difficulties and pitfalls that lie in ambush along the way to true thought.*

368 - This is an issue given attention to by de Tocqueville in the context of Western civilization. He notes (1840, part 2, ch. xv):

> I am no believer in the prosperity, any more than in the durability, of official philosophies; and as to state religions, I have always held, that if they be sometimes of momentary service to the interests of political power, they always, sooner or later, become fatal to the Church. Nor do I think with those who assert, that to raise religion in the eyes of the people, and to make them do honor to her spiritual doctrines, it is desirable indirectly to give her ministers a political influence which the laws deny them.

369 - Or between different religions?

370 - That is, as established by mass media (women, gays, Blacks, Native Americans, etc.). The status of victim is politically very useful. It should be understood that in the present context, 'victimhood' is, above all, a packaging method for postmodern values and assumptions.

371 - In this regard, the **Universalis Encyclopaedia** notes the mythical origin of this ritual (2003 Entry: Shiva and Shaivism):

> The wife of Shiva was first known as Sati, daughter of Daksha. Her father having failed to honour Shiva with a great sacrifice, Sati could not bear the shame of seeing her husband humiliated and killed himself by jumping into the sacrificial fire. Shiva had revenge in the form Virabhadramurti, destroying the sacrifice and manhandling all the participants. Sati was reborn as the daughter of Himalaya, known as Parvati or Uma.*

372 - Although "discussions", where no material issues are at stake, are always desirable and useful for marketing purposes...

373 - A principle succinctly described by Girard (1999/2001: 103):

> If there are only differences between religions, they make up one big undifferentiated conglomerate. We can no longer say they are true or false [any more] than we could say a story by Flaubert or Maupassant is true or false. To regard one of these stories as more true or false than the other would be absurd.

374 - And if one observes that many of these achievements are linked to the Judeo-Christian worldview, one may consider this as further indication that the postmodern is inherently a reaction to this worldview (as well as a reaction to the modern worldview, of course).

375 - That is to say, as something existing independently of the observer's will or imagination and providing the context of his existence. Philosophers call this realism and if it is denied then the experimental method becomes bogus if reality is not considered independent and cannot tell us things we do not already know...

376 - These individuals sometimes claim not to advance new dogmas, not to influence or lead. They may claim that the ethicist's role is not to assert any exclusive "illumination" or sacred knowledge, but simply to aid others to find truth, to think and judge for themselves. They help others along in their questionings, suggesting tools for understanding and discussion, but always maintaining perfect neutrality. What a load of... It should be noted that such ethics committees often do not settle ethical issues. Deciding to kill a man or a child is of course an ethical issue. Whether this is done by hanging, the guillotine, a morphine overdose or food deprivation, is simply a technical (or aesthetic) matter.

377 - That is taking morality for granted.

378 - The postmodern religion can, of course, accommodate any number of flexible, "open-minded" and inconsequential deities in its pantheon.

379 - Sade is thinking of a life-long marriage commitment here. Sade (1795/1972: 111) thus distinguishes between what he calls "exclusive property rights" (marriage), which he rejects, and the right to universal and opportunistic pleasure, which he accepts (and promotes). The rock musician Marilyn Manson pushed the logic even further. On the cover of his **Mechanical Animals** (1998) album containing the song "User Friendly" (or "Use-her"?, also addressing gender relations) one finds at the bottom, computer keyboard keys: [CTRL] [ESC] [DEL], that is to say Control (dominate), Escape (flee) and Delete (eliminate).

380 - That for a long time de Sade's writings were "forgotten" (unpublished for over a century) is perhaps due to the fact that he was an "uncomfortably consistent" modern thinker.

381 - On this issue, Pearcey observes (2004: 211-212):

> When one of the authors, Randy Thornhill, appeared on National Public Radio, he found himself deluged by angry calls, until finally he

insisted that the logic is inescapable: If evolution is true, then "every feature of every living thing, including human beings, has an underlying evolutionary background. That's not a debatable matter." Three times during the program, he hammered home the same phrase: It's "not a debatable matter." This explains why opponents of evolutionary psychology have failed to halt its rapid growth: Many accept the same evolutionary premise, which means ultimately they have no defense against its application to human behavior.... There was an amusing episode in the NPR program when Thornhill faced off against a leading feminist, Susan Brownmiller, who authored an influential book on rape many years ago called Against Our Wills. Not surprisingly, she objected strenuously to the rape thesis, and Thornhill fired back with the worst insult he could dream up: He said she was starting to sound just like "the extreme religious right." No doubt she was insulted, but the underlying point was actually serious. Thornhill was saying that evolution and evolutionary ethics are a package deal. If you accept the premise, then you must accept the conclusion. And if you don't like it, you may as well join the "religious right" and challenge evolution itself.

382 - Sometimes it can be useful to look at things from another angle. One could rephrase this by saying that the Darwinian cosmology does not demand altruism. It allows it of course, but does not demand it. This is a critical distinction. Taking into account the logical structure of Darwinian cosmology, modern and postmodern religions may then support any ethical stance, nothing is excluded. The French historian of science André Pichot explores the flexibility of the altruism concept in evolutionary thought (2000: 145):

> In short, evolutionary altruism was the source of a pseudo-naturalistic morality, making it possible to reconcile the law of the jungle with the noble savage ideology. Applied to human society, it animalizes humans by considering them as [no more than] biological organisms. Applied to animal society, it humanizes animals, through anthropomorphism, attributing to them the psychological and moral dimensions of human social behaviour. Hence the inherent reversibility of these concepts justifies both the love of animals as well as the extermination of "inferior races". This lends itself to anything and everything, from feel-good emotionalism to ruthless business dealings. Everyone found this concept convenient and everyone identified with it.*

383 - Infanticide was practiced by the ancient Phoenicians and Romans as well as by Australian aborigines (Pfeiffer 1972: 355).

384 - C. S. Lewis explored the *Tao* concept in **Mere Christianity** (Book I) as well as in **Abolition of Man**. The *Tao*, in this context, does not refer to Chinese Taoism, but rather to a universal concept of absolute and basic moral law, that is to say, accepted (with some variations) by all (ancient)

civilizations.

385 - For those old enough to remember, in the late 60s and early 70s the initial public outrage in the West at the suggestion that abortion be legalized was huge. In Canada for example, in 1975 a petition against the legalization of abortion was signed by 1 million Canadians (an unheard of number) and was sent to the Canadian federal government, but was quickly forgotten. The public reaction was so efficiently managed by media and judicial elites that now this matter is under control to the point where it is deemed "uncontroversial"...

386 - The moral of the story is of course, do NOT connect the dots... When the typical modern historian or critic examines Nazi ideology, given that he shares the same basic cosmological assumptions (materialism) as the Nazis, he finds himself forced to call the conclusions drawn by the Nazis from Darwinism "abuses". As an example, the lawyer and politician Robert Cecil once remarked (1972: 69):

> Its [Nazi ideology] primarily Germanic character derived partly from exaggerated German nationalism and partly from a peculiarly perverse adaptation of Social Darwinism. Men like Lagarde and Moeller v.d. Bruck, who had even less claim to scientific knowledge than H. S. Chamberlain, had applied to human beings the hypothesis of the survival of the fittest, in its crude physical sense, and gone on from there, by analogy, to regard nations and races as subject to the same inexorable law. Where Metzsche had rejected this perversion of Darwin's original theory, these shallow minds extended it beyond all reason by dividing nations arbitrarily into those which were still young, vigorous and destined to survive, and those which were old, sated and condemned to decline.

Several theoretical elements associated with Haeckel's and Galton's Darwinism in the nineteenth and early twentieth centuries were rejected by the generation that followed the Final Solution, as they were now perceived as tainted, of ill repute. Marketing issues seem to play a decisive role here in the final analysis. At the end of his book **The Meaning of Evolution,** professor of the history of science Robert Richards, perhaps a bit too smugly, observed (1992: 179):

> But neo-Darwinians seem to have reached general agreement that three older proposals should be dismissed: that species evolution should be modeled on individual evolution, that embryogenesis recapitulates phylogenesis; that that evolution is progressive. It is thus surprising to discover that these ideas nonetheless served in the Bauplan of Darwin's thought. Darwin was indeed the architect of the theory that has become reconstructed as neo-Darwinism. But the architect was our ancestor, who dwelt happily enough in the nineteenth-century.

Disconnection is bliss, apparently...

387 - Whereas the Reformation came to oppose centralized power in soci-

ety, the Enlightenment typically reinforced it. Early Enlightenment thinkers such as Hobbes (in **Leviathan**) grasped for familiar institutions, such as kingship, that focussed much power in the hands of one individual. Later followers of the Enlightenment dropped kingship as a proper vehicle for their ideologico-religious system and rather preferred elite groups such as science gurus, technocrats as well as cultural elites.

388 - This is linked to the fact that postmodernism is in part a reaction to the 20th century totalitarian ideologies and regimes generated by the modern religion.

389 - It seems that Thomas Jefferson was the owner of 187 slaves. One of them, Sally Hemings, became his concubine and there is reason to believe that Jefferson had several children by her.

390 - Nazism was a very pragmatic ideology. One sometimes hears the claim that Hitler was a "Christian". Hitler did in fact exploit anti-Semitism existing among German Christians (Catholics and Protestants) and used religious language to do so, but such claims typically overlook the fact that Hitler ruthlessly attacked any Christian group opposing his political objectives. Hitler's true view of Christianity (and incompatibility with Nazism) comes out of the closet in his private conversations published under the title: **Table-Talks** (1944/1973: 51, October 10th, 1941):

> War has returned to its primitive form. The war of people against people is giving place to another war — a war for the possession of the great spaces. Originally war was nothing but a struggle for pasture-grounds. Today war is nothing but a struggle for the riches of nature. By virtue of an inherent law, these riches belong to him who conquers them. The great migrations set out from the East. With us begins the ebb, from West to East. That's in accordance with the laws of nature. By means of the struggle, the elites are continually renewed. The law of selection justifies the incessant struggle by allowing the survival of the fittest. Christianity is a rebellion against natural law, a protest against nature. Taken to its logical extreme, Christianity would mean the systematic cultivation of the human failure.

In this regard, Hitler echoed attitudes previously put forward by Nietzsche in his essay **Antichrist** (1889) where he stated that Christianity is the religion of the weak and sick. Albert Camus, for his part, made this comment regarding Hitler's rhetorical exploitation of the God concept (1951: 178):

> As for Hitler, his professed religion unhesitatingly juxtaposed the God-Providence and Valhalla. Actually his god was an argument at the end of a political meeting and a manner of reaching an impressive climax at the end of speeches.

Taking into account his experience with interwar Germany, Albert Einstein can be called in as a witness in this case (in Anonymous 1940: 38):

> Being a lover of freedom, when the (Nazi) revolution came, I looked to the universities to defend it, knowing that they had

always boasted of their devotion to the cause of truth; but no, the universities were immediately silenced. Then I looked to the great editors of the newspapers, whose flaming editorials in days gone by had proclaimed their love of freedom; but they, like the universities, were silenced in a few short weeks.... Only the Church stood squarely across the path of Hitler's campaign for suppressing truth. I never had any special interest in the Church before, but now I feel a great affection and admiration for it because the Church alone has had the courage and persistence to stand for intellectual and moral freedom. I am forced to confess that what I once despised I now praise unreservedly.

Furthermore, the German historian K. D. Bracher brings to light a little known point regarding the Nazi regime (1970: 390):

The Nazi rulers to the very end were greatly concerned about the actual or potential resistance of the churches, which, according to the 1940 census, still counted 95 per cent of the population as nominal members. The elimination of this obstacle to total domination was a prime postwar objective of the regime.

391 - This an excerpt drawn from a debate that took place on April 30th, 1994 between William B. Provine and Phillip E. Johnson at Stanford University.

392 - A concept also rejected by Nietzsche in **The Twilight of the Idols**, The Four Great Errors: The Error of Free Will.

393 - Or the subjects of some other form of determinism, such as hormonal, neural or molecular.

394 - The "Kingdom" to which Monod alludes to here is obviously not the kingdom of heaven, as a Christian might conceive it, but the world of progress that moderns dream of where all will be led by a scientific, rational, enlightened and self-righteous elite. Science, becomes a means of salvation and the key to utopia!

395 - Obviously, one should expect our postmodern criminal to reject the concept of crime, consistently claiming, that such a concept is demanded by social morality, which he feels no obligation to recognize.

396 - Morality, defined in a way to ensure its compatibility with materialist cosmology, would be of no help in this context. The French philosopher Pascal Engel observes (2004: 12):

... morality is a set of attitudes or judgments involving the normative privilege of certain practical options over others regardless of the contingent goals that an individual may choose. The evolutionary perspective on ethics can be expressed in the following manner: a set of coordinated mechanisms serving a set of basic needs and interests.*

397 - This expression is apparently drawn from a book by Richard Weaver (1948) with the same title.

398 - The psychiatrist Viktor Frankl opposed determinism and noted

(1959/1971: 213):

A human being is not one thing among others; things determine each other, but man is ultimately self-determining. What he becomes — within the limits of endowment and environment — he has made out of himself. In the concentration camps, for example, in this living laboratory and on this testing ground, we watched and witnessed some of our comrades behave like swine while others behaved like saints. Man has both potentialities within himself; which one is actualized depends on decisions but not on conditions.

In this regard it may be useful to evoke an ironic quip attributed to the mathematician Henri Poincaré "One freely chooses to be a determinist."

399 - These were small Russian landowning peasants, who opposed the collectivization of land and means of production after the Soviets took power. In 1930 to 1931 the process of *dekulakization*, involved, according to Solzhenitsyn, the arrest and deportation of 15 million peasants. See **The Gulag Archipelago**, Part VI, chap. 2.

400 - Some have already given thought to how human clones could be used as organ banks. Their identity as human beings would merely be deleted, a simple administrative matter...

401 - On the other hand, a Christian researcher (a consistent Christian, it goes without saying) engaged in biotechnology research projects would have an additional moral constraint. This researcher would be accountable not only to the shareholders of the company paying his salary, but first of all to the Author of life. Accepting this premise changes everything. Of course, a Christian under postmodern influence, having assimilated the concept that religion should keep its place (in private life), will make no link between his Christian beliefs and his job. In such a case, there would be no reason to expect his behaviour or views to be distinguishable from that of any other colleague.

402 - In the former case, one can think of Alexander Solzhenitsyn and in the latter, the German philosopher Martin Heidegger, Heidegger is an interesting case as he is considered a precursor of postmodernism and remains popular with postmodern intellectuals though from 1933 to the end of WWII he was a member of the Nazi party. Gauging whether or not to commit to a fashionable position is risky business…

403 - Which recalls another verse: "The Word became flesh and made his dwelling among us. We have seen his glory, the glory of the one and only Son, who came from the Father, full of grace and truth." (John 1: 14 NIV)

404 - It seems psychological and physiological diseases contributed to his condition. Some claim he was also suffering from syphilis. In any case Nietzsche saw with great clarity the emptiness at the edge of this abyss (1883/1999: part 1, s. XVII)

Thou lonesome one, thou goest the way of the creating one: a God wilt thou create for thyself out of thy seven devils! ... With my tears, go into thine isolation, my brother. I love him who seeketh to create beyond himself, and thus succumbeth.

405 - Despite the fact that Nietzsche, for his part, rejected anti-Semitism (in contrast to his friend Richard Wagner).

406 - This paragraph contains ideas drawn from conversations with LR.

407 - That is a critical postmodern presupposition.

408 - For the present, that is...

409 - This brings to mind the Richard Sternberg case. In 2004 Sternberg lost his job at the National Museum of Natural History, Smithsonian Institution, Washington, DC for allowing the publication of a critique, in a prestigious scientific publication, of the theory of evolution, a central component of the modern cosmology. Cf: www.rsternberg.net This also brings to mind Canadian or French politicians who dared take a stand against gay marriage. How were they treated by the media?

410 - That is, when traditional religions conflict with postmodern presuppositions.

411 - Like wild animals, kept in a zoo, safe and fun to look at.

412 - If Christianity dares bring up issues such as sin or immorality for example.

413 - Though an academic would put it somewhat differently. For example: "All metanarratives must be deconstructed."

414 - This could be compared to the domestic divinities widely revered by the ancient Romans, but such rituals were never the basis for questioning, in public life, the imperial cult, which considered the emperor a god.

415 - Events where the postmodern religion is deficient and provides little meaning.

416 - Gregorian chant, for example, may be of use in soothing postmoderns' stressed-out nerves.

417 - While over a number of generations "religion" [Christianity] has been despised by Western elites expressing themselves mainly by means of verbal violence, in the long-term physical violence would be the next plausible and logical step (though this would require a break with the "tolerant" postmodern facade).

418 - Examined in preceding chapters.

419 - For more information about these issues it is pointless to consult mainstream media, particularly in French. One must seek out alternative voices, especially on the Internet. Here are some sources:

Compass Direct: www.compassdirect.org/

Voice of the Martyrs: www.persecution.com/

Or publications such as:

Nina Shea, **In the Lion's Den: Persecuted Christians**. (Broadman Holman, 1997) Paul Marshall & Lela Gilbert, **Their Blood Cries Out: The Growing Worldwide Persecution of Christians**. Word. 304 p.

420 - This may be true in the context of the marriage contract, but the Jewish woman in the ancient world did not seem particularly restricted in her economic activities as outlined in Proverbs 31: 10-16 (NIV):

A wife of noble character who can find? She is worth far more than rubies. Her husband has full confidence in her and lacks nothing of value. She brings him good, not harm, all the days of her life. She selects wool and flax and works with eager hands. She is like the merchant ships, bringing her food from afar. She gets up while it is still night; she provides food for her family and portions for her female servants. She considers a field and buys it; out of her earnings she plants a vineyard.

421 - One should not attempt to gloss over the paradoxes implied by Christianity when considering gender relations. If one consults Scripture, the woman is clearly subject to her husband (Eph 5: 24), but also equal in status (Gal 3: 28), while the man is clearly the head of the household (1 Cor 11: 3), as well as a servant to his wife (Eph 5: 25-33, Mark 9: 35). All these pieces of the puzzle are necessary to understand the Judeo-Christian perspective. In the so-called "Christian West", the empirical shortcomings in the behaviour of both sexes should not obscure the fixed goal. One should also take into account the obscuring effect of the postmodern context where the simplistic, but very widespread assumption is held that in gender relations, women are always "victims" and men always "oppressors".

422 - Julius Cesar, in his **Gallic Wars**, makes the following blunt observation on male-female relations among the ancestors of the French, the pre-Christian Gauls (1915: 6, 19):

Husbands have power of life and death over their wives as well as over their children: and when the father of a family, born in a more than commonly distinguished rank, has died, his relations assemble, and, if the circumstances of his death are suspicious, hold an investigation upon the wives in the manner adopted towards slaves; and if proof be obtained, put them to severe torture, and kill them.

423 - Is this just a coincidence? At a time when many concepts promoted by the Enlightenment had become socially dominant at the institutional level?

424 - Postmoderns on the other hand, depart somewhat from such restrictions. This plays a part in the debate in the West about alternative medicine.

425 - Chances are that a scientist challenging the dominant Darwinian cosmology will suffer career marginalization. The issue is discussed in an article by Richard Halvorson in the Harvard Political Review (2002):

At Baylor University, professor and I.D. theorist William Dembski experienced what he called "academic McCarthyism" from science faculty who withdrew funding from Dembski's research facility after discovering that his research challenged Darwinism. He compares doubting the Darwinian Orthodoxy to opposing the party line of a Stalinist regime. "What would you do if you were in Stalin's Russia and wanted to argue that Lysenko was wrong? That's the sort of situation we're in. You have to play your cards very close to the chest, and you can't really say what you're about," Dembski told the HPR. Michael Behe, a Lehigh University biochemist and I.D. theorist, told the HPR that questioning Darwinism endangers one's career. "There's good reason to be afraid. Even if you're not fired from your job, you will easily be passed over for promotions. I would strongly advise graduate students who are skeptical of Darwinian theory not to make their views known."

426 - Christianity in particular.

427 - Troubling in that it is a strong indicator of the erosion, if not the failure of their worldview. Postmodernism seems to be plan B.

428 - While Christianity has been rather efficiently marginalized in public life in Europe, the growth of Islam in Europe poses a huge challenge and will inevitably upset the apple cart... Like modernism and postmodernism, Islam targets control of key social institutions, in particular the State. The stage is set for many battles to come.

429 - 1973 is the year in which the U.S. Supreme Court, in Roe vs. Wade, issued it's decision, making abortion legal in the U.S.

430 - Or in many places in the Third world where Islam is dominant.

431 - The naked body of a man (later called Tollund Man) was discovered in a bog in 1950 near Bjaeldskor Denmark. A rope around his neck attested to the method of his execution. Because the body was so well preserved by acidic bog water it was initially believed to have been a recent murder. Human sacrifice was known in America among the Aztecs. In the ancient Middle East, several societies, including the Phoenicians, practiced child sacrifice. The Universalis encyclopaedia (2003: entry on burial)

> Both in China as well as in Mesopotamia, perhaps even among the Celts, the servants and slaves, sometimes relatives and wives of a deceased king, could became part of the funeral escort. Human sacrifices often accompanied the funeral, and victims were buried with their lord. There is evidence of this in the tombs of Ur. Subsequently, substitutions occurred, and figurines demonstrate the permanence of a rite considered too bloody. Over many years this changed in many primitive societies.

Cf also, Iron Age 'bog bodies' unveiled.

http://news.bbc.co.uk/2/hi/science/nature/4589638.stm

In the ancient world, cf:

Heinrichs, Albert. Human Sacrifice in Greek Religion. pp. 195-242 in Le sacrifice dans l'antiquité, J. Rudhardt and O. Reverdin, eds. Entretiens sur l'antiquité classique, 27. Geneva: Vandoeuvres, 1981

Twyman, Briggs L. Metus Gallicus: The Celts and Roman Human Sacrifice. pp. 1-11 The Ancient History Bulletin 11.1 1997.

Seawright, Caroline Human Sacrifice in Ancient Egypt. 11 Oct. 2003 www.thekeep.org/%7Ekunoichi/kunoichi/themestream/egypt_ humansacrifice.html

Green, A.R.W. The Roles of Human Sacrifice in the Ancient Near East. Missoula, MT: Scholars Press, 1975

Green, M. Dying for the Gods: Human Sacrifice in Iron Age and Roman

Europe. Arcadia, 2001.

Lincoln, Bruce. The Druids and Human Sacrifice. pp. 176-87 in Death, War and Sacrifice: Studies in Ideology and Practice. Univ. of Chicago Press, Chicago 1991

Lawrence E. Stager and Samuel R. Wolff, Child Sacrifice at Carthage: Religious Rite or Population Control?, Biblical Archaeology Review, Jan. - Feb., 1984, pp. 31-51

Brien K. Garnand, From Infant Sacrifice to the ABC's: Ancient Phoenicians and Modern Identities. Stanford Journal of Archeology vol. 1 2002. www.stanford.edu/dept/archaeology/journal/newdraft/garnand/paper. pdf

432 - http://en.wikipedia.org/wiki/File:Gundestrupkarret3.jpg

433 - Made of gilded bronze, decorated with gold filigree and studs. See: http://www.museum.ie/en/list/artefacts.aspx?article=bfcd87b3-c3b1-489c-84f3-5c8bc08cc471
http://en.wikipedia.org/wiki/Ardagh_Hoard

434 - Of course, some will view this position as going "too far", as it implies a limited admission of dependence on the Judeo-Christian worldview.

435 - This painting was done in 1898 while Gauguin was living in Tahiti and seriously thinking of suicide. After its completion, he took arsenic. He wanted to die, but vomited the poison. He would live.

436 - Many years before, discussing Enlightenment thinkers of his time, Pascal arrived at much the same conclusion (1670/1908: section II, 77):

> I cannot forgive Descartes. In all his philosophy he would have been quite willing to dispense with God. But he had to make Him give a fillip to set the world in motion; beyond this, he has no further need of God.

437 - But of course repackaged and marketed using progressive, postmodern rhetoric.

438 - The codename for this operation was drawn from the Berlin main office address, "4, Tiergartenstrasse" (in English, Zoo Street).

439 - If the story line sounds familiar to our postmodern generation, it should...

440 - And related traits such as having interests, tastes, etc. But a further question arises: How does one go about developing an identity if not by interacting with others who differ from me? But what if the momentum of deconstruction should be pursued here too? What if others are only arbitrary constructs? Why should they limit my identity (even if only in contrast)?

441 - This issue is examined in the first chapter of C. S. Lewis' book **Mere Christianity.**

442 - Either as a potential mating partner or as an edible object...

443 - One should take into consideration that Borisov's comments were written before the fall of the Iron Curtain, which occurred in the USSR in the late 1980's.

444 - If one rejects absolute moral standards, everyday life may at times call this into question, as in the following anecdote narrated by Francis Schaeffer (1982/1994: v. 1, 110):

> One day I was talking to a group of people in the room of a young South African in Cambridge University. Among others, there was present a young Indian who was of Sikh background, but a Hindu by religion. He started to speak strongly against Christianity, but did not really understand the problems of his own beliefs. So I said, "Am I not correct in saying that on the basis of your system, cruelty and noncruelty are ultimately equal, that here is no intrinsic difference between them?" He agreed. The people who listened and knew him as a delightful person, an "English gentleman" of the very best kind, looked up in amazement. But the student in whose room we met, who had clearly understood the implications of what the Sikh had admitted, picked up his kettle of boiling water with which he was about to make tea, and stood with it steaming over the Indian's head. The man looked up and asked him what he was doing, and he said with a cold yet gentle finality, "There is no difference between cruelty and noncruelty." Thereupon the Hindu walked out into the night.

445 - One may compare, for example, the views of the father of modern eugenics movement (Charles Darwin's cousin) Francis Galton and the actions of the Nazis. Durant notes regarding Galton (1981: 428):

> In 1865, he published his first article on these subjects, arguing that in man mental ability is heavily influenced by inheritance. From this basis, Galton made the following rather startling prediction: 'what an extraordinary effect might be produced on our race if its object was to unite in marriage those who possessed the finest and most suitable natures, mental, moral and physical!' (...) With this suggestion the modern eugenics movement was born.

And what did Hitler say in **Mein Kampf**? That which Galton could only dream of, Hitler had the power to accomplish... (1925/1941: 608-609):

> He who is not physically and mentally healthy and worthy must not perpetuate his misery in the body of his child.... The prevention of the procreative faculty and possibility on the part of physically degenerated and mentally sick people, for only six hundred years, would not only free mankind of immeasurable misfortune, but would also contribute to a restoration that appears hardly believable today. If thus the conscious methodical promotion of the fertility of the most healthy bearers of the nationality is realized, the result will be a race which, at least at first, will have eliminated the germs of our present physical, and with it of the spiritual, decline.

The logic is identical; the only difference lies in these individuals power to implement their beliefs and aspirations. And in this respect, Hitler and Galton echoed Darwin's thoughts, as brutally expressed in **The Descent of**

Man (1871: 168):

> We civilized men... do our utmost to check the process of elimination; we build asylums for the imbecile, the maimed, and the sick; we institute poor laws; and our medical men exert their utmost skill to save the life of everyone to the last moment.... Thus the weak members of civilized societies propagate their kind. No one who has attended to the breeding of domestic animals will doubt that this must be highly injurious to the race of man. It is surprising how soon a want of care, or care wrongly directed, leads to the degeneration of a domestic race; but excepting in the case of man himself, hardly anyone is so ignorant as to allow his worst animals to breed.

446 - Except perhaps in proffering subjective feelings of indignation or disgust...

447 - In a text written in the early 1970's, amidst student protest movements, the sociologist (and Catholic priest) Andrew M. Greeley echoed Borisov's comments regarding the autonomy of ethics from religious beliefs, where ethics finds its source (1972: 212):

> The assumption of the conventional wisdom, then, that ethics can be divorced from religion and that men can make moral judgments without reference to principles or powers outside themselves seems to be both unreal and too optimistic. The profoundly religious outrage of some segments of the young against what they take to be the moral abuses of adult society is based on the implicit assumption that there is not only evil in the world, but sinfulness. Why else be angry at a man for doing evil unless you think he is responsible for his evil? Why else demand that people be moral, save if you believe they are capable of giving up their immorality? Why else try to reform society unless one believes that there are certain absolute social principles which ought to characterize human behavior? And if they are absolute, whence comes this absolutism? Here the conventional wisdom is able to provide no answer; but then if it can't even explain — not as long as it is following its own principles of rational and scientific progressivism — why there should be either immorality or outrage when both are profoundly nonrational activities.

448 - Translator's note: The original French term "esprit" is not easily translated as it combines concepts such as mind and spirit.

449 - That is to say, based solely on materialistic assumptions.

450 - Among twentieth-century behaviorists, determinism was generally viewed as environmental (or more specifically, social). The Judeo-Christian perspective offers a way out of determinism, though a rather paradoxical way out. It claims that at the end of time all the acts and words of men will be judged. This judgement implies that man is responsible for his actions. This responsibility implies, in turn, the capacity to make good and bad choices. And choosing involves being free, not determined, with the ability to discern between good and evil as well as being held accountable for

the use of this ability... To fill in the picture, one must add the concepts of the Fall and man's fallen nature, that is to say, that humans have the ability to recognize good, but still do evil nonetheless (Rom. 7: 21-24).

451 - In Social Anthropology, this is precisely what Franz Boas proposed in the early twentieth-century. In his view, anthropology should be only concerned with empirical evidence, rejecting the development of theories and generalizations. Hatch notes that before the Second World War, the influence of the empiricist attitude was crumbling as it offered no answers to the serious questions confronting twentieth-century man (1983: 106):

> Perhaps this development was not unrelated to world affairs. The general pessimism of the 1920s, the worldwide economic collapse of the 1930s and World War II stimulated a sense of crisis within the discipline. The world was in trouble, deep trouble, and the best anthropologists could do in response, it seemed, was to gather coyote tales and moccasin designs. What was needed was a scientific understanding of humanity that the world could use and that would distinguish the discipline.

It is clear from the context here that at the heart of the anthropological endeavour one finds an ideologico-religious objective, that is to say the urge to establish a cosmology providing a framework of meaning for human life.

452 - Of course the disintegration of the family in the West has contributed to this burden.

453 - In many cases, disillusioned intellectuals from the Left, set adrift by the failure of socialism in the twentieth-century.

454 - Postmoderns talk about the end of History (with a capital), in the sense that they reject the Western concept of history as something objective, but view it rather as a cultural construct. From that point on, there are only stories, tales, legends...

455 - This is not the only such conceptual taboo, but we will return to this matter later on...

456 - This link was pointed out to me by Gib McInnnis.

457 - This challenge to the postulate of an external world, subject to laws, had already been foreseen by David Hume in his **Treatise of Human Nature** (1740) in which he offered several objections to the concept of causality, a principle essential to scientific research.

458 - Later on, Pepperell provides the reason for this assumption (1997: 23):

> In a political sense, materialism seemed to prove what was obvious to many: that humans were responsible for their own conduct and conditions without reference to a mysterious outside agency such as God.

If materialism's sole objective was to get rid of the Great Busybody in the sky, this seems consistent enough, but attempting to develop morality and human responsibility on this basis embodies a rather naive optimism.

459 - Which does not propose a Creator making his own moral demands.

460 - Or a slave to…

461 - Perhaps the expression "the Matrix" would be just as appropriate…

462 - Specifically, Pepperell says (1997: 186):

> The Post-Human is entirely open to ideas of 'paranormality', "immateriality", the "supernatural", and the "occult". The Post-Human does not accept that faith in scientific methods is superior to faith in other belief systems.

463 - Such as Raymond Kurzweil, Marvin Minsky, Hayles and Pepperell.

464 - If a supercomputer like Deep Blue can beat a chess grandmaster such as Gary Kasparov (in some matches) does this prove that a computer "thinks" or is "superior" to man? What exactly does this prove? Other questions arise, including: Did Kasparov really play chess against a computer or should we consider rather that he played against a team of programmers and chess experts, aided by a machine? To challenge a grandmaster, one certainly cannot simply supply a cage full of monkeys with keyboards to fiddle on as a reply to Kasparov's moves. In actual fact, Deep Blue physically represents a large team of experienced programmers and chess experts. In this context, how is one then to determine the machine's own specific contribution to the outcome? Would such a machine even know what its particular strengths (such as massive memory or processing power) were if humans weren't there to recognize and exploit them?

465 - Or a lesser-known movie such as **Android** (1982), directed by Aaron Lipstadt.

466 - Perhaps it should come as no surprise that this work was voted science fiction's most influential twentieth-century movie by the BBC in 2004.

467 - That is memories of a childhood and parents they never had…

468 - In the novel **Do Androids Dream of Electric Sheep?**, Dick examines the concept of empathy and presents this [via Deckard's thoughts] as a paradox, for all intents and purposes, incompatible with the logic of the evolutionary cosmology (1968/1982: 26):

> For one thing, the empathic faculty probably required an unimpaired group instinct; a solitary organism, such as a spider, would have no use for it; in fact it would tend to abort a spider's ability to survive. It would make him conscious of the desire to live on the part of his prey. Hence all predators, even highly developed mammals such as cats, would starve. Empathy, he once had decided, must be limited to herbivores or anyhow omnivores who could depart from a meat diet. Because, ultimately, the empathic gift blurred the boundaries between hunter and victim, between the successful and the defeated.

469 - Which does not appear in the book.

470 - Dyson was involved in the Manhattan Project, which produced the first atomic bomb during World War II.

471 - Philips notes that with respect to consciousness, AI devotees defend contradictory perspectives. In some contexts, they argue that mind and brain are identical and in others, that spirit (or consciousness) is distinct

and can be downloaded (2000: chap 2):

> While they don't want to say that the mind is a "substance" distinct from the brain, and wish rather to think of the mind as in some sense nothing more than the brain or even identical to the brain, they also tend to think of it as the program that the brain runs when it is operating. On this analogy, the mind is to the brain as a program is to a computer and as software is to hardware. We need to keep this metaphor or model in mind in trying to understand the viewpoint of our authors. Our authors have humans in the future being able to "port" themselves all over the place from machine to machine as the need arises. If they don't think of the mind as a piece of software, of the type of stored program that runs in a von Neumann architecture, it is hard to see how they could envision this sort of thing happening. But the mind as software is more than a metaphor to them. Their predominant view is that the mind is literally a program. For example, Moravec (1999, p. 210) thinks that humans will exist in the extraordinary future as artificial intelligence programs running on platforms other than the human brain. As programs, our minds might be laser-beamed at the speed of light to inhabit distant robot brains (Moravec, 1988, p. 214).

472 - Asimov's solution to this story's central question is ambiguous, full of irony (for an atheist with a Jewish background).

473 - Which is linked to sex of course, one of the means of salvation offered by pomos.

474 - She is the author of the book **Close to the Machine** (1997).

475 - This is more than gratuitous irony involved here as Minsky himself entitles his article **Will Robots Inherit the Earth?**, making a thinly veiled allusion to the Gospels (in fact to the Beatitudes) where Christ said that: "The meek shall inherit the Earth."

476 - From this point on, the story line from **I-Robot** (Asimov 1950) becomes a real world possibility.

477 - When Turing first formulated this idea, he included gender as a significant factor. One of the contestants had to be female while the other attempted to imitate a woman's style of conversation. Later, Turing ignored this distinction.

478 - At present, the test is done through the exchange of text messages only. The unrestricted test would involve the ability to process audio and visual data as well.

479 - The ALICE system (developed by Richard Wallace) has won the competition a number of times (as the most human-like computer).

480 - At the time of writing (2006).

481 - Though of course the research done may be of interest for other purposes.

482 - This is pertinent regarding the existence of messages [which must be contrasted with the concept of information, that the author confuses in the

following quote] in the biological world. Stephen Meyer, a director at the controversial Discovery Institute and Ph.D. in history of science at Cambridge, writes (in Glassman 1997):

> When we encounter information in any other domain of life, and we know the causal story about how that information came about, whether it's a headline on a newspaper, or an ancient inscription, or a message coming in on a radio signal, we infer that there is an intelligence behind that. And what you have in the cell is what Bill Gates called a software program, only much more complex than any we've been able to devise. And we know that the information in a software program came from a programmer. And many scientists are beginning to suspect that the same thing is true of DNA. On the DNA, you have a four-letter chemical alphabet, complete with punctuation. It has stop and start codons to indicate the beginning and end of the message. And this information on DNA has created the suspicion, I think, among a lot of scientists, that what they're looking at is a hallmark of mind, or an artifact of intelligence.

483 - This issue was explored over 30 years ago by R. L. Purtill (1971: 294):

> Let me get away entirely from the "imitation game" and state my most basic objection in this way: any output of any computer presently existing or foreseeable on the basis of present technology can be explained as the result of a program, inserted into the machine by a human programmer or the interaction of such a program and inputs of various kinds (e.q. data). Except for mechanical malfunctions the output is totally determined by the program and the input. In some programs a random element is inserted into the program, but even in such cases the range of possible outputs, the relative frequency of various outputs, etc., is determined by the program and the nature of the randomizing device. Any computer output can be explained along these lines.

And even when one adds a random element, the fact remains that this element is still part of the program. Its presence and interventions are linked to the programmers' objectives. Ultimately, the computer's behaviour is always strictly determined by the content of its programming and whether it includes random elements or not. An acquaintance who is an engineer and experienced in developing real time resource management software, made the following remarks on this subject: "If Artificial Intelligence had truly fulfilled its promises, all the research labs in the world would be empty and staffed only with machines. I think I have pushed computers as far as they can go in real time applications (at present) and I come away with the following findings:

- A computer system (including all software and peripherals) is essentially the representation of a process as the designer understands it, **no more**. It is not radically different from other means used by humans to process information and produce conclusions such as philosophy, mathematics, chemistry or politics.

- The notion that a computer can "learn" is an assumption, as "learning" and the human learning process do not have precise and unquestionable definitions. "Artificial intelligence" also demands precise definitions and understanding of human intelligence (as a minimum, considering other intelligence forms may exist!), which we do not have (and are far from having in my opinion). To emulate intelligence "artificially", you need a firm understanding of the nature and structure of the "real thing" and we're not even close to such knowledge yet!

- Even if a computer system can correct itself (a simplistic and misguided characterisation of intelligent behaviour…), it can only do so to the extent that it has been developed to perceive defined deviations. It cannot detect problems which it was not made aware of or given means to evaluate (a critical issue in practice)… while humans seem to perceive issues they were not even looking for or did not suspect initially.

- And this sensibility to meaning and knowledge elements (concepts, troubleshooting, analysis, discrepancies, hidden consequences,..) is very complex to even describe and even more so to comprehend or predict. It is not programmable in any type of computer system, while repetitive and systematic processes can be. These latter can be made to correct themselves, within a given paradigm, but never outside it, an extremely limiting factor.

- Furthermore, the fact that a computer system can produce results that are unexpected is far from proof of intelligence. In most cases it is a demonstration of the system designer's lack of comprehension of the examined process (frequently the case) or simply the consequence of a faulty system at the operation or design level (or both…).

- The computer's speed of calculation and the flow of information it can put out are so large that the designer's feedback capability in the design process of the system is severely limited to the point where mistakes made in development may only be noticed at a very late point or not at all;

- Computers and software provide amplified means to manipulate a huge number of factors that can be analyzed within a study or a process of reflection, over and into a stunning number of dimensions, structured in vast and complex relations. Human ability to conceptualize and efficiently use such inference systems is extraordinarily low, even among researchers. This highlights the fact that the mental models we develop attempt to model processes we do not yet understand. This demonstrates, in my opinion, that man simply does not understand how he thinks!

Computers can pour out torrents of data, totally indifferent to meaning or purpose, leaving bewildered humans, confronted with an overwhelming blast of "information" (whatever that is). This is of course a huge, stupefying adrenaline rush, but it is also confusing and disorienting. Big clouds of smoke can be thrown in people's faces and labelled "knowledge", to intimidate them, but not for the sake of legitimate science. From this point of view, when men seek to build a machine that thinks like him (or better), it's like a kid putting on a Superman costume and thinking he can then fly off the balcony... Something just hasn't clicked...!"

484 - If one were to naïvely take the Loebner competition at face value, one might as well watch a sci-fi movie and think everything was filmed as is, without a director, actors, set designers, musicians, costume designers, stuntmen, CGI or video editors.

485 - The first such encounter took place in 1989, when the Deep Thought software-computer package was opposed on several occasions to Gary Kasparov and Anatoly Karpov (with a rematch in 1991). Deep Thought was not able to win any of these matches. In May 1997, Gary Kasparov played a series of six matches against Deep Blue. Final verdict: Kasparov: 2.5; Deep Blue: 3.5. For information on the team responsible for the development of Deep Blue, see (Hsu 1990) and: www.research.ibm.com/deepblue/meet/html/d.4.html

486 - This does not make any judgement about the teenager's intelligence, but pertains more to his motivation to express his intelligence...

487 - Unless, of course, the programmer also had a sudden inspiration just before the test.

488 - And of course, this demands that his programming skills allow him to put such information to use.

489 - Turing did not consider this matter.

490 - This also demands that the hardware must be up to the task required by the software.

491 - And what happens if you erase the computer's software (or operating system)? What's left? The computer then becomes no more than a clunky and useless knick-knack.

492 - Not to mention the computer's hardware design features and processing power which owe their existence to the engineer's creativity and hard work.

493 - Or perhaps a priest with long experience with the ritual of confession.

494 - Despite dramatic advances in computer technology since 1950, one of Turing's rather over-confident predictions has not been fulfilled (1950: 442):

> I believe that in about fifty years' time, it will be possible to programme computers with a storage capacity of about 10^9, to make them play the imitation game so well that an average interrogator will not have more than 70 per-cent chance of making the right identification after five minutes of questioning. The original question, 'Can machines think?' I believe to be too meaningless to deserve discussion.

495 - As an argument, solipsism states that the thinking subject will only accept the existence of its self and its manifestations. This is a form of subjectivity carried to great extremes, ultimately involving the denial of an external world.

496 - One of the objections to Searle's argument is that although one can assume that Searle-in-the-Chinese-room does not understand Chinese, the whole system does. This type of argument involves a somewhat magical conception of a critical component of the system, that is to say, the reference book. In the real world, such books are not produced without the involvement of intelligent agents. This being the case, in considering the entire system, it would then be unacceptable to exclude the agent responsible for writing the reference book.

497 - Already in section 7 (Learning Machines) of his paper, Turing does not hesitate to use this kind of rhetoric (1950):

> These last two paragraphs do not claim to be convincing arguments. They should rather be described as 'recitations tending to produce belief'.

498 - Halpern would agree and in the same article notes on this matter (1987: 79):

> It has achieved this unprecedented celebrity by providing what I shall call a thought-drama: a script for an unperformed, and perhaps unperformable, coup de théâtre that provides, as is traditional for drama, an arena in which abstract and elusive issues become concrete and immediate, at whatever cost to clarity and rigour. This thought-drama, commonly known as Turing's Test, is often appealed to by the practitioners and publicists of Artificial Intelligence (AI) as if it were a thought-experiment that provided strong evidential support for an AI hypothesis. What it in fact provides is a myth, and what it supports is not a hypothesis but an ideology. My purpose here is to examine the remarkable career of Turing's paper and in particular of Turing's Test, and to explore the ideology that, finding in the Test such powerful emotional support, has made it the best known philosophical image since that of Plato's Cave.

I would add a more specific claim, namely that the TT can be legitimately viewed as an origins myth and, in much the same way that Darwin's **Origin of the Species** broke the cosmological Man/Animal distinction, the TT lays low the old Man/Inanimate world distinction.

499 - This would apply as well to what Turing calls the "heads in the sand objection", to which it is linked.

500 - Here is the comment from another Brit, a contemporary who may have encountered Turing's comments. In a way, C. S. Lewis returns Turing's irony (Lewis 1961/2001: 81-82):

> Can a mortal ask questions which God finds unanswerable? Quite easily, I should think. All nonsense questions are unanswerable. How many hours are there in a mile? Is yellow square or round?

Probably half the questions we ask — half our great theological and metaphysical problems — are like that.

501 - That said, there remain certain paradoxes in a character like Turing. Jorion observes (2000: 264):

> The only significant event mentioned by those close to him as a harbinger of his death (this event occurred about ten days before) was an — an unusually long — appointment with a fortune teller which left him pale and obviously in acute distress.*

502 - Clearly such "reluctance" may have other causes since an individual making coherent use of Gödel's theorem would also have to dare question a fundamental assumption of the modern ideologico-religious system, that is to say that the cosmos is a closed system. To the preceding, Lucas adds (1961):

> Goedel's theorem must apply to cybernetical machines, because it is of the essence of being a machine, that it should be a concrete instantiation of a formal system. It follows that given any machine which is consistent and capable of doing simple arithmetic, there is a formula which it is incapable of producing as being true — i.e., the formula is unprovable-in-the-system-but which we can see to be true. It follows that no machine can be a complete or adequate model of the mind, that minds are essentially different from machines.

503 - Cf. Jorion (2000: 252):

> Regarding the actual possibility of an "artificial intelligence", it is curious that the Turing machine is seen as an argument in the same mathematical discussion (the "Hilbert program") as Gödel's famous "incompleteness theorem", which is usually raised to prove that such an endeavour is impossible. Indeed, while the Turing machine is seen as supporting the point of view of feasibility, "Gödel's theorem" is always invoked (for example, by Penrose [1989, 1994]) to prove that a machine will never be able to reproduce human-like thinking. The reason for this apparent paradox is that the actors in the artificial intelligence debate refer to Gödel or Turing to support views on different levels: Turing, when emphasizing the impossibility of distinguishing [human] thought processes from those of complex software, Gödel, when suggesting that the human mind, which can conceptualize the incompleteness of arithmetic, exceeds it in some way, and is therefore able to operate on a different level.*

Although he published before Gödel, there is a curious parallel, in terms of logic, when Wittgenstein states, in the context of a discussion on ethics (1921/1922: 6.41-42): "The sense of the world must lie outside the world. In the world everything is as it is and happens as it does happen. In it there is no value — and if there were, it would be of no value. If there is a value which is of value, it must lie outside all happening and being-so. For all happening and being-so is accidental."

504 - One suspects a scientist such as Victor Frankenstein would have

387

admired such a composite creature.

505 - Whose main function is to profitably exploit science's sacred aura...

506 - But since a statement of this kind would be "irritating" for the average posthuman proponent, they will inevitably ignore it or deny it at all costs.

507 - According to J. - F. Lyotard, even in a cosy university setting, such questions also arise (1979/1984: 51):

> The question (overt or implied) now asked by the professionalist student, the State, or institutions of higher education is no longer "Is it true?" but "What use is it?" In the context of the mercantilization of knowledge, more often than not this question is equivalent to: "Is it saleable?" And in a context of power-growth: "Is it efficient?"

508 - Though there is good reason to be optimistic about postmodern man's technical capabilities, regarding his ethical capacities, it would perhaps better to be prudent (and rather pessimistic).

509 - It seems likely that this danger may result mainly from multinational economic interests rather than from a military, racist ideology as was the case with the Nazis.

510 - On this matter, the philosopher Francis Schaeffer mentions (1982/1994, vol. 5: 124):

> It is important that the Bible sets forth true knowledge about mankind. The biblical teaching gives meaning to all particulars, but this is especially so in regard to that particular which is the most important to man, namely, the individual himself or herself. It gives a reason for the individual being great. The ironic fact here is that humanism, which began with Man's being central, eventually had no real meaning for people. On the other hand, if one begins with the Bible's position that a person is created by God and created in the image of God, there is a basis for that person's dignity. People, the Bible teaches, are made in the image of God, they are nonprogrammed. Each is thus Man with dignity.

511 - As Freud would have claimed?

512 - The Old Testament alludes to these matters: "Those who trust in their wealth and boast of their great riches? No one can redeem the life of another or give to God a ransom for them the ransom for a life is costly, no payment is ever enough." (Ps. 49: 6-8 NIV). In the New Testament, when questioned by the Pharisees about the legitimacy of healing a man on the Sabbath, Jesus responded, "If any of you has a sheep and it falls into a pit on the Sabbath, will you not take hold of it and lift it out? How much more valuable is a person than a sheep! Therefore it is lawful to do good on the Sabbath." (Matthew 12: 11-12 NIV).

513 - This quote appears in the postscript (The Case For A Tragic Optimism) of the 1984 edition.

514 - Or Genetically Modified Organisms.

515 - Further information is available in "Nazi human experimentation", http://encyclopedia.thefreedictionary.com/Nazi%20human%20experi-

388

Notes

mentation
516 - The French Universalis encyclopaedia notes (2003, entry: Shoah):
   In 1941 genocide was launched in Europe. In this regard we now have access to a crucial document, the minutes of the famous Wannsee Conference, held in Berlin, on January 20, 1942. According to testimony given by Eichmann in Jerusalem, the minutes were "cleaned up", not everything that had been said was disclosed, but most important matters were covered. Convened by Reinhard Heydrich, one of Heinrich Himmler's assistants who was directly responsible for Nazi police, the conference brought together state secretaries of key ministries. Himmler and Heydrich, who bore the responsibility of executing this crime, needed the cooperation of the German bureaucracy.*
517 - From a consistent Judeo-Christian perspective, humans are not part of one "race", but rather all humans belong to one family, a family fallen from its original condition.
518 - As well as the mentally and physically handicapped, Poles, homosexuals and others deemed "inferior" or "undesirable" by the Nazi's racial genetics program.
519 - Commenting this passage, André Pichot writes (2009: 62-63):
   It is amusing to see Haeckel disguise himself as St. Francis of Assisi, especially after he has classified human races in a pitiless evolutionary hierarchy. ... In actual fact, Haeckel's hatred of Christianity is above all antipapism, bound up in his case with a pan-Germanism that is both political and racial, in particular asserting the superiority of the Indo-Germanics ... The Monist League that Haeckel founded to propagate his doctrine is today viewed as one of the nurseries in which the ideas that would develop into Nazi biological-political doctrine were elaborated.
520 - See also: www.ccac.ca/fr/publications/publicat/resource/vol221/art2221e.htm
And a French article: Cédric Gouverneur, **Vers une écologie radicale: Les guérilleros de la cause animale**. Le Monde Diplomatique août 2004 pp. 1, 12-13
www.monde-diplomatique.fr/2004/08/gouverneur/11463
521 - CSIS is the Canadian Security Intelligence Service. A 1992 CSIS report discusses violent acts by animal rights groups.
www.csis.gc.ca/pblctns/cmmntr/cm21-eng.asp
522 - The Universal Declaration of Animal Rights was proclaimed in Paris, October 15th, 1978, at UNESCO Headquarters. The text was revised in 1989 by the International League of Animal Rights and released in 1990. Cf: http://league-animal-rights.org/duda.html
www.ch-br.net/quatropatasecia/e/infos/animal_rights.htm
523 - While the concept of "rights" appears completely out of nowhere. How an evolutionary cosmology might coherently support this concept is not

justified by the authors of the declaration and one wonders if it might simply evaporate in a context where survival of the fittest is bottom line.

524 - An "antispecist" is someone who rejects speciesism, which is the assigning of different values or rights to beings on the basis of their species membership (in particular humans). It should be noted that no non-humans are known to be antispecists.

525 - Putallaz offers two criticisms of Singer's views that are worthy of attention (2003):

It is rather easy to ridicule Singer's views by turning one of his arguments against him and state that when Singer is sleeping he is not a rational self-conscious being [and no longer human]. But the serious point I think is the issue of pain assessment. Who gets to assess [capacity for] pain? Who measures one's total amount of happiness? Singer himself does this. I think this is outrageous and very dangerous. It amounts to, as they say in the English-speaking world, taking on a Godlike position in ethics.*

526 - Considering man as just one animal among others involves a paradox and a contradiction which most generally miss. Genetics does not send us a clear message; sometimes we appear closer to, sometimes more distant from other primates. Studies on certain sets of chromosomes show greater differences than expected between men and chimpanzees. It all depends on the genetic reference point that is used for these comparisons. Cathy Holding **Chimps are not like humans**. www.freerepublic.com/focus/f-news/1151270/posts

That said, in the cosmological context in which Singer operates, he is entirely consistent in his reasoning.

527 - The operation is usually invisible as it involves recycling values drawn from the West's cultural baggage, artefacts inherited from Christianity. Because these values and attitudes have been around for so long, they seem "natural" or commonsensical, but when taken out of their Christian context, they can easily dissipate in the winds of social change.

528 - Isn't this just another example of typical Western arrogance? Is it fair to say this? How ironic when such rhetoric comes from the mouth of postmodern materialists! If they grant themselves the right to criticize the Christian Middle Ages and the Inquisition, their criticisms typically go unchallenged, but mostly because of logical inertia. If a Christian criticises the Inquisition, his criticism is coherent as this institution violated the image of God inscribed in man, particularly man's freedom. His criticism is justified, as it is founded on a logical and cosmological plane. When a postmodern criticizes the Inquisition, on what basis can he do so? To which universal concept of justice will he appeal to criticize this institution, so far away from him in time as well as in terms of culture? And if he does, where does he get this universal concept of justice? Does his cosmology demand such an attitude? Is his behaviour really coherent?

529 - This phrase is attributed to Irina Dunn, an Australian educator, jour-

nalist and politician (possibly shortly after her divorce with Brett Collins?).
530 - And, possibly, discarded when this need is no longer felt ?
531 - Of course moralistic remarks of this kind would be despised by gay elites in the West. What they seek is not "understanding", but rather the acceptance of their ideological and religious presuppositions, in other words, conversion (to their worldview).
532 - With Schaeffer, the "line of despair" concept, involves the abandonment of Reason as a guide as well as the development of a coherent cosmology. In basic terms, it is a rejection of the Enlightenment. This leads therefore to systems of thought stressing the need for an act of faith or the irrational (a leap of faith) in order to ensure morality or salvation/fulfilment. It is also an admission of the impossibility of erecting a coherent worldview, one capable of accounting for all aspects of human experience upon the Enlightenment basis. The observed impotence of the Enlightenment worldview typically leads to syncretism. Stephen Jay Gould's NOMA concept is one manifestation (among others) of such an outcome. Several schools of twentieth-century Western thought, including existentialism and surrealism promote such a perspective.
533 - Cf: **Three of Hearts: A Postmodern Family**. Reviewed by Stephen Holden NY Times 2004. http://movies2.nytimes.com/gst/movies/movie.html?v_id=314759
www.imdb.com/title/tt0424496/
534 - Cf: **Here Come the Brides**. Stanley Kurtz
www.weeklystandard.com/Content/PublicArticles/000/000/006/494pqobc.asp?pg=1
535 - What might the rather shocking discovery of the normality of complementarity mean to a postmodern couple, a discovery in conflict with the surrounding culture and their education? A US travel magazine published an account of a typical young postmodern couple who went out and bought a sailboat (named "Lucy") in view of going off on an adventure cruise around the world or, at least, attempting to cross a few oceans. On ce at sea, they find themselves having to take responsibility for all the tasks involved in such an enterprise. How do you divide things up, how do you decide who does what? They were surprised at their own behaviour (Bennett 2005: 83):

> After a couple of weeks aboard Lucy, we woke up one morning to find that we'd divided all the onboard duties into pink tasks and blue tasks. It was as if we'd sailed back in time 40 years. And it was this way for nearly every other boat we ran into. The woman aboard was in charge of organizing and cleaning and maintaining the living space below decks; the man was in charge of making sure everything worked. She was June Cleaver and he was Mr. Goodwrench — even if in real life she was a trial lawyer and he was a science teacher. The division left us constantly bewildered. Were we more content in these traditional roles? It was a somewhat unsettling idea.

536 - This was the technology used to produce "Dolly", the cloned sheep, the first mammal developed from a cell of an adult animal.

537 - To produce pharmaceuticals based on genetic engineering.

538 - 'Fluorescent fish' give the green light to GM pets. Robin McKie, The Observer, June 15, 2003. http://education.guardian.co.uk/higher/news/story/0,9830,978391,00.html

539 - A Latin expression, meaning: Out of nothing.

540 - Now of course cars cannot "magically" reproduce by themselves, but organisms can do so.

541 - For further information on this subject, see: the Center for Environmental Risk Assessment, GM Crop Database: http://www.cera-gmc.org/?action=gm_crop_database

542 - On this subject, see: Maryann Mott, Animal-Human Hybrids Spark Controversy. January 25, 2005 http://news.nationalgeographic.com/news/2005/01/0125_050125_chimeras.html
Rabbit Eggs Used to Grow Human Stem Cells. www.medtech1.com/new_tech/new_tech_pf.cfm?newsarticle=138

543 - Several scientific journals have refused to publish articles discussing experiments on human embryos.

544 - Even if one considers the influence of traditional breeders, using selection to favour certain genetic traits in the animals or plants they raise, such efforts are always limited by the traits available in the species gene pool.

545 - It is possible of course that other genetic techniques (presently existing or under development) may further challenge human corporeality, our biological nature.

546 - Programs such as the *Ahnenerbe* (Ancestral Heritage) and the *Lebensborn* (Spring of Life) offered their contributions. It should be noted that Germany was not the only nation to impose eugenic laws. In fact, the United States was the first to enact such legislation (later inspiring the Nazis) and Denmark and Sweden were among the last to abolish such laws. In this regard see Pichot (2009: chapter 9). The Nazis were not the only ones developing such projects. The American eugenicist, Hermann Joseph Muller, a Nobel Prize in Physiology and Medicine (1946), suggested the idea of a sperm bank which was later founded by Robert K. Graham in New York under the name of The Repository for Germinal Choice (now in California), which consisted of a collection of semen samples from great men, some of whom were Nobel Prize winners (Pichot 2000: 233).

547 - But this is not always the case, as recently it has been found that one could recover stem cells from the bone marrow of adult humans rather than human embryos.

548 - That is when taking in consideration only existing technologies...

549 - In 1983, Canada allowed the commercial production of insulin drawn from genetically modified E. coli bacteria. Today, this insulin is used in

diabetes treatment.

550 - This is not the case for all biotechnologies: cloning for example typically deals only with genetic material from one individual.

551 - Cf. **Asilomar and Recombinant DNA.** Paul Berg (section: Voluntary Moratorium) http://nobelprize.org/chemistry/articles/berg/
Les enjeux des OGM: Un peu d'histoire.
www.cirad.fr/fr/dossier/ogm/enjeux.html

552 - Initially, I thought of adding the cosmological assumptions of political leaders and scientists to this list, but since their core beliefs are postmodern, it would be pointless to do so. As noted above by P. - P. Grasse (1980: 44), in the 1930s German scientific and cultural elites, sharing the same cosmological assumptions as the Nazis, overwhelmingly supported Nazi programs when these were put into action.

553 - The credit for this accomplishment must be shared by The Human Genome Project (with financial backing by the US government) and the project directed by Craig Venter at Celera Genomics.

554 - Inserting genes from one species into another.

555 - Of course, a Darwinian may suggest society as a substitute for the Divine Judge, but that would be a dubious proposition. Historically, the needs or attitudes of specific societies have varied widely. To rely on "Society" will not get you very far in moral terms. One might as well refer to the Unicorn or the Loch Ness Monster, as to which concrete society should one refer to, that of the Nazis in the 1930s - 1940s or Soviet society, with its purges under Stalin or Cambodia with its Killing Fields under Pol-Pot?

556 - Gould, in the context of the debate on the speed of the evolutionary process (opposing neo-Darwinian gradualists and Gould's followers, advocating rapid, punctuated evolution), came to recognize the ideological or cosmological dimension of scientific concepts. He wrote (1980: 153-154):

If gradualism is more a product of Western thought than a fact of nature, then we should consider alternate philosophies of change to enlarge our realm of constraining prejudices. In the Soviet Union, for example, scientists are trained with a very different philosophy of change — the so-called dialectical laws... The dialectical laws are explicitly punctuational.... The dialectical laws express an ideology quite openly; our Western preference for gradualism does the same more subtly.

557 - Though before Darwin, the Frenchman Jean-Baptiste de Monet de Lamarck had taken some of the first steps to challenge this concept.

558 - This brings to mind the Coelacanth, a fish whose first live specimen was caught in 1938 off the Comoros in the Indian Ocean. It had been thought to be the worthy predecessor of the amphibians, but researchers were surprised to find that it showed no trace of internal organs preadapted for use in a terrestrial environment. Today it is recognized that "coelacanths represent a surprisingly conservative or stable group»…

559 - Or perhaps one could put it differently, "a series of rather well-coor-

dinated fortuitous events". But, some may ask why do we use the term "miracle" here? It is because Gould's view demands the sudden appearance of many new (and integrated) features in an organism, without the intervention of any intelligent Agent. This is basically an effect without a sufficient cause.

560 - This is discussed in the first chapter of Genesis.

>And God created great whales, and every living creature that moveth, which the waters brought forth abundantly, **after their kind**, and every winged fowl **after his kind**: and God saw that it was good. (Gn 1: 21 also Gn 1: 24)

More recent research into the "kind" concept goes under the term "baramin" or "baraminology", an approach where inter-fertility is the bottom line for classification. A baramin is then a wider, more inclusive classification group than the term species. Members of one baramin may show much phenotypic variety. For example, using the more common morphological definition of species, lions and tigers are considered as belonging to separate species, despite the fact that in captivity they have been observed to be inter-fertile over more than two generations. Based on fertility then they would be considered members of the same baramin.

561 - This refers to the concept of the Fall, affecting both man and the cosmos. Gen ch. 3.

562 - Here is the definition proposed by Ernst Mayr for his Biological Species Concept (1942: 120):

>Species are groups of actually or potentially interbreeding natural populations, which are reproductively isolated from other such groups.

563 - Kurzweil is a prolific inventor and innovator, holding numerous patents. In the late 1970s, he developed one of the first optical character recognition (OCR) applications as well as a voice synthesizer, which were incorporated into the Kurzweil Reading Machine, giving the blind access to printed texts and books. In the 1980s, he invented the Kurzweil K250 digital synthesizer, a project involving Stevie Wonder. Kurzweil also invented one of the first voice recognition applications for a personal computer, Voice Xpress Plus.

564 - Concerning extinctions, Stephen Jay Gould comments (in Campbell 1993: 502):

>All paleontologists are probably agreed that there are five really large extinctions that stand out. I don't know the exact ranking, but by far the biggest is the one at the end of the Permian, 225 million years ago. The estimates for that mass extinction range as high as 96% of all marine invertebrate species. The other four came at the end of the Ordovician, of the Triassic, and of the Cretaceous. and the one that came near the top of the Devonian.

565 - And if man nevertheless insists on taking on the role of manager of evolution, a self-managed process up until now, doesn't this move imply

that something is inherently "wrong" with evolution?

566 - In effect, this fits rather well with Charles Darwin's view, as stated in **The Descent of Man** (1871: 104-105):

There can be no doubt that the difference between the mind of the lowest man and that of the highest animal is immense.... Nevertheless the difference in mind between man and the higher animals, great as it is, certainly is one of degree and not of kind.

567 - As well as finding itself in conflict with the laws of several ancient civilizations.

568 - An analysis has been done by Dennis Bonnette (2003, ch. 5): **Significance of Recent Ape-Language Studies**. pp. 73-102.

569 - Which could easily be replaced by the term "humanism" in the author's view.

570 - In the Judeo-Christian context, it should be noted that man was made the steward or manager of nature and, as such, answering to God for what he does with/to it. Man then does not have carte blanche to exploit nature in any way he likes. Discussing the last judgements, Revelation (11: 18 NIV), states: "The nations were angry, and your wrath has come. The time has come for judging the dead, and for rewarding your servants the prophets and your people who revere your name, both great and small — **and for destroying those who destroy the earth**."

571 - Mayr appears to be echoing statements originally made by Julian Huxley in his introduction to the **Origin** (1958).

572 - On such matters Genesis chap. 1: 28-31 is a good starting point. For further details cf: Francis Schaeffer's **Pollution and The Death of Man** (1970), in particular chap. 4 (included in volume 5 of the **Complete Works**).

573 - Which was signed, amongst others by Julian and Aldous Huxley, the British playwright George Bernard Shaw and mathematician Bertrand Russell. The first version was published in 1933 followed by other versions in 1973 and in 2003 (www.americanhumanist.org). The evolution of this manifesto is interesting as it documents and reflects the (implicit) self-examination forced on moderns in response to the outcome of materialistic (deterministic) ideologies that the geopolitical events of the twentieth-century so horrendously exposed.

574 - Their web site states (2004): "We demand the extension of the community of equals to include all great apes: human beings, chimpanzees, bonobos, gorillas and orang-utans. The community of equals is the moral community within which we accept certain basic moral principles or rights as governing our relations with each other and enforceable at law. Among these principles or rights are the following: 1. The Right to Life ... 2. The Protection of Individual Liberty ... 3. The Prohibition of Torture." Furthermore, the site adds: "The organization is an international group founded to work for the removal of the non-human great apes from the category of property, and for their immediate inclusion within the category of persons." (www.greatapeproject.org)

575 - Eighteenth-century Enlightenment thinkers such as Jean-Jacques Rousseau already seem to have given some thought to man's relation to primates and actually made "prudent" allusions to an experiment attempting to bridge the gap between humans and primates. Is this a thinly veiled reference to a human and ape bedding down together? (Rousseau 1755/1985: 171):

> These experiments do not appear to have been made on the pongo [gorilla?] and the orang-utan with sufficient care to be able to draw the same conclusion. There would, however, be a means by which, if the orang-utan and others were of the human species, even the crudest observers could be provided with proof, but seeing one generation would not suffice for this experiment, it must be considered impractical since that which is only a hypothesis would have to be shown to be true before the test might be innocently attempted.*

576 - Chimpanzees are known to have attacked their guardians or owners at times, one of them losing a finger. There is a documented case of an attack by Washoe the monkey on one of his guardians. See: Bonnette **A Philosophical Critical Analysis of Recent Ape-Language Studies**. 1996. www.godandscience.org/evolution/ape-language.html

577 - A letter from Charles Darwin to W. Graham, dated July 3, 1881.

578 - Or put in a zoo? But in a zoo, they would not have access to TV, the Internet or to pool tables…

579 - Possibly he was thinking of Pascal who wrote (1670/1908: s. II, 72):

> So, if we are simply material, we can know nothing at all; and if we are composed of mind and matter, we cannot know perfectly things which are simple, whether spiritual or corporeal.

580 - This question will be examined in volume II of this essay.

581 - Taking into account the Fall and its consequences, for example, it is unacceptable to claim that human reason be considered an infallible source of Truth.

582 - Perhaps it would be more accurate to claim that Descartes was pre-Enlightenment thinker. Many consider Descartes as an important influence on the "Lumières" in setting up science as an important alterative to religion for TRUTH. One of his (unpublished in his lifetime) works was actually entitled: "Recherche de la vérité par les lumières naturelles", (published in the **Opuscula posthuma**, 1701) or a "Search for truth by the light…". Though Enlightenment thinkers did criticize Descartes on minor issues such as his views of the soul, they carried over entire his concept of science as a source of truth (inevitably becoming a competitor with Scripture).

583 - It is an ill-kept secret that empirical knowledge requires reference points. A surveyor cannot do anything without markers or boundaries. Managing human labour and schedules requires an absolute zero hour. Historians, for their part, when classifying data from past ages, rely on a timeline with a zero year. And if empirical knowledge demands such benchmarks, why would this not be the case for thought itself?

584 - French novelist Victor Hugo relates this anecdote (1987: 686) "Mr. Arago had a favourite story. When Laplace's **Celestial Mechanics** was published, he said, the emperor summoned him. The Emperor [Napoléon] was furious and exclaimed when he saw Laplace: How is it that you describe the whole system of the world, giving the laws of all creation and yet you do not speak once in your book of the existence of God! - Sire, Laplace replied, I did not need this assumption."*

585 - See **Luna, the Orphaned Orca**.
www.whale-museum.org/education/library/luna/luna_main.html
But the concluding episode is admittedly rather sad (died, March 2006): http://news.bbc.co.uk/2/hi/americas/4796106.stm

586 - Or, to use the Judeo-Christian expression, man is a "steward of Creation".

587 - Of course it is unlikely that Dawkins would ever acknowledge empirical data contradicting this statement, even if it could be shown to exist.

588 - At the end of winter, male polar bears have been observed cannibalizing cubs of their own species. Cf: Taylor, M., T. Larsen, and R.E. Schweinsburg 1985 **Observations of intraspecific aggression and cannibalism in polar bears (Ursus maritimus)**. Arctic, Vol. 38, no 4, pp. 303-309 .
http://pubs.aina.ucalgary.ca/arctic/Arctic55-2-190.pdf

589 - A more politically correct term would be "transhumanism".

590 - Available in some European countries, in addition to dog meat eaten in Asia or monkeys in equatorial Africa.

591 - It could be a good idea to put these wares near the pig meat, as urban legends have it that human meat is closest to pork in terms of flavour... Perhaps as follow-up, cookbooks could be published with recipes for marinating and grilling one's favourite politician on the BBQ.

592 - A fictional character in novels by Thomas Harris and their movie adaptations such as **Silence of the Lambs** (1991).

593 - On such matters: **Concern over 'spare part' babies.**
http://news.bbc.co.uk/2/hi/health/4663396.stm

594 - If here and there we have examined works drawn from popular culture in this study, it is for one simple reason. These works are vehicles for cosmological assumptions and are as significant as others meeting the highest academic demands. Cosmological presuppositions are to be found in any means of expression and can be packaged in a multitude of ways. The important thing is communicating meaning.

595 - "Heresy" would have been the term used in past times...

596 - This paragraph is derived from exchanges with LR.

597 - A shorter version of this article was published in the French magazine, Le Nouvel Observateur, Thurs. 27 May 2004.

598 - Peter Morton noted (1984) concerning this volume:
There was a revised edition of part I in 1894. This work, despite being Wells' first book, is very little known. It is not mentioned, for

instance, in Ingvald Raknem's meticulous bibliography H.G. Wells and His Critics. Indeed, the only published reference to it by Wells himself seems to have been in a chatty letter to Grant Richards of 6 November 1895, where he calls it 'a cram book - and pure hack-work... facts imagined' (from the unpublished letter as quoted by Bernard Bergonzi, The Early H.G. Wells: A Study of the Scientific Romances, p. 24). These contemptuous remarks - which are untrue may have been occasioned by Wells not, in his own opinion, having been given sufficient credit for some revision undertaken by himself and a friend. There are some relevant letters in the Wells Archive, University of Illinois. The Textbook was reissued in 1898, fully revised by A.M. Davies.

9 / Index

404

Index

Index

10 / Acknowledgements

The author would like to thank:

In a virtual world, my wife Margot, for her tangible support.

Jim Erickson, who proofread the present text and for help above and beyond the call of duty.

And others who have contributed to this work in various ways: Rodrigue Allard, Marie-Claude Bernard, Jerry Bergman, Mark Billington, Francine Bilodeau, David Bump, George Cooper, Pascal Daleau, René Delorme, Ronald Dilworth, Denis Duguay, Annélie Gagnon, Alain Gendron, Louis Gosselin, Jimi Hendrix, Lisette Jobin, Donald Martin, Gib McInnis, Roger C. Ouellette, Jean-Guy Paquet, Jacques Robitaille, Louis Robitaille, Nicolas Savard, Walt Stumper, Nadia Tawbi.

And for the Internet…

11 / Technical Considerations

A quotation in the text, followed by an asterisk * indicates the quote has been translated by the author.

In addition, references accompanying quotations typically proceed as follows:

Example: A sentence at the end of a paragraph mentions the author Bertrand Russell and is followed by the reference (1946/1975: 135) refers to a book whose first edition is dated 1946 and the cited edition is 1975. The number following the colon provides the page number from which the following quote is drawn. If it is an author quoted in a collective work, then the name of the editor is added to the parenthesis. And if one checks the bibliography of this volume, one will see that the above quote is drawn from the book "Western Philosophical Thought".

In the case of an article published in a collection of essays, the quotation reference will take the following form (in Curval 1990: 98-99) and refers to the editor of the book, not the author of the quoted article. The same applies in the case of an individual quote appearing in an article published by another author (an interview for example). In rare cases, this book includes different references from the same author and published the same year. To differentiate such references, a letter is added to the year of publication (appearing both before the quote as well as in the bibliography).

In rare cases the author may have added a comment or note inside a quote. When this occurs, the added words are enclosed in brackets [].

Bible quotes: Unless otherwise indicated, Bible quotes are drawn from the King James (1769 authorized) version of the Bible.

Order Form
(North America)

I would like to order _____ copies of **Flight From the Absolute: Cynical Observations on the Postmodern West. Volume I** by Paul Gosselin ($CND 33.95 /copy)

Shipping fees/country
Canada: $8/copy ($2 for each additional copy)
USA: $10/copy ($3 for each additional copy)

SUB-TOTAL $ /_____

SHIPPING $/_____

TOTAL $/_____

Personal cheques and money orders should be made out to **Samizdat** *(Canadian funds only)*.

Shipping address

name: _____

street: _____

city/state/province: _____

code postal: _____

country: _____

email: _____
(optional: for shipping confirmation only)

Get in touch about the 20% discount on orders of 10 copies or more.
Your order will be processed within 2 working days after receipt of payment.
Send the order form and payment to:

Samizdat
Succursale Jean-Gauvin
C. P. 25019
Quebec, QC
G1X 5A3 - CANADA

publications@samizdat.qc.ca
www.samizdat.qc.ca/publications

CPSIA information can be obtained at www.ICGtesting.com
Printed in the USA
LVOW06s2314170714

394905LV00003B/271/P